AMERICAN POLITICS
Ideals and Realities

AMERICAN POLITICS
Ideals and Realities | George McKenna

Department of Political Science
The City College of New York

McGRAW-HILL BOOK COMPANY

New York   St. Louis   San Francisco   Auckland   Düsseldorf
Johannesburg   Kuala Lumpur   London   Mexico   Montreal   New Delhi
Panama   Paris   São Paulo   Singapore   Sydney   Tokyo   Toronto

This book was set in Times Roman by National ShareGraphics, Inc.
The editors were Lyle Linder and John M. Morriss;
the cover was designed by J. E. O'Connor;
the production supervisor was Charles Hess.
Kingsport Press, Inc., was printer and binder.

Cover painting: "The Art Institute of Chicago."
Jack Levine, "The Trial." Oil on Canvas, 1953-54/72" x 63".
Courtesy of the Art Institute of Chicago.

AMERICAN POLITICS: IDEALS AND REALITIES

Copyright © 1976 by McGraw-Hill, Inc.
All rights reserved. Printed in the United States of America.
No part of this publication may be reproduced, stored in a retrieval system,
or transmitted, in any form or by any means, electronic, mechanical,
photocopying, recording, or otherwise, without the
prior written permission of the publisher.

234567890KPKP79876

Library of Congress Cataloging in Publication Data

McKenna, George.
    American politics.

    Includes index.
    1. United States—Politics and government—Handbooks,
manuals, etc.   2. Political participation—United
States.   I. Title.
JK274.M24   320.9′73′092   75-20094
ISBN 0-07-045355-1

TO LAURA,
MARIA, AND
CHRISTOPHER

Contents

Preface	xi
Introduction: Post-Watergate Politics	1
Watergate: The End of an Era	4
Some Lessons of Watergate	6
. . . But Will the Lessons Be Learned?	10
Democracy: The Socialization of Conflict	13
Outline of This Book	16

PART ONE   PREREQUISITES FOR DEMOCRACY

1 Liberty: The Free Trade in Ideas	23
Democracy—Some Common Definitions	23
Free Speech: The Dynamo of Democracy	26
Direct Coercion	29
Indirect Coercion	38
Monopoly	42
Some Conclusions	51
2 Equality: Rich and Poor in America	56
Heritage of the New Deal: Three Flawed Antipoverty Programs	56
AFDC	66

	The Search in the Sixties for Better Solutions: Self-Help and the OEO	69
	New Antipoverty Approaches	73
	Summary and Conclusion	84
3	**Fraternity: Races and Groups in America**	89
	Cultural Autonomy versus Assimilation	91
	The Indians: The Original Victims	92
	The Blacks: Imported Victims	97
	The White Ethnics: "Forgotten" Victims?	107
	Conclusion: Toward Intergroup Coalition	110

PART TWO   PROCESSES OF DEMOCRACY

4	**Campaigns and Elections: Are They Worth the Bother?**	115
	How Rational Is the Voter?	117
	How Rational Are American Political Campaigns?	121
	Is It Really "One Man, One Vote"?	126
	Conclusion	136
5	**"Special Interests" and the Public Interest**	140
	Group Theory	141
	Interest Groups in Congress	148
	Interest Groups and the Executive	154
	Interest Groups and the Public	161
	Summary	166
6	**Parties: Remembrance of Glories Past**	171
	"Party" Defined	173
	American Parties	174
	"Responsible" Parties: Some Pros and Cons	175
	The Emergence of American Parties	178
	Some Functions of Parties	180
	Historical Developments Undermining Party Strength	185
	Weakening of Party Ties: An Irreversible Process	187
	Progressivism: A Perennial Movement	188
	The Future of American Political Parties	194
	Conclusion: Parties as Instruments	197

PART THREE   COMPONENTS OF AMERICAN DEMOCRACY

7	**Congress: The Abdication of Power**	205
	Symptoms of Decline	207
	Unchecked Power: Who is Really to Blame?	208

	The Legislative Ordeal	209
	Negative Checks: Pro and Con	215
	Seniority	216
	Congressional Folkways	218
	Fragmentation of Authority	220
	Casework: Missing the Forest for the Trees	224
	Summary and Conclusions	227
8	**The President: Powers**	**236**
	The Strange Case of Richard Nixon	236
	Cult of Activism	239
	Constitutional Provisions	241
	The President as Commander-in-Chief	244
	The President as Chief Executive	249
	The President as Chief of State	256
9	**The President: Limits**	**264**
	Congress as a Check	265
	The Judiciary as a Check	276
	The Bureaucracy as a Check	278
	Political Parties as a Check	282
	The Press as a Check	283
	The Ballot Box as a Check	285
	Some Proposed Checks	287
	The Last Best Check: The People	290
10	**Democracy and Judicial Review**	**296**
	Origins of Judicial Review	296
	Checks on the Court	301
	Does the Court "Make" Laws?	305
	The Warren Court	311
	The Burger Court	315
	Future of the Court	317
	Conclusion: What Is America?	**321**
	National Identity—A False Solution	324
	The Question Again: What Are We?	325
	Citizen Leadership: The Range of Possibilities	328
	What Is America? Some Answers in Brief	331
	Index	**335**

Preface

In writing this book I was aware of the limitations both of orthodox textbooks and of the so-called point-of-view introductions to American politics.

The ills to which orthodox textbooks are susceptible include a leaden prose style; a dense array of facts with insufficient explanation of why the reader has to know them; a spurious air of objectivity; a tendency, in explaining how the system "works," to assume that it *does* work the way it is supposed to; flatness, blandness, and a lack of critical analysis. In trying to avoid these ills, the point-of-view textbooks sometimes slide into ills of a different sort; shrillness; idiosyncratic organization (or no organization at all); thinness of content; lack of balance in presenting arguments opposed to the book's point of view.

Yet both kinds of textbook have their strengths. The best of the orthodox texts have been well organized, rich in content, full of good section headings, summaries, and other guides for students and teachers. The virtues peculiar to the best point-of-view textbooks tend to be of a different kind: a lively, provocative style; a certain humanity, a sense that the author is really trying to talk with the student instead of hurling down verities from Mount Olympus.

In writing this book, I made a conscious effort to combine the virtues and avoid the vices of the two kinds of textbook. The book is held together by an overall point of view (to be discussed in a moment), but the point of view is broad enough to allow for a considerable range of content. Moreover, I believe—and I kept this belief in mind as I wrote the book—that certain basic facts about the American political system cannot be left out of any text on the subject, whether or not they are directly relevant to the textbook writer's point of view. Exactly which facts are "basic" is of course a debatable question. But after thirteen years of teaching American government, I have reached the conclusion that the subject cannot be understood even on a rudimentary level if one has no knowledge of how a bill becomes a law, how judicial review originated, what the powers of the President are, what functions the party system serves, what the famous school desegregation case of 1954 said, how civil liberties are protected and limited in America, and what such terms as "democracy," "pressure groups," and "checks and balances" mean in an American context. These and other facts which I judged to be "basic" are presented here with as much objectivity as one opinionated person can muster; they are labeled and organized as plainly as possible. Thus, even if one rejects the point of view running through this book, one may at the very minimum find it useful as a source of information about American government and politics.

Yet students need more than information to participate in the learning process. They must also be exposed to the issues—the "disputed questions," as the old schoolmen used to call them. Has the Presidency gotten too powerful? Are we moving toward "the coming Caesars"? Is Congress starting to make a comeback, or is it likely to remain a passive branch of government? What is the future of our party system—or does it have a future? What about civil liberties: Is there any danger that America is headed toward a police state? Are "pressure groups" always bad, or do they sometimes serve a useful purpose? It is the nature of an issue to have at least two sides. While I have not been coy about indicating which side I favor, I have tried to present other points of view as fairly as possible.

The attempt, in short, is to have it both ways: to combine the virtues and leave out the vices of both orthodox and point-of-view textbooks in American politics. Needless to say, the attempt may not have been completely successful—not at least from every reader's standpoint. Even though the book's conceptual framework is relatively broad and flexible, it has not been broad enough to include all the topics usually found in orthodox texts. Thus, for example, it does not include a discussion of obscenity under the category of civil liberty, since obscenity raises a wholly different set of questions than those connected with political expression. Other topics, such as bureaucracy and foreign policy, are covered in this book, but only indirectly, as parts of broader topics within its overall framework. These decisions may be regrettable, but some hard choices must always be made in a book which studies American politics from a particular perspective. The hope is that this book will still be able to stand by itself without a whole battery of supplementary reference works to back it up.

The overall point of view running through this book might be characterized as that of "pre-cold war liberalism." It harkens back to a tradition at least as old as Thomas Jefferson, a tradition which has been appealed to by a number of reform movements over the past two centuries. The tradition became dormant not long after the death of Senator George Norris in 1944, but parts of it were awakened in the 1960s by the New Left and the New Politics, and other parts were revived at the beginning of the 1970s in the form of neopopulism.

This tradition emphasizes certain ideals which it identifies with America: openness, honesty, liberty, limited and responsible government, spontaneous action from the grass roots. Underlying the tradition are certain assumptions: that ordinary people are not necessarily fools or ignoramuses, that people with modest education are often wiser and more prophetic than college professors, that seemingly solid fortresses can be stormed by the most unlikely troops, that seemingly changeless situations can be changed rather quickly, that spirit in the long run is more important than hardware. When the cold war came along at the end of the forties it became fashionable to deride all of this naïve, unrealistic, sentimental, unscientific, and possibly fanatical. But in recent years, for reasons I try to make clear in the introduction and conclusion of this book, the cold war approach has demonstrated its own pitfalls: Its "realism" has left out a whole side of reality, its "pragmatism" has not worked very well, its "empiricism" has ignored too many facts.

This book is an attempt to analyze American political institutions and processes from the standpoint of the old liberal ideals, which, I am convinced, can provide a more realistic framework for analysis than much of what has passed for "realism" over the past quarter-century. In any case, is it not better at least to *start* with the ideals, correcting them for harsh reality when necessary, than to start at the other end, with the most pessimistic expectations, and to find oneself having to explain away altruism and decency when they do appear?

There is nothing startling or even very original in the point of view of this book. It was adumbrated in the Declaration of Independence in 1776, and since that time it has worked its way through our history, our institutions, our political grammar and rhetoric. From a pedagogical standpoint the advantage of it is that the beginning student should have no difficulty either in understanding it or accepting it. For some, however, it might sound too commonplace, too unoriginal, too close to the platitudinous rhetoric of the Fourth of July. In answer to this criticism we might cite the reply of Thomas Jefferson to John Adams' rather caustic observations concerning the Declaration of Independence. Adams noted that the Declaration "contained no new ideas," that "it is a common-place compilation, its sentiments hackneyed in Congress for two years before." Jefferson replied that the object of the Declaration was "not to find out new principles or new arguments never before thought of, not merely to say things which had never been said before, but to place before mankind the common sense of the subject"—and to say it plainly.

ACKNOWLEDGMENTS

A number of people helped me prepare this textbook. Professor Thomas Karis, a colleague in the Political Science Department of The City College of New York, read an early draft of Chapter 1 and provided helpful comments. Professor Joyce

Gelb, also of City College's Political Science Department, gave me some valuable bibliographical information on political parties. Professor Judson James of the Virginia Polytechnic Institute discussed his own work on parties with me and provided a manuscript copy of a forthcoming revision of his *American Political Parties*. Richard Tropp, a former student of mine who is now a member of President Ford's White House staff, wrote a very detailed review of Chapter 2 which led to extensive revisions of it. Conversations with former New York Congressman John Dow have proven helpful in understanding some of the forces which shape the collective behavior of Congress. Neil Upmeier of Common Cause and Russell Hemenway, National Director of the National Committee for an Effective Congress, also gave interviews and informational material. David Iafolla, my father-in-law, has over the past twelve years contributed the benefits of seventy years of shrewd observation. On the other side of the generation gap, the students in political science classes at The City College of New York have been enormously helpful over the past thirteen years in forcing me to explain myself as clearly and coherently as I could. I am also grateful to Professor Randolph Braham, Chairman of City College's Political Science Department, and to the other members of various departmental and university committees, for granting me a sabbatical and leave of absence to write this book.

Robert Rainier, Editor-in-Chief of McGraw-Hill's Social Science and Humanities Division, deserves warm thanks for his support and encouragement of this project from its earliest beginnings. The late Ronald Kissack of McGraw-Hill, whose untimely death in 1974 was a sad event to all who knew him, served as a valuable editor, supporter, and adviser during the early stages of the manuscript. Lyle Linder, Political Science Editor of McGraw-Hill, took over the overall supervision of this manuscript during its later stages, and John Morriss served as the Editing Manager.

Particular thanks go to John Hendry, an editor associated with McGraw-Hill, for his craftsmanlike comments on every chapter of the manuscript. He ferreted out many begged questions and fuzzy thoughts, and he provided a combination of basic and detailed criticism which was of enormous value when it came to revising the original manuscript.

Needless to add, any remaining errors of fact, logic, concept, organization, or anything else are solely mine.

A final word, which can be stated very simply: Nothing at all would have emerged without the love and support of my wife, Sylvia.

George McKenna

Introduction: Post-Watergate Politics

Shortly after one o'clock in the morning of June 17, 1972, Frank Wills, a twenty-four-year-old security guard at the Watergate Office Building in Washington, D.C., was making his rounds.[1] As he passed the building's garage-level doors, something caught his eye: a piece of tape. The tape had been placed around the doorlatch to keep it from locking when pulled shut.

Thinking that the tape had been left by one of the maintenance men, Wills removed it and continued his rounds. Soon afterwards, he strolled across the street for a cup of coffee. When he returned, he checked the door again. To his surprise and alarm, he discovered that someone had put the tape back on. Wills called the police.

At nine o'clock Saturday morning, Bob Woodward, a reporter for the *Washington Post*, was awakened at home by a phone call. It was the city editor. Five men had been arrested earlier that morning in a burglary at Democratic headquarters, carrying photographic equipment and electronic gear. Could he come in? Woodward was unenthusiastic. It sounded like a burglary of some local Democratic storefront—a routine police assignment. Not until he got down to the office did he discover that it was in fact a break-in of the Democratic National Committee's headquarters.

Assigned to cover the story with Woodward was another reporter: Carl Bernstein, twenty-eight, a year younger than Woodward. After checking with the police and other sources, the reporters were able to write the next day that one of the burglars, James McCord, was security coordinator for the Committee for the Re-election of the President (CREEP). On the day that story appeared, Woodward got a phone call from the *Post*'s police reporter. One of the burglars was carrying two address books containing the name and phone number of somebody named E. Howard Hunt, followed by the notations "W. House" and "W. H." After some more checking the reporters wrote a story which was headlined: "WHITE HOUSE CONSULTANT TIED TO BUGGING FIGURE." When reporters asked Presidential News Secretary Ronald Ziegler about the story, Ziegler dismissed the Watergate incident as a "third-rate burglary attempt," not worthy of further White House comment. "Certain elements," Ziegler said, "may try to stretch this beyond what it is."

Judge John J. Sirica, driving to work in the early morning, was troubled. Each day before his court went into session he would read the *Washington Post,* and each day there seemed to be a new disclosure. He would read stories about a secret White House fund, fed by illegal campaign contributions, controlled by H. R. Haldeman, the President's Chief of Staff, and used to finance the Watergate burglary; stories about other strange doings, even political sabotage, paid for out of the same fund; stories about two of the accused Watergate burglars being employed previously by the White House in some sort of investigative unit called the "plumbers," and supervised by John Ehrlichman, the President's chief domestic adviser; stories about payoffs to the defendants for the purpose of keeping them quiet.

Those were the stories Judge Sirica had been reading in the morning newspaper before going to work. Yet when he walked into his courtroom to preside over the trial of the burglary defendants, it was as if he were in another world. There no one, neither the Justice Department prosecutors nor the defendants' attorneys, made any references to the controversial charges swirling around the case. The prosecutors treated it as if it were simply a break-in by seven cranks acting entirely on their own. The prosecutors seemed satisfied when they obtained guilty pleas from five of the defendants and guilty verdicts against the other two. As the trial continued, Judge Sirica became increasingly exasperated. He began questioning witnesses himself and urging the prosecution to call others. He suspected a far wider conspiracy and was "not satisfied that all the pertinent facts that might have been available have been placed before an American jury."

James W. McCord, Jr.: ex-CIA man, bugging expert, Sunday school teacher, CREEP official, undercover agent for the White House—and convicted Watergate burglar. All during the fall and winter of 1972, McCord had been pressured to plead guilty. He had resisted the pressure, but it had not been easy. John Caulfield, a CREEP official and former member of the White House staff, had told McCord that he was authorized by "the very highest levels of the White

House" to promise McCord Presidential clemency if he would plead guilty. Caulfield kept warning him: "Everybody is on the game plan but you. You are not following the game plan. Keep silent."

If McCord was annoyed at these tactics, he was more than annoyed—he was furious—at the White House effort to blame Watergate on the CIA. James McCord was deeply loyal to the agency he had served for more than twenty years. Before his trial he had written Caulfield that if "the Watergate operation is laid at the CIA's feet, where it does not belong, every tree in the forest will fall." Now that McCord had been convicted, his temptation to clear-cut the forest was strengthened by a new consideration. He had been found guilty on eight counts of burglary; he could get thirty-five years in prison, and the presiding judge was known around Washington as "Maximum John." But Judge Sirica had prudently delayed sentencing, hinting that a full disclosure of the truth from the convicted men might constitute grounds for leniency. James McCord decided that it was time to talk. He wrote to Judge Sirica that there were others involved in the break-in who "were not identified during the trial."

"He was a pilot fish. You know, the little fish who follow beside the sharks." That is how a colleague of John Wesley Dean III characterized him. As Counsel to the President and former Deputy Attorney General, the thirty-four-year-old attorney had been swimming beside some very big fish: Attorney General John Mitchell, John Ehrlichman, and Richard Nixon himself. He had served them all faithfully and efficiently. He knew his place. According to one Justice Department official, he rose to the position of Counsel to the President not only because he was bright and good-looking, but because "John Ehrlichman didn't want someone in that job who would challenge him."

But even a pilot fish has to protect himself. In April of 1973 John Dean was becoming very fearful that the sharks were turning on *him*—in less metaphorical language, that they were setting him up as the man responsible for the whole Watergate cover-up. So the time had come to swim free. After announcing that he was not about to be made a "scapegoat," Dean began plea-bargaining with federal prosecutors, meanwhile notifying the newly created Senate Watergate Committee that he would cooperate in its investigation of the affair.

Staff members of the Senate Watergate Committee called it a "throwaway question"—one of those questions asked in passing which will most likely lead nowhere. Still, their curiosity was mildly aroused by a remark John Dean had made during the course of his long and sensational public testimony before the Watergate Committee. During one of their private conversations in the Oval Office, Dean said, Nixon started asking him a number of leading questions "which made me think the conversation was being taped." One staff member, certain that he would get a "no" answer, nevertheless asked Federal Aviation Administrator Alexander B. Butterfield, Nixon's former appointments secretary, whether he knew anything about any taping system in the President's office. Butterfield remained calm, but he was clearly troubled. "I was hoping you fellows wouldn't ask me that."

WATERGATE: THE END OF AN ERA?

The scenes above are fragments from a very significant episode in American political history. It is difficult, and perhaps presumptuous, to mark beginnings and ends in history, but it is hard to avoid the thought that Watergate signified the end of an era in American politics—an era begun nearly thirty years earlier with the advent of the cold war.

Within two or three years after the end of World War II the nation had committed itself to a new, open-ended struggle against a new enemy—"the Communist conspiracy." The cold war produced a remarkable and long-lasting consensus in America; the keystone of that consensus was the Manichean notion of cosmic war between the forces of darkness and light. The human race inhabited a divided, bipolar world, and as head of the "free world," America had to lead the struggle against the "Communist world." Even the bitterest liberal opponents of Senator Joseph McCarthy tended to accept his basic premise, "that we are now engaged in a show-down fight—not the usual war between nations for land area or other material gains, but a war between two diametrically opposed ideologies."[2] A full decade after those words were spoken, liberals enthusiastically applauded the inaugural address of President Kennedy, which sounded exactly the same theme of cataclysmic, global struggle between the good guys and the bad guys. ("Let the word go forth" that "a new generation of Americans" is "unwilling to witness or permit the slow undoing of those human rights to which this nation has always been committed, and to which we are committed today at home and around the world." We "shall pay any price, bear any burden, meet any hardship, support any friend, oppose any foe to assure the survival and the success of liberty.")[3]

The *objective* basis for cold war thinking began to disintegrate in the early sixties. "Communism" could no longer be considered monolithic when the Soviet Union and China, the two largest Communist countries, were exchanging bitter polemics and arming themselves against one another. (Indeed, as early as 1948, a crack had developed within the "Communist bloc" when Communist Yugoslavia refused to take orders from Moscow and was expelled from the Comintern.) It soon became clear that there existed many national variants of communism, and some of them were in no way puppets of either Moscow or Peking. In the meantime, the idea of "peaceful coexistence" had made steady gains, heralding a new day when diplomatic relationships between Western and Communist countries would thaw. But *subjectively,* cold war habits of mind persisted, leading to a curious form of doublethink: As late as 1972 President Nixon could drink toasts to Chairman Mao in Peking, then come home and order the mining of Haiphong in order to save South Vietnam from something called "communism." As the waves of the sea keep rolling long after the wind has died down, the political thought of America—or at least of America's leaders—during the sixties and early seventies was still being conditioned by the traumas of the late forties: We were involved in an "all-out" fight to contain the spread of world communism; we must sterilize the homefront against this contagion, and remove the germs of it elsewhere in the world, or else country after country will (to change the metaphor) "fall" to communism like so many dominoes.

Beating the Communists at Their Own Game

If there was anything that ran through the thinking of the cold war period, it was the compulsion to match, and if possible one-up, the strategies and tactics of the "enemy." The Communists used force and violence to get their way; *we* must not shrink from using these methods. The Communists laughed at civil liberties; *we* must not be so absolutist about such things as free speech and the right of privacy as to give aid and comfort to the enemy. The Communists were directed by a strong executive, which was one reason they could act so swiftly; *we* must have a strong President, without too many restraints upon him by our talkative Congress. The Communists directed a worldwide network of spies, saboteurs, and assassins; *we* need a CIA. The Communists operate on the principle that power comes out of the barrel of a gun; *we,* as President Kennedy said, "dare not tempt them with weakness. For only when our arms are sufficient beyond doubt can we be certain beyond doubt that they will never be employed."[4] Above all, the Communists were "toughminded." They were crafty, deceitful, and utterly without scruple. They had no respect for ideals, and they sneered at "sentimentalism." Let *us* not be so high-minded about political ideals and legal niceties. Let us frankly recognize that there is a fight going on in the back alleys of the world, a fight in which no quarter is given and none is expected. Let us fight fire with fire.

The unfortunate effect of this preoccupation with beating the Commies at their own game was that we began to lose sight of our own traditional ideals: openness, honesty, liberty, equality, fair play, and the other values which we associate with democracy. To be sure, America has not always practiced these ideals, but at least the ideals were always held up as models by which to shame the nation into making reforms. But during the cold war period it became fashionable to dismiss ideals for being just that: "mere" ideals. They might be nice, the thinking went, but we couldn't afford the luxury of dreaming about them right then, not with the enemy at the gates. "Idealists" were derided as quixotic souls—harmless dreamers at best, at worst dupes of the Communists. Cold war thinking emphasized "realism," tough-minded "empirical" analysis. An "end of ideology" was proclaimed. It was a bad season for those who wanted basic reforms of the political process in America or fundamental changes in the way America looked at the world.

As early as the mid-sixties, when the Johnson administration invaded the Dominican Republic and began escalating the Vietnam war—both acts justified in the name of anticommunism—the thinking of the cold war began to be challenged by significant numbers of Americans. But the "doubters and cussers," as Johnson called them, were a minority, and their tactics provoked a backlash. As the seventies began, the doubter-cusser elements seemed to be disappearing from the American scene. It was not Eugene McCarthy but Richard M. Nixon who had taken over the Presidency the year before. The campuses were getting quieter. "Vietniks" were getting beaten in the streets by "hardhats," Nixon's favorite blue-collar constituency, while the police looked on. Automobile windows were being decorated with American flag decals, and bumper stickers announced the alternatives: "Love it or leave it." In 1972 Senator George McGovern, the candidate associated with the "new politics," was overwhelmingly defeated by President Nixon, who, even as he visited China and talked about "détente" with Russia, epitomized the essential ingredients of cold war thinking—its "tough-mindedness," its love for "pragmatic" solutions, its emphasis on "national security," its preoccupation with foreign "crises," its rather loose interpretation of the Bill of Rights, its disdain for political reformers and other domestic "idealists." The 1972 election seemed like the last hurrah for political reform in America. It was 1920 all over again: back to "normalcy." Before the campaign was over, even the "radical" challenger was trying to look like a "centrist." This was not a time to reexamine things but to accept reality. Four more years. . . .

Then it happened. Slowly at first, the earliest headlines hardly making an impression—relatively few people knew what "Watergate" meant in the winter of 1972. Yet within a year the facade of "normalcy" had been ripped away, revealing the crouching figures in rubber gloves, the spies and the saboteurs, the bugs and telephone taps, the "enemies" lists, and, on top of everything, a "law and order" President who conspired with his aides to cover up crimes and pay hush money to criminals. It was Watergate, far more than the Vietnam war or any other event since 1945, which showed how dangerously far cold war thinking could be carried, and what damage it had done to the nation's traditions.

SOME LESSONS OF WATERGATE

Let us examine a few of the lessons of Watergate.

1 The Pathology of "Toughness" The determination to fight fire with fire was, as we have noted, a prominent feature in the thinking of the cold war. President Kennedy and his advisers liked to be considered "tough-minded" in their dealing with the Communists; hence the eyeball-to-eyeball confrontations in the Caribbean and the James Bond adventures with Green Berets in Vietnam. President Johnson adapted his own Texas-style *machismo* to the requirements of the cold war: He, too, would show the Communists how tough he was. ("I didn't just screw Ho Chi Minh," he said after his first bombing raid on North Vietnam, "I cut his pecker off.")[5] Nixon and his advisers were thoroughly steeped in this kind of climate when they came into office. White House aide Charles Colson hung a slogan of the Green Berets on the wall of his den: "If you've got 'em by the balls, their hearts and minds will follow."[6] Violence had already become a substitute for diplomacy in the international sphere. What Nixon and his White House team did was to bring it home, turning the sphere of American politics into a combat zone. The goal was "victory," and the point was to win. All the rest was essentially a matter of technique. Ideals and sentiments possessed no intrinsic worth; they were, like fears and lusts, useful levers for manipulating people.

The corollary to this kind of toughness was naïve faith in technology as the key to victory. The tough guy is cynical about ideals, so he idealizes the tangible—the things that touch, or are touched by, the surface of the body rather than the heart or mind. The human yearning for ideals becomes in him a passion for mechanical ingenuity, hence for apparatus and gimmickry of all kinds. If previous administrations had placed great faith in such things as spy planes, "smart" bombs, "surgical" air strikes, electronic Maginot lines, and computerized battle reports, the Nixon administration, once again, brought the cold war home. Domestic "enemies" were fought with equipment borrowed from the CIA: secret microphones, tape recorders, walkie-talkies, voice-disguisers, and pellet guns. It was all crazy, of course. Nixon himself was shocked by the senselessness of placing electronic bugs in the headquarters of one of the leakiest, most gossipy organizations in the country, and no less an authority than Anthony Ulasewicz, the former police officer who delivered hush money to the Watergate burglars, scornfully testified that if "any old retired man in the New York City Police Department" were to bug an office, "he would not have walked in with an army, that's for sure."[7]

Watergate may have been the ultimate insanity, but it was really no more than the logical conclusion to cold war "toughness." As early as the 1950s, the sociologist and social critic C. Wright Mills called it "crackpot realism." By installing or supporting right-wing dictators throughout the world, America prepared the way for its own loss of influence as these dictatorships began to crumble. Our nation, founded in revolution, became associated with a kind of mean-spirited reaction. And by trying to match the Communists in ruthlessness and stealth, American policy makers further depleted the enormous reservoir of good will America enjoyed at the end of World War II. The same self-defeating result occurred when "crackpot realism" was infused into domestic politics: The two Presidents who relied so heavily on manipulation to influence America opinion ended up by not being believed even when they were telling the truth.

2 The Imperial Presidency   Cold war thinking was preoccupied with "crises." There was the "U-2 crisis," the "Cuban Missile Crisis," Richard Nixon's "Six Crises," and a general, all-around "crisis in confidence." A book of readings on American government published in 1963 was entitled *Continuing Crisis in American Politics*. Most of these "crises" were in the area of foreign policy, and they resulted from America's global "commitment" to save the world from communism. Anything which upset the status quo anywhere in the world became a new "crisis" for America to resolve. "Each day the crises multiply," President Kennedy warned. "Each day their solution grows more difficult. Each day we draw nearer the hour of maximum danger. . . ."[8]

To protect us in our "hour of maximum danger" we needed a strong President. Only he could make the quick decisions necessary in a crisis atmosphere. Only he had the national mandate and the personal guts to take the responsibility for his acts. ("The buck stops here," said the sign on President Truman's desk.) Only he could serve as the symbol of the nation's unity as it faced its chief adversary in the world. Only he could inspire the people, through the use of what Theodore Roosevelt had once called his "bully pulpit," to make the necessary sacrifices for fighting the cold war. ("Ask not what your country can do for you. . . .")

It was Watergate which finally deflated the pretensions of the cold war Presidency. By exposing some almost incredible abuses of the powers Presidents had been accumulating over the past quarter-century, the scandal made a central issue of presidential power and the need for checks upon it. At the same time, it thoroughly debunked the mystique of the modern Presidency. After Watergate, nobody could be blamed for raising an eyebrow at this confident assertion, published just before the scandal broke open: "No wholly dishonorable or cruel or corrupt citizen has ever been able to capture the office."[9] Even the doctored transcripts of Nixon's White House conversations interred the notion, so commonly accepted during the cold war years, that the presidential office somehow screened out rascals or transformed them into men of virtue.

By the same token, Watergate may have readjusted the balance between President and Congress. The disintegration of the Nixon administration permitted Congress, sometimes forced it, to recover some of the old congressional powers which had either lain dormant or drifted into the hands of the President during the long period of cold war: the power to participate in the making of foreign policy, to set limits to presidential warmaking, to spend money according to its own priorities, to exercise legislative oversight, to conduct a full-scale investigation of the President's activities. Even the old blunderbuss, impeachment, which had rusted long before the cold war began, was oiled and ready for use if Nixon had not resigned. The public's attitude of condescension toward Congress, which the cold war had reinforced, also seemed about ready for a change. The televised Watergate hearings and impeachment deliberations showed members of Congress to be far more serious and intelligent than the bourbon-and-branchwater stereotype had made them out to be. The post-Watergate flood of freshmen members of Congress in the fall of 1974 seemed to many observers to bring a promise of better days for the image—and the reality—of the legislative branch.

3 The Threats to Civil Liberties The atmosphere of crisis and the cult of "toughness" combined to produce an unhealthy environment for civil liberties during the cold war period. From the outset "national security" had at least two meanings. On the one hand it meant the external fight against communism, and was used to justify an ever-escalating defense budget. On the other hand, it meant combating internal "subversion"—a term which could mean anything from throwing bombs to "conspiring to advocate." "National security" was the excuse for jailing Communists in the late forties, and presumably was the excuse for breaking into embassies during the fifties, for spying on college students in the sixties, and for trying to censor newspapers in the early seventies. But not until Watergate was it clear how frightfully far the term "national security" could be pushed. It was used as a justification for the burglary of a doctor's office, for the tapping of news reporters' telephones, and for an elaborate scheme of domestic espionage which even FBI chief J. Edgar Hoover wanted no part of. The Watergate burglary itself was to be secretly justified as a "national security" matter: After the break-in, Nixon and Haldeman planned to tell this to the FBI in order to justify their command to "stay to hell out of it." John Dean later described Watergate as

> an inevitable outgrowth of a climate of excessive concern over the political impact of demonstrators, excessive concern over leaks, an insatiable appetite for political intelligence, all coupled with a do-it-yourself White House staff, regardless of the law.[10]

But Watergate was more than that. In the longer perspective it was the culmination of a long era during which "national security" had become a kind of all-purpose excuse for invading the liberty and privacy of American citizens.

Can we not be grateful for the dropping of the Watergate "bombshells"? They not only blasted away the camouflage of those who, in Senator Lowell Weicker's words, "almost stole America" during the Nixon years; they also set off a series of secondary explosions which continued into the post-Nixon era. In 1975 Congress began to undertake comprehensive and public investigations—the first time it had ever done so—of just what the FBI and the CIA had been doing in the name of "national security" over the past quarter-century. Newspapers and other media also began to zero in on what these agencies had been doing: spying on Americans, keeping massive files on Americans' personal lives, opening mail, blackmailing members of Congress and civil rights leaders, and generally acting on the principle that traditional Anglo-Saxon rights have been, in John Ehrlichman's words, "considerably eroded over the years."[11] The exposure of how far our rights *had* eroded in the minds of those sworn to protect them resulted in a changed attitude toward "national security." Suddenly it had lost its appeal as an excuse for violating the Constitution. Indeed, the public would accept no excuse for the activities listed above. Even the radical-right *New York News* admitted that New York Congresswoman Bella Abzug had "a legitimate beef" over the fact that the CIA had been opening her mail for the past twenty years. In the wake of Watergate, the popular climate for civil liberties was better than it had been in a generation.

4 The Hazards of "Politics as Usual" The counterpart to the crusading zeal of American policy makers as they faced the world was a spirit of complacency and self-congratulation when it came to the question of reforming America's domestic political process. "Emergencies in policy with politics as usual" was the way political scientist Richard E. Neustadt summed up the spirit of "mid-century America" in 1960.[12] The "usual" politics was a politics of wheeling and dealing, bargaining and horsetrading among elites. Politicians were to play the role of brokers, mediating the disputes between the representatives of organized pressure groups—business, labor, farmers, and so on. The opinion leaders of the cold war era tended either to accept this arrangement as part of the nature of things, or to celebrate it as a positive good. After all, the system "worked," didn't it? ("Tough-mindedness" again.) We had enough to do holding world communism at bay without tearing apart the structure of American politics in pursuit of some unworkable "ideal."

Even before Watergate, "politics as usual" had began to falter. Large numbers of young people, poor people, racial minorities, and others had obviously been left out of the system of established pressure groups, and their frustration sometimes boiled over into violence. Critics also noted that pressure-group politics lacked any vision of the common good; it seemed to be concerned only with appeasing the most powerful interest groups in the country. The system, in Theodore Lowi's words, "lacks justice." But not until Watergate was the implicit cynicism of "politics as usual" brought out into the open for all to see. As the machinations of ITT and the milk lobby demonstrated, payoffs by special interests could play an important role in government decision making, even—perhaps especially—at the highest levels of the administration. The activities of the Watergate burglars and saboteurs were paid for out of a campaign fund bloated with illegal contributions which had been extorted from large corporations. Meanwhile, Congress, which was supposed to be keeping an eye on the executive branch, was itself deeply immersed in "politics as usual." The milk lobby had contributed generously toward the reelection of key committee chairmen, and members of Congress seemed to be more concerned with servicing local districts—or the leading pressure groups in them—than with governing the nation.

What Watergate did was to force up all the bile secreted during the long years of national celebration. In cultivating "patriotism" and searching for "national purpose," American leaders had ignored one basic source of discontent and disunity: the widespread suspicion that the American political process is rigged on behalf of special interests. The politics of barter and negotiation meant accepting, in the name of "realism," closed-door committee meetings and the rule of minorities in the legislative process, big campaign contributions by special interests, oil depletion allowances and other tax loopholes, and the whole existing structure of wealth and power in the nation. The average citizen was no political expert, but he or she knew enough about the facts of life to have become a political cynic. Turnout at the polls had been steadily declining since 1960, until in 1972 only slightly more than 55 percent of eligible voters even bothered to show up at the polls. For some time now the average American had been losing respect for the system, had been suspecting that venality and cupidity were bound up with the decision-making process at the highest levels of government. What Watergate did was to bring these suspicions out into the open. During the Watergate investigations it was revealed that there *were* lies galore from the highest public officials; there *were* attempts to cover up crimes and to prejudice justice and to call off investigations. The most lurid images of the most irresponsible muckraker—suitcases full of laundered greenbacks, incriminating documents being stuffed into shredders or immolated in fireplaces, furtive meetings in parks, hasty conversations on pay phones, threats, disguises, code names, hush money, bag men—were now revealed as established facts, confirming the worst suspicions about dirty politics in America. The lesson was clear: The reputation of "politics as usual" had hit rock bottom; the time had arrived for basic reforms in the operation of our domestic political system.

. . . BUT WILL THE LESSONS BE LEARNED?

In summary, Watergate marked the end of a quarter-century era in American politics. For those in power, the era which ended with Watergate was an era in which "tough-minded" politics—marked by the use of dubious means in the pursuit of what were often illusory goals—were pursued with very little questioning or even notice by the public at large. For many, perhaps most Americans, during this era, it was a time to rally behind the government. Especially in the area of foreign policy, it was a time of faith—all too often blind and unmerited faith—in the powers that be: "They have facts we don't have; therefore they know better than we do; therefore they must be doing the right thing," whether it be the bombing of Indochina or the wiretapping at home.

And the era was itself the culmination and conclusion of a larger period in American history: an age of innocence; a period during which we not only looked up to our government but expected the world to look up to America. Uncle Sam was at once the policeman of the world and the supreme model for how other governments and societies should operate. That age of terrifying confidence in "the American way of life" was not ended by Hiroshima, nor by the McCarthy period, nor by the Bay of Pigs. But the combination of Watergate and Vietnam did shake that confidence to its roots.

But are we really learning the lessons of Watergate? There are signs that we may indeed be learning. By bringing to light some of the seamiest results of the "usual" politics, Watergate may have paved the way for reform. In the wake of the scandal there was much talk about a "post-Watergate morality" in Washington. Some of that talk was frankly rueful, much of it was plainly sarcastic, and the morality itself threatened to be short-lived, even assuming that it was genuine. Having made all these allowances on the side of caution, we can note that the "post-Watergate morality" did help to produce changes: By 1975 the power of committee chairmen was being curbed, the seniority system in Congress had been struck a mighty blow, government secrecy was being challenged as never before, the Senate filibuster was modified, the oil depletion allowance, at least for the major oil companies, had been eliminated, and the mood was more favorable to reform than retrenchment—for opening up the system instead of sealing it against change. But it is still too early to tell whether the lessons of Watergate will stay in our consciousness very long. A flurry of procedural and substantive reforms are all very well, but it is change over the longer run which will determine whether Watergate will go down in history as a fundamental moment of truth for America.

If the lessons of Watergate are *not* learned, then the age of innocence will still be over—innocence, like virginity, can never be restored—but instead of being replaced by a new age of maturity it may, possibly, skip that stage and go right into senility. There are countries in the world where the citizens, having lost their old illusions of their country's "mission," have simply lapsed into the pursuit of their own private interests, letting the nation be damned. The citizens have lost their illusions—but also their spirit. Corruption and decadence have become ways of life, and the nation simply disintegrates. Whether this happens to America depends in no small part on whether Americans are able to put aside their old illusions and to put together a better, more credible version of the American dream. Leonard J. Fein, a professor of politics and social policy at Brandeis University, put it this way:

> Though we cannot renew the old dream, we can yet make a new one, and the task that awaits . . . is to define its terms and limits. It will be less grand, less compelling, perhaps, but more credible, more proximate to its promise.[13]

In part, this book is an attempt to reflect upon the lessons of Watergate. It will examine the components and processes of American government with particular emphasis upon the events and the changing concepts of politics and government over the past quarter-century. Running through every chapter of this book is the first lesson of Watergate: that the cult of "toughness," which flourished during the cold war years, needs to be put aside in the post-Watergate era; we need to begin talking about ideals again—usable ideals, derived from the American experience, by which to measure the present realities of America. We need more than empirical description of America as it is; we also need normative projections of America as it should be, based upon reasonable hopes of what America could be.

This book, then, is intended not merely to ruminate upon the lessons of the past, lessons which we can only hope were branded into our consciousness by Watergate. It is intended not merely to look back but to look around us at the present and to look forward to the future. And we intend not merely to look at the facts but to judge the facts, and not to be reticent about making suggestions as to how the facts should be changed. Value judgments are not taboo in this book. Indeed, hovering over its analysis of American politics and government is a guiding ideal.

What ideal? Whose ideal?

Nothing very original or newfangled. The seeds of it are in the Declaration of Independence. It was translated into the vernacular by Andrew Jackson. It was appealed to by all sides during the Civil War. It was held up as the supreme standard by Lincoln, and it was made into poetry by Walt Whitman. It was taken up by the populists in the 1890s, and brought into the new cities by the progressives in the early 1900s. It was honored all during the 1930s by poets, politicians, and folk singers. The ideal is called by a number of names—self-government, majority rule, government "of the people, by the people, for the people"—but the most common name for it is "democracy." What on earth does it mean?

"Democracy" is one of those terms bandied about so much that it seems to have lost any definite meaning. In the beginning of Chapter 1 and again at the beginning of Chapter 4 we attempt some definitions of the term. Here we are more concerned with how it works in a modern industrial nation of over two hundred million people, a difficult task in itself. For we all know that we cannot expect this country to be run like ancient Athens or an old New England town meeting, where the people governed themselves directly, without bothering with representatives. We all know that day-to-day decision making is always in the hands of elites. We all know that people have jobs to go to and work to do, and cannot spend all their time on politics. We may even suspect that most of the people most of the time do not much care about politics, and would just as soon leave it in the hands of those who do care. We can grant all of this, yet still maintain that "democracy" is a meaningful term, and that, while no country is a perfect democracy, some are more democratic than others.

Let us start with a system which ranks very low on the democratic scale, that of the Soviet Union. But why is it undemocratic? After all, it does hold elections.

The Soviet Union, of course, sharply curtails civil liberties, but it is not yet clear what the relationship is between civil liberties and majority rule. (This will be explored in Chapter 1.) The representatives of the Soviet Union claim that the majority of people there do not *want* to read Solzhenitsyn. If this were correct, it might suggest that the people are illiberal or illiterate, but not necessarily that the system is undemocratic. Yet we persist in saying that it is. Why?

Suppose we suggest this answer: The Soviet Union is undemocratic because *all conflicts there are more or less successfully contained within a small ruling clique.* Within the Kremlin walls there exists a considerable amount of in-fighting—the Kremlinologists assure us of that—but very little of it gets out of those walls. The ruling clique holds elections, but it permits no real competition at the polls. Again, conflict is suppressed. Modern oligarchies and dictatorships often exalt "the people," and sponsor marches, rallies, and all kinds of popular spectacles. But the mark of a phony democracy is that the real decisions have already been made—*the real conflicts have already been settled*—and the purpose of the "people's" gathering is to applaud the decisions.

DEMOCRACY: THE SOCIALIZATION OF CONFLICT

If the mark of an undemocratic system is that conflict is successfully contained, it follows that democracy means the *socialization of conflict.*[14] In a democracy conflict has a way of getting "out of hand." A conflict which began within a narrow circle of ruling elites expands beyond its borders and becomes a matter of concern to the whole society. Conflict is inherently contagious, and a democratic society is one which facilitates the spread of the contagion. Like the effect produced when a stone is dropped into the water, democracy is always associated with rippling rings of controversy. In a modern democracy the day-to-day business of government is left up to elites. But democracy always leaves open the possibility that at any time the circle may greatly expand, that the number of participants may be greatly enlarged.

Ordinarily, for example, the average American may not be very interested in how the Federal Reserve Board operates. But if the members of the Board, by their money policies, were to worsen an economic recession, then the whole question of the Board's priorities and methods could become public controversy. The Board members' gut reaction might be to think, if not to say out loud, "this matter is too complicated for the public to understand," or "this is just going to get the masses confused and upset." In nondemocratic systems these elitist notions underly the rules of the game. A critic of the Board might appeal to some politburo or czar or council, but he or she would know better than to communicate to the public at large. Even in a democracy the expansion of controversy often begins slowly and tentatively. The critic of a government agency might first try to work within the agency itself, hoping to persuade its members to change their ways. Getting nowhere, the critic might then bring up the matter behind the closed doors of a congressional committee or subcommittee. Finding the committee mainly interested in sheltering the agency from criticism, the critic might persuade a member of Congress to bring it up on the floor of the House or Senate. If the criticism still fell on deaf ears, he or she might turn to the media. If the critic's complaints were to get it aired on radio or TV, or printed in the public press, it would then reach the furthest, outermost circle, and possibly become a public controversy. A democracy is of course a form of government which permits the public to appoint or remove its governing officials. But even prior to that, a democracy is a form of government which airs controversies, which permits dissenters to appeal to the public at large, and which thus holds over the head of governing officials the sword of public accountability. And the process is spontaneous, not a stage-managed orgy of "confession" and "self-criticism" directed from someplace else in the governing establishment.

Watergate itself provides an example of democracy as the spontaneous expansion of a controversy. No single person or group arranged the whole sequence of events which began this chapter. It was more a matter of one event simply leading to another, in a constantly escalating controversy which began with a small piece of tape around a doorlatch and culminated in the expulsion of an administration and a sweeping reexamination of the premises which the nation had accepted for a generation. Despite Nixon's increasingly frantic efforts to "keep the cap on the bottle," the Watergate genie got out—and kept growing. First it was a police matter, a "third-rate burglary attempt," then a newspaper exposé, then a very extraordinary judicial proceding, then a congressional investigation and a daily television show, finally a deadly juggernaut that could neither be steered nor "stonewalled." Even as this book goes to press the ramifications of Watergate are still being felt: It has helped to put a new spirit, and new people, into Congress, it has opened new investigations into the espionage establishment, it has whetted the appetite of the press for new information about what various administrations had been doing all during the cold war period, it has affected the balance of forces within and between our political parties, and it has raised the basic question of whether "politics as usual" is tolerable any longer.

Watergate, of course, was a special case. Conflicts do not have to be as sensational and melodramatic as Watergate, and it is not necessary that they involve actual crimes by government officials. Without even getting into crimes, there are enough blunders and follies committed in government to keep the critics sufficiently occupied. When critics from within the Pentagon aired their charges of wasteful military spending, they were not charging corruption or theft but simply the mindless use of taxpayers' money. When other critics point to the extremely cozy, mutually protective relationship which exists between government agencies and the industries they are supposed to be regulating, the critics are not always charging bribery or other criminal acts; more often than not, they are simply calling attention to a set of attitudes among our governing officials, attitudes reinforced by years of congenial association with industry officials. Nor is it necessary to say that critics of the "establishment" are always right in order to appreciate their invaluable contribution to the democratic process. Whether they are right or wrong, they serve the public function of bringing controversies out into the open, bringing issues before the public, letting *us* decide whether a charge is, to use the favorite word of governing elites, "irresponsible."

The theory of democracy which underlies this book does not require that all the people be involved in politics all the time. It recognizes the necessary role of elites in day-to-day decision making. But it does require that the many participate some of the time, and that they be allowed to do so. This means, first, keeping the process of communication open—allowing free and uninhibited debate, open files of government records, open committee meetings in Congress, perhaps televised floor debates, open caucuses in political parties, and so on. Secondly, it means a political process which facilitates public involvement: a political party system which welcomes amateurs and newcomers instead of regarding them as troublemakers, executive agencies which are at least as cordial to consumer groups as they are to drug-company representatives, a Congress which makes it possible for nonmillionaires to run for office without mortgaging themselves to special interests. A democracy does not require that the majority always rules, only that the majority is always invited to rule.

But it is futile to wait for governing elites to send out invitations. Their tendency is the reverse—to discourage public participation. They like to contain controversy and limit the spread of embarrassing information. They invoke a variety of reasons for doing so: the need for privacy, the danger of "irresponsibility," their own "expertise," the need for protecting "classified information," "executive privilege," and so on. Sometimes these excuses are valid, but it is risky to rely upon the self-serving claims of public officials. If democracy is to work, if it is to be more than a pious hope that our ruling elites will open up the channels of participation, it requires the actions of counterelites—those who throw wrenches into the smooth operation of governmental machinery. In the early sixties they threw their bodies in the way of "states' rights" and "gradualism," forcing a very reluctant Kennedy administration to sponsor a major civil rights bill. In the late sixties they blasted apart President Johnson's "consensus" to make a national issue of the undeclared war in Asia which everyone else seemed to be trying to forget. In the seventies the protesting minorities were more inclined toward legal means, but the same spirit was there in the muckrakers and the whistle-blowers: the conscience-stricken RAND employees who delivered the Pentagon Papers to the nation's leading newspapers, the citizen-lobbyists who sued the Finance Committee to Re-Elect the President to force disclosure of illegal campaign contributions, the Pentagon employees who risked their government jobs by exposing the massive amount of waste in defense spending, the reporters who dug out the real stories behind the government's facade of public relations. These are examples of the counterelites, whose struggles with the elites of the government at the center of the arena have had this effect: They have, on occasion, moved people off the sidelines and into the fray. At the end of 1973, Special Prosecutor Archibald Cox refused to drop his law suit against Richard Nixon for possession of the White House tapes. He was fired—and a public "firestorm" followed. People who had only been spectators to the unfolding Watergate scandal suddenly became participants. Congressional offices were flooded with letters, telegrams, and phone calls demanding the impeachment of President Nixon. By the time the storm had subsided, the most powerful man in the United States had been forced to appoint a new Special Prosecutor and yield some of his tapes; and

Congress itself had been nudged a step closer to impeaching him. The act of Archibald Cox which had set off this series of ripples was part of an old American tradition of prophetic "witness," which assigns preeminent importance to the "honest man" in a democracy. In 1849 Henry David Thoreau wrote:

> I know this well, that if ten thousand, if one hundred, if ten men whom I could name,—if ten *honest* men only,—ay, if *one* HONEST man, in this state of Massachusetts, *ceasing to hold slaves,* were actually to withdraw from this copartnership, and be locked up in the county jail therefor, it would be the abolition of slavery in America.[15]

The counterelites: Columunist Jack Newfield called them the "prophetic minority," but for Lyndon Johnson they were the "doubters and the cussers," and for Spiro Agnew "the impudent snobs." They are not necessarily pleasant people, and they are not usually distinguished by their humility; to some they come across like Puritan saints. But they are the heroes of this book, because they serve as catalysts of democracy: They socialize conflict.[16]

OUTLINE OF THIS BOOK

This book deals with the possibilities and evidences of democracy in America, and it points out when and how democracy is frustrated in America. Its chapters are grouped into three basic division: *prerequisites* of democracy, *processes* of American democracy, and *components* of democratic government in America, followed by a concluding chapter.

Prerequisites: Chapters 1–3. If democracy is like a primitive football game— the kind that permits the spectators to join the players—then before the people in the grandstands can get involved at least three conditions must be fulfilled. First, they must be given an unobstructed view of the action on the field. Secondly, they must be free enough from worries about food, shelter, and so on to pay attention to what they do see—starving people make poor spectators and even less likely participants. Thirdly, there must be reasonable harmony among the spectators so that they can pay attention to what is happening at the center of the arena instead of skirmishing among themselves in the grandstands.

The three prerequisites above are considered in the first three chapters of this book, which deal, respectively, with liberty, equality, and fraternity. The "liberty" in Chapter 1 is not taken as an end in itself but as a means—an absolutely essential means—by which the majority learns the facts and debates the alternatives. Chapter 2 considers the second prerequisite to democratic participation: freedom from need. Its thesis is that relieving poverty is a prepolitical task: It must be undertaken *before* we can expect "maximum feasible participation" from people. Chapter 3, on "fraternity," raises this question: can we reach a new *political* consensus among races and ethnic groups in America without flattening out or obliterating America's *social* and *cultural* diversity?

Processes: Chapters 4–6. The second part of this book deals with the processes of democracy in America. Chapter 4, on campaigns and elections, comes to grips with some questions which no believer in democracy can avoid. If the people can be trusted to govern, why are they so apathetic about politics in America? And why are they, at least seemingly, so ignorant and confused when they go to the polls to vote? The chapter reviews some of the research on voting behavior and concludes, with political scientist V. O. Key, that, "voters are not fools" The problem is rather with our system of nominations, campaigns, and elections, which has bred so much cynicism and insincerity. Another aspect of our "politics as usual" system is studied in Chapter 5: the cozy relationship between special interests and government. But Chapter 5 also studies another kind of interest group—the kind that claims to represent the interests common to the entire nation. Are these presumptuous claims? Such self-proclaimed "citizen's lobbies" as Ralph Nader's and Common Cause are studied in terms of that question. Chapter 6 brings us to the study of larger organizations than interest groups: It examines the politics of parties in America. If the democratic process can be compared to the effects of a stone dropped into the water, nowhere is this process more neatly illustrated than in the history of American political parties. The chapter shows how parties have widened the circles of participation, bringing more and more people into the political process through such devices as the caucus and the nominating convention. But the chapter also raises the question whether parties have lost their capacity to democratize and innovate. For primary elections and other more recent devices to open the channels of participation are not the work of parties but *movements*—which will also be studied in Chapter 6.

Components: Chapters 8–10. Here we are concerned with the three major components of the federal government: the Congress, the President, and the Supreme Court. Each of them has a vital role to play, and each should perform vigorously if we are to preserve balance in our system. The need for political power cannot be wished away in our modern world. The way to prevent the abuse of power is not to enfeeble any organ of government but to make sure that each of the three components is healthy enough to stand guard against abuses from either of the other components.

The sick man in our system has been Congress. Chapter 7 discusses some of the factors that have prevented Congress from reaching its full potential as an instrument of representative democracy. Chapters 8 and 9 take a long look at the chief beneficiary of congressional infirmity: the President. As the Congress has abdicated, the President has aggrandized. The dangers to democracy of the imperial Presidency should be obvious enough. Chapter 8 systematically examines the enormous powers gathered into the hands of one person. Chapter 9 considers some of the limitations on those powers, and reviews some proposals for additional checks. Chapter 10 turns to the third branch of the federal government, a branch which has also taken up some of the slack left during the years of legislative stagnation. It studies the Supreme Court in terms of this basic question: Is the Supreme Court, exercising its powers of judicial review, compatible with democracy?

Conclusion: What is America? Returning to the model of democracy sketched above, the concluding chapter of this book discusses the meaning of America, speculates on its future, and offers some hints as to what citizens can do to affect that future. For now, we can only briefly anticipate some of these themes by taking a last look at the beginning of this chapter—the uncovering of the Watergate scandal. It has often been debated whether Watergate proved that "the system works." The problem at the very outset is the ambiguity of the word "system."

If the "system" means *only* our official or quasi-official organs of government and politics—Congress, the courts, the executive branch, our two major political parties—then the whole Watergate episode points up some critical flaws in it. From the very day of the break-in, the FBI, under the direction of a Nixon loyalist, L. Patrick Gray, systematically reported on the status of its investigation to Nixon's chief aides; it continued to do so even when evidence began to accumulate that these same aides were involved in the break-in, or at least the cover-up. The FBI thus enabled suspects to rehearse their answers in advance of the questions and to know who it was who was doing the talking to the FBI. As for the Justice Department, its prosecutors seemed unprepared to search for culprits beyond the original seven burglars. The transcripts of the White House tapes show that Henry Peterson, the Assistant Attorney General who headed the Watergate inquiry, was easily intimidated and bamboozled by Nixon. Nor were either of our political parties very zealous to get at the facts behind the mysterious burglary attempt in the headquarters of one of them. Senator Hugh Scott of Pennsylvania was typical of the Republican leadership, defending Nixon with a loyalty which Nixon had never shown to the Republican party, excoriating the press with all the fervor of a Ronald Ziegler, and accepting at face value the increasingly incredible statements emanating from the Nixon White House. Even the Democrats soft-pedaled Watergate, making little effort to smoke out the conspirators for fear of being accused of "partisanship." Turning to Congress, the branch of government which supposedly exercises "oversight" of the executive branch, we note that not until nearly a year after the break-in did a Senate investigation get under way. What had Congress done to find the Watergate leviathan *before* it blundered to the surface on June 17, 1972? For over three years, right under the nose of Congress in the nation's capital, the Nixon administration had been able to assemble its own domestic CIA, to illegally tap phones, to break into buildings, and to plan an extensive program of espionage and sabotage. In this context congressional "oversight" became a grotesque pun.

But suppose that the American political "system" is taken in the larger sense, to include not merely the governmental apparatus but all the observers and political actors who operate outside of the official government, and sometimes in opposition to it—everyone from the people who write letters to newspapers, to the newspapers themselves and the various activist organizations throughout the country. Even though very few newspapers and reporters pursued the Watergate case with any degree of vigor, it was exposed through the work of reporters like Bernstein and Woodward of the *Washington Post*. Organizations like Common Cause also helped to uncover Watergate-related scandals by forcing the Nixon administration to disclose the sources of its campaign funds. And American society itself was free enough to reverberate with all the controversy and discussion surrounding Watergate, widening the circles of the scandal until it became a national issue and a historical turning point. If *this* is what is meant by the "system"—a grand assembly of amateur and professional politicians, reporters, columnists, gadflies, whistle-blowers, team, and nonteam players—if, in short, everybody in America who talks and argues and cares about politics is also part of "the system," then Richard Nixon's 1973 prophecy makes some sort of ironic sense after all: "It was the system that brought the facts to light and that will bring the guilty to justice."[17]

NOTES

1. The scenes which follow are taken from a variety of sources, but particularly these three: J. Anthony Lukas, "The Story So Far," *New York Times Magazine,* July 22, 1973, passim; Carl Bernstein and Bob Woodward, "All the President's Men," *Playboy,* XXI (May 1974), pp. 86–90; Congressional Quarterly, *Guide to Current American Government,* Fall 1974, p. 2.
2. George McKenna, ed., *American Populism* (New York: G. P. Putnam's Sons, 1974), p. 214.
3. Hillman M. Bishop and Samuel Hendel, eds., *Basic Issues of American Democracy,* 5th ed. (New York: Appleton-Century-Crofts, Inc., 1965), pp. 582–584.
4. Ibid., p. 583.
5. David Halberstam, *The Best and the Brightest* (Greenwich, Conn.: Fawcett Publications, Inc., 1973), p. 503.
6. Lukas, op. cit., p. 8.
7. Congressional Quarterly, *Watergate: Chronology of a Crisis* (Washington: Congressional Quarterly, Inc., 1973), p. 82.
8. Quoted in Theodore C. Sorensen, *Kennedy* (New York: Harper & Row, Publishers, Incorporated, 1965), p. 292.
9. Emmet John Hughes, *The Living Presidency* (New York: Coward, McCann & Geoghegan, Inc., 1972), p. 76
10. *The Watergate Hearings: Break-in and Cover-up, New York Times* edition (New York: Bantam Books, Inc.) p. 266
11. Ibid., p. 521.
12. Richard E. Neustadt, *Presidential Power: The Politics of Leadership* (New York: John Wiley & Sons, Inc., 1960), p. 3.
13. Leonard J. Fein, "To Try to Dream Again," *New York Times,* Feb. 11, 1973, sec. 4, p. 13.
14. The following model of democracy is taken from E. E. Schattschneider, *The Semisovereign People* (New York: Holt, Rinehart and Winston, Inc., 1960), chap. 1.
15. Henry David Thoreau, "Civil Disobedience," in Robert A. Goldwin, ed., *On Civil Disobedience: Essays Old and New* (Chicago: Rand McNally & Company, 1968), p. 20.
16. The counterelites honored in this book must not be confused with revolutionaries, and certainly not with the various crazies (Weathermen, Symbionese Liberationists, and so on) who imagine themselves revolutionaries. These latter groups are properly studied in a textbook on abnormal psychology; there is nothing to say about them here except to recall Lenin's contempt for "infantile" leftists. As for nonpsychotic revolutionaries, they may someday be proven correct that the only way to produce meaningful change is to overthrow everything, by violence if necessary, and start anew. But this book proceeds on the assumption that their conclusion is, to say the

least, premature. The difficulty at the very outset is to find an agreement about goals. If the revolutionary desires heaven on earth, he or she is absolutely correct in concluding that the American political system will never deliver. But if we are talking about secular goals—a substantially smaller military budget, a substantially larger expenditure on health, education, and welfare, a much flatter curve of income distribution, a wide availability of social services and health care, an end to slums and to outright privation, a clean environment, an industrial system which serves the public interest—if goals of this sort are what the revolutionary wants, it remains to be seen whether they are attainable without revolution. The assumption in this book is that they can be attained, or at least that we should have a try at attaining them, without resorting to revolution.

The reformer is often distinguished from the revolutionary on the grounds that he or she works "within the system." The characterization contains a core of truth, but it is also misleading. To be a reformer one does not have to settle for only minor, marginal changes in the status quo, nor does one have to profess a "higher loyalty" to those who run the government, or, indeed, to the government itself. But it is necessary for the reformer to believe in the American political community. By "community" we mean the people at large insofar as they constitute a political whole and share certain basic political convictions. The community includes the *unofficial* political agents and organizations—the media and its commentators, interest groups, voters, and even all the unaffiliated activists, talkers, viewers, readers, and spectators. But for the revolutionary there is no such thing as "the community"; the very term seems to such a person a kind of mystification used by the ruling class to disguise the ugly fact of oppression. Or, even if the revolutionary concedes that the term has any meaning, he or she will deny that it now exists; it can exist only after the revolution. The reformer, on the other hand, acts as if the community already exists. It is never far from his mind as he muckrakes, or exposes, or commits civil disobedience. He is always, ultimately, appealing to the public at large. He calls himself a "citizen," a member of the *civitas,* the city, the *polis,* the commonwealth—the community. No modern revolutionary worthy of the name would ever call himself a citizen. The term sounds too respectable, and in a way it is: It implies the acceptance of an inviolable politcal structure, a prior organization of society, an organization put together without the help of the revolutionary. It is their contrasting attitudes not toward the government but toward the community which distinguishes the reformers from the revolutionaries. Both types may play havoc with the smooth operation of government, but the reformer recognizes the sovereignty of the community. In throwing a wrench into governmental machinery, therefore, the reformer is not trying to destroy the community. She or he is trying to communicate with it.

17 Broadcast Address, Apr. 30, 1973, in *The Watergate Hearings,* op. cit., p. 689.

Part One

Prerequisites for Democracy

Chapter 1

Liberty: The Free Trade in Ideas

Let truth and falsehood grapple: who ever knew truth put to the worse, in a free and open encounter. . . .
John Milton
The method of democracy is the method of debate.
Sir Ernest Barker *

This chapter will discuss liberty, especially liberty of expression: free speech, free press, freedom to petition and demonstrate peacefully. Free expression, of course, is only one area of liberty. Among the other liberties considered basic are the liberty to worship (or not to worship) according to conscience, the liberty to travel and move about as we please, the liberty to live in our homes without being bugged or tapped or arbitrarily invaded or searched by others, the liberty to keep one's private life confidential, the liberty to associate with whom we please, the liberty to vote for the candidate we think best qualified, and, indeed, the liberty to stay away from politics if we prefer. To these traditional Western ideals of liberty, President Roosevelt added another in his famous "four freedoms" speech of 1941: freedom from want.

Freedom from want will be discussed in the next chapter in considering the

---

* *Reflections on Government* (New York: Oxford University Press, 1958).

question of equality. As for all the other freedoms mentioned above, we can only pause here to pay our respects, before narrowing in on the one that most interests us in this chapter: freedom of expression.

Freedom of expression is especially interesting to us, first, because it covers a lot of ground (in discussing indirect threats to free speech we can hardly avoid talking about other liberties, especially the liberty to enjoy privacy,* secondly, because of its integral connection with democracy.

Democracy is one of the main themes running through this book, and this chapter will argue that liberty of expression is in fact a prerequisite to it. To see why it is a prerequisite, it will be necessary to examine the meaning of democracy. If the reader will just be patient for a few pages, we shall come back to liberty after taking a closer look at that elusive word "democracy".

DEMOCRACY—SOME COMMON DEFINITIONS

Ask any group of Americans how they define the term "democracy." You will probably get a variety of responses:

"It's when the people run their own government."
"It means that people have the right to vote."
"Democracy means that all people are treated equally."
"In a democracy people are secure in their homes; there's no midnight knock at the door."
"It means people can say what they please without fear of intimidation."
"Democracy means individualism—it's the opposite of totalitarianism."
"Democracy is essentially a matter of counting heads."
"Democracy means respecting the rights of minorities."

One reason for the bewildering variety of responses is that "democracy" has become a kind of all purpose "hurrah-word," in the same league as the good, the true, and the beautiful. Yet the definitions cited above, which are rather typical ones, are not altogether without pattern, Broadly, they seem to fall into two categories: democracy as a method and democracy as a set of values. We can fit them into a table, like this:

Democracy as:

Method	Values
"The people run their own government"	"All people are treated equally"
"The right to vote"	"People are secure in their homes"
"Counting heads"	"People can say what they please."
	"Individualism"
	"Respecting the rights of minorities"

* See below, pp 38–42.

A semanticist might object that only those definitions in the left-hand column apply to the term "democracy." The roots of the term are the two Greek words, *demos* and *kratia*, meaning *people* and *rule*. A democracy implies some variant of popular rule; it involves numbers, not values. The items listed above in the right-hand column seem to suggest that democracy must be decent and reasonable, but there is nothing in the etymology or the history of democracy which requires it to be. In Oscar Wilde's opinion, "democracy simply means the bludgeoning of the people by the people for the people."[1] A democracy put Socrates death for saying the wrong things to the youth of Athens, and democracy in America has often accorded the same treatment to unpopular individuals and minorities. If numbers only are taken into account, what is more democratic than a lynch mob?

Americans, fortunately, have not been content to define democracy merely in terms of numbers. We speak of "majority rule," but we usually add, "and minority rights." These rights, we seem to agree (in theory, if not always in practice), include the right of minorities to express themselves freely, even if their opinions are anathema to the majority. The First Amendment is a legal expression of this commitment: It explicitly prevents the majority, as represented in the national legislature, from tampering with free speech: "Congress shall make no law" abridging it. Thomas Jefferson was one of the Founders who insisted that the First Amendment be added to the Constitution, as a necessary safeguard against "the tyranny of legislatures." This is all the more remarkable, since Jefferson was one of the few Founders who retained an almost boundless faith in the fairness and decency of the majority. Even Jefferson, then, hedged his faith with some important qualifications. In his first inaugural address, the same speech in which he called for "absolute acquiescence in the decisions of the majority," he reminded his audience of "this sacred principle,"

> that, though the will of the majority is in all cases to prevail, that will, to be rightful, must be reasonable; that the minority possess their equal rights, which equal law must protect and to violate which would be oppression.[2]

A logician might object that Jefferson is trying to eat his cake and have it too. Once he says that "the will of the majority is in *all* cases to prevail," what point is there in talking about minority rights? What he really should say is that "the majority is in *some* cases to prevail," i.e., in those cases when it is "reasonable," when it does not oppress the minority. To say that, however, would open up a new and dangerous area for discussion: Who is to say what is "reasonable"? Should the majority be allowed to judge in its own case? Or should we give the power to some elite body, such as the Supreme Court? If the latter, what happens to the "absolute acquiesence in the decisions of the majority"?

One is tempted to draw a gloomy conclusion: Majority rule and minority rights (democracy as a method and democratic values) are not only unrelated but downright contradictory at times. We "pays our money and takes our choice." Once we commit ourselves to democratic method, we must accept whatever results from that method, however objectionable it may seem from the standpoint of civil liberties. If, on the other hand, we opt for civil liberties, we may wind up being elitists if a democratic majority decides to become oppressive.

This dilemma is a serious and perennial one in the theory of democracy. It may even be insoluble as a matter of logic. But democracy involves more than logic.

When we turn from abstract formulations to the actual setting of democracy, majority rule and minority rights are by no means unconnected. Let us take note of the fact that it is not really accurate to talk about "the" majority. Today's majority can become tomorrow's minority, and vice versa. Presidents Johnson and Nixon learned this lesson painfully, and even seemingly stable majorities have melted away in time. The lesson here is not only that the majority, or those who claim to speak for them, may someday find themselves on the receiving end of the oppression they once dealt out, but also that it is difficult even to say what *is* the majority over an extended period of time. In fact, "the" majority is not a static monolith but a potentially unstable coalition of minorities. Democracy is thus a dynamic process. And the heart of the dynamo is the communications process—argument, persuasion, discussion, and debate.

FREE SPEECH: THE DYNAMO OF DEMOCRACY

The political actor tries to persuade members of his or her opponent's coalition to break away and join his or hers. The political actor may appeal to their ideals or their self-interest, but some sort of pitch must be made. Such a person's opponents, naturally, do the same. And what about the people in the "audience"? It is to *their* interest to hear as many points of view as possible so as to make the wisest choice. They may even feel that in order to "hear" properly they should be able to cross-examine, to question, to bring up counterarguments. Finally, they may decide to become activists themselves, not being content merely to vote for candidates or causes but to speak out on their own behalf. It is hard to imagine a working democracy, therefore, without free speech. To artificially "freeze" a majority, to try to prevent its erosion by prohibiting free speech, is really to rig the whole system of majority rule. Even if elections are permitted in such a situation, the elections are meaningless because the voter has been denied an essential means of finding out what he or she is voting for.

In choosing democracy as our form of government, said Alexander Meiklejohn, we Americans have made "a momentous decision. We have decided to be self-governed." Now we really get down to the hard-core defense of liberty. Sometimes liberty is defended as some sort of abstract, mystical "natural right," inscribed in the universe by the hand of the Creator—and of course immediately intelligible to anyone with eyes to see and ears to hear. In the eighteenth century the signers of the Declaration of Independence held that the "unalienable" right to liberty was a "self-evident" truth. In our more skeptical century, however, there aren't many "self-evident" truths lying around. Liberty in particular needs a better defense than the bare assertion than that it happens to be one of "the

Laws of Nature and of Nature's God." Meiklejohn's defense of liberty answers that need by picturing liberty not as an end but as a means—a means by which a self-governing people keeps itself informed. Freedom does not have to be seen as some "natural right" written in the heavens but as a very down-to-earch vehicle for obtaining information.

> Shall we give a hearing to those who hate and despise freedom, to those who, if they had the power, would destroy our institutions? Certainly, yes! Our action must be guided, not by their principles, but by ours. We listen, not because they desire to speak, but because we need to hear. If there are arguments against our theory of government, our policies in war or in peace, we the citizens, the rulers, must hear and consider them for ourselves. That is the way of public safety. It is the program of self-government.[3]

Let us now consider the implications of the argument. This chapter forgoes any defense of liberty as an end in itself. The argument is rather that freedom is valuable because it is *useful*. Oliver Wendell Holmes, Jr., once put it in the form of an economic metaphor: The best way to find truth in the political arena is through "the free trade in ideas."[4] The majority is pictured as a kind of comparison-shopper. The shopper wanders in and out of the stalls, lets each proponent hawk his or her wares, and finally chooses the product which combines the best features. Needless to say, the economic marketplace no longer works that way, if it ever did. But that need not detain us. We are talking about speech, not commerce, and we are positing an ideal, not describing the reality. In fact, we shall use that ideal in order to compare it with the reality in America.

The "free trade in ideas" may be disrupted in at least three different ways: by *direct coercion,* by *indirect coercion,* and by *monopoly.* We could call the coercion *direct* if, for example, the police arrested either the "seller" or the "buyer" of a particular set of ideas. We could also speak of direct coercion if a howling mob disrupted the transaction, or lynched one of the buyers or sellers. *Indirect* coercion would imply the use of threats or other forms of pressure. The buyer could buy and the seller could sell, but they both might find their phones tapped or their tax returns singled out for auditing. Indirect coercion might also come from neighbors or employers or former friends: The idea-traders might find themselves snubbed, insulted, socially ostracized, or unemployed. *Monopoly,* unlike direct or indirect coercion, doesn't have to be nasty. It could just happen that one of the sellers buys out all the rest. Yet this particular act, which might be concluded with smiles and handshakes, is at least as effective as coercion when it comes to choking off "the free trade in ideas." It might even be more effective because it operates quietly and smoothly, without any melodrama.

Note that each of these restraints on idea-trading—direct coercion, indirect coercion, and monopoly—can come either from government or from society, i.e., the private sphere. When the police arrest a speaker, the source of coercion is the government, but when the speaker is shouted down or beaten up by a mob, we ordinarily attribute the coercion to some element of society. (Unless the mob is egged on by the government! One of the most disturbing features of the Nixon administration was its preoccupation with inflaming social prejudices against its critics by "getting the story out" on them.) We can at once sum up and illustrate with this table:

Threats to "The Free Trade in Ideas"

	Direct coercion	Indirect coercion	Monoply
From government	jail, censorship	threats, surveillance, etc.	exclusive government control
From society	mob violence, vigilantism	social ostracism, loss of job, etc.	exclusive control by one point of view

Before taking a closer look at these threats to "the free trade in ideas," let us put together some of the things we have been saying in the preceding pages. The best way to assemble the pieces is to see if we can arrive at a definition of liberty. The term "liberty" is sometimes defined as "the absence of restraint." The trouble with that definition is that it fails to account for the *purpose* of liberty: *Why* does a speaker or writer or demonstrator want liberty? Surely the answer is that liberty is desired in order to communicate, to make a point, to *affect the minds* of the audience. If the speaker is hauled off to jail that purpose is frustrated, but the purpose can also be frustrated if no one happens to be listening. Sane people do not go around talking to themselves. Their purpose is to reach others and get a response.

To speak—yet be deprived of an audience? Is that possible? Everyone, of course, can find someone to listen, but not very many can find a mass audience. And mass audiences, in today's world, are where the action is.

We live today in an age of loudspeakers, and those who control access to those loudspeakers are the ones who determine what will be heard by the public at large. The unamplified human voice is no match for a coast-to-coast network of electronic communication or a national chain of newspapers. That is why soapbox oratory has become so quaint. The circle of listeners is small (unless a TV camera is present) and Americans today are simply not tuned in to local oratory; they are wired to the nation and the world. Those who control those wires are the ones who really enjoy free speech, or enjoy it to the fullest degree. It is not enough, therefore, to define liberty negatively as "the absence of restraint." It has to be defined affirmatively, as "the right to communicate through the media from which Americans customarily receive news and opinion." When the First Amendment was written those media were mainly two: the vocal cords (more or less equally distributed throughout the population) and the printing press (to which it was easy to gain access). Today, when the media of communication serve mass audiences through wire services, sophisticated printing equipment, audio and visual electronics, the problem is to find some way of opening these up to all who wish to communicate. Such a goal may never be fully attainable, but it can hardly be forgotten if we are to strive for "liberty" in the proper sense of the term, which is to say *effective* liberty.

More will be said on the subject of effective liberty when we consider monopoly as a threat to free speech. But let us begin at the beginning, by considering some of the more obvious restraints on "the free trade in ideas." The first of these threats is direct coercion.

DIRECT COERCION

Until the twentieth century, America saw few instances of direct governmental coercion. True, as early as 1798 the Federalists passed a draconic series of laws, known collectively as the Alien and Sedition Acts, which prescribed fines and imprisonment for anyone who should "write, print, utter, or publish . . . any false, scandalous, and malicious writing or writings against the government of the United States or any of its officers." But the furor caused by the passage and enforcement of these laws was to have a boomerang effect upon their authors. The acts became a campaign issue in the election of 1800, and helped to ensure the defeat of John Adams and his party at the hands of the Jeffersonians. For more than a century afterward the instances of direct government interference with free speech were few, and usually temporary, such as those used against pro-Southern newspaper editors during the Civil War.

Not until the time of America's entry into World War I did the federal government get back into the business of writing and enforcing statutes against dissenters. The Espionage Act of 1917 punished, among other things, any attempt to "willfully obstruct . . . the recruiting or enlistment service of the United States." Under the terms of the Sedition Act of 1918 Americans were forbidden to "willfully utter, print, write, or publish any disloyal, profane, scurrilous or abusive language about the form of government of the United States, or the military or naval forces of the United States, or the uniform of the Army or Navy of the United States." Nearly a thousand persons were convicted under these two acts. The Justice Department raided newspaper offices, arrested people without warrants and held them without bail. People were sent to jail for opinions uttered "in the heat of private altercation, on a railroad train, in a hotel lobby, or at that battle ground of disputation, a boardinghouse table."[5] Men and women were imprisoned for saying that the war should be financed by higher taxes instead of bond sales and for criticizing the Red Cross or the YMCA. One woman was sentenced to ten years in jail for saying, "I am for the people, and the government is for the profiteers."[6]

Shouting "Fire!"

The constitutionality of the Espionage and Sedition Acts was sustained in six cases which came before the Supreme Court. The most memorable and durable of the opinions in these cases was that of Justice Oliver Wendell Holmes in *Schenck v. United States* (1919),[7] which sustained the conviction of an antiwar publicist for violating the Espionage Act. Schenck had circulated leaflets arguing that military conscription violated the Thirteenth (antislavery) Amendment and urging men to "Assert Your Rights" by petitioning for repeal of the draft. He was convicted of violating the provision in the Espionage Act which prohibits the obstruction of recruitment. Holmes rejected Schenck's contention that his First Amendment rights were being violated by the conviction.

Holmes, did you say? The reader may be puzzled. Was this the same Oliver Wendell Holmes whose "free trade in ideas" is the central theme of this chapter? The answer is yes. How, then, can he uphold the conviction of someone for the "crime" of circulating opinions on the military draft?

Holmes's reply is that more than opinions were involved in the *Schenck* case. "The character of every act depends upon the circumstances in which it is done." Speech loses its character as mere opinion when it takes place in an atmosphere in which a resultant action is imminent. For example, "the most stringent protection of free speech would not protect a man in falsely shouting fire in a crowded theater and causing a panic." Holmes's conclusion: Words that would normally be protected by the First Amendment may be punished if they occur in circumstances where their utterance would create a "clear and present danger" of an evil which Congress has a right to prevent—in this case an obstruction of the military draft during wartime.

It is hard to disagree with Holmes that falsely shouting fire in a crowded theater is an intolerable incitement. But the difficulty appears when we try to apply the "clear and present danger" test to cases involving political dissent instead of psychotic practical jokes. In the *Schenck* case, for example, the defendant had done no more than mail out leaflets protesting the draft. Schenck had urged only peaceful means, such as petitioning for repeal of the draft. Is this the same as shouting fire in a crowded theater?

Whatever its difficulties, Holmes's effort to balance liberty and security was surely more favorable to the side of liberty than some of the other tests used by the Court at various times. Consider, for example, a famous case decided by the Court in 1951.

The "Dennis" Case: Conspiring to Advocate Although Congress passed the Smith Act in 1940, and the Justice Department used it a few times against American Nazis at the beginning of the Second World War, its wholesale application did not begin until the late 1940s, when it was used against Communists. The act made it a federal crime:

1 "to knowingly or willfully advocate, abet, advise, or teach the duty, necessity, desirability, or propriety of overthrowing or destroying any government in the United States by force or violence, or by the assassination of any officer of such government"
2 to organize or be a member of a group which advocates such measures
3 to *conspire* to advocate or organize

In 1948 the eleven top leaders of the American Communist party were indicted under the act for "willfully and knowingly conspiring to teach and advocate the overthrow of government by force and violence, and conspiring to organize the Communist Party for the purpose of so doing." The Supreme Court affirmed their convictions in a landmark case, *Dennis v. United States* (1951).[8]

Note: The defendants were not charged with doing anything, conspiring to do anything, or even with advocating anything, but with *conspiring to advocate.* The Court majority paid homage to the clear and present danger test, but reinterpreted it in such a way as to change its essential meaning. It was now sufficient for the government to demonstrate a "grave and probable" danger: If the danger is grave enough its imminence need not be proven, only its probability. Chief Justice Vinson said: "Obviously [clear and present danger] cannot mean that before the Government may act, it must await until the *putsch* is about to be executed, the plans have been laid and the signal is awaited." If we can prosecute the person who shouts fire in a crowded theater, why not prosecute such a person if we catch her at home plotting to do it? The urge "to kill the serpent in the egg," as Zechariah Chafee once put it, was a prominent feature of the early cold war period in America.

Toward the end of the 1950s, when official anxiety about secret plans and putsches seemed to subside, the Court tightened the requirement for prosecution under the Smith Act. In *Yates v. United States* (1957)[9] the Court interpreted the statute as punishing advocacy only when such advocacy is "in language reasonably and ordinarily calculated to incite." Prosecution under the Smith Act and related laws became increasingly subject to successful court challenges, and the Justice Department became increasingly hesitant to seek prosecutions. The "red scare" of the early 1950s seemed to have subsided by the end of the decade. Although the Court sustained the membership clause of the Smith Act in 1961 by a narrow 5-4 majority, it interpreted the statute to ban only "active" membership, i.e., membership in the organization with specific intent to overthrow the government by force and violence *(Scales v. United States).*[10] In a related case, the Court reversed the conviction of another party member because such intent had not been demonstrated *(Noto v. U.S.).*[11]

Vietnam Era Hardly had the fears of quiet subversion been laid to rest than a new specter began haunting the nation's lawmakers. The House Committee on Internal Security, successor to the House Un-American Activities Committee, called it "revolutionary violence." Others preferred terms like "guerrilla theater." Whatever the name, the sixties gave us a new kind of politics: existential politics, the politics of acting out. Vietnam protest began with marches on Washington and ended with Daniel Ellsberg's sensational leak of secret documents. "Counterculture" emphasized changes in style and manners. Draft cards were burned or handed in during solemn ceremonies. Countless angry speeches or morality skits were staged in front of TV cameras.

The authorities reacted predictably—with statutes, prosecutions, and investigations. In 1965 Congress made it a crime for anyone to burn his draft card. A year later, David P. O'Brien did precisely that, on the steps of a Boston courthouse. He was sentenced to six years in prison, but the Court of Appeals reversed the conviction as a violation of the First Amendment. In 1968, however, the Supreme Court, in *United States v. O'Brien,*[12] upheld the conviction, rejecting O'Brien's contention that the burning of his card was "symbolic speech" protected by the First Amendment.

O'Brien's protest was the act of one man. More typical were the activities of groups of protestors. The government's attempt to punish those it regarded as the ringleaders of the protest movement led to a series of sensational show-trials. Guerrilla theater moved from the streets into the courtroom as government prosecutors, sometimes with the support of judges, clashed with defendants who often sounded more like accusers. Numbers and towns were to mark the various trials: the Catonsville Nine (a trial which resulted in the conviction of two Catholic priests, Daniel and Phillip Berrigan, and seven others for burning draft records with homemade napalm); the Milwaukee Fourteen (another draft-record immolation by Catholic peace activists—all found guilty); the Harrisburg Seven (in which the government tried, unsuccessfully, to convict Phillip Berrigan and the six others on a variety of bizarre charges, including a conspiracy to kidnap Henry Kissinger); the Gainesville Eight (seven antiwar Vietnam veterans accused of assaulting the 1972 Republican convention with automatic weapons, a crossbow, and a slingshot). The two group-trials which perhaps best capture the flavor of the period were the trials of the Boston Four and the Chicago Seven.

The Boston Four In 1968, Benjamin Spock, the noted baby doctor, was indicted with four others and charged with a conspiracy to "counsel, aid and abet diverse selective service registrants to unlawfully . . . evade service in the armed forces of the United States. . . ." Like the *Dennis* indictments of a generation earlier they did not charge the defendants with committing any illegal overt acts, or even with causing them to be committed, but with a *conspiracy* to cause them to be committed. A conspiracy does not have to be successful to be punishable.

Aside from the government's reliance upon conspiracy charges, however, the circumstances and the defendants in the Spock trial could hardly be more different from those in the *Dennis* case. Spock's codefendants included: William Sloan Coffin, Jr., chaplain at Yale University and a former CIA member; Michael Ferber, a graduate student at Harvard; and Marcus Raskin, former disarmament adviser to President Kennedy and codirector of The Institute for Policy Studies. These were not political pariahs but prominent, even establishmentarian figures in America. Their dissent was not based on fundamental opposition to the American system of government, but merely on opposition to the war policies of the Johnson administration.

The government's "conspiracy" charge had an ironic flavor—not only because some of these "conspirators" hardly knew one another, but also because their acts were open, in full view of cameras, reporters, and government agents. One of the government's exhibits, "A Call to Resist Illegitimate Authority," signed by four of the defendants (plus hundreds of others), was published in a newspaper and subsequently in a book. Some of the defendants actively sought indictments for the purpose of testing the legality of the draft law, and of the war itself. But their hopes for making the Spock trial a test case were dealt a fatal blow when the eighty-five-year-old judge ruled out of order any discussion of the draft or the war. Four of the defendants, including Dr. Spock, were found guilty. Their convictions were reversed in 1969 on equally anticlimactic grounds: The judge had improperly instructed the jury.

The Chicago Seven This trial shared some common features with the Spock trial: an elderly judge; a group of defendants who "couldn't agree on lunch," as one of them put it, being charged with conspiracy; an attempt by the defendants to turn the tables on their accusers by raising the question of official illegality. The Chicago Seven, however, were not as respectful of courtroom decorum as their counterparts in the Boston trial. The Chicago trial was thus the scene of some of the most uproarious confrontations ever seen in a United States District Court.

The trial, which was heard before District Judge Julius Hoffman in 1969–1970, grew out of events in Chicago during the 1968 Democratic convention. The defendants were accused of violating a 1968 federal statute prescribing criminal penalties for crossing state lines with "intent" to "incite a riot." The statute has been called the "Rap Brown" law, after an itinerant black militant whose speeches were frequently cited by proponents of the statute as part of the reason for its necessity.

The Chicago Seven, who included Yippie spokesman Abby Hoffman, former SDS Chairman Thomas Hayden, and Black Panther leader Bobby Seale, had little in common ideologically, but symbolically they represented virtually every faction of the so-called New Left—which, the defendants believed, was why the government singled them out for prosecution. The trial was punctuated with shouts, curses, melodramatic speeches, and verbal duels between Judge Hoffman and the defendants' lawyers. At one point Bobby Seale was bound and gagged for continuing to insist upon being represented by his own lawyer. Judge Hoffman meted out a total of forty-one contempt citations to the defendants and their lawyers for offenses ranging from talking out of turn to blowing kisses to the jury and wheeling a birthday cake into the courtroom. Five of the seven were convicted, but their convictions were reversed by a Court of Appeals in 1972 because of the manner in which Judge Hoffman conducted the trial. Since the reversal was based entirely on procedural grounds, the "Rap Brown" law remains on the books.

Burning and returning draft cards, setting fire to draft records, demonstrating in city streets during a highly volatile period—are these valid contributions to "the free trade in ideas"? Or are they abuses which can only lead to chaos and anarchy? While many, including most leaders in government, saw the protesters as either traitors or spoiled show-offs, they saw themselves as representatives of a higher patriotism, resorting to dramatic devices in order to break through the shell of politics-as-usual. The intensity both of the demonstrations and of the official reactions reached a peak in the early seventies, as the Nixon administration became entangled in what had once been "Johnson's war." In May 1970, after United States troops invaded Cambodia, student strikes and demonstrations broke out on campuses throughout the nation. During one of these, on the campus of Kent State University in Ohio, National Guardsmen fired live rounds into a large mass of demonstrators, killing four. A year later the momentum of Cambodia had produced a massive antiwar demonstration in Washington. On Attorney General John Mitchell's orders 13,000 were summarily arrested, although the cases were all dismissed later in the courts.

After 1971 mass demonstrations began to wane, but the same spirit of "bearing witness" against the government took a new form: muckraking and exposure of the government's secrets.

The Paper and the Papers   Sometime late in March 1971, Daniel Ellsberg, a former RAND Corporation employee, supplied the *New York Times* (and eventually several other newspapers) with copies of a top-secret Pentagon study of American involvement in Indochina since the late 1940s. After spending months going through the documents, the *Times* began publishing excerpts on June 12, 1971. Three days later Attorney General Mitchell took the *Times* to court and obtained an injunction prohibiting it from publishing any more of the Pentagon Papers until the legal issue of whether it could do so was resolved. It was the first time in the nation's history that a newspaper was restrained in advance by a court for publishing a specific article.*

During this period the *Times* appealed its case to the Supreme Court, which—in an unusual move resented by some of its members—agreed to hear the case in record time and thus tell the *Times* whether it could go ahead and publish. On June 30, 1971 the Court majority, by 6 to 3, upheld the newspaper.[13] It was, however, a precarious majority. Justices Burger and Blackmun, two Nixon appointees, dissented, along with Justice Harlan. (Before the end of 1971, Nixon had appointed two additional Justices.) What is more, the majority was fragmented into five separate opinions, ranging from Justice Black's insistence that First Amendment liberties are absolute to Justice White's willingness to approve of prior restraint under certain curcumstances.

What was the attitude of the nation's Chief Executive during all of this? The evidence suggests that Richard M. Nixon did not for a moment regard Ellsberg's leaks as endangering national security,[14] but he saw in the uproar surrounding them an excellent opportunity to discredit Ellsberg, the peace movement, the Democratic party, and prior administrations. John Ehrlichman's handwritten notes, taken during his meetings with the President in June and July of 1971, show Nixon making these comments: "Win PR, not just court case," and "Win the case but the NB [next best] thing is to get the public view right. Hang it all on LBJ." Nixon adivsed Ehrlichman to read the chapter on Alger Hiss in his book *Six Crises,* observing, "It was won in the press." On July 6, according to Ehrlichman's notes, Nixon said to Attorney General Mitchell: "Must be tried in the papers. Not Ellsberg (since already indicted). Get conspiracy smoked out

---

*Forty years earlier, in the case of *Near v. Minnesota,* 283 U.S. 697 (1931), the Court had expressly prohibited the use of prior restraint. A Minnesota statute had given judges the authority to restrain from further publication any newspaper which they found to be "malicious, scandalous and defamatory." In finding the statute unconstitutional the Court compared it to the practice, dear to the monarchs of the Old World, of requiring a state license or *imprimatur* before publishing. The Court reaffirmed the dictum of Blackstone, an eighteenth-century English jurist: "The liberty of the press is indeed essential to a free state; but this consists in laying no previous restraints upon publication, and not in freedom from censure for criminal matter when published. Every freeman has an undoubted right to lay what sentiments he pleases before the public; to forbid this, is to destroy the freedom of the press; but if he publishes what is improper, mischievous or illegal, he must take the consequences of his own temerity." For fourteen days, from June 16 to June 30, 1971, *Near v. Minnesota*—and Blackstone—were overturned.

thru the papers." The overall goal was recorded in Ehrlichman's note of July 10: "Goal—Do to McNamara, Bundy, JFK elite the same destructive job that was done on Herbert Hoover years ago."[15] It was, at least in part, to implement the goal of what came to be known as "Project Ellsberg" that the President authorized the creation of a special investigations unit within the White House. The mission of "the plumbers," as the unit came to be known, was to investigate and plug security leaks, but its first job was to dig up dirt on Daniel Ellsberg. The "plumbers" were to be supervised by Ehrlichman, but they were to report to Egil Krogh, another White House aide. Their membership would include some of those who were later caught burglarizing Democratic headquarters in the Watergate hotel: G. Gordon Liddy, E. Howard Hunt, Eugenio R. Martinez, and Bernard Barker. In early September of 1971 a "plumbers" team broke into the office of Ellsberg's psychiatrist in order to film his psychiatric file.

The Trial of Ellsberg and Russo None of this, of course, was known to Ellsberg and his fellow-defendant Anthony Russo (another former RAND employee who helped Ellsberg make Xerox copies of the papers) when they went to trial in 1972. The trial began as expected, with the government trying to prove that the defendants' leak of classified documents constituted a violation of criminal law. The government's burden of proof was not a light one. Leaking "classified" information, in and of itself, is not a crime; the whole classification system rests not upon statutes but executive orders—unilateral declarations by various Presidents. The highest penalty for violating an executive order is dismissal from government service.

One statute relied upon by the government was the Espionage Act of 1917, which provides criminal penalties for delivering "to any person not entitled to receive it" any document which the deliverer "has reason to believe could be used to the injury of the United States or to the advantage of any foreign nation." Did Ellsberg and Russo indeed have "reason to believe" that their disclosures would "cause injury to the United States"? Their contention was directly opposite: that the publication of the Pentagon Papers would help get the United States out of a war which they believed disastrous to the public interest.

Ellsberg and Russo were also charged with the theft of government documents. On its face the charge was patently unsupportable, since they returned the documents after duplicating them. But the government claimed ownership not only of the documents but of the *information* contained in them. If this view were upheld, the administration could dispense with the Espionage Act. Any leak of information, regardless of whether it endangered national security, could be punished as theft. In March of 1973 President Nixon proposed legislation which would convert this interpretation into statute. His proposal would make it a crime to leak *any* classified information, without the government having to prove that it endangered national security.

Nixon thus became the first President of the United States to propose an American version of the British "official Secrets Act." Britain's wide-ranging statute, dating back to 1911, not only prohibits collecting or communicating defense information "prejudicial to the safety or interests of the State," but bans "unauthorized" persons from giving or receiving any information which the government decides to keep secret. For years the CIA had been quietly lobbying for such a law in America, but Ellsberg's leaks brought new pressure for it. "We need a severe Official Secrets Act," former Secretary of State Dean Acheson wrote, "to prevent irresponsible or corrupt transfer of secret papers from the government to publishers."[16] The staff of Senator John L. McClellan of Arkansas drafted a proposed revision of the criminal code which would have made it a felony to disclose "classified information." Momentum was building for an Official Secrets Act in the spring of 1973—until the first big Watergate "bombshell" burst.

On April 27, Judge Matthew Byrnes, presiding over the Ellsberg-Russo trial, disclosed a Justice Department memorandum revealing the burglary of Ellsberg's psychiatrist's office by the White House "plumbers." (For a month Nixon had tried to keep this information from reaching the judge; he allowed it to be communicated only after Assistant Attorney General Henry Peterson threatened to resign.) Three days later, with what seemed to be some chagrin, Judge Byrnes also disclosed that presidential adviser John Ehrlichman had met with him twice while the trial was in progress, and, on the President's behalf, asked him if he might be interested in the directorship of the FBI. Some days later, another disclosure: The government had tapped Ellsberg's phone sometime in 1969 or 1970, though the logs of the conversations were missing. Judge Byrnes then threw the whole case out of court on the grounds of government misconduct. About a month later Daniel Ellsberg found himself sitting in the audience watching the Senate Watergate Committee grill some of the key participants in "Project Ellsberg." The conspiracy "smoked out thru the papers" turned out to be the government's own conspiracy, and "official secrets" began to take on a sinister connotation.

All well and good, the reader may say, but—despite all the abuses of it—is there not still a legitimate case for government secrecy? Perhaps there is, but the present system of classification is so unwieldy and irrational that it actually threatens the credibility of any security stamp.

The classification system began during World War II, when Americans began copying the British system. In 1951 President Truman issued the first executive order extending the secrecy system to civilian departments. Two years later President Eisenhower replaced Truman's system with a new one, which provided the basic framework for today's three-tiered classification scheme. "Top Secret" is information which, if disclosed, "could reasonably be expected to cause exceptionally grave damage to the national security." "Secret" means that the information could cause "serious damage." "Confidential" information could simply "cause damage." These definitions leave considerable leeway for interpretation, and bureaucrats usually prefer to err on the side of caution. Consequently, security stamps are placed on the most innocuous documents, and "Secret" and "Top Secret" are notoriously overused. In 1958 a congressional subcommittee headed by Congressman John E. Moss of California found that the Army had placed a security stamp on a monograph study of the bow and arrow (which a Major General, testifying before the subcommittee, called "a report on silent flashless weapons"). The Navy, meanwhile, had stamped "Top Secret" on a 1916 treatise entitled "The Shark Situation in the Waters about New York."[17] Because of this promiscuous use of "Secret" and "Top Secret," few people in government take the classifications seriously. As Justice Stewart remarked in the Pentagon Papers case, "when everything is classified, then nothing is classified."[18] Because the boy cried "wolf" so many times, nobody believed him when a real wolf appeared. This realization has led various administrations to invent new, special categories for truly wolfish information. There is a special "Q" clearance for atomic energy information, a "Special Intelligence" clearance relating to intercepted information, special "eyes only" stamps, Orwellian-sounding labels like NODIS, EXDIS, and LIMDIS, which limit who may see a given document, and special priority categories like CRITIC, meaning a "critical crisis." Several other categories also exist, the names of which are themselves classified. This proliferation of special categories tends to devalue the original ones all the more, making it necessary for the classifiers to invent still newer and more emphatic categories. The following conversation, which seems to be straight out of a *Doonesbury* comic strip, actually took place in the White House on July 24, 1971; the participants are President Nixon ("P"), John Ehrlichman ("E"), and Egil Krogh ("K"):

P. And maybe another approach to it would be . . . to set up a new classification. *E.* Right.
P. Which we would call what? Let's just call it a new classifica—Don't use top secret for me ever again. I never want to see top secret in this God damn office. I think we just solved—shall we call it—Uh, John, what would be a good name? "President's Secure—" Or, uh—"Eyes Only" is a silly thing too. It doesn't mean anything anymore. Uh—
K. We used "Presidential Document" before with one of the counsel we were working with, but that didn't—There's some—
E. How about—Uh, uh, looking forward to the court case, I wonder if we could get the words "National Security" in it. *P.* Yeah.
E. So that "National," uh, just say "National Security Classified" or National Security—*K.* [Unintelligible].
E. "Secret" or uh—*P.* Well, uh, not the word "Secret" should not be used.
E. All right, uh, uh—*P.* Because you see "Secret" has been now compromised.
E. How about "Privilege"? *P.* "Privilege" is, is not strong.
E. Too soft. Too soft. *P.* "National Security—" uh, "National Security—" uh—
E. "Restricted." "Restricted." *P.* Right, "National Security—" and, uh—I agree to "National, Na—, National Security—"
E. "Restriction." *P.* "Priority."
E. "Controlled"? *P.* Or "National Security"— "Priority"— "Restricted"— "Controlled." *E.* Oh, we'll—Let us work on it.[19]

Let *us* now return to the main topic. The concern so far in this chapter has been with direct constraints upon free speech: laws punishing people for advocating certain actions or "conspiring to advocate"; court decisions permitting the government to bypass the First Amendment in cases of a "clear and present danger"; attempts by the government to "get" certain well-known figures in protest movements. As the Ellsberg case demonstrates, however, direct coercion can sometimes merge with indirect constraints upon "the free trade in ideas." Nixon was not so much interested in jailing Ellsberg as he was in discrediting and intimidating those whom he considered his real enemies. The goal was "to win PR, not just court case," to "get the public view right," to try a case "in the papers." The Ellsberg case thus straddles the line between direct coercion and indirect coercion. Let us finally cross that ill-defined border.

INDIRECT COERCION

Indirect Coercion from Society Since Puritan times free speech in America has been hedged in by a variety of social constraints. In some cases the restraints have been brutally direct—lynchings, tar-and-feathers, and so on—but more commonly the method has been indirect. Social ostracism is a good example of indirect coercion, and it has been used with great effectiveness in America. During the 1830s Alexis DeTocqueville, a French visitor to this country, was particularly impressed by this hedge surrounding free discussion:

> In America, the majority raises very formidable barriers to liberty of opinion: within these barriers an author may write whatever he pleases, but he will repent it if he ever step beyond them. Not that he is exposed to the terrors of an *auto-da-fe* [burning at the stake] but he is tormented by the slights and persecutions of daily obloquy. His political career is closed forever, since he has offended the only authority which is able to promote his success.[20]

By the 1950s DeTocqueville seemed remarkably prophetic. In the long transition from the America of Andrew Jackson to the America of Joe McCarthy, public opinion had become an increasingly powerful factor in political life. Our political parties courted it as never before, our pollsters were constantly taking its pulse, our new communications media both amplified it and transmitted it instantly throughout the nation. When the cold war began, therefore, the charge of "Communist conspiracy" became an extremely potent weapon in the arsenal of American orthodoxy. Many people lost their jobs or their friends, or both, because of some "pink" organization they might have joined during the thirties, or even because of some petition they might have signed or some words they might have said years earlier. Without being convicted of any crime, they were punished by "the slights and persecutions of daily obloquy." It did not take long for prudent people to get the message: If you care about your career, keep away from controversy, don't protest too much, play it safe. Conformity was enforced not by the threat of jail but by the terror of public prejudice—and by those who knew how to manipulate it. In the process, indirect coercion was transformed from a social force into a very useful political instrument. President Eisenhower disdained to use it. He left that to others, including his Vice President.

Indirect Coercion by Government Richard M. Nixon was not only a close observer but a participant in the red-hunting spectaculars of the late forties and early fifties. After winning an upset victory in a 1946 congressional race (he associated his opponent with Communist labor unions) Nixon achieved national fame by his aggressive pursuit of Alger Hiss, a former high State Department official accused of being a Communist spy. Nixon followed the same pattern in his successful bids for the Senate and Vice-Presidency. His Senate opponent,

Representative Helen Gahagan Douglas, was characterized as "the pink lady" and accused of siding with the Communists in her voting record. When he ran for the Vice-Presidency Nixon associated the Democrats with treason and subversion.

The "new Nixon" elected in 1968 was prepared to negotiate with Communist countries, wind down the Vietnam war, fraternize with Soviet leaders, and visit mainland China. But the old pattern of vindictiveness and vilification emerged when it came to dealing with "enemies" on the home front. The specter of communism was no longer so frightening as it was in the fifties, but within a year of Nixon's inauguration Vice President Spiro Agnew was denouncing the new bogeymen: "radical liberals" (or "radiclibs"), the "Eastern establishment," the "effete corps of impudent snobs." The Communist Conspiracy had become the Gay Snob Conspiracy, but the tactics used against the enemy were essentially the same: the mobilization of public prejudice combined with the maximum use of the weapons available to an officeholder. The campaign against criticism took a variety of forms:

Threats "You're going to find something done in the area of antitrust action," White House aide Patrick Buchanan warned in 1972, if the networks persisted in giving the "negative" side of the President.[21] Clay T. Whitehead, Director of the White House Office of Telecommunications, complained about "elitist gossip" and "ideological plugola" on network news shows, and warned that station managers and network officials who failed to "correct imbalance" or who "acquiesce by silence" might not get their licenses renewed.[22] These attacks, coordinated with Agnew's were designed to intimidate.[23] It is less certain that they succeeded in their purpose, although even the venerable Walter Cronkite worried about its "subconscious effect" on his reporting.[24]

Smears Acting under instructions from White House aide Charles Colson, E. Howard Hunt falsified 1963 State Department cables to make it appear that President Kennedy had ordered the assassination of Ngo Dinh Diem, then-president of South Vietnam. President Nixon later said at a news conference that "the way we got into Vietnam [in 1963] was through overthrowing and complicity in the murder of Diem." The fake cable was then leaked to the press. Hunt and others were also assigned the task of finding and disseminating information about Senator Edward Kennedy's sex life. The role of the "plumbers" in using the Ellsberg case to get at the Kennedys "thru the press" has already been discussed.

Administrative "Punishments" Special Counsel John Dean compiled a White House "enemies" list of 218 Americans. The intention was, in Dean's words, to "screw" them in various ways: tax audits, antitrust suits, and so on. Patrick Buchanan, meanwhile, urged the use of the Internal Revenue Service against "leftist" foundations and institutions. A reporter for the *Long Island Press* who wrote a series of exposés on Nixon's friend Bebe Rebozo was subjected to a special tax investigation. High on the list of priority targets were the TV networks and the *Washington Post*. According to CBS reporter Dan Rather, John Ehrlichman told him that the networks were "anti-Nixon" and that "they are going to have to pay for that sooner or later, one way or another."[25] After the Nixon administration began an antitrust action against CBS, Charles Colson called the network's president, Frank Stanton (according to Stanton's sworn testimony) and threatened the network with financial ruin. "Things will get much worse for CBS," Colson said, according to Stanton. "You didn't play ball during the campaign . . . we'll bring you to your knees in Wall Street and on Madison Avenue."[26] In the summer of 1973 Katherine Graham, publisher of the *Washington Post,* alleged that the licenses of two Florida stations owned by her company were challenged because of the *Post's* role in uncovering the Watergate scandal. What lent substance to her allegations was the threat made the previous fall by former Attorney General John Mitchell. He told a *Post* reporter that "Katie Graham's gonna get her tit caught in a big fat wringer if that's published."[27]

Surveillance   The Watergate and Ellsberg break-ins were only the tip of the iceberg. President Nixon on July 23, 1970 adopted the "Huston plan," named after its author, twenty-eight-year-old Tom Charles Huston. It called for the surveillance of dissenters, political opponents, news reporters, and government employees through burglary, wiretapping, eavesdropping, mail covers, and spying by the CIA and other agencies. Although the "Huston plan" was supposedly abrogated five days later because of J. Edgar Hoover's objections, surveillance was a common practice in the Nixon administration. The CIA, in violation of its 1947 charter, became deeply involved in domestic espionage. The targets were antiwar activists and other dissidents inside the United States. Intelligence files on at least 10,000 American citizens were compiled. Not to be outdone by the CIA, the White House engaged in its own spying programs. The phones of several newsmen were tapped. CBS reporter Daniel Schorr was subjected to an extensive FBI investigation, and when this was discovered administration officials claimed that Schorr was being considered for an appointment—a story which was regarded with considerable amusement by Schorr's colleagues.

Sabotage   In 1971 and 1972 at least twenty undercover agents, including Donald Segretti, were hired to disrupt Democratic events, circulate false charges about Democratic candidates, and cause confusion in the Democratic ranks by throwing campaign schedules into disarray, forging letters, planting provocateurs in Democratic rallies, and leaking false information.

The Nixon years are over. Why bring these incidents up today? The answer, as Attorney General William B. Saxbe later acknowledged, is that "you could have Watergate happen again."[28] Precedents, once set, have a way of recurring. Joe McCarthy died in 1957, but his style of smear and innuendo resurfaced in the Nixon administration. Since the fifties the CIA had been conducting James Bond-type "covert operations" and "dirty tricks" in foreign countries; during the Nixon years James Bond—in the person of E. Howard Hunt—came home. The FBI had long been involved in burglarizing embassies, forging credentials, setting up sham organizations, sending anonymous letters, and leaking derogatory information;[29] Nixon simply borrowed the same techniques to use against his political opponents. The question, then, is whether the acts of the Nixon administration will themselves become precedents for some future administration to build upon.

If it were all a matter of one man's psyche, we could be reassured. But the climate of vindictiveness during the Nixon years extended far beyond the administration, and far beyond Washington itself. Throughout the nation it was a season for "getting tough." Construction workers, the "hard-hats" so actively courted by the administration, charged into crowds of long-haired demonstrators; at Jackson State University in Mississippi and Kent State in Ohio, unarmed students were shot and killed by state authorities; state police sent undercover agents and provocateurs to campus rallies; "law 'n' order" mayors like Frank Rizzo of Philadelphia suddenly became national figures. It was also a time for investigations: In 1971 alone, at least thirteen federal grand juries were used to investigate political dissenters; anyone refusing to testify was threatened with a jail term. Both federal and local grand juries began subpoenaing newsmen to testify against confidential sources of information.

The Nixon years are over. But some alarming precedents were set during that period. One of them, to which we now turn, was hardened into law by a Supreme Court decision.

The *Caldwell* Case In December of 1969, Earl Caldwell, a reporter for the *New York Times,* wrote a series of articles on the Black Panthers. The Panthers consented to the interview only after Caldwell accepted their ground rules, which included a promise from him not to talk about the interview to any government officials. After his series on the Panthers appeared in the *Times,* he was subpoenaed by a federal grand jury. He refused to appear, claiming that even his appearance before the grand jury would compromise his promise of confidentiality, destroy his ability to gather sensitive information in the future, and interfere with freedom of the press. By five to four (the four Nixon appointees plus Justice White) the Supreme Court ruled against Caldwell, claiming that "newsmen are not exempt from the normal duty of appearing before a grand jury and answering questions relevant to a criminal investigation."[30]

The significance of *Caldwell* was not lost on the nation's law-enforcement officials. In less than a year, twelve newsmen went to jail—one of them for sixty days of solitary confinement—rather than testify about confidential sources. In November of 1972 a Harvard professor named Samuel Popkin became the first American scholar imprisoned for refusing to name the source of his information. Popkin had gathered information about the Pentagon Papers from lower-level officials in the Nixon administration; he was jailed for contempt when he refused to tell a grand jury the source of his information. Despite this show of resistance, many researchers and reporters found their sources drying up. These sources included government employees afraid to talk about impropriety in their departments for fear of being identified and losing their jobs, welfare clients afraid to testify to abuses in the system for fear being denied benefits,* and others fearful

---

* "Ike Kleinerman, a C.B.S. News producer, took a camera crew through the South recently to develop material for a documentary on the problems of children in America. He hoped to arrange an interview with a mother who could describe vividly how the welfare system, with its prohibitions against payments to families with working fathers, has encouraged the breakup of homes. He finally found just such a woman. She was a welfare client who spoke eloquently from experience of the

of reprisals of one kind or another. From the standpoint of the communications process in a democracy—the free flow of information—this drying up of sources may have been worse than the actual jailing of newsmen. It happened quietly, without melodrama, without making the front page of the newspaper, without bringing matters to a head or shaming the government. And the ultimate loser was neither the reporter nor his would-be informer, but the public at large.

To remedy the damage caused by *Caldwell,* a number of different "shield" laws, laws to protect news reporters from having to disclose their sources, have been proposed in Congress. Most members of Congress apparently agree on the overall aim of such legislation, but its proposed scope and application have raised a number of thorny questions. Should the news reporter's immunity be absolute? What about cases involving slander by anonymous "sources?" What about those cases involving serious crimes? And should immunity be limited to news reporters? What about scholars? Or pamphleteers? By the middle of 1973 Senator Sam Ervin's Judiciary Committee was considering at least thirty different proposals for immunity, and Senator Ervin confessed that "this is the most difficult field I've ever had to write a bill in."[31]

We have been discussing coercion as a threat to "the free trade in ideas." Coercion may be direct or indirect, but it always implies punishment of some sort: prison, harassment, sabotage, threats, smears, social ostracism. Coercion is a nasty way of limiting free speech.

But it is not the only way. Speech can be restrained more subtly—perhaps even more effectively—without antagonism or bad feelings, without violence, or enemies' lists, without any of the clumsy paraphernalia of repression. Speech can be limited simply because one source or point of view has a monopoly of speakers. Let us consider this third restraint on "the free trade in ideas."

MONOPOLY

In 1969 the Supreme Court said:

> It is the purpose of the First Amendment to preserve an uninhibited marketplace of ideas in which the truth will ultimately prevail, rather than to countenance monopolization of that market, whether it be by the Government itself or a private licensee.[32]

Monopoly "by the Government itself" is standard—and, on the whole, effective—procedure in totalitarian countries. In such places as China and the Soviet Union, the people know only what the government wishes them to know about events through the government-controlled media. Even in more or less demo-

---

system's inequities. She agreed to be interviewed on camera, but only with her face averted and with absolute assurances she would not be identified by name. She had been recently harboring her husband in her home and feared that this would be discovered if she spoke out publicly. Although promises to withhold names have traditionally been routine in journalism, Kleinerman called C.B.S. headquarters in New York to check. The matter was referred to the legal department, where the judgment was swift. Kleinerman was told not to give the requested assurance. The interview was cancelled." Brit Hume, "A Chilling Effect on the Press," *The New York Times Magazine,* Dec. 17, 1972, p. 13.

cratic countries such as France and Italy, the government's monopoly of the electronic media sometimes results in censorship, although newspapers and periodicals remain free of government control. In Britain and America, as we have seen, government monopoly takes a different form—not a media monopoly, but, at least in the area of "national security," an information monopoly. Official secrecy in both countries operates to the advantage of government officials because it permits them to *selectively* leak materials which are stamped "Top Secret." Presidents and other top officials have long made it a practice to make public parts of classified documents—the parts that make them look good. News reporters or researchers who demand to see the rest of the files are told that "national security" forbids further disclosure. As a way of eliminating (or at least modifying) this catch, Congress in 1974 passed a series of amendments to the 1966 Freedom of Information Act. The 1966 act had forced the government to provide access to its files, but had made an exception in the case of classified information. One of the amendments passed in 1974 would permit a petitioner to ask that a federal judge privately review classified information to determine if it should be made public. The amendment was strenuously opposed by President Ford, but his veto was overridden by large margins in both houses of Congress. The mood of Congress may have been summed up by Representative Bill Alexander, an Arkansas Democrat, who reminded his colleagues of the Watergate scandal and shouted this rhetorical question: "Hasn't the White House learned that Government secrecy is the real enemy of democracy?"[33]

Despite the problem of official secrecy, the American media are free from government monopoly when it comes to disseminating the information that does reach them. Whatever gets into their hands is fair game—even classified information like the Pentagon Papers. Americans, it is fair to say, have little to fear from a government monopoly of the media. Our news media have exposed government corruption, run programs like "The Selling of the Pentagon," freely criticized the highest officials in the land. The only serious campaign against the media by an administration ended when that administration was swept away by Watergate. The media emerged victorious, stronger than ever for having played such a key role in uncovering the scandal. Many of their reporters had become heroes and celebrities.

A victory for the media, however, is not necessarily a victory for the public. Americans, if they ever did, no longer have to worry about a government media monopoly. The real problem, when it comes to the dissemination of news and opinion, is that of private monopoly. "The stifling weight of censorship is to be found, not in the hearing rooms of the Federal Communications Commission, but in the conference rooms of this nation's television networks."[34] The author of that statement was not Spiro Agnew but Nicholas Johnson, former FCC Commissioner and a staunch believer in the free trade in ideas. Lest there be any doubt about Johnson's commitment to civil liberties, it should be noted that Johnson also staunchly opposed the Nixon-Agnew campaign against the media. Even more interesting is his reason for opposing it. He saw it as nothing more than an attempt to transfer power "from a handful of men in New York to a handful of men in the White House."[35] By the end of 1974, the "handful of men in the White House" had left office in disgrace, some of them to serve time in country-club penitentiaries. This makes it all the more important that we examine the power of those whom the White House "handful" saw as their adversaries.

Since ancient times the power of the word has played an enormous role in shaping events. Words—"mere words" to the unwary—have chipped away at the foundations of empires and helped to create new ones. Particularly since the eighteenth century and the appearance of the "general will" (or "popular mandate") as a badge of legitimacy, those who would get and keep power have known that they must somehow influence public opinion. In today's America the dissemination of news and opinion has become a major industry. It has also become a major component of political power. The press has been called the "fourth branch of government"[36] because the rise and fall of political regimes is closely connected with what gets into the media. This is particularly true of the modern media. Over the past two centuries the revolution in communications technology and the increasing sophistication of news reporters have combined to change the context in which "news" is reported and perceived. As Theodore White has pointed out, we are no longer told merely "what happened" but "what is happening."[37] Past, present, and future are fused as news reporters and analysts discuss "trends" and "developments." Thus, "events" are seen not as isolated occurrences but as parts of the "Watergate story" or the "Middle East situation." Within certain bounds (a presidential assassination or some other catastrophe could hardly be ignored) the media exercise almost unlimited discretion in deciding what is "eventful." What does not get reported is simply not an "event," and can have no impact on public opinion. Even if it does get reported, the "angle" in which it is presented will shape its meaning. Is an antibusing riot presented in terms of the rocks thrown—or the grievances of those who threw them? Is an antiabortion drive presented as another example of the Catholic Church's power—or as another effort to preserve life? The choice of contexts thus becomes an important part of an event's meaning and impact on public opinion.

It is pointless, then, to argue whether reporters or editors are biased. Of course they are biased. Any human perspective is biased. The real question is whether the American people are being given a *multiplicity of competing biases*. Let us examine this question as it pertains both to print and to electronic media.

Shrinking Newspapers

Were it left to him, Jefferson said in 1787, "to decide whether we should have a government without newspapers or newspapers without a government, I should not hesitate a moment to prefer the latter."[38] Jefferson held newspapers in such high esteem because he remembered the democratizing role they had played in colonial America. A Tory writer in the Boston Evening-Post complained that the Whig press had made it possible for "the peasants and their housewives in every part of the land . . . to dispute on politics and positively to determine upon our liberties."[39]

In Jefferson's time most newspapers made no pretense of objectivity—they were frankly partisan sheets—but the great variety of them afforded the widest range of biases for readers to consider. Today the opposite situation prevails: Reporting has become more professional, but the variety of newspapers has drastically shrunk. In 1923, 552 American cities had competing daily newspapers; in 1945 the number was 117; today only 58 towns and cities offer their readers more than one established paper. Hartford, Connecticut, provides a typical example of this trend. When it had only 13,000 people it had thirteen newspapers. Today, with half a million people, it has two.

A number of factors have combined to produce this decrease in the number of competing newspapers: high labor costs, expensive equipment and other overhead, plus the growth of the great national newspaper chains, such as Hearst, Gannett, and Scripps-Howard (which not only put some newspapers out of business but also, in some cases, impose editorial points of view on their member newspapers). Our tax laws have facilitated the growth of chains by giving them tax loopholes for cash invested in still more communications media. The competition from television has also had an adverse effect upon the number of competing newspapers, since it has drained away advertising revenues and thus helped to kill off the less established papers. Finally, the growing centralization of government in America, coupled with the increased importance of foreign affairs, has turned our attention toward Washington and the world for "news." Not many local newspapers can afford to keep a full-time reporter in their state capital, much less in Washington or Moscow or Tel Aviv. Thus, even the newspapers which have not been absorbed into the national chains have become more and more dependent on standardized sources of news and opinion: wire services, syndicated columns, and press releases. (Ben Bagdikian, media critic for the *Washington Post,* watched a friend of his who runs a newspaper-clipping service select at random an edition of one of our leading newspapers, analyze its contents, and discover that 82 percent of its nonadvertising matter originated from press handouts.)[40] All these factors have combined to produce a growing homogeneity of news reporting and analysis in our nation's press. As a class project, the author had his students subscribe to papers from a number of states during the course of the 1972 presidential campaign.[41] Students and teacher were shocked at how little variety was found in the coverage of events. When it came to the front pages, papers from Iowa and Nebraska were practically identical to those in New York and California. In national news, local papers exercised discretion mainly in one area: where all the canned items appeared on the pages.

Television

Since the end of World War II, newspapers have given way to electronic media as the chief source of news and opinion. As early as the 1930s, radio had made a breakthrough, as President Roosevelt was quick to perceive. His radio addresses and "fireside chats" enabled him to appeal to the public over the heads of a generally hostile press. During the war, radio reporting became dramatic and professional as men like Edward R. Murrow brought reports on the bombing of London into American living rooms. But within a generation the family's radio had been moved to the kitchen to make room for a new electronic box, one which is now installed in 98 percent of American homes. By 1961 the news presented on television was considered more believable by Americans (39%) than that presented by newspapers (24%), radio (10%), or magazines (10%). Television, which is watched on the average of five hours per day by Americans, has largely supplanted other means of communicating with mass audiences. "Certainly the thinking of a third of the politically articulate American public is shaped by Mr. Cronkite," observed Joseph C. Harsche of the *Christian Science Monitor,* and "well over half is influenced by Mr. Cronkite, David Brinkley, Harry Reasoner, and Howard K. Smith."[42]

TV possesses great potential for promoting "the free trade in ideas." As a picture medium, it can provide a lively forum for argument and discussion; it can expose wrongdoing in a particularly graphic way; it can get people involved in the political process by giving them a vicarious sense of participation—which might later be transformed into real participation. Because of the televised hearings in 1973 and 1974 Americans were able to learn first-hand the sordid details of Watergate. A generation earlier the Army-McCarthy hearings helped lead to McCarthy's undoing: The Senator's demagogic style was disastrously ill-suited to a "cool" medium like TV.[43] Even the Kennedy-Nixon debates, which have been the object of considerable debunking, apparently stimulated large numbers of people, got them thinking about the candidates and their arguments.[44] Such documentaries as "Hunger in America" and "The Selling of the Pentagon" were seriously and perhaps maliciously flawed in parts,[45] but they at least stirred controversy and helped counterbalance the government's own public relations.

Yet television is far from realizing its full potential. Most of it is still geared toward bland and mindless entertainment: quiz shows and soap operas during the day, "comedy hours" and "action" dramas in the evening, plus a few neatly packaged "news" segments. All this programming is regularly interrupted by dramatizations of grown men and women gravely comparing laxatives, stomach remedies, and dog foods. One reason, then, for the blandness and lack of true diversity is that television in America is a business—and, like much of American business, it has become a conglomerate.

Coast-to-coast television in America is served by three networks: the National Broadcasting Company (owned by the Radio Corporation of America, which is also a major defense and space contractor, a washing machine and dishwasher manufacturer, and owner of Random House, Pantheon, and Knopf book companies), the Columbia Broadcasting System (which also controls $21 million in the credit affiliates of Ford, General Motors, and Chrysler, television stations in the Caribbean and Latin America, Creative Playthings, and Columbia Records), and the American Broadcasting Company (which also owns 399 theaters, ABC-Paramount Records, and three farm newspapers). Television, in other words, fits John Kenneth Galbraith's model of "oligopoly."[46] Three big businesses provide us with news, entertainment, and a continuing din of commercials (which are, of course, necessary because they pay the broadcasting bills). These three conglomerates depend, then, upon other businesses for the sponsorship of programs: About 85 percent of broadcasting's total revenue is derived from advertising.

Needless to add, the sponsors of these programs are not anxious to drive away potential customers. Some of them have even promulgated rules for the nonnews programs they will support. The broadcasting industry's largest sponsor, Procter and Gamble, has established the following policy:

> There will be no material that may give offense, either directly or by inference, to any minority group, lodge, or other organizations, institutions, residents of any State or section of the country, or a commercial organization of any sort. This will be taken to include political organizations, religious orders, civic clubs, memorial and patriotic societies, philanthropic and reform societies . . . athletic organizations, women's groups, etc., which are in good standing.[47]

The Ford Motor Company reviews "story lines, characterization and dialogue for every program we sponsor"; General Motors wants nothing to do with "anything of a controversial nature concerning any national or regional issue"; DuPont avoids sponsoring anything that approaches "involvement in domestic or international subjects."[48] Understandably, then, some critics suspect that the TV news shows ignore those events which may injure the interests of their sponsors. Very sparse coverage, for example, was given to the 1966 Senate hearings on the "truth in packaging" bill. This prompted one critic to ask: "Could it be that such behavior reflects a concern for the best interests of, say, the top 50 grocery-products advertisers who spent $1,314,983,000 in television in 1965, 52.3% of television's total advertising income?"[49]

In the past, at least, some documentaries were apparently watered down in the interest of sponsors. ABC-News producer Stephen Fleishman once described the dilemma very simply: "You can't get a documentary on the air unless you get a sponsor, and if you get a sponsor, you've got to do a bland show."[50] Fred Friendly, former CBS news director, looked back over his years with the network and admitted that "I found myself subconsciously applying a new kind of conformity to our documentaries. Looking back now, I suppose that I was subtly influenced to do controversial subjects in a noncontroversial manner."[51]

What is controversial, of course, varies with the times. Abortion and premarital sex, to take two examples, are no longer taboo subjects on TV. But this is part of the problem. American television is a fashionable medium. It stays abreast of "the times," rejecting those ideas which are either "ahead" of or "behind" them. But "the free trade in ideas" must mean more than the selling of modish products. It must also provide the choice of old-fashioned ones, odd and eccentric ones, and ones *too* advanced to be stylish. On programs like the "Mary Tyler Moore Show" and "Maude" abortion and premarital sex are not simply treated openly, but openly condoned—to the exclusion of dissenting views.[52] Also missing from TV's marketplace of ideas are those which, in the opinion of network executives are too far "ahead" of the times. In 1973 CBS abruptly cancelled *Sticks and Bones,* a bitter drama about the Vietnam war, because "it might be unnecessarily abrasive to the feelings of millions of Americans. . . . "[53] In summary, if we use "the free trade in ideas" as our touchstone, the contrast between ideal and reality becomes apparent. What Americans need is an electronic medium which allows the wides range of ideas: "abrasive" and soothing ones, radical and reactionary ones, pious, irreverent, religious, atheistic, communistic, Birchite, authoritarian, anarchistic ideas. What Americans get is a corporate media monopoly which tends to flatten out controversy and tune out dominance.

Increasing the Free Trade in Ideas: Some Suggested Reforms

Lest we conclude this section too gloomily, it might be well to consider some suggested reforms. One of them is to open up more communications channels, which the development of cable television makes technically feasible.

Cable TV At present about 9 percent of American homes receive television by way of coaxial cables capable of carrying a thousand times the capacity of telephone wires. By 1980 40 to 60 percent of our homes could be similarly wired. Cables permit a significant increase in the number of channels: In August of 1971 the FCC proposed a minimum capacity of twenty, and several communities

"*Attention out there! We now bring you an opposing viewpoint to a CBS editorial!*"

Drawing by Richter; © 1975 The New Yorker Magazine, Inc.

have already activated twice that number through the use of cables. By using communication satellites this number could be linked coast to coast, so that the citizen would have a choice not of three but of forty networks.

Serious problems cloud this potentially dazzling development. One of them is the lack of funds, which leads to some very dull programming. A related problem is that the same commercial oligopolies which run the existing networks may take over the cable networks. One proposal for avoiding these pitfalls is to levy some form or other of a broadcast tax, which many European countries use to finance TV. Aside from the practical difficulties in getting such a law passed, however, there remains the question of who would get the money. Can we trust the government to run cable TV? One way of resolving this problem might be the adoption of the Dutch method. In Holland any group of 15,000 people can organize a "TV station" and turn over their broadcast tax to any group of their choice, which is then allotted air time proportionate to its number of supporters. Dutch viewers can see groups representing every conceivable interest and viewpoint on their TV screens. Something along these lines has already been proposed by former FCC Commisioner Nicholas Johnson: Community groups of a certain size could win the right to air time; once they qualified, a cable system's technical staff would be required to give them assistance. This could open up the possibility of a more inclusive dialogue than America has ever experienced in the media.[54]

However exhilarating its potential, cable TV still remains largely in the future. Nor is the free trade in ideas guaranteed merely by opening up more channels. If diversity of ideas, not merely a multiplicity of forums, is the ultimate aim, one might consider some of the possibilities at hand.

The Affirmative Duty to Air Controversies Section 315 of the Communications Act of 1933 requires broadcasters "to operate in the public interest and to afford reasonable opportunity for discussion of conflicting views on issues of public importance." Since 1949 the FCC has interpreted the statute in terms of its "fairness doctrine": Broadcasters must provide the opportunity for counterarguments on controversial issues—*if* one side of the controversy has been presented. As a consequence, many broadcasters simply stay away from *any* controversy in order to avoid the duty of presenting all sides to it. This in turn reinforces the political status quo and the power of political incumbents. The stations, for example, have no obligation to provide free air time or coverage for those running against an incumbent President before he officially announces his intention to run again. Hence the plethora of "nonpolitical speeches" and staged "events" by Presidents during election years. If stations had an affirmative duty to take the initiative in airing controversies, this advantage to incumbents would be minimized.

At least one critic has suggested sanctions against stations which make it a practice of playing it safe and avoiding controversial discussion.[55] Station licenses must be renewed every three years, at which time the FCC is empowered to mete out penalties ranging from cease-and-desist orders to revocation of licenses.

If these sanctions, and the willingness to use them, sound a little too much like the threats against the media which used to emanate from the Nixon White

House, let this crucial difference be kept in mind: Nixon's men were threatening to use sanctions against the networks not for avoiding controversy but for getting involved in it. Broadcasters generally argue that sanctions are sanctions, and no matter what the purpose, their use impinges upon First Amendment rights. This argument, however, fails to acknowledge the fact that television is a limited-access medium. In such a medium the broadcaster has a serious responsibility to air all points of view, and this responsibility is not met by refusing to air *any* point of view. Besides, as another critic observed, "it does take remarkable gall on the part of the purveyors of 'The Beverly Hillbillies,' 'Laugh-In,' 'Hee-Haw,' 'Hogan's Heroes,' 'The Secret Storm' and the Every-Night-of-the-Week Movie to keep presenting themselves as the defenders of our intellectual freedom."[56]

Public TV A third means of increasing "the free trade in ideas" is to give the public an alternative to commercial broadcasting. But can we provide some form of public TV which is independent *both* of industry *and* government? In the Public Broadcasting Act of 1967 Congress established a Corporation for Public Broadcasting (CPB), a fifteen-member board of presidential appointees, to supervise the programming of a tax-supported network. Under its first president, John W. Macy, Jr., the CPB created a subordinate but semiindependent agency, the Public Broadcasting Service (PBS), composed of nineteen members largely made up of local station managers, for the purpose of creating and distributing programs. CPB decided to delegate its power of programming to PBS in order to insulate programming decisions from the hot breath of politics.[57] PBS was to be a "heat shield" against censorship and manipulation by government officials. By leaving daily decision making in the hands of a body not directly appointed by the President of the United States, it was hoped that noncommercial public broadcasting could be independent in fact as well as in name. In Britain, for example, the BBC retains nearly complete independence from government interference even though it is supported by official license fees.

America's experiment in independent broadcasting has not been as successful as Britain's. Part of the reason for the BBC's rugged independence is that it gets its money from license fees without having to go to Parliament with its hat in its hand, but a bill that would have given American TV some measure of a similar independence—by providing for two-year funding instead of annual appropriations by Congress—was vetoed by President Nixon in 1972. This was before Watergate shattered his power, and some observers saw it as part of a campaign to enfeeble public TV, which Nixon staffers associated with "leftist" bias. Shortly afterwards the Nixon administration took over CPB, the fifteen-member parent board, replaced its chairman, and announced that henceforward it would assume full programming responsibilities. PBS, the nonpolitical "heat shield," had been penetrated; all decision making was now in the hands of Presidential appointees, the majority of them Republicans. (Henry Loomis, the new chairman, wasted no time in telling people his own philosophy: He was "concerned about the propriety of using public funds to be competitive with commercial networks.")[58] But by July of 1974, after two years of Watergate, the Nixon White House was itself enfeebled. The White House Office of Telecommunications gave in to pressure from public broadcasters and urged Congress to enact a five-year funding plan. Not long afterward the Senate Commerce Committee reported out an even stronger bill, which would appropriate over $600 million over a five-year period. In its report the committee said that "although public broadcasting has admirably served the American public, its contribution to the quality of our life is only a hint of the potential it offers, if adequately funded."[59]

SOME CONCLUSIONS

In this chapter we have discussed three restraints on "the free trade in ideas": direct coercion, indirect coercion, and monopoly. Let us now try to put them in perspective.

Direct coercion, if it ever was a major threat to free speech, no longer seems to be. Even during the darkest days of reaction to the Vietnam war dissenters, nobody went to jail (as they did during the World War I period) for saying, "I am for the people, and the government is for the profiteers." Draconic laws such as the Smith Act have been whittled down or overturned by Supreme Court decisions. More recent statutes (such as the "Rap Brown" amendment) have been so far from silencing dissenters that they have produced the opposite effect, by giving them new forums for speech making.

Indirect coercion may be a more promising means of controlling speech in today's America. Modern electronics have provided our rulers with a variety of devices, from computer data banks to supersensitive bugs, for keeping tabs on dissenters. Popular credulity and the appetite for gossip have made critics vulnerable to smears and leaks. The enormous responsibilities of modern government have given its operators a number of devices to "screw" its critics: singling them out for tax audits, denying them appropriations, jobs, contracts, interviews, licenses; harassing and punishing them in a thousand little ways without making public martyrs of them. Like Gulliver, the critic may find herself subdued not by chains but by Lilliputian threads.

Americans today must also consider this restraint upon "the free trade in ideas": monopoly, or at least oligopoly. In the present era the powers that be have little to fear from soapbox oratory. Americans are not much attuned to this form of communication anymore. They hurry from their jobs to their homes, eat dinner, glance at the paper—and watch TV. Nixon's instincts, then, were sound. He never really worried about the speakers at bughouse square. He perceived his real enemies to be the networks and newspapers like the *Washington Post* and the *New York Times*. The *Times* and the *Post* are opinion leaders with enormous influence in Washington and throughout the country; the networks have cornered the market on national television. Having despaired of getting these giants on his "team," Nixon set out to reduce their power. He knew, in other words, that we live an an age of loudspeakers, and that those who decide what is said through those loudspeakers play a decisive role in shaping public opinion.

For six years Americans watched a war between two giants, the Nixon administration and the media; the Nixon administration lost. The succeeding administration knew better than to renew the hostilities.

From the standpoint of "the free trade in ideas" this truce may be a mixed blessing. The media conglomerates now occupy the field without anyone of comparable influence to challenge them. Whatever his motives, whatever his misdeeds, Spiro Agnew was right when he said that "the American people should be made aware of the trend toward the monopolization of the great public information vehicles and the concentration of more and more power over public opinion in fewer and fewer hands."[60] The trend still continues. It may even be more difficult to reverse today, thanks to the Nixon administration. Any effort to do so can now be stigmatized as an assault on "civil liberties."

Actually, as this chapter has tried to indicate, civil liberties can be paradoxical at times. It may be necessary, for example, to curtail a broadcaster's liberty to dodge controversy in order to give her listeners the liberty to hear controversy. At this point government enters the picture, as the agency for regulation. We must not minimize the dangers of abuse once the government gets into the business of regulating the media. Indeed, this chapter had devoted many pages to documenting some of those abuses. But neither can we pretend that "the free trade in ideas" will result from a policy of laissez faire. Private monopoly is just as stifling as public monopoly, and self-censorship deprives us of new ideas just as surely as does government censorship. The arrogance of power is a vice which appears wherever great power is wielded without adequate checks upon it. Surely such power is wielded by those, like Walter Cronkite, who can tell millions of people every night, "that's the way it is." Surely the power to decide, as the editors of the *New York Times* decide, what news is "fit to print"—and to put into worldwide circulation—is a very considerable power. Yet there seems to be very little check upon it.

Let us close this chapter with a case which illustrates the paradox of civil liberties. On September 20 and 29, 1972, the *Miami Herald* accused a candidate for the state legislature of being a "czar," of engaging in "shakedown statesmanship," and of fattening his private business at public expense. The *Herald* then refused to print his replies to these charges. The candidate sought relief under a Florida "right to reply" statute, but when the case reached the Supreme Court it was held to be an unconstitutional interference with free speech.[61]

But was it? Considering the fact that America has so few competing newspapers, when one of them refuses to print someone's reply to serious charges made against him in its pages, it deprives the person of a chance to correct what might be a vicious and damaging untruth. Nor is the individual the only victim in such situations. The ultimate victim is *we*—the public, the comparison-shoppers among competing ideas. We have been deprived of an essential means of hearing both sides to a controversy.

Of course, "right of reply" laws, such as the Florida law struck down in the *Miami Herald* case, contain their own dangers. In the hands of vindictive government officials they can be used as a device to chill criticism and intimidate the press. In judging such situations as those presented by the *Miami Herald* case, therefore, it may be necessary for us to balance off the danger of one evil against the existence of another. In making such choices, the important point is that we not lose sight of the real *purpose* of liberty, which is to provide us with the widest range of options from which to choose as we exercise our responsibilities as citizens in a democracy. This has been the theme running through the present chapter, and it was ably summed up by a critic of the *Miami Herald* decision:

> The First Amendment's guarantee for freedoms of speech was not designed simply to protect abstract rights to speak and print. These are only means for obtaining an informed public that can reason its way, through public discussion, to the popular consensus on which a democracy functions.[62]

NOTES

1. Quoted in Saul K. Padover, *The Meaning of Democracy* (New York: Frederick A. Praeger, Inc., 1963), p. 90
2. Quoted in Edward Dumbauld, ed., *The Political Writings of Thomas Jefferson* (Indianapolis, Ind: The Bobbs-Merrill Company, Inc., 1955), p. 42.
3. Alexander Meiklejohn, *Free Speech and Its Relation to Self-Government* (New York: Harper Brothers, 1948).
4. See Holmes's dissent in *Abrams v. United States*, 250 U.S. 616, 624 (1919).
5. Zechariah Chafee, Jr., *Free Speech in the United States* (Cambridge, Mass.: Harvard University Press, 1941), p. 53.
6. Harry J. Carman and Harold C. Syrett, *A History of the American People* (New York: Alfred A. Knopf, Inc., 1957), II, p. 429.
7. 249 U.S. 47 (1919).
8. 341 U.S. 494 (1951).
9. 354 U.S. 298 (1957).
10. 367 U.S. 203 (1961).
11. 367 U.S. 290 (1961).
12. 391 U.S. 367 (1968).
13. *New York Times Company v. United States*, 403 U.S. 712 (1971).
14. See Chapter 8, note 37.
15. From the House Judiciary Committee's summary of evidence of possible grounds for impeachment of President Nixon, reprinted in *New York Times*, July 23, 1974, p. 23.
16. Quoted in David Wise, *The Politics of Lying* (New York: Vintage Books, Random House, Inc., 1973), p. 228.
17. Ibid., pp. 96–97.
18. See Note 13, above.
19. From transcripts of White House tapes, as reprinted in *New York Times*, July 19, 1974, p. 14.
20. Alexis de Tocqueville, *Democracy in America* (New York: Vintage Books, Random House, Inc., 1945), I, p. 274. First published in English translation by Henry Reeve in 1835 and 1840.
21. Julius Duscha, "The White House Watch over T.V. and the Press," *The New York Times Magazine*, Aug. 20, 1972, p. 92.
22. *New York Times*, Dec. 19, 1972, p. 1.
23. *Newsweek*, Mar. 2, 1970.
24. *New York Times*, Mar. 12, 1973, p. 33.
25. *New York Times*, Apr. 30, 1974, p. 28.
26. Ibid.
27. Carl Bernstein and Bob Woodward, "All the President's Men," *Playboy*, XXI (May 1974), p. 214.
28. *New York Times*, Nov. 24, 1974, sec. 4, p. 3.
29. Ibid.

30. The *Caldwell* case (*United States v. Caldwell*) was actually one of three cases heard together by the Court on February 22 and 23, 1972. The other two were *Branzburg v. Hayes* and *In re Pappas*.
31. *New York Times,* Mar. 15, 1973, p. 12.
32. *Red Lion Broadcasting Co., Inc. v. Federal Communications Commission,* 89 S. Ct. 1794 (1969).
33. *New York Times,* Nov. 21, 1974, p. 19.
34. Quoted in Morton Mintz and Jerry S. Cohen, *America, Inc.: Who Owns and Operates the United States* (New York: Dell Publishing Co., Inc., 1971), pp. 112–113.
35. Quoted in ibid., p. 157.
36. Douglas Cater, *The Fourth Branch of Government* (New York: Vintage Books, Random House, Inc., 1959).
37. Theodore H. White, *The Making of the President 1972* (New York: Bantam Books, 1973), p. 333. White believes that this new time frame began with the appearance of muckraking journals at the turn of the century.
38. Quoted in Dumbauld, op. cit., p. 94.
39. Clinton Rossiter, *The Political Thought of the American Revolution* (New York: Harcourt Harvest Book, 1963), p. 11.
40. Ben H. Bagdikian, *The Effete Conspiracy* (New York: Harper & Row, Publishers, Incorporated, 1972), p. 27.
41. The author is grateful to two of his friends and colleagues, Professors Jeffrey Morris and Frank Macchiarola, for suggesting this project. See their "Teaching Notes," in *P.S.,* III (Summer 1970), pp. 336–340.
42. Quoted in John S. Saloma III and Frederick H. Sontag, *Parties: The Real Opportunity for Effective Citizen Politics* (New York: Alfred A. Knopf, Inc., 1972), p. 251.
43. Harold Mendelsohn and Irving Crespi, *Polls, Television, and the New Politics* (Scranton, Pa.: Chandler Publishing Company, 1970), p. 312
44. Elihu Katz and Jacob J. Feldman, "The Kennedy-Nixon Debates: A Survey of Surveys," in William J. Crotty, ed., *Public Opinion and Politics: A Reader* (New York: Holt, Rinehart and Winston, Inc., 1970), pp. 421–422.
45. Martin Mayer, "Television" section, *Harper's,* CCXLIII (December 1971), p. 42.
46. John K. Galbraith, *American Capitalism* (New York: Houghton Mifflin Company, 1952).
47. Quoted in Newton Minow, *Equal Time* (New York: Atheneum Publishers, 1964), p. 18.
48. Les Brown, *Television: The Business behind the Box* (New York: Harcourt Brace Jovanovich, Inc., 1971), p. 65.
49. Bryce Rucker, *The First Freedom* (Carbondale, Ill.: Southern Illinois University Press, 1968). p. 106
50. Quoted in *Control of Information,* Network Project Notebook Number Three, March 1973, p. 23.
51. Quoted in ibid., p. 31.
52. Robert B. Beusse and Russell Shaw, "Maude's Abortion: Spontaneous or Induced?," *America,* CXXIX (Nov. 3, 1973), pp. 324–326.
53. *New York Times,* Mar. 7, 1973, p. 87.
54. Jack Newfield and Jeff Greenfield, *A Populist Manifesto: The Making of a New Majority* (New York: Frederick A. Praeger, Inc., 1972), chap. 9.
55. Jerome A. Barron, "An Emerging First Amendment Right of Access to the Media?", in Michael P. Smith, ed., *American Politics and Public Policy* (New York: Random House, Inc., 1973), p. 305.

56 Robert Stein, *Media Power: Who Is Shaping Your Picture of the World?* (Boston: Houghton Mifflin Company, 1972), p. 28.
57 *New York Times,* Jan. 31, 1973, p. 83.
58 Quoted in Anthony Lewis, "The Public Airwaves," *New York Times,* Nov. 20, 1972, p. 37.
59 Congressional Quarterly, *Weekly Report,* Aug. 31, 1974, p. 2384.
60 Quoted in Mintz and Cohen, op. cit., p. 158.
61 *Miami Herald Publishing Company, Inc. v. Tornillo,* 94 S. Ct. 2831 (1974).
62 Nathan Lewin, "What's Happening to Free Speech?", *New Republic,* CLXXI (July 27 and Apr. 3, 1974), p. 17.

Chapter 2

Equality: Rich and Poor in America

The poison that destroys a democracy—the poison that Marx was sure was going to destroy Western democracy—is the growth of the feeling that some people are in and others are out.
Charles Frankel*

He [the plantation owner] doesn't want us trying to vote like that—and first I'd like to feed my kids, before I go trying to vote.
Wife of Mississippi Plantation Worker†

The Two Park Avenues

At 68th Street and Park Avenue in New York City the rhododendrons are blooming in front of Hunter College. Crossing the avenue at 69th Street is a uniformed maid, pushing a baby in an English pram. 700 and 710 Park Avenue are imposing fourteen-story penthoused apartment buildings with roof gardens. Across the avenue are some particularly handsome brownstones, brass carriage lamps ready to light their doorways. A man of perhaps sixty is walking past, sporting a bow tie, and two boys about ten, one of them carrying a baseball bat

---

* *The Democratic Prospect* (New York and Evanston: Harper & Row, Publishers, Incorporated, 1964), p. 20.
† Nick Katz, "The Subcommittee Chairman: Politics of Fear," in Michael P. Smith, ed., *American Politics and Public Policy*, (New York: Random House, Inc., 1973), p. 144.

which appears not to have been used. On the corner of 75th and Park, a shop: "Flowers By Cort." A Cadillac limousine, windows shut, idles its engine while the chauffeur runs inside.

At 86th a hint of change appears. On this busy throughstreet people seem more hurried, less sure of themselves. Some black faces (aside from servants) can be seen among the pedestrians.

At 96th Street everything comes apart. The avenue's green center mall disappears and is replaced by a rusty iron fence. Twenty feet below runs the Penn Central railroad. The penthouse-topped luxury apartments have also vanished, their places taken by run-down tenements half a block long, their backs linked by clotheslines. A bent old woman, with a shopping bag in each hand, peers into the garbage cans in front of the "Spanish-American Grocery."

At 100th and Park the railroad tracks slope upward and Park Avenue slopes the other way. It is now divided by a stone wall several feet high, forcing traffic into a narrow lane with the wall on one side and tenements on the other. The smell of dampness mixes with other smells: urine and uncollected garbage. At 103rd Street a young man, staring aimlessly, sits on a box in front of New York Marble Works.

At 115th Street the stone wall is replaced by giant rusty stilts holding up the railroad tracks. Below are some abandoned cars, shattered glass, a litter of handbills announcing "EL BOY: Orquestra de Jazz." Transistor radios are blaring. Even on this weekday afternoon, men and teen-age boys seem to be sitting and standing everywhere—idle, bored, full of despair and defeat.

The trip between the two Park Avenues of New York City takes slightly more than five minutes by car. It can be duplicated in almost any American city—in Chicago, by driving from North State Street to South State Street; in Boston, by driving from Beacon Hill to South Boston; in San Francisco, by driving from the Marina to the Fillmore area; in Los Angeles, by driving from Westwood to Watts; and so on.

Journeys of this kind illustrate the extremes of rich and poor in urban America. But to see the very worst degree of poverty one must leave the Northern cities and travel to the rural hollows of America, particularly those in the South and Southwest.

Starvation in America

One out of every ten people in America does not have enough of the proper kind of food to maintain health; some do not even get enough to maintain life. In 1968 the U. S. Public Health Service began a National Nutritional Survey, a study of the eating habits and health conditions of poor people in ten states. In January 1969, Dr. Arnold E. Schaefer of the Service reported to a Senate subcommittee some of its preliminary findings. Children were found afflicted with kwashiorkor (a Ghanian word meaning "the disease that takes the child after it leaves the mother's breast"), a disease of extreme protein deficiency previously thought to exist only in the most underdeveloped countries. Even more astounding were cases of marasmus, a disease resulting from caloric deficiencies. In stunned silence the senators watched a film of a marasmus victim, a tiny baby with emaciated limbs and bulging eyes. Dr. Schaefer commented:

> We did not expect to find such cases in the United States. In many of the developing areas where we have worked—Africa, Latin America and Asia—these severe cases of malnutrition only rarely are found. They either are hospitalized or have died.[1]

These were cases of outright starvation. Other cases, even more numerous, involved children dying of starvation-related diseases. Dr. Robert Coles of Harvard University Health Services told the same Senate subcommittee what he and his committee of physicians personally observed:

> We saw, bluntly, hungry, malnourished children with swollen ankles, swollen bellies, widely infected skin, wasting muscles, and for practically each part of the body, I am sad to say, signs of illness. Hearts had murmurs. Percussion of chests indicated lung infections. Teeth were in awful condition. Children needed glasses, needed antibiotics, needed drugs that would rid them of worms; they needed to have their hearing checked or their heart or nose and throat or bones and joints checked. Children had, almost universally, anemia and unhealed sores and chronic sinus conditions and, in the words of one mother, "colds, colds, colds; they never get over them, even when the temperature goes over 100."[2]

When Dr. Coles reported his findings to the then-Secretary of Agriculture, Orville Freeman,

> We were told that we and all the hungry children we had examined and all the other hungry Americans . . . would have to reckon with Mr. James L. Whitten, as indeed must the Secretary of Agriculture, whose funds come to him through the kindness of the same Mr. Whitten. We were told of the problems that the Agriculture Department has with Congress, and we left feeling we ought to weigh those problems as somehow of the same order as the problems we had met in the South—and that we know from our work elsewhere existed all over the country.[3]

Representative Jamie Whitten, of Mississippi, the chairman of the House Appropriation Committee's Agriculture subcommittee, exercises iron control over funds appropriated for rural areas. Preventing starvation, he believes, has to be balanced against other priorities. "When you start giving people something for nothing, just giving them all they want for nothing, I wonder if you don't destroy character more than you might improve nutrition."[4] Yet Whitten's subcommittee approves five billion dollars in farm subsidies every year; 7 percent go to the poorest 41 percent of American farms, while the richest 7 percent get 32 percent of the benefits.[5] Senator James O. Eastland, Whitten's fellow Mississippian who sits on the Senate Agriculture Committee, received $159,000 in agricultural subsidies in 1971[6]—without anyone worrying about its effect on his character. But life is different for Jamie Whitten's black neighbors in Tallahatchie County. Of its 24,081 residents in 1969, 18,000 had family incomes of less than $3,000 a year, and 15,197 made less than $2,000. "Only a few blocks from Whitten's own frame house, Negroes live in shacks without toilets, running water, electricity—or food."[7]

The recent experience of "stagflation"—combined recession and inflation—

has made life even more desperate for America's poor. In June of 1974 a panel of experts reporting to the Senate Select Committee on Nutrition and Human Needs concluded that the poor in this country were hungrier and poorer than they were four years previously, despite increases in spending on food programs. One of the experts, after noting that federal spending on food programs had increased threefold between 1970 and 1974, added:

> I would be pleased to tell you that we have made substantial progress in the effort to eradicate hunger. However, to do so would be untruthful. For the sad and tragic truth is that, over the past several years, we have moved backwards in our struggle to end hunger, poverty and malnutrition.[8]

The rapid increases in food prices were bad for the middle classes, but devastating to the poor. Middle-class shoppers began "spending down," buying cheaper cuts of meat and otherwise reducing food expenditures. But there was no more "down" for many of the poor to go to, and the pressure of demand from middle-class consumers was driving up the price of even the cheapest foods. The experts reported visiting one Indian family surviving on chocolate bars and stale coffee, and another family in Georgia eating nothing but stale bread and pig jowls. There were rumors of elderly poor eating dog food. ("Makes 'em chase after cars," comedian Johnny Carson told his late-show audience. An official of the Food and Drug Administration was more sober. Pet foods, he said, "are absolutely not for humans. In a time of intensifying food shortage, we may change our concepts of what is edible, of course.")[9] Unemployment, which was above 8 percent in 1975, was at least double that figure in the nation's ghettos.

The Rich Get Richer

Social welfare for the rich, free enterprise for the poor; subsidies and price supports for plantation owners, character development for their starving neighbors; boutiques and mod shops at one end of town, poverty and hopelessness a few blocks away—these are the realities of rich and poor in America today, realities which may become even more stark in the years to come. The gap between rich and poor in America seems, if anything, to be widening. In 1970 S. M. Miller and Pamela Roby offered the "discouraging report" that "the percentage of total money income that goes to the bottom 20 percent of families has hovered around 5 percent since 1947."[10] More recent studies reveal an even more discouraging picture. A study of the salaries of male workers, published by the U. S. Labor Department in December 1971, indicated that from 1958 to 1970 the share of aggregate wage and salary earned by the lowest fifth of male workers declined from 5.10 percent to 4.60 percent. At the same time, the share of the highest fifth of male wage and salary earners rose from 38.15 to 40.55 percent.[11] The development of technology and civil-service employment is leaving the poor further and further behind. New jobs in the higher echelons of these areas are going to the children of the upper-middle class.

The Labor Department's study reflects only wage and salary. To measure the full extent of income disparity, we must take into account all sources of income. America's rich make their money from a variety of sources besides wages and salaries. These include earnings from assets and in-kind (nonmonetized) earnings, such as bond interest, capital gains, expense accounts, "business trip" vacations, stock dividends, and so on. It is very difficult to find reliable data on all the sources of wealth, however, because they do not appear on pay checks and are thus not automatically report to the IRS. As Bertram Gross has put it:

> While the majority of America's almost eighty million employees have their income automatically reported through payroll taxes, rich individuals and corporations escape reporting through a wide variety of tricks, including padded expense accounts, company-provided luxuries, tax (and income) havens and loopholes, undistributed profits, the international shell game of conglomerates and holding companies, and the foundation shell game for dodging inheritance taxes.[12]

It appears that these gimmicks have proliferated since 1941, the year when high tax rates were put into effect. "It is surely no coincidence," Gabriel Kolko wrote in 1961, "that the high tax rates and the decline in the before-taxes income-share of the top 5 percent began in the same year."[13]

Census data, which are based upon uncritical reporting of family income, are an unreliable index of income disparity, but data developed by Joseph Pechman of the Brookings Institution have given us a better look at the disparity of income in America. According to Pechman's data, the poorest fifth of all Americans obtain only about 3 percent of the country's annual income; the next poorest fifth get 11 percent. but the richest fifth receive 46 percent of the annual income, and the topmost sliver of the population—the very richest one-twentieth—get 20 percent of all income.[14] If we express the figures not in terms of income but wealth (the value of assets owned), the contrast is more striking: One-third of all individual wealth in the United States belongs to 1 percent of the people. Many Americans, for example, own stocks, but 2 percent of all individual stockholders own about two-thirds of the individually held stocks.[15]

The superrich: These are the people who do not have to worry much about inflation and recession. In 1974 the middle classes tightened their belts and the poor became desperate. But at the Mauna Kea Beach Hotel, the highest priced resort in Hawaii, business from America was brisk. "The very well-to-do, those who are used to traveling in style, are still traveling in style," said one travel agent, echoing the views of many others. Sales of luxury Cadillacs and Rolls Royces were also up 15 percent from the previous year, and Tiffany's reported no fall-off in sales of diamonds and expensive gifts.[16]

And what about the poor—what is their life like? Part of the difficulty in answering that question appears when we try to define "poor." What is poverty?

The federal government has developed a poverty measure by which families are called poor if their income falls below a specified level prescribed by the Social Security Administration. This level takes account of such factors as family size, number of children, and nonfarm residence, as well as the amount of family income. It is based upon the Department of Agriculture's estimate of a minimum nutritionally sound food plan (an "economy" diet for "emergency or temporary use when funds are low"), and it assumes that the poor family should spend no more than one-third of its income for food. A household is statistically classed as "poor" if its total money income is less than three times the cost of the "economy" food plan. In 1972 the poverty line for a family of four was $4,140.

If we were to accept the official definition of poverty we could make some firm assertions about poverty in this country. We could say that about 12 percent of our people can be defined as poor. We could also have some cause for optimism, since the number of such poor has declined from 22 percent in 1959. But the government's definition of poverty contains some serious flaws. For one, it takes no account of regional differences in the price of food and other necessities. Perhaps a family of four could get by on $4,140 per year in Georgia, but not in the New York City area without some form of supplement. Second, the Department of Agriculture's "economy" food budget was developed for "temporary or emergency use," and is inadequate for a permanent diet. Third, and most important, it uses a fixed standard to define what is in essence a relative condition.

Today's poor in America might be well-off compared, say, to the lower classes of medieval Europe, or to the starving people in Ethiopia, but they are certainly not well-off when measured by what Americans in the seventies consider a "decent standard of living." To live decently in today's America is to live in a house or apartment which is adequately heated in winter and ventilated in summer, under a roof that doesn't leak, without crowding, or broken plumbing, or rats. It means having the money to live in a neighborhood which has adequate schools, police protection, and other services. It means being able to eat more than an "emergency" diet, being able to buy new clothes when needed, to afford medical and dental services, and to have some money left over for a little entertainment once in a while, and for such things as household furnishings and appliances. It is hard to see how a family of four could live in this manner anywhere in America today on an annual budget of $4,140.

Of course these standards are shot through with subjective considerations (What is "adequate" police protection? How often are new clothes "needed," etc.?), but it is hard to see how we can avoid subjectivity if we are to understand what it means to to be poor. "Poverty in its truest sense," wrote one authority on the subject, "is more than want; it is want mixed with a lack of hope."[17] To be poor means to be left out, left back, to see oneself stuck at the low end of the economic scale while others move upward. How can this be measured in statistics? In the fullest measure, it probably cannot be quantified, but some, like the sociologist Herbert Gans, argue that *relative* standards of poverty ought to be used for measurement.[18] One way of doing this would be to peg the poverty line at some percentage of the median income. (The most common figure suggested is 50 percent of the median income, though Gans believes it should be 60 percent.) Defined in this way, poverty becomes less tractable than it appears when we apply absolute standards. As we have seen, income distribution, if it has changed at all since 1941, has changed in the direction of greater inequality. A relative standard of poverty would also imply a more radical means of attacking the problem. It would mean not only raising the incomes of the poor but narrowing the gap between the poor and the rich in America. Will that ever happen? The prospects do not seem very good.

If anything, the poor seem to be more forgotten today than they were during the sixties. In 1964 President Lyndon Johnson, at the height of his power, proposed an "unconditional war on poverty." The legislative fruit of his proposal was the Office of Economic Opportunity, a great umbrella agency which sponsored several projects designed to eradicate poverty once and for all. But by the second term of the Nixon administration it was clear that this was at least one war which had ground to a halt. President Nixon's proposed budget for 1974 leveled off the amount spent for social welfare measures, suspending housing subsidies to low-income families, cutting back on funds for education and training of the poor, school milk programs, urban renewal, public employment, and hospital care for disabled veterans. The Office of Economic Opportunity, which had been established as the chief vehicle for fighting poverty, was to be dismantled, and legal aid services for the poor were to be turned over to the states. After the Watergate scandal weakened his power, Nixon was forced to retreat from his plans to dismantle the Office of Economic Opportunity, but otherwise the policy remained the same. If anything, "Watergate politics" drove Nixon further away even from such modest programs as Family Assistance (which he had supported during his first term) in order to win support from the conservative wing of his party. When Nixon was finally forced to resign, the optimistic view was that Gerald Ford, whose personality was the opposite of Nixon's, would pursue different policies. But when it came to the question of spending for social programs, Ford soon made it clear that austerity was to be the order of the day. In November of 1974 the new President proposed spending cuts totalling $4.6 billion, about three quarters of which would come from such social programs as Medicare, food stamps, veterans' education benefits, and welfare.

Inequality and Democracy

Democracy does not depend upon absolute equality of condition, but it is certainly flawed by extremes of poverty and wealth. Its minimum requirement is that all must be equal before the law. Yet legal equality becomes an empty formalism if the real conditions in a society give a special power to one class at the expense of another. The contradiction between formal rights and actual conditions is what prompted the famous sarcastic remark of Anatole France: "The law, in all its majesty, forbids rich as well as poor to sleep under bridges on rainy nights, to beg in the streets and to steal bread." It is hard to assure a hungry man that he is, after all, your equal before the law. He knows better, and so do those who have studied the problem and found that the ability to be protected against bureaucratic and legal mistreatment depends upon income and education.[19] It is also hard to expect poor people to be effective participants in a democracy. Statistics demonstrate that participation, like justice, varies with income. Less than half of the poor vote, as contrasted with nearly 85 percent of the better-off.[20] Several studies show that membership in voluntary associations increases with status. In a study of New York City poor, David Caplovitz showed that, *within* the lower classes, the less the financial stability of the family, "the less its participation in the life of the broader community."[21]

What can be done about poverty in America? To prevent the question from being loaded, it might be well to ask first *whether* anything can or should be done.

Let Poverty Be: The "Solution" of Laissez Faire

Laissez faire (literally, "leave to do" or "leave alone") has a long tradition in American social thought. The fact that it has been respected more in theory than practice (America has always provided tax breaks, subsidies, tariffs, and free land to commercial enterprises) has not dimmed its attractiveness as an "explanation" for why nothing can be done for the poor.

The slogan "I fight poverty—I work for a living" epitomizes the attitude of many middle-class people toward those in the class immediately below them. President Nixon called it "the work ethic," and considered it part of his mandate for reelection. " . . . I feel very strongly what this country wants and this election will demonstrate what the American people want and the American people will thrive upon a new feeling of responsibility, a new feeling of self-discipline, rather than go back to the thoughts . . . that it was the government's job every time there was a problem, to make people more and more dependent upon it. . . ." The basic task of government is "to allow people to do more for themselves. . . ."[22] His second inaugural address contained a revised version of President Kennedy's famous "ask not" quotation from his inaugural twelve years earlier. Whereas Kennedy had appealed to the ideal of service, Nixon appealed to the ideal of self-reliance: "Ask not what your country can do for you, ask what you can do for yourself."

But it must be asked: What can single mothers with preschool children, or a teen-ager with no skills, or nonunionized migrant workers, or penniless old people, do to help themselves? About 18 percent of the poor are sixty-five and older;[23] 41 percent are children under eighteen; one-third live in homes where the head works full-time, and another one-quarter where he or she works part-time.[24] "I fight poverty—I work for a living" is thus a cruel and silly slogan, at least when applied to the overwhelming majority of poor people in America today, who either do work for a living, or would if they could.

"The work ethic"—Nixon did not want to say "the Protestant ethic"—is another one of those high-sounding expressions, like "law 'n' order," which elude us when we search for concrete meanings. How many of those who applauded the expression belonged to labor unions which demand higher wages without asking their members to work harder? How many were businessmen who benefited from fair-trade laws, tax write-offs, government subsidies, loans, and tarrifs? How many were farmers who got federal money to *not* grow crops, or veterans who went to school on the GI Bill, or students at low-tuition municipal and state colleges, or homeowners who benefited from FHA mortgages or tax write-offs on their mortgage interest? We don't know the actual numbers, but we should know this: American society today is honeycombed with various social programs which hand out money, services, tax credits, and exemptions to all sorts of people, including some very rich people. Relatively few people in America can without hypocrisy declare themselves rugged individualists, and those few will include a sizable portion of the poorest people in the nation.

Despite the lip service Americans give to rugged individualism, large numbers of them benefit at some time or another from the interventionist state. They seem to be aware of this fact, too, because when it comes to concrete measures they are often willing to approve state intervention in the economy. During the Depression in the 1930s the Roosevelt administration experimented with a variety of programs for dealing with poverty, and some of them remain in existence today. Let us examine three of these programs.

HERITAGE OF THE NEW DEAL: THREE FLAWED ANTIPOVERTY PROGRAMS

Social Security

The most popular of these was the Social Security Act. Although this program has been amended several times since its enactment in 1935, its basic principles remain the same. It is an insurance program for wage-earners. The wage-earner and his employer contribute equal amounts to a fund held in trust by the federal government. At some point in his life the wage-earner will receive monthly cash benefits in accordance with the size of his family and the money he has earned during his lifetime. Its main purpose is to provide for retirement; a male worker may start collecting these benefits at 62, a woman at 60. It also provides money for widows, orphans, and the disabled.

Social Security contains a number of attractive features. It is entirely a federal program. This means that its standards do not vary from state to state, that its records are kept in Washington or in regional offices, that it uses the most modern and efficient data processing systems, and that its checks arrive on time by mail at the end of every month without any hitches, questions, or red tape. More important, Social Security is viewed as a person's *right*. Those receiving it can assure themselves that they earned it, or at least part of it. This sense of dignity is enhanced by the way the program is administered: No one calls at the person's house to see whether he or she is needy or deserving. All members, rich and poor alike, receive their Social Security checks without having to submit to demeaning examinations by welfare bureaucrats.

The above features of Social Security are so attractive that they have served as models for those who would reform other aspects of our welfare system. But they are offset by features which prevent Social Security from being very effective in relieving hard-core poverty. First, it applies only to retired or disabled people and their dependents. It is thus useless as a means of combating poverty caused by unemployment or underemployment among younger and able-bodied people. Second, even among the elderly, two million people do not receive Social Security, either because they have not worked at jobs covered by it, or they have not worked at them long enough. Third, and most important, payments are pitifully low, averaging $293 per month for a retired worker and his wife. In today's inflated economy this is not enough to live on. Yet if the retiree tries to supplement it by getting a job, he will find his Social Security benefits cut by fifty cents for every dollar he earns above $200 per month. But this applies only to *earned* income, such as wages and income from self-employment. It does not apply to money made from annuities, interest, capital assets, inheritances, rents, or dividends on investments. The retiree could get $1,000 per month from these sources—or $5,000, or whatever, since there is no limit—and still get his full

Social Security benefits. In other words, the system penalizes those who work for a living, while favoring those who get their money from inheritances, rents, and investments. Meanwhile, at the very bottom of the income ladder, those poor who have suffered years of unemployment or underemployment—who are most likely to need financial assistance in their old age—receive the least amount in Social Security benefits. In 1973 Congress passed a Supplementary Security Income program (S. S. I.), setting a floor of $219 per month for a couple as a minimum payment to those poor who had contributed little or nothing to Social Security, but nobody has yet explained how a couple today can live on $2,628 per year.

Coupled with the inequities in Social Security payments are inequities in the way the monies are collected. Social Security funds are derived from a flat-rate tax on earnings up to the first $14,100 of a worker's salary. This makes it a regressive tax, since the higher a person makes above $14,100 the lower is his or her effective tax rate. And there is no Social Security tax at all on unearned income: dividends, interest, capital gains, and so on. Once again, the system seems to be biased toward the well-to-do and against the lower middle-class. It is also biased against working wives. In some cases a wife who has been earning money (and, not incidentally, paying Social Security taxes) will get no more in payments than one who has stayed at home. And the system is regressive: If husband and wife were both to work, each earning $14,100, both would pay the maximum Social Security tax, while a family with only one worker earning $28,200 would have to pay only half as much.

Unemployment Insurance

Also established under the Social Security Act of 1935 is a system of insurance designed to relieve the financial situation of workers temporarily unemployed. Unlike old-age, disability, and survivor's insurance, however, this aspect of the program is administered in cooperation with the states. As a result, the eligibility requirements, procedures, and payments vary widely from state to state. Typically, unemployed workers must wait two weeks before receiving any payment, during which time they must prove themselves able and willing to work; they will then receive payments for a specified period, the amount and duration of which will depend upon a number of factors, including the average earnings they made while employed and the region of the country they live in.

Unemployment Compensation is useless as a means of combating chronic and long-term unemployment. It was not meant to do so. But even given its objectives—to help workers over periods of temporary layoffs—Unemployment Compensation contains critical flaws. The *scope* of the coverage, for example, is too narrow: Many low-income and poorly organized occupations are not covered. Also, those employed for less than the specified period of time are not eligible for benefits. Thus the poor, who are likely to be in and out of jobs for short periods, are the ones left out.

Public Assistance

When Americans speak of "welfare," they usually mean the public assistance program that has provided aid to various categories of dependent people. The

Social Security Act of 1935 established federal participation in public assistance, with the purpose of giving immediate help to destitute persons who could not wait for aid under the social insurance programs initiated under the same law. The main difference between public assistance and the other programs discussed so far is that it is in no way connected with any monies paid into the program by the recipient, but is based solely on "need." The problem lies in the definition of "need."

Federal grants to state public assistance programs are available under four categories: Old-age Assistance (OAA): Aid to Families with Dependent Children (AFDC); Aid to the Blind (AB); and Aid to the Permanently and Totally Disabled (APTD). Until 1973 the states were given discretion to define "need," with the result that standards varied widely depending upon the states. In 1968, for example, Cleveland accepted 80 percent of those applying for public assistance, while in Houston the figure was 30 percent. The amount paid was also subject to great regional fluctuations. In October of 1973 Congress alleviated this problem somewhat by federalizing the standards for three of these categories: aid to the blind, to the disabled, and to the aged. Individuals in these categories with no other income receive a minimum monthly federal payment of $130 ($195 for a couple). But the largest category of federally funded public assistance, Aid to Families with Dependent Children (AFDC), is still administered by the individual states.

AFDC

AFDC has proven to be the most controversial item in the welfare program. Southern states, while relatively generous in their other programs, have been particularly stingy in providing aid for these families. A number of factors, including racial prejudice, the stigma against illigitimacy, and the belief that aid to these families will encourage more child-bearing, have militated against more generous allowances. (Senator Russell Long of Louisiana has called welfare mothers "black brood mares.") But even in the North the program tends to be regarded as a "confession of failure" or "the welfare mess," and campaigns against "chiselers" have become ritualized features in every electoral contest.

Pressures to "do something about welfare" mounted greatly during the Nixon years, and largely because of an important fact: a massive increase in AFDC rolls since the mid-sixties. Figure 2-1 provides some idea of the dimensions of this leap.

At the end of the fifties, the number of families on AFDC was not much higher than the number of individuals receiving old-age assistance or other forms of public assistance. By the middle of the sixties the climb of AFDC rolls suddenly steepened, and by the early seventies its line of ascent was nearly vertical, leaving all other forms of welfare at the bottom of the chart. Why?

Swelling Welfare Rolls: Why?

Daniel P. Moynihan, who served first as one of Nixon's chief domestic counsellors (later as Ambassador to India and now as Ambassador to the UN), considers the reasons to be connected with the breakdown of the black family structure

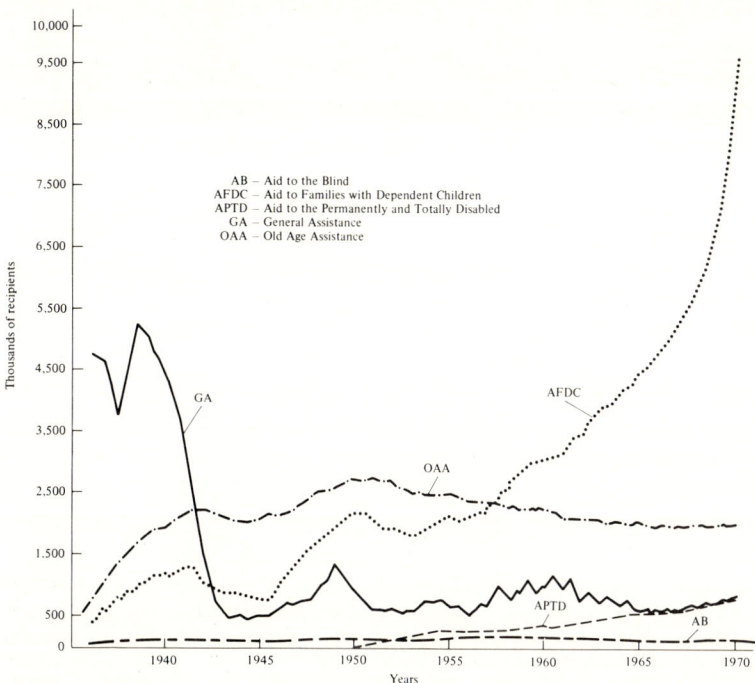

Figure 2-1 Number of public assistance recipients of money payments by program. June and December of each year, 1936 to date. [*Source: Reprinted from Welfare Mothers Speak Out: We Ain't Gonna Shuffle Anymore, p. 23, by Milwaukee County Welfare Rights Organization. By permission of W. W. Norton & Company, Inc. Copyright © 1972 by W. W. Norton & Company, Inc.*]

during the sixties. In *The Politics of a Guaranteed Income* Moynihan summed up the analysis he had presented to President Nixon on the problem when Nixon first came into office in 1969. The strongest probability, Moynihan told Nixon, was that the number of welfare cases had shot up during the sixties because *(a)* liberalized standards for receiving it had increased the number of families eligible for it, *(b)* the number of female-headed families in metropolitan areas also increased, *(c)* illigitimacy increased, and *(d)* black families on AFDC—who are more likely to receive AFDC than poor whites—had similarly increased.

These conclusions were not without political relevance. President Nixon was greatly interested in Moynihan's reports, because the thrust of Nixon's approach to the welfare program was "reform," i. e., getting people *off* welfare. Since Moynihan's analysis seemed to point toward the breakdown of the black family structure as the underlying cause for the increase in the welfare rolls, it seemed appropriate to devise an approach to welfare that would aim at keeping families together without destroying the incentive to find work.

The late George A. Wiley, executive director of the National Welfare Rights Organization (NWRO), emphatically disagreed with Moynihan's thesis. The increase in recipients, Dr. Wiley contended, simply meant "that more people in need of public assistance are now getting it," and he believed that his organization, by acquainting people with their "right to welfare," could take some of the credit for the increase in AFDC cases.

> The real welfare crisis . . . is not how many but how few poor people are receiving benefits. Now that the welfare system is finally being forced to deliver what it is supposed to under the law, everyone says there is a crisis, but the real crisis has been going on for a long time. It will continue until all the poor people in this country get their right to welfare.[25]

At the bottom of these contrasting analyses is a basic philosophical disagreement. Is welfare a right? Or is it, as Moynihan argued, a sign of dependency, as demeaning to the recipient as it is burdening to the rest of society? Wiley's position was that, since most Americans (including the rich) are on some form of welfare anyway, it is unfair to apply pinchpenny economics only to those who happen to be black, female ghetto residents with children. What is demeaning in the present system is not the fact that people are given money without work, but that some of them—the poor—are stigmatized and humiliated by the *manner* in which it is handed out (the imperious attitude of many caseworkers, the investigations, the bureaucracy) and the paltry sums received. Moynihan, on the other hand, shares the Nixonian view that the only real solution to poverty, both in its economic and psychological aspects, is to get people to work. Any poverty program, therefore, which destroys the incentive to work for money will finally bankrupt the society and demoralize those it was intended to benefit. These contrasting philosophies played a role in dividing the original supporters of President Nixon's proposed Family Assistance Program in 1970–1971, thus ensuring the program's defeat in Congress. This episode will be explored in more detail later in the chapter.

Weaknesses of AFDC

What both Moynihan and Wiley, and for that matter Americans of every persuasion, seemed to agree upon is this: The present welfare system is indeed a "mess." AFDC suffers from three major weaknesses:

1 The system *discourages* families from staying together. Payments are cut off if an adult male is found living in the home. A father must desert his children if he wants them to receive benefits. Take this hypothetical example from New York City:

> A dishwasher who earned $60 per week and had a wife and three children could receive welfare payments of $48 per family per month. *If he left his family,* New York City payments for a family of four in 1969 averaged $249.75 per month, or $62 per person per month, plus medical aid and other services—*and the income was tax free.*[26]

The United States is the only industrialized country in the world that provides public welfare only *after* the family has broken up.

2 The system is ridden with red tape and punitive features. One would think that in an age of computers the administration of welfare could be vastly simplified. But the administration of public assistance is part and parcel of the administration of local governments, with their antiquated procedures and pork-barrel hiring practices. Recipients and caseworkers are constantly occupied in filling out innumerable forms, in several copies, which are then shuffled and reshuffled, passed through more hands, filed and misfiled.* Further complicating the administration in many states is the requirement that the poor be "worthy" of help. Case workers are sometimes so preoccupied with seeing if the rules have been violated that they have little time to help the recipients.

3   The system constitutes a gigantic invasion of privacy. The Louisiana Department of Public Welfare includes the following item in its manual for caseworkers:

> It is recognized that the client has the right to participate in social activities, including dating. The fact that a mother has dates with a man does not establish that a non-legal marital union exists. However, the worker shall be alert to and follow up on clues which indicate that the relationship is more than that of dating. . . . When there is indication that the relationship may be more than that of normal courtship, this should be discussed with the client, who should be asked where she usually sees him, the frequency of their dates, and where they go.[27]

This may be an extreme example, but throughout the country welfare workers are expected to ask the most personal questions and keep the most careful eye on the recipients to see if they are keeping within the rules, Social workers have been known to knock on doors in the middle of the night to see if welfare mothers are sleeping with men. Although the practice was declared unconstitutional by the Supreme Court in 1968, it reportedly still continues.

THE SEARCH IN THE SIXTIES FOR BETTER SOLUTIONS: SELF-HELP AND THE OEO

Why has this kind of welfare system, with these obvious shortcomings built into it, been tolerated for so long? One reason is that Americans for years deceived

---

* Some idea of what happens to human beings while all this is going on is provided by the following account, written by a former New York City caseworker:

The Diaz family was burned out of their third-floor walk-up on Christmas Eve, 1969. Since their apartment had already been scheduled for razing, the Department of Urban Relocation was contacted for help in finding them new accommodations. This agency acted quickly. They placed the Diaz family, in 10° temperatures, in an abandoned third-floor three-room walk-up without heat or plumbing. There were five people in this three-generation family. Margaret, the mother, had suffered severe injuries to her feet in escaping the fire, which made navigation of the stairs painful at first, ultimately impossible. Her daughter, Luz, had moved in with her mother when her common-law husband first locked her out, then disappeared with all their belongings. Luz had a two-month-old baby from this union. Ricardo, fourteen, and Juanita, seven, Margaret's other children, completed the family.

Luz had made formal application for ADC for herself and her child a month earlier. She had not been given any help, nor any word on the status of her case. (The Department frequently disregards the legal time limit of four weeks for reaching a decision on new applications.) Margaret took her family to the Social Service Center on the 24th to apply for an emergency check for a week's food for herself and two children—Luz and her baby being nonpeople as far as the Department was concerned. The Center kept her there four hours, processing the check and paperworking the move to the new address. Consequently, the family did not arrive at the Urban Relocation office to pick up the keys to their new home until after 5:00 P.M. The office was locked, and would not reopen until the 26th. The center was also closed through Christmas Day. The family, of necessity, spent that holiday in the misery and mess of their burned-out building. [Edythe A. Shewbridge, *Portraits of Poverty* (New York: W. W. Norton & Company, Inc., 1972), pp. 23–24.]

themselves that poverty was largely a thing of the past. The full employment generated by World War II put an end to the Depression, and New Deal policies seemed sufficient to take care of any remnant of poverty. In the 1950s, liberals and conservatives alike saw no need to undertake any new initiatives against a problem that seemed to be quickly fading away. When John F. Kennedy campaigned in West Virginia in 1960 he was shocked to see half-starved people living in shacks amid the abandoned coal fields, and one of the first bills supported by his administration was the Area Redevelopment Act of 1961, which sought to move industry into these hard-pressed areas. They were still thought of as mere "pockets of poverty," however, and not parts of a larger problem.

In 1962, Michael Harrington's book *The Other America,* along with other studies on the extent of poverty in the affluent society, finally jolted the public's consciousness into a recognition that poverty in modern America is both widespread and deeply rooted. Harrington's book, based in part on his experience as a poverty worker in some of New York's seamiest areas, not only brought poverty to the public's attention (one of his observations was that today's poor are "invisible"), but also underscored the chronic features of the problem. Today's poverty, Harrington argued, tends to perpetuate itself because the poor suffer not just from lack of money but also from the sense of futility and frustration. Since today's poor are mired in hopelessness, we need nothing less than a comprehensive program which seeks not merely to provide the poor with money, but with spirit, "elan" (a word which recurs several times in his book), so that they can help themselves.

And how do we provide the poor with elan? "There are . . . housing administrators, welfare workers, and city planners with dedication and vision. They are working on the local level, and their main frustration is the lack of funds."[28] Harrington's approach to poverty epitomized the attitude of many liberals in the early sixties. If the poor can be *taught* to participate in their own solutions to their own problems, the reasoning went, they can then break out of the culture of poverty. The task of government, therefore, is to supply funds to dedicated leaders in the local communities, who will use them to help the poor through training and organization. This basic philosophy was embodied in the Economic Opportunity Act, passed by Congress in August of 1964.

The Economic Opportunity Act was to be a vehicle for fulfilling Lyndon Johnson's promise to wage a "total, unconditional war on poverty." Its "services" approach to the causes of poverty was underscored by the appointment of R. Sargent Shriver, earlier the Peace Corps Director, as its chief coordinator. Just as dedicated young Americans were serving abroad to help indigenous people to help themselves, so also was self-help to be encouraged and developed in the domestic sphere: An Office of Economic Opportunity was to coordinate a series of programs in local communities designed to train, educate, and motivate the poor in the solution to their own problems.

VISTA (Volunteers in Service to America), also known as the "domestic Peace Corps," was one of the first programs created in 1964. Its aim was to provide trained, dedicated persons to assist the underprivileged throughout the nation—on Indian reservations, among migrant workers, in hospitals, mental institutions, city slums. The Job Corps was to train low-skilled young people for entering today's work force. The Neighborhood Youth Corps was to provide part-time jobs to youngsters to give them enough incentive and money to stay in school. The Comprehensive Employment Program was to find jobs and develop marketable skills for poor people. The Upward Bound program sought to help bright underachieving children from low-income families gain admission to college. Project Headstart enrolled preschool children from poverty areas in an effort to improve basic learning skills.

The Economic Opportunity Act provided other services as well, such as legal assistance and family planning. But the basic philosophy behind all of them was the same: The key to eliminating poverty is motivation. The keystone of the poverty program, therefore, was the Community Action Agency (CAA). Community Action was aimed at organizing the poor in their local communities to participate in the administration of the various poverty programs. Local, grass-roots councils of poor people were to be given a certain responsibility for the operation of their own poverty programs. How much responsibility? On this question the act was vague, specifying only that the poor should be provided "maximum feasible participation" in the various Community Action Agencies throughout the nation. Patterns of participation thus varied widely. In some places, activists from the poor themselves dominated the local CAA; in others, middle-class professionals exercised de facto control; in still others the CAAs were taken over by the local political machine.

The OEO approach to poverty was an experiment noble in purpose, but its accomplishments never matched its rhetoric. A decade after its enactment the poverty problem in America remains severe, and the gap between the rich and poor seems, if anything, to be widening. What went wrong?

Shortcomings of the OEO Approach

One factor may have been lack of proper funding. One year after President Johnson's declared war against poverty, he found himself deeply committed to an undeclared war in Southeast Asia, and that war was to drain vital resources from his domestic programs. The level of funding for OEO thus never reached above $2 billion per year (compared to $20 billion or more per year on the Vietnam war), and a series of increasingly conservative Congresses became ever more chary about appropriating money for "nonessentials" during wartime. Indeed, within the Johnson administration itself, attention turned away from the problems of the poor in America to the escalating war in Southeast Asia. "Vietnam took it all away, every goddamned dollar," former director Shriver was later to complain.

But money, or the lack of it, was not the only reason why the war on poverty was a losing war. Part of the problem may have been inherent in the "services strategy" as a means of fighting poverty. Johnnie Tillmon, a welfare mother and Founding Chairman of the National Welfare Rights Organization, later provided this perspective:

> We always have a lot of programs—poverty programs, Model Cities programs—and

they all are geared around the poor. But nothing is actually filtered down to the poor. There are a lot of jobs created for other people, and when we do have an opportunity to participate in the jobs, we have the lowest-paying ones. Most of the jobs throughout the programs are no larger than a welfare check.[29]

If all poverty program administrators were as dedicated as Michael Harrington, it might be possible to reply that, if little money filters down to the poor, at least services do. But Betty Niedzwiecki, another welfare mother, echoed a familiar complaint in relating the following anecdote about Inner City Development Project, an OEO-funded program, in Detroit:

> Let me tell you a story about one guy who works at an ICPD center. He was talking to a friend of mine one night and said, "Boy, did I have a busy day, I referred eleven people." My friend said, "Okay, but what'd you do for them?" He said, "Man, I referred 'em, I referred 'em."[30]

There can be no question that the war on poverty was helpful to a number of businesses. Between 1964 and 1970 about $600 million was spent on contracts for the study, evaluation, revision, and operation of the poverty program; 254 companies received $100,000 or more in OEO contracts, including forty-four separate evaluations of Project Headstart.[31] Nor is there any doubt that many young, middle-class college graduates were hired for the better-paying positions in the poverty program. There is no need to go to the lengths of Dr. George Wiley, who called these administrators "poverty pimps," to observe that the war on poverty put a good deal of money into the pockets of the nonpoor.

Some of these administrators did nothing to earn their money. Others, perhaps, did too much. The Community Action Program stressed "maximum feasible participation" of the poor. This placed the program on a collision course with big-city mayors and other local politicians, who wanted the funds to filter through their organizations, in the manner of traditional public assistance programs. In the meantime, the local Community Action agencies, fed by OEO funds, had begun to build up their own counterestablishments with their own vested interests. The clash between the local establishments and counterestablishments began to embroil the whole poverty program in controversy. The local establishments appealed to their congressmen and senators for help, which was usually granted because these federal officeholders depended upon local party organizations for money and votes. The counterestablishments responded by getting the poor involved in protest marches, confrontations, and media events.*
"Maximum feasible participation," which began as a means of integrating the poor into the American political community, suddenly turned, in the apocalyptic

---

* For a fascinating study of one such clash, see Huey Perry, *"They'll Cut Off Your Project": A Mingo County Chronicle* (New York: Frederick A. Praeger, Inc., 1972). The author, an earnest young poverty administrator in West Virginia, describes his showdown with the local politicians in Mingo County. The book is all the more interesting for its unintentional revelations. Perry becomes increasingly militant as the story unfolds, and increasingly diverted from his task of relieving poverty to that of confronting and unmasking the establishment. He is shocked and indignant when the establishment fights back. By the end of the chronicle, the establishment has won, Perry has moved to another job, and the poor are left just as poor as they were at the beginning.

atmosphere of the late sixties, into a force for destroying the "system." What the Community Action militants apparently forgot was that they were being *funded* by the system.

The state giveth and the state taketh away. By 1970 Community Action had been subdued; by 1974, it was nearly abolished. One cannot expect the system to subsidize its own destruction.

The tragedy of Community Action was that it sought to relieve an economic problem by political means. True political participation requires economic independence. The wife of a worker on a cotton plantation in Mississippi told Robert Coles the reasons why she and her husband did not vote: "He [the plantation owner] doesn't want us trying to vote and like that—and first I'd like to feed my kids, before I go trying to vote."[32] The ancient Greeks considered politics an activity proper only to free people. This woman and her husband are unfree in two ways: First, they are preoccupied with physical survival; second, they are utterly dependent on the plantation owner for the little they do receive. It is unrealistic, therefore, to expect her to be interested in political participation without *first* doing something about her husband's dependence and her family's starvation. The main trouble with "maximum feasible participation" is that it attempted to put the cart before the horse. Poverty is a prepolitical condition. It must be alleviated, as directly and expeditiously as possible, before we can even hope to involve its sufferers in true political action. If the "system" is to be challenged, it can only be challenged by people who are not obviously dependent upon it for their daily bread and butter. In 1970, before the CAAs were abolished, one author spoke approvingly about their demand for "no services without representation,"[33] presumably an updated version of the American prerevolutionary slogan, "No taxation without representation." On closer examination, however, the analogy is false and the CAA slogan turns out to be absurd. The American colonists were economically independent. They were in fact the givers, and they were threatening to withhold their gift—taxes—unless provided representation in return. But welfare recipients have nothing to give, and their slogan amounts to a threat not to *receive* services unless given representation—biting their noses to spite their faces. During the Nixon administration the government responded by saying, in effect, "No services without representation? Very well, then, no services!"

NEW ANTIPOVERTY APPROACHES

By the early 1970s a consensus seemed to be developing around the following propositions:

    1 The "services" strategy of OEO had used up too much precious money on administrative salaries and fees, had raised false expectations among the poor, and had promoted an extremely fragile kind of militancy which did little to help the poor out of their central predicament—poverty.

    2 People are poor for a variety of reasons, but the most direct reason why they are poor is that they have no money.

3   Instead of searching for long-range, "ultimate" solutions for the "underlying causes" of poverty, therefore, let us at least begin with simplicity itself: Let us give poor people money.

Even before the seventies this conclusion, that an "income" strategy was better than a "services" strategy, had been reached by social thinkers from the widest range of ideologies. On the left, Michael Reagan had argued for a "guaranteed income" as early as 1964.[34] On the right, the libertarian economist Milton Friedman had set forth the tenets of his "negative income tax" proposal in a book published in 1962.[35] Somewhere in between was Daniel P. Moynihan's proposal for "family allowances" based on the European mode.[36] At the beginning of the seventies these separate ideological strands seemed, for one brief moment, almost ready to be woven into one of the strangest coalitions in the history of American politics.

The Left: A Guaranteed Annual Income

Proponents of a guaranteed income point out the fact that our increasingly automated economy is leaving behind millions of Americans who can never hope to step into the relatively narrow range of high-skill jobs available. Some of these people have worked all their lives in industries which are now declining, such as hand cottonpicking, and are too old for retraining, much less for pulling up stakes and moving to a new area. Other workers may be highly trained but find themselves, perhaps permanently, out of work because of shifts in government priorities (some categories of aerospace engineers, for example). Still others, scarred from childhood, simply cannot be educated to step into a high-skill job.

Once these facts are accepted, the argument goes, they lead inexorably in the direction of a guaranteed annual income. The rising welfare rolls prove that the number of dependent people is rapidly increasing. We provide them welfare already—but grudgingly, unevenly, and in such a manner as to destroy their self-respect. Why not guarantee to every American an adequate income without all the forms, the caseworkers, the red tape, and the prying questions? Why not send them monthly checks, much as senior citizens are sent monthly Social Security checks, as a matter of right? As for the amount of a guaranteed income, proposals vary from Michael Reagan's proposal in 1964 of $3,000 annually to George Wiley's 1972 proposal of $6,500. In the 1972 presidential campaign George McGovern tentatively proposed a guarantee of $1,000 annually for every man, woman, and child in the country.

Whatever the economic merits of these proposals, their very name dooms them to political defeat. Anything with the name "guaranteed annual income," or even "guaranteed *adequate* income," as Wiley called it, affronts the American "work ethic." Even the proposal of a modest guaranteed annual income of $3,200 was disapproved by 58 percent of those polled by Gallup in 1968, and there is no reason to imagine that approval is more likely today. The typical sentiment reported was the "nobody should get something for nothing."[37] McGovern's $1,000 proposal in 1972 was undoubtedly one of the factors contributing to his "radical" image.

The Right: A Negative Income Tax

Yet the proposal of Professor Milton Friedman, Barry Goldwater's economic adviser in the campaign of 1964, is in some ways at least as radical as a guaranteed annual income. Friedman has proposed that subsidies should be given on a sliding scale, with people making less than a given amount not only exempt from taxes but eligible to receive a benefit, which is then adjusted upward or downward according to income. Since we already have federal income-tax exemptions for people making less than certain amounts per year, Friedman believes that the same principle can be extended: People making less than a certain amount should not only be exempted from paying taxes but should receive payments, which will then increase as earned income decreases. In a way, Friedman's proposal can be considered radical. It compromises the work ethic: Friedman frankly proposes that people should be provided a certain annual income floor regardless of whether they work for it or not. He also states, in agreement with the proponents of a guaranteed annual income, that the income strategy "gives help in the form most useful to the individual, namely, cash."[38]

But the Friedman proposal is also conservative because of the very small amount of money it would allow to poor families. In the hypothetical example provided in his 1962 book, *Capitalism and Freedom,* Friedman discussed a negative income tax maximum of $300 per person annually. What is more, and this is crucial to Friedman's concept, the negative income tax is to be a *substitute* for existing welfare programs. In other words, everything, from food stamps to AFDC payments, must be discontinued once the negative income tax is enacted. Otherwise, Friedman believes—here reverting to the work ethic after all—the program would destroy the incentive to look for a job. In some states the Friedman proposal would have the effect of *reducing* assistance to the poor.

A Middle Way: Family Allowances

America is the only industrial democracy in the world without a system of family allowances. This observation, which Daniel P. Moynihan makes repeatedly throughout his memoir of the Nixon administration's effort to pass its Family Assistance Program, forms the basis for his own approach to income supplements.

Family allowances, first tried in England 170 years ago, are now a standard feature in every European country and in about a third of the nations outside Europe, including Canada. Like a guaranteed annual income or a negative income tax, the family allowance system can provide money on a standardized and routinized basis, with a minimum of red tape and no questions asked about anyone's personal life. It also has an additional advantage: Since every family, regardless of income, is provided with these grants, it will cause no resentment among the better-off and will give no special stigma of dependency to the poor.*

---

* Nor is there any evidence that family allowances induce people to have more children. Canada, with family allowances, has the same birth rate as the United States. Some nations introduced family allowances as an inducement to larger families during the thirties, and found the allowances to be completely ineffective in increasing the birth rate. James C. Vadakin, *Family Allowances* (Coral Gables, Fla.: University of Miami Press, 1958), p. 120.

The disadvantage of the family allowance approach is that it is a relatively inefficient means of disbursing funds to fight poverty. Since the money is awarded on the basis of family size rather than income, the Kennedy and Rockefeller families would receive large grants while poverty-stricken couples would get the least. Generally, poor families are larger, but this is by no means a universal rule.

The Family Assistance Program

On August 8, 1969, President Nixon delivered a major address in which he set forth his administration's proposed version of the family allowance scheme. Nixon's proposal was an attempt to combine the better features of the Moynihan and Friedman proposals. FAP, as it came to be known, provided a series of income supplements keyed to family size and amount of earned income. In the form in which it was originally proposed it would provide a minimum of $1,600 for a family of four. As the family's earnings increased beyond zero, the $1,600 would be reduced by fifty cents for every dollar earned. However, the family would be allowed their first $720 in earnings without any reduction of the $1,600 supplement. The following chart illustrates the sliding-scale principle of FAP:

Earnings	Benefits	Total
$ 720	$1,600	$2,320
1,000	1,460	2,460
2,000	960	2,960
3,000	460	3,460
3,920	0	3,920

In principle, at least, FAP would seem to have a number of advantages over the existing AFDC system. First, it would not force fathers to leave their families, since it would be given regardless of whether or not a man lived in the house. Second, the work-disincentive features of AFDC would be lessened, since there would be no *sudden* cutoff of welfare as soon as the recipient found a job. Third, it would eliminate much of the bureaucracy and paternalism involved in AFDC, since it would be administered by the federal government on the basis of a simple declaration of income by the applicant.

Mayors and governors throughout the nation strongly supported the program, which was remarkable since on no other major legislation over the previous four years had there been agreement between governors as a group and the mayors as a group (much less between governors and mayors from different regions of the country). This powerful coalition behind FAP, which included men and women of the most diverse ideologies, was built upon the rock of self-interest. One of the critical flaws of AFDC is that it requires very costly state administration. It also requires state matching of AFDC payments. As a result of these two factors, the rise in welfare rolls during the sixties was proving very costly to states and cities. FAP proposed to take the whole problem off their hands by federalizing everything, from the payments themselves to the administration of them. Consequently the nation's mayors and governors proved to be FAP's strongest boosters, and this in turn put pressure on Congress to pass it, since the reelection of members of congress depends in no small measure upon governors' party machines and mayors' support.

In one sense, FAP was a daring plan, far more daring than anything ever offered by a Democratic administration. It was a proposal for a guaranteed annual income—direct cash payments to families with no demeaning investigations and no dubious "services" by social therapists. FAP appeared for a moment to be a domestic equivalent to Nixon's China visit: a liberal initiative by a conservative President. It was hailed by most of the press and praised even by long-time Nixon critics. To some, it seemed the kind of measure around which a new right-left consensus might be built. What eventually happened, however, was the opposite: Both sides rejected it.

From the very outset the Nixon plan was opposed by the far right. Vice President Agnew opposed it as politically dangerous, and Agnew's constituency of Southern whites and conservative Republicans lent substance to his predictions. Governor Lester Maddox of Georgia was described as "horrified" by it, and one of Georgia's congressmen was quoted as saying, "There's not going to be anybody to roll these wheelbarrows and press these shirts. They're all going to be on welfare."[39] Milton Friedman opposed it because it departed from the pure theory of the negative income tax, which would abolish all other forms of social welfare. FAP left undisturbed the existing welfare system, only supplementing it in states where payments were less than $1,600. This, in the opinion of Friedman and other conservatives, was a sure means of destroying the incentive to work for a living.

President Nixon anticipated—perhaps all too well—this reaction from the right. From the very outset he tried to portray his program not as welfare but as welfare *reform*, or "workfare." FAP was not, he insisted, a "guaranteed income."

> During the Presidential campaign last year, I opposed such a plan. I oppose it now and I will continue to oppose it, and this is the reason: A guaranteed income would undermine the incentive to work; the family assistance plan that I propose increases the incentive to work.[40]

To prevent his plan from running afoul of the "work ethic," Nixon opposed any major increases in the amount of the "floor" to be provided, and included in the plan a work requirement compelling all family heads except mothers with preschool children to accept any "suitable" job offered by the state welfare department. These two features of FAP won no support from conservatives (William F. Buckley called them "boob bait"), but did succeed in alienating the left. For George Wiley's National Welfare Rights Organization (NWRO) these features amounted to "institutional racism" and "subsidizing slave-wage employers at the expense of poor people."[41]

Despite these opponents on the left and right, a centrist coalition carried FAP through the House of Representatives on April 16, 1970, by a margin of 243 to 155. In the Senate, however, the plan became snagged in the Finance Committee. Its chairman, Russell Long of Louisiana, a staunch supporter of oil depletion allowances and other corporate tax exemptions, became an equally staunch opponent of FAP. ("I can't get anybody to iron my shirts!")[42] Senator John J.

Williams, a Republican from Delaware, subjected administration witnesses to withering questions about FAP's system of decreasing payments to the working poor. In doing so, he zeroed in on one of FAP's chief weaknesses—its work disincentives.

The more money a person earned, the less he or she would get from FAP. What is more, the worker would have to start paying taxes, including the regressive Social Security tax. Finally, the working poor would find their existing welfare benefits, such as food stamps and housing allowances, diminished or cut off at some point. In short, Nixon's "workfare" was so structured as to make it worthwhile for some people in certain income categories to stay away from work.

Under Williams's relentless questioning, administration witnesses admitted that FAP needed some revisions. But their revisions satisfied neither the conservatives, who considered FAP a colossal giveaway program, nor the liberals, who kept pushing for larger amounts. George Wiley and the welfare mothers in NWRO insisted on a guaranteed income of $5,500 (later raised to $6,500), which would have cost about $60 billion per year. Wiley's group may not have influenced many liberal senators, but his demands and tactics (which included disrupting meeting of pro-FAP pressure groups like Common Cause) supplied considerable ammunition to the conservative enemies of FAP, who could say to their wavering colleagues: "See what we're getting into once we start down the road to income maintenance!"

Although FAP died on the floor of the Senate in December of 1970, Nixon sought to revive it in 1971, calling it "White House priority number one." Once again it passed the House in short order, as part of an omnibus Social Security bill (H. R. 1), and once again got stuck in the Senate. To please liberal critics, Nixon increased the maximum it would provide for a family of four, from $1,600 to $2,400, but to please conservatives he proposed cutting off food stamps and strengthening the work requirements. Neither side was pleased, and the revised FAP remained bottled up in the Senate Finance Committee until 1972.

Yet for a time passage of the bill seemed to be near. In May of 1972 administration lobbyists and leading liberals on the Senate Finance Committee struck a bargain, which included a $2,600 maximum payment for a family of four. Unfortunately, however, 1972 was a presidential election year, and the Democratic front-runner had already put his foot in his mouth by proposing a flat grant of $1,000 annually to every man, woman, and child in the nation. McGovern's ill-considered proposal made him seem fiscally irresponsible to the voters, which of course was pleasing to Nixon's chief strategists (notably Haldeman and Ehrlichman). The danger was that if Nixon got too committed to FAP, especially at the $2,600 level which was agreeable to Senate liberals, he might also be perceived as a give-away artist. Why let McGovern off the hook?[43]

Whether or not campaign considerations played the decisive role, Nixon at any rate retreated from the deal his lobbyists had made with the liberals on the Senate Finance Committee. He stuck to his $2,400 level proposal, refusing to accept the $2,600 compromise. With neither side giving any more ground, FAP was doomed. At the end of 1972, H. R. 1 was passed, but minus the plan which Nixon had once considered his "priority number one." One member of Congress described H. R. 1 in its final form as "an emasculated, mangled and toothless shadow of the original proposal."[44]

Who killed FAP? Administration officials put much of the blame on NWRO and the liberal senators who responded to it. "Had three liberals on the Finance Committee not heeded NWRO's pleas that FAP was inadequate, and voted with delighted conservatives to scuttle it, we would have a bill today,"[45] one HEW official later contended. Other observers blamed the death on Senator Williams's aggressive cross-examination of administration witnesses, on the lack of adequate homework on the part of administration officials, and on the hostility of Chairman Long to anything resembling income maintenance. But FAP's leading supporter in the Senate, Abraham Ribicoff of Connecticut, laid the ultimate blame on one man. "It was the failure of support from President Nixon that sealed the doom of welfare reform."[46]

Whoever it was who killed FAP, its passing was a blow to America's poorest families. Despite his homage to "the work ethic," Nixon managed to propose a plan which would have paid a guaranteed income to poor people while eliminating much of the capriciousness, discrimination, red tape, and paternalism of the present system. A national "floor" would be established, below which no family in the country would be allowed to fall. In many places—particularly in those rural areas of the South and Southwest where hunger and malnutrition are not uncommon—this could make a big difference.

It is true, of course, that FAP's payments were pitifully small. Even accepting the government's poverty line of $4,140 for a family of four, the maximum amount provided such a family ($1,600 in the original plan, $2,400 in the 1971 version) would hardly suffice. Yet these figures were based upon zero earnings. Most of the poor earn something, and the income supplements in FAP would not be phased out completely until earnings reached nearly $4,000. The $1,600 version of FAP would also be supplemented by food stamps, and by any programs of public assistance the individual states might administer. Recipients in high-paying welfare areas, like New York and California, would be guaranteed that existing levels of AFDC would not be cut back. Finally, and perhaps most importantly, FAP was at least a foot in the door. The fears of FAP's conservative critics were probably well founded: Once the precedent of income-by-right had been set, it would not have been so difficult for subsequent Congresses to increase the level of payments.

A Revised FAP?

With all its weaknesses, then, FAP remains a promising concept in the fight against poverty. The moderate-liberal coalition which originally sponsored it—or a new one, which would include many of the younger members of Congress elected in 1974—might be put together again, especially since the nation's recession has once again focused public attention upon economic problems. As more and more "middle Americans" worry about food bills and job security instead of hippies and protestors, the mood of the 1930s might be reborn. Poverty is no longer "invisible" once the possibility of sinking into it is not altogether remote. If that does not lead to an increased empathy for the poor, it might at any rate lead to a demand for economic reforms, reforms which could benefit the poor as well as the middle class.

Yet the opposite effect might be produced: As the nation's economic pie gets smaller, the fight for its slices might become more intense, with middle Americans elbowing the poor aside in order to "get theirs."

There were some indications, in the mid-seventies, that middle-class Americans were drifting in *both* directions: toward economic reform and toward fighting the poor for scarce resources. Congress at the end of 1974 increased the coverage and length of unemployment compensation; it also created 100,000 federally financed jobs for the unemployed, a move reminiscent of the 1930s, when the Works Projects Administration put people to work on WPA projects sponsored by the government. On the other hand, as the economic crisis deepened and the cities began laying off public employees, animosity toward the poor sometimes flared into the open. In New York City, for example, the head of the Patrolmen's Benevolent Association charged that "welfare thieves" were siphoning off money that could save the jobs of police officers threatened with layoffs.

What the scramble for public funds may do is to revive the old question of priorities, which could be glossed over during times of prosperity, when there seemed to be enough money for everything. Now we have to ask the question: Who is getting what? What are we spending our money on in this country? These questions can hardly be avoided if we are going to finance any kind of meaningful war on poverty. Such a war would be an expensive one.

In its original form FAP would have cost the nation an annual $4 billion. In its revived form, with a $2,400 minimum for a family of four, it would have cost $5.5 billion. Under Senator Ribicoff's proposal, which would have raised the benefit level to $2,600, the cost would have been close to $7.5 billion per year. With today's cost of living, even that figure seems pathetically low. Yet if we were to raise it, say, to $3,600—double the original Nixon proposal—it would cost $25 billion per year.[47] And even this version of FAP would not bring up the payment level of the official poverty line of $4,140.

Moreover, FAP by itself would only be one weapon in the fight against poverty. It would do nothing about joblessness and dependency. Yet WPA-type projects or other means of finding work for people can also be costly. The Senate version of the emergency job bill passed at the end of 1974 would have cost $4 billion, and would have made only a dent in the unemployment situation.

Nor is this all. America's poor seem to have little choice between dilapidated housing and sterile, institutionalized public housing projects which turn out to be vertical ghettos. The poor also suffer from inadequate health care because of the prohibitive costs. Yet even a modest program of housing subsidies to the poor—say, $1,200 each for the five million families below the poverty line and $400 for every individual similarly situated—would cost $8 billion, not counting administrative expenses.[48] As for medical care, the cost of a national health insurance program, depending upon the scope and amount of the coverage, could add another $5 to $10 billion. Putting all these costs together, it can be seen that a basic "poverty package" which used an income strategy for dealing with the problem might cost somewhere between forty and fifty billion dollars annually.

Where are we going to get that kind of money? What follows are a few tentative suggestions.

Paying for a Poverty War: Some Suggestions

1 Cut the Military Budget The largest single item in our budget is defense appropriations, which now reach the level of $100 billion. Because of the massive size of this budget and the secrecy which surrounds it, enormous amounts can be spent on all sorts of questionable projects. We can pick up the newspaper on almost any day and run across items like this:

> "WASHINGTON, May 9 [1973]: Unknown to Defense Secretary Elliot L. Richardson, the Army has ordered several thousand new nuclear shells for its large cannons in Europe."
>
> "The cost of the Army's 'nuclear ammunition modernization program' is being kept secret by the Pentagon, but Congressional sources who have been briefed on the plan say it will run into 'millions and millions of dollars.'"
>
> On the same day: "A Nixon Administration official told the Senate Foreign Relations Committee today that despite the Vietnam and Laos cease-fires, 15,000 to 20,000 Thai 'irregular' troops—financed by the United States—were now based in Laos."
>
> ". . . [The official] said that the Thai forces in Laos were being paid about $26-million yearly."[49]

The amount of sheer waste in the military budget is mind-boggling. From 1963 to 1973 the value of weapons programs that were simply abandoned, without any usable hardware at all to show for the time and effort, totaled $7 billion. In 1973 government accountants audited forty-five major weapons systems under development and found cost overruns of $31.5 billion over original estimates.[50] Because of the enormous bulk of the defense budget, inflation is also a major problem. Television viewers are by now familiar with news reports on "grocery baskets," in which reporters fill up shopping carts with selected items and compare their costs over a certain period of time. One *Washington Post* reporter decided to do the same with a selected group of Pentagon weapons. He found an increase of $16.9 billion on his selected "weapons basket" over a three-*month* period in 1974.[51]

How much could safely be slashed from the defense budget? Estimates range from those of Pentagon officials, who say it is already dangerously low, to those of Professor Seymour Melman of Columbia University, who believes that more than $50 billion could be cut from the military budget without endangering national security.[52] Somewhere between these two extremes, William D. White, a former Defense Department official, has estimated that by eliminating unnecessary weapons systems the Pentagon could save $30 billion by 1980 and $8 billion to $9 billion in the years following.[53] Studies by the Brookings Institution and the Center for Defense Information have also set forth a series of alternate weapons programs that could generate significant savings.[54]

2 Eliminate Unproductive Social-service Programs Some programs in the field of health and social service are either anachronistic, likely to become so if a guaranteed income were given to the poor, or useless from the start. The Hill-Burton hospital construction program is one of those projects which belongs in the anachronistic category. Enacted after World War II, when hospital construction was badly needed, it still goes on spending millions every year even though today's problem is not shortage of hospitals but of staff to service them. In the category of programs which would *become* anachonistic if a substantial FAP program were enacted is the $5.9 billion nutrition and food stamp program. As for the third category, useless-from-the-start projects, one example is the annual $300 million spent for training people on welfare, which has produced only a handful of jobs.

3 Tax the Rich The federal income tax was first instituted by the Sixteenth Amendment in 1913. It was supposed to be a progressive income tax, meaning that those who could afford to pay more should do so. Today's marginal income tax rates reach 70% on individual incomes and 48% on corporate income. Despite these nominal rates, the highest effective rates are less than 35% on individual income and about 30% on corporate income. Why the discrepancy? The main reason is that various tax loopholes have been inserted into our tax laws by Congress over the past sixty years or more. Money made from municipal bonds, for example, is completely tax free, and this form of investment is concentrated heavily in the hands of upper-income individuals and banks. Another example: Only one-half of capital gains, such as the profit from stockmarket sales, is taxable. Tax shelters of various kinds have also proliferated. By investing in real estate, oil drilling, cattle, and other farm activities, those with money to spare can shelter it from taxation.

It has been argued that these tax loopholes actually serve the public at large by providing investors with an incentive to put money into needed areas. The answer to this argument is that if Americans want to put money into some needed area they ought to vote for direct subsidies to it instead of waiting for timid or capricious private investors to put money into it. In the long run, the direct-subsidy method might be cheaper. As Jack T. Conway, president of Common Cause, contended before the House Ways and Means Committee in 1973:

> In fact, they [tax loopholes] either fail in their stated purpose altogether or achieve limited objectives at excessive cost to the general treasury. Most loopholes disproportionately benefit the wealthiest members of our society. Experts say that some $50 billion in federal revenues are lost each year through existing loopholes. If this revenue were added to existing collections, we could finance all present federal programs, balance the budget and have enough surplus to reduce general tax rates.[55]

Tax loopholes actually provide a kind of social welfare to the rich—at the expense of the poor and middle class. It is the rich who have the money to invest in tax shelters, the rich who make a significant proportion of their income from the stock market, municipal bonds, and other investments. Some of the more spectacular cases of tax avoidance by the rich have been cited by such groups as former Senator Fred Harris's Tax Action Committee: Some 1,300 people with

EQUALITY: RICH AND POOR IN AMERICA

Table 2-1 Who Gets Tax "Welfare"?

Income group	Number of families	Total yearly tax "welfare"
Under $3,000	6,000,000	$92 Million
Over $1 Million	3,000	$2.2 Billion

Source: Philip Stern, testimony before U.S. Congress, Joint Economic Committee, Subcommittee on Priorities and Economy in Government, *The Economics of Federal Subsidy Programs,* 92d Congress, First Sess., 1972, p. 83.

incomes over $50,000 paid zero income tax in 1970; J. Paul Getty, the richest man in the world, who reportedly has a *daily* income of $30,000, should be paying $70 million in taxes each year, but was able to get away with paying only a few thousand dollars a year during the early sixties.[56] Such critics of the tax system as Philip Stern, author of the *The Rape of the Taxpayer,* have illustrated its upper-class bias by preparing charts on tax "welfare" (the amount saved the taxpayer through loopholes). One of Stern's charts is reproduced in Table 2-1.

Since the average taxpayer does not enjoy the variety of loopholes available to the rich, he or she is really carrying the rich when it comes to paying for the expenses of government. Government is expensive today. When wealthy taxpayers avoid paying their full share of the burden, the money must come from someplace else. That leaves the average "working stiff"—the person who is not a big investor, or a gentleman farmer, or an upper-echelon corporate executive, or an oil millionaire—holding the bag, or rather filling it up. Philip Stern may have scored his most effective rhetorical point when he reminded the members of a congressional committee that they, too, were being victimized by the vagaries of our tax laws.

> MR. STERN. . . . I think among the people who are most discriminated against . . . are you gentlemen in the Congress. You work very hard . . . for your $42,500 a year. If I take some of my money and invest it, let's say in Xerox and don't lift a finger thereafter and the people at Xerox do all the work and I get a huge gain, I might pay a lower marginal rate than you would on your earned income and I think that is an outrage. I don't see why you put up with it. [laughter.]
> Representative [Henry S.] REUSS. Mr. Stern, you may have done more for tax reform with that last observation than we have been able to do in many years.[57]

Without going into specific plans for tax reform, it seems clear that by closing some of the more gaping loopholes in our system we could generate considerable income to help finance a war on poverty. The effect of this would be to skim off income from the top and redistribute it toward the bottom of the income ladder—in blunter language, to take from the rich and give to the poor. If this be characterized as a kind of romantic Robin Hood-ism, we can only answer that the whole concept of a progressive income tax is Robin Hood-ism. The American people by large margins favor the progressive income tax ("Raising the taxes of the rich and lowering them for lower income people" was favored by 71 to 18 percent of respondents to a Harris poll taken in 1972),[58] so it is not at all un-American to propose a closing of tax loopholes. As for the complaint that income redistribution robs Peter to pay Paul, we might quote Bertram Gross's rejoinder: "My own judgment is that if there were more attention to the rich Peter we would find . . . that *he* has been robbing Paul."[59]

SUMMARY AND CONCLUSION

This chapter has made the following points:

1 America is a country in which the most abject poverty coexists with the most conspicuous wealth. Often the two are separated by a short drive through one of our cities.

2 Despite a much heralded "war on poverty" launched during the sixties, the gap between rich and poor has not narrowed. There is some evidence that it is growing wider.

3 Poverty is inimical to democracy. It makes the claim of "equality before the law" sound like a hollow abstraction. It is also related to a low rate of political participation, which in turn leaves the poor even more shut out of the system. Poverty—and the gap between rich and poor, both in terms of money and political participation—lends substance to the Marxist claim that Western democracy is class-biased.

4 President Johnson's "war on poverty" made little headway toward its goal of eliminating poverty from the land. One reason for its shortcomings has been the lack of proper funding, but another factor was its preoccupation with a "service" strategy, which sought to combat poverty by training and motivating the poor. This put money into the hands of middle-class "poverty workers," but little of it percolated down to the poor. It also radicalized some of the poor, but without giving them a secure income base from which to participate in the political process. Poverty is a prepolitical problem: It must be dealt with *before* there can be meaningful participation.

5 President Nixon's "income strategy" sought to take the bull by the horns by putting money directly into the hands of the poor. FAP had the merit of eliminating middlemen and standardizing payments, although its architects never completely solved the problem of disincentives. Its payments were very small, although subsequent Congresses may have been able to expand them. FAP failed to pass for a variety of reasons: lack of preparation by administration supporters of FAP, the implacable hostility of conservative congressmen, the refusal by liberals to accept lower funding levels, and, in the end, lukewarm support from the White House.

6 A revised FAP, together with national health insurance, housing subsidies, and public-service jobs, might constitute an effective beginning for a new war on poverty. It would, however, be an expensive war.

7 Resources for fighting such a war might be gotten from savings in our defense budget, from cutting back unproductive social-services programs, and from eliminating tax loopholes.

We ought not to delude ourselves that such a strategy as suggested here will "eliminate" poverty. If poverty is defined in relative terms, there will always be those who are less well-off than others. Even if we use some absolute figure, like the Social Security Administration's $4,140 for a family of four, bringing people up to that level would not be easy or inexpensive. And if we take into account the more intangible factors connected with poverty today, such as the feeling of hopelessness, the lack of training, the self-reinforcing aspects of poverty culture, then we will be on our guard against utopian expectations. We have underscored the "income strategy" in the fight against poverty and criticized the "services strategy" of the Johnson administration, but we may have overstated the argument. Some services, such as legal assistance, have been successful ones, and these should be retained as part of a blend of strategies for fighting poverty.

As for the method for funding a renewed war on poverty, we have no assurance that the three suggestions at the end of this chapter would produce enough revenue to do so without having to raise the taxes of the middle-class taxpayer. The suggestions, moreover, carry their own dangers. If the defense budget were cut, what would happen to the people who work in defense-related industries? If we stopped building hospitals by discontinuing the Hill-Burton construction program, what would happen to the construction workers who have been building them? If the rich were heavily taxed, what would happen to the foundations, which make grants from which the poor benefit? And what about the workers in the various industries which serve the rich if the rich began cutting back on their purchases? We can always reply that these losses would be compensated by more purchasing power flowing into the economy from the other end of the income scale. The poor would have more money to spend, which would lead to greater employment in those industries which serve people with modest incomes. Nevertheless, there would surely be at least temporary dislocations, as workers shifted from one type of industry to another, and some workers might not be able to make the shift.

The costs of fighting poverty and redistributing income in America cannot be ignored. Social scientists can help to calculate the costs of fighting poverty, and visionaries can help to inspire the nation into making the effort, but ultimately some hard judgments would have to be made—judgments which cannot be made by slide rules or glossed over by inspirational rhetoric. "Trade-offs" of various kinds would have to be made as the various options for fighting poverty were to be considered. How much economic dislocation is acceptable in order to shift from defense to domestic spending? What mix of "service" and "income" strategies is the most desirable? What would be the "good" and "bad" effects of a particular program or shift in priority? At what point would the "bad" effects outbalance the "good" ones? Judgments of this sort—conscious judgments, in which costs are taken into account instead of being wished away—would have to be made if America were to fight poverty without the illusions which lead to disillusionment.

The proposals made in this chapter, then, are not intended as part of any finished "answer" to the problem of rich and poor in America, but only as grist for argument and discussion. Sometimes it is necessary to rush in where angels—and experts—fear to tread, in order to get *some* proposal on the table. This seems particularly important today. After all the great expectations of the sixties, America in the present decade seems to be afflicted with a paralysis of will. From the one extreme of inflated rhetoric and grandiose promises we have perhaps gone to the other extreme of promising nothing, hoping for little, and fearing the worst. Pessimism and cynicism are no more realistic than excessive optimism, and they have the additional defect of being sterile. By themselves they produce nothing and lead nowhere.

In the meantime the problems remain, problems which are personified in the malnourished children, the senior citizens trying to make ends meet with increasing desperation, the teenagers standing around the streets with nothing to do, the people of all ages who lack proper food, housing, and medical care. The two Park Avenues remain, as starkly defined as ever, five minutes away from each other, and worlds apart.

NOTES

1 Quoted in Robert A. Liston, *The American Poor: A Report on Poverty in the United States* (New York: Delacorte Press, Dell Publishing Co., Inc., 1970, p. 126.
2 U. S. Congress, Senate, Select Committee on Nutrition and Human Needs, *Hearing, Nutrition and Human Needs,* 90th Congress, 2d Sess., 1968, Part 4, p. 1215.
3 Nick Kotz, "The Subcommittee Chairman: Politics of Fear," in Michael P. Smith, ed., *American Politics and Public Policy* (New York: Random House, Inc., 1973), p. 144.
4 Ibid., pp. 147–148.
5 U. S. Congress, Joint Economic Committee, Subcommittee on Priorities and Economy in Government, *The Economics of Federal Subsidy Programs,* A Compendium of Papers, 93d Congress, 1st Sess., 1973, Part 7, pp. 907–909, 912.
6 Mark J. Green, James M. Fallows, and David R. Zwick, *Who Runs Congress?* (New York: Bantam/Grossman Books, 1972), p. 140.
7 Kotz, op. cit., p. 150.
8 *New York Times* June 20, 1974, p. 17.
9 *New York Times,* Nov. 26, 1974, p. 44.
10 S. M. Miller and Pamela A. Roby, *The Future of Inequality* (New York: Basic Books, Inc., Publishers, 1970), p. 37.
11 Peter Henle, "Distribution of Earned Income," *Monthly Labor Review,* December 1972, pp. 16–27.
12 Bertram Gross, "A Closer Look at Income Distribution," *Social Policy,* III (May–June 1972), p. 61.
13 Gabriel Kolko, *Wealth and Power in America* (New York: Frederick A. Prager, Inc., 1962), p. 28.
14 Reported in Letitia Upton and Nancy Lyons, *Basic Facts: Distribution of Personal Income and Wealth in the United States* (Cambridge, Mass.: Cambridge Institute, 1972), table 2.
15 These data were developed by Edward Budd, and were reported in ibid., table 6.
16 *New York Times*, Aug. 16, 1974, p. 34.
17 Herman P. Miller, *Rich Man, Poor Man,* (New York: Thomas Y. Crowell Company, 1971), p. 111.
18 Herbert Gans, *More Equality* (New York: Pantheon Books, Random House, Inc., 1972), pp. 66ff.
19 Charles A. Reich, "Individual Rights and Social Welfare: The Emerging Legal Issues," *The Yale Law Journal,* LXXIV (June 1965), pp. 269–275.
20 Richard M. Scammon, "Electoral Participation," *The Annals of the American Academy of Political and Social Science,* CCCLXXI (May 1967), p. 63. Cf. Sidney Verba and Norman H. Nie, *Participation in America: Political Democracy and Social Equality* (New York: Harper & Row, Publishers, Incorporated, 1972), passim.

21 David Caplovitz, *The Poor Pay More* (New York: The Free Press, 1963), pp. 133–134.
22 *New York Times,* Dec. 10, 1972, p. 20.
23 Dorothy James, *Poverty, Politics, and Change* (Englewood Cliffs, N. J.: Prentice-Hall, Inc., 1972), p. 9.
24 Liston, op. cit., p. 54.
25 Milwaukee County Welfare Rights Organization, *Welfare Mothers Speak Out: We Ain't Gonna Shuffle Anymore* (New York: W. W. Norton & Company, Inc., 1972), p. 24.
26 James, op. cit., p. 52.
27 Quoted in Stanley Esterly and Glenn Esterly, *Freedom from Dependence: Welfare Reform as a Solution to Poverty* (Washington: Public Affairs Press, 1971), p. 14.
28 Michael Harrington, *The Other America: Poverty in the United States* (New York: The Macmillan Company, 1963), p. 171.
29 Milwaukee County Welfare Rights Organization, op. cit., p. 31.
30 Ibid., p. 44.
31 *New York Times,* Nov. 8, 1970, p. 54.
32 Kotz, op. cit., p. 149.
33 Miller and Roby, op. cit., p. 235.
34 Michael D. Reagan, "For a Guaranteed Income," *The New York Times Magazine,"* June 7, 1964, pp. 20ff.
35 Milton Friedman, *Capitalism and Freedom* (Chicago: The University of Chicago Press, 1962), Chap. 12.
36 See Moynihan's Foreword to James C. Vadakin's *Children, Poverty and Family Allowances* (New York: Basic Books, Inc., Publishers, 1968).
37 Cited in Moynihan, op. cit., p. 245.
38 Friedman, op. cit., p. 192.
39 Quoted in Moynihan, op. cit., pp. 388–389.
40 Nationwide Radio and Television Address, Aug. 8, 1969.
41 The "institutional racism" quote is cited in Moynihan, op. cit., p. 226. The second quote is in the Milwaukee County Welfare Rights Organization, op. cit., p. 108.
42 James Welsh, "Welfare Reform: Born Aug. 8, 1969; Died October 4, 1972," *The New York Times Magazine,* Jan. 7, 1973, p. 16.
43 Ibid., pp. 21–22.
44 Congressional Quarterly, *Weekly Report,* Oct. 21, 1972, p. 2765.
45 Letter to the author, July 27, 1973.
46 See Ribicoff's review of Moynihan's *The Politics of a Guaranteed Income* in *The New Republic,* Feb. 17, 1973, p. 26.
47 Moynihan, op. cit., p. 344.
48 Herbert J. Gans, "A Poor Man's Home Is His Poorhouse," *The New York Times Magazine,* Mar. 31, 1974, p. 52.
49 *New York Times,* May 10, 1973, p. 1.
50 Associated Press Dispatch, *The Journal-News* (Nyack, N. Y.), May 21, 1973, p. 7A.
51 *The Washington Monthly,* VI (December 1974), p. 17.
52 Seymour Melman, *American Capitalism in Decline* (New York: Simon & Schuster, Inc., 1974).
53 William D. White, "P-38, Where Are You?" *The Washington Monthly,* VI (December 1974), p. 37.
54 Alton H. Quanbeck and Barry M. Blechman, *Strategic Forces: Issues for the Mid-Seventies* (Washington: The Brookings Institution, 1973); Charles L. Schultze, Edward R. Fried, Nancy H. Peters, and Alice M. Rivlin, *Setting National Priorities* (Washington: The Brookings Institution, 1973).

55 "Testimony of Jack T. Conway, President, Common Cause, before the Ways and Means Committee of the U. S. House of Representatives, Thursday, March 8, 1973" (mimeo.), p. 2.
56 "Take the Rich Off Welfare," brochure of Fred Harris's Tax Action Campaign, 1973. Cf. Jack Anderson's column, *The Journal-News* (Nyack, N. Y.), Apr. 7, 1973, p. 4A.
57 U. S. Congress, Joint Economic Committee, Subcommittee on Priorities and Economy in Government, *The Economics of Federal Subsidy Programs,* 92d Congress, First Sess., 1971, p. 92.
58 *Chicago Tribune,* Oct. 9, 1972.
59 Gross, op. cit.

Chapter 3

Fraternity: Races and Groups in America

The idea of unity seems to possess a peculiar fascination for the average human mind. Only a savage or a philospher may be content with, or rise to, the conception of a pluralistic universe.

James Truslow Adams

Should races and ethnic groups be integrated in America? And what does "integration" mean? Is it the same as desegregation, or is its meaning closer to assimilation? Does equality have to mean identity? Is there some valid concept of "separate but equal" for races and groups in America?

These are the kinds of questions Americans in all groups and races find themselves wrestling with in the 1970s. The most thoughtful among them will admit their own ambivalence and uncertainty in providing answers.

A generation ago everything seemed, at least in theory, much simpler.

In 1954 the United States Supreme Court had ordered Jim Crow out of the schools *(Brown v. Board of Education)*, and was in the process of extending its ruling to other areas of segregation. A reluctant President Eisenhower had finally begun to enforce the Court's decision. Many Southern whites—who talked and even looked like authentic villains—were putting up fierce resistance, but it seemed only a matter of time until the black and white races would become integrated and the color of a person's skin would become as irrelevant as any other physical characteristic. This general prognosis was widely accepted by black and white liberals alike. It hinged upon three assumptions:

1   The Negro is *the* oppressed minority in America. The American crisis was, to borrow the title of a book published in the early sixties, a "crisis in black and white."
2   What was primarily wrong about race relations in America was that Negroes were being kept out of the "mainstream" of white society.
3   The problem (or at least its most tenacious roots) was mainly regional. The black comedian Dick Gregory remembered that when he worked as a mail sorter in the Chicago Post Office, he dropped Mississippi mail in the "foreign" slot.

All three of these assumptions were demolished by the end of the 1960s.

The first rumblings had actually come at the beginning of the sixties. James Baldwin, a black novelist, wondered out loud if blacks should *want* to become integrated into the "burning building" of white America. Within the black community a separatist sect known as the Nation of Islam began to acquire notoriety, largely through the efforts of a charismatic spokesman named Malcolm X. By 1963, stories had begun to drift back from the South of tension between black and white civil rights workers. And racial violence had drifted North: Martin Luther King was greeted by howling white mobs on the outskirts of Chicago, and the first black riots since 1943 had begun in New York's Harlem.

By the middle of the sixties, one former civil rights worker named Stokeley Carmichael coined a term, "black power," which was to become a symbol of a new spirit of independence, autonomy—and anger—among blacks. Instead of journeying from Berkeley to the deep South to patronize blacks, Carmichael and others argued, white liberals should stay in their own communities and teach their own people not to be racists. Black power also became identified with a new cultural self-consciousness among blacks. "You dig where we coming from? We coming from a black thing, from a black thing, that's where we coming from."[1] This kind of talk would have been unthinkable in the 1950s. Critics of black power called it reckless and arrogant, and Carmichael finally abandoned America at the end of the 1960s, but not before the theme of black consciousness had caught on and become respectable in the black community. A Louis Harris Survey in 1970 disclosed that 85 percent of the black Americans polled endorsed black studies programs in high schools and colleges and considered such programs an "important sign of black identity and pride."[2]

Black power, however, has turned out to be a game in which any number can play, as shown in the following developments:

• Mexican-Americans—or Chicanos, a term no longer of derision but pride—constitute the second largest minority in America, yet traditionally they have kept a low profile. Since the advent of black power they have also moved toward preserving their own culture against the pressures of assimilating into that of the Anglos. They have developed their own aggressive political leadership including Cesar Chavez, a kind of Catholic Martin Luther King, and others not so religious or nonviolent. They scorn the "Tio Tacos" (Uncle Toms) in their midst.

• In 1964 a group of young Indians from the National Indian Youth Council held a press conference in New York City. Tongue-in-cheek, they began to discuss their plans for building "red power," the need of radicalizing their community's self-consciousness and throwing out all the "Uncle Tomahawks" in their leadership. Less than a decade later "red power" was more than a joke. By 1974 Indians had seized and held Alcatraz Island for several months, broken into the U. S. Bureau of Indian Affairs in Washington, stolen and publicized documents about broken treaties, occupied the South Dakota town of Wounded Knee, and exchanged gunfire with federal officials which resulted in three deaths.

• American Jews, particularly young Jews, seemed to be losing their identity at the beginning of the sixties, but by the seventies many had discovered a new awareness of themselves as a unique and persecuted minority. Organizations like the Jewish Defense League, founded by Rabbi Meier Kahane at the end of the sixties, attracted the more militant. But even moderate Jewish opinion began to turn inward, toward greater awareness of what it means to be a Jew in a predominantly Gentile country.

• "White ethnics," a term which usually applies to Catholic working-class citizens of Italian and Slavic ancestry, began to assert their own claims. Many of them lived on the edge of poverty and could recall their own experiences with discrimination, yet their needs and their hardships, their religion and their culture, were either ignored or misunderstood as media reporters concentrated upon the plight of blacks. Some joined organizations such as the Italian-American Civil Rights League or PIGS (Poles, Italians, Greeks, and Slavs). Others took refuge in right-wing slogans, welcoming Spiro Agnew's attacks on the media and applauding the pugnacity of George Wallace. "Suddenly," one commentator noted at the end of the sixties, "Suddenly there are demands for Italian power and Polish power and Ukranian power. In Cleveland the Poles demand a seat on the school board, and get it, and in Pittsburgh John Pankuch, the seventy-three-year-old president of the National Slovak Society, demands 'action, plenty of it, to make up for lost time.' "[3]

• Even among the sexes an analog to Black Power has appeared. The leaders of women's liberation compare their plight to that of an oppressed race. "We are all niggers" is the judgment of Gloria Steinem, the editor of *Ms.* magazine. Male and female homosexuals have also joined the battle for sexual liberation, claiming that they, too, should be considered oppressed minorities, since they have suffered everything from ridicule to imprisonment because of their life-style.

CULTURAL AUTONOMY VERSUS ASSIMILATION

The claims of all these groups may not be equally valid or serious, but their drive for self-assertion and cultural autonomy represents a major change in America over the past decade. The concept of "Americanism" as a cultural ideal is being called into question as never before in America. Helter-skelter, our nation's minorities are leaping out of the melting pot.

Is this development a good or a bad one? Let us consider the potential for both.

On the one hand it may lead to more diversity in American life, acting as an antidote to those commercial and industrial forces which threaten us with cultural homogeneity, standardization, conformity, and blandness. Pride in one's group may also increase aspiration and thus energize the political process in America. Finally, these various subgroups tend to give individuals a spiritual "home," helping to counter the rootlessness and alienation of modern society.

But the promising side of the new ethnicity must be set off against the risks involved.

In Europe's Balkan peninsula at the beginning of this century at least six ethnic nationalties struggled with one another for dominance, each bitterly aware of its own grievances, each unwilling to recognize the claims of the others. The struggles between Serbs, Bulgarians, Croats, Greeks, Turks, and Albanians led to two small wars in two years, and finally to a big one—World War I—which ultimately benefited no one. If the resurgence of ethnicity in the New World were to lead to a similar "Balkanization," the results could be at least as disastrous. A viable democracy does not depend upon cultural uniformity, but it does require a spirit of accommodation and dialogue. "In unstable democracies," Charles Frankel has noted, "politics has the shape of a play by Chekov; everyone carries on a loud monologue with himself and nobody ever answers anybody else."[4] With Balkanization each *group* talks only with itself, and the danger in this situation is that it becomes less and less aware that other groups also have legitimate claims and aspirations. Black Power advocates have been known to assert that whites should be happy to call themselves "honkies."* For many white ethnics, blacks are "animals." For some of the WASPs in women's liberation, the ethnic women who prefer a different life-style are assumed to be "brainwashed." Unless groups learn to talk—and listen—to one another, the new ethnicity may sour into old-fashioned bigotry. Worse, it could turn into an *ideology* of bigotry, converting inchoate prejudices into self-conscious political dogmas.[5]

One way of avoiding Balkanization is to try to understand each group from its own point of view. Without attempting to be exhaustive, let us survey some of the claims and grievances of three groups in America—Indians, blacks, and white ethnics—and see what progress has been made in satisfying claims and redressing grievances.

THE INDIANS: THE ORIGINAL VICTIMS

Since the time of Jamestown and Plymouth the dominant American viewpoint has been that the Indians should either become "civilized" or remove themselves from the path of the white man's civilization. A typical view among the Puritan settlers was that the Indian was a "great naked dirty beast,"[6] and this expressed in one phrase the English Protestant's obsession with cleanliness and his

---

*Julius Lester, "Look Out, Whitey! Black Power's Gon' Get Your Mama," in Herbert J. Storing, ed., *What Country Have I?: Political Writings by Black Americans* (New York: St. Martin's Press, Inc., 1970), p. 196. Cf. Lerone Bennett, Jr., *The Challenge of Blackness* (Chicago: Johnson Publishing Company, Inc., 1972): "For racism to end here, whites must condemn themselves and their institutions." And from James Baldwin: "It is not necessary for a black man to hate a white man, or to have any particular feelings about him at all, in order to realize that he must kill him." *No Name in the Street* (New York: The Dial Press, Inc., 1972), p. 191.

thoroughly un-Christian attitude toward cultures different from his own.* The French fur traders adapted easily to Indian ways, and while the Spanish conquistadores slaughtered Indians without pity, they ended up by merging with them. But the English marched across America, methodically removing the Indians as they went, driving them westward, and slaughtering those who would not be routed. To the English Protestant, everything about the Indians was appalling—their "heathen" religion, their exotic appearance, their tribal organization—but especially their attitude toward property. Although some Indians farmed the land, they lived communally, never fencing it off as the exclusive property of individuals. The Indians were pantheists, finding the divine in everything and living in organic relation to the soil. To chop the earth into plots and sell it as a commodity seemed to them both impious and nonsensical.

For the Anglo-American settlers this was precisely the reason why the Indians were uncivilized. They were letting potentially "useful" lands lie idle. Private property sharpens the competitive instincts of individuals, with each striving to "get more from his property. The result is "progress," a concept that was meaningful to the white settlers but was quite alien to the Indians.

In other words, the Indians showed their lack of civilization because they merely lived upon the land without "doing anything" with it.† Even the tolerant Ben Franklin showed the most arrogant contempt for this aspect of Indian culture, even suggesting that rum might be useful for getting rid of Indians.[7]

In executing this design of Providence the Anglo-American employed the following means: White settlers and frontiersmen would encroach upon Indian lands, slaughtering the game and destroying its habitat. The Indians were thus deprived of food. The Indians were then persuaded, sometimes after a war, to sell their lands to the whites and let themselves be deported to the west. There, they were promised, they could live forever without molestation. A few years later the

---

* The Puritan's image of Indians as beasts—and fair game—has been perpetuated in folklore, dime novels, Western movies, and by hucksters who sell toy guns to children. In 1964, the back of a Cheerios package advertised a plastic "Old Wild West Carbine" in these terms: "They sure came in powerful handy for shooting Indians and rattlesnakes and varmits and such." When the author complained to the General Mills corporation in Minneapolis, the makers of Cheerios, he received a reply from Jack Lemmel, Promotion Supervisor, apologizing for the "incorrect phraseology" in the advertisement. "We agree with your comments as they are so correct." As proof that General Mills "supports organizations who are working in the interests of American Indians" he cited an example: "At the present time we are employing a large number of American Indians on a reservation in Northern Minnesota. They are performing sewing work for us on a large Puppet-Doll Premium Promotion." Then, not to let a sales opportunity slip, he added: "This premium offer will be in the stores in the Spring of 1965."

† "Every now and then I am impressed with the thinking of the non-Indian. I was in Cleveland last year and got to talking with a non-Indian about American history. He said that he was really sorry about what had happened to Indians, but there was good reason for it. The continent had to be developed and he felt that Indians had stood in the way and thus had to be removed. 'After all,' he remarked, 'what did you do with the land when you had it?' I didn't understand him until later when I discovered that the Cuyahoga River running through Cleveland is inflammable. So many combustible pollutants are dumped into the river that the inhabitants have to take special precautions during the summer to avoid accidentally setting it on fire. After reviewing the argument of my non-Indian friend I decided that he was probably correct. Whites had made better use of the land. How many Indians could have thought of creating an inflammable river?" Vine Deloria, Jr., *We Talk, You Listen* (New York: Dell Publishing Co., Inc.—A Delta Book, 1970), p. 10.

process would be repeated: squatters and frontiersmen chopping down the forests and killing or scaring off the animals, traders selling rum and missionaries selling Christianity, hooligans plundering and starting trouble. Starvation. Then another solemn treaty and another forced march westward.

These periodic Indian removals were accompanied by the most terrible suffering. In 1838, when five tribes were removed to Oklahoma territory, 4,000 Indians died from exhaustion and cold on the way. One of their chiefs, captured under a flag of truce, died from mistreatment.

When the Indians finally realized that the removals would never end they banded together and put up a fierce resistance. But by then it was too late. The whites were too numerous, well organized, and determined to fulfill what they justified as a divine mission. The last armed confrontation between whites and Indians was not a war but a massacre of Indian men, women, and children at Wounded Knee, South Dakota, by the U. S. Cavalry in 1890. From roughly this period onward the defeated Indians no longer had to fear anything from their enemies. It was their friends they had to worry about.

Dawes Act of 1887

Having defeated the Indians and banished them to reservations, the government was now determined to "civilize" them.* The Dawes General Allotment Act of 1887 sought to expedite this process in two ways: Culturally, it forced children off reservations and into large boarding schools many miles away, where they were forbidden to speak their tribal language or practice their customs. Economically, the Dawes Act sought to make rugged individualists of the Indians by dividing up tribal lands and distributing them into individual plots for farms. Any reservation lands remaining after this parcelling-out were to be sold at public auction and the proceeds deposited to the credit of the tribe.

Indian culture was wholly unprepared for this sudden transformation to individualism. Even if it had been, the lands were largely dry and arid, unsuitable for farming. Many sold their land to whites at bargain prices; others were simply swindled out of them. By 1934 the Indians had lost 90,000,000 acres of the 138,000,000 they had owned in 1887. The money promised them by the government in return for their lands was often witheld from them under a variety of devices. Cheated of their lands, their cultural continuity destroyed, the Indians became almost totally helpless and dependent.

Indian Reorganization Act of 1934

In 1928 an officially commissioned report by Lewis Merriam and Associates, called *The Problems of Indian Administration*, outlined the full extent of the damage done to the Indians by the policy of forced assimilation. This famous report spurred efforts toward reform, and in 1934 Congress finally responded by passing

---

*Many of the facts and statistics presented in the next two pages are taken from the writings of Alvin M. Josephy, Jr. *Red Power,* edited by him in 1971 (New York: McGraw-Hill Book Company), contains valuable notes as well as articles by and about Indians. His contributions to the Dushkin Publishing Group's *American Governemnt '73/'74 Text* (Guilford, Conn.: Dushkin Publishing Group, Inc., 1973), pp. 345–352, were also useful to me. Josephy's *The Indian Heritage of America* (New York: Alfred A. Knopf, Inc., 1970), especially chapters 26–27, was an additional source of information.

the Indian Reorganization Act. This represented a new departure in Indian policy. It stopped the parcelling out of Indian lands, set up scholarships and loan funds, and provided for the establishment of new reservations. Although the ultimate goal of assimilation was not abandoned, the Reorganization Act at least slowed its pace and allowed greater discretion to the tribes as to its manner.

The administration of the Reorganization Act was flawed by red tape and inadequate funding, but it did help to undo the worst depredations of the 1887 act. From 1934 to 1947 the total Indian land base increased by 3,700,000 acres. Indian livestock income increased from less than $2 million to $47 million.

Termination Resolution of 1953
During World War II, however, new pressure began to mount for assimilating the Indians. Complaints also grew louder that the Reorganization Act was costing the taxpayers too much money. In 1953 Congress responded to these pressures with House Concurrent Resolution 108—the most disastrous piece of Indian legislation since the Dawes Act of 1887. It declared Congress's intent to end the "segregation" of Indians by terminating all federal relations with them: treaty obligations, protection of their lands, federal services and tax exemptions. This termination was to be imposed unilaterally, without the consent of the Indians.

For all the hardship of the reservations, they represented a homeland to many Indians and permitted them to mingle with their own people and culture. In breaking up these reservations the government damaged both the economic autonomy and the cultural continuity of tribal life. In Wisconsin, for example, the Menominee tribe had been prospering for a generation thanks to large timber holdings and their operation of a sawmill. After the passage of the 1953 termination legislation, the state of Wisconsin broke up the reservation, destroyed its economic base, and forced so many of its members onto the state welfare rolls that Wisconsin was soon appealing to the federal government for help.

In 1958 the Secretary of the Interior announced an important modification of its termination policy. Hereafter no tribe would be terminated without its consent. Despite this change of direction, much of the damage had already been done. Many of the Indians who had left their tribes and gone to the cities had slipped into despair and alcoholism. Those left behind on the reservations found themselves stripped of lands, money, and dignity.

Indian Policy in the 1960s
In the 1960s the Kennedy and Johnson administrations attempted to reverse some of the damage wrought earlier. They began dealing with social problems within the reservations instead of trying to break them up. They also recognized the right of Indians to determine their own way of life. These steps represented an improvement over the policies of the previous decade, but the well-meaning theorists of the Great Society still could not resist the attempt to "motivate" Indians without a proper understanding of how Indians motivate themselves. The Economic Opportunity Act of 1964 was thus a mixed blessing to the Indians. It channeled much-needed poverty funds into areas where unemployment reached as high as 60 percent, and it provided Indians with a voice in the distribution of these funds. On the other hand, it sent in more helpful outsiders to save the souls

of people they scarcely understood. The "expert" is the modern missionary, trying to teach the natives the new gospel of social engineering. One Indian expressed his misgivings about OEO in this way:

> We have many rulers. They are called social workers, "cops," school teachers, churches, etc., and now OEO employees. They call us into meetings to tell us what is good for us and how they've programmed us, or they come into our homes to instruct us and their manners are not always what one would call polite by Indian standards or perhaps by any standards.[8]

Nixon's Indian Policies

By the 1970s some progress in Indian affairs had been made, at least in the area of presidential speech-writing. For the first time in history an American President went on record against the policy of "civilizing" the Indians. In a message to Congress in 1970 President Nixon said:

> Both as a matter of justice and as a matter of enlightened social policy, we must begin to act on the basis of what the Indians themselves have long been telling us. The time has come to break decisively with the past and to create the conditions for a new era in which the Indian future is determined by Indian acts and Indian decisions.[9]

This commitment to "break decisively with the past," like Nixon's Family Assistance Program, was a surprisingly radical initiative from a conservative President. His message called for legislation explicitly repealing the termination resolution of 1953, granting autonomy to the tribes in the administration of service programs, restoring some Indian lands, providing greater financial and legal assistance to the tribes, and giving the Indians a new voice in the Department of Interior.

Unfortunately, the administration failed to press for the enactment of these proposals in Congress. Within a year Nixon's priorities had shifted from domestic innovation to foreign invasions, blockades, bombing, and "internal security." But before the shift in priorities, the Nixon administration did institute some reforms of its own within the Bureau of Indian Affairs (BIA). In November of 1970 the following changes were announced by the BIA: decision making would henceforth be on reservations instead of field offices; personnel shifts would be instituted; there would now be greater evaluation and inspection of the work of Indian agents; reservation "superintendents" were renamed "field administrators," reflecting the new mood of assisting the Indians instead of managing them.

But these reforms are largely symbolic. By themselves they can do little to ease the burden of America's poorest minority. Indians average $1,500 per year in income; their average unemployment rate is 40 percent; their average life expectancy is forty-seven years; the suicide rate among their teenagers is one hundred times that of whites; 50 percent of their schoolchildren drop out; their infant mortality is three times the national average. On and off reservations they live in debilitated housing, often without running water or electricity. They continue to be patronized by bureaucrats, victimized by land speculators, gaped at by tourists.

A heightened indignation over these conditions, together with a new awareness of the past—the massacres, the thefts, and the broken treaties—have contributed to Indian militance in recent years. Although at least one reporter regarded the seventy-day takeover of Wounded Knee in 1972–1973 as little more than a crude media event, a replay of the black and student takeovers in the sixties,[10] it was also a symptom of anger and impatience. Indians will no longer passively wait for the white man to act.

In recent years a number of Indian self-help organizations have attempted to direct the new militance into nonviolent and legal channels. The Americans for Indian Opportunity was founded in 1969 as a technical assistance organization to put Indians in touch with resources and expertise in order to develop projects and protect themselves against abuses. Its president, La Donna Harris, a half-Comanche who is the wife of former Senator Fred Harris, has expressed her own contempt for the melting-pot approach to minorities: "Dark skins don't melt. . . . We want to retain our individual tribal culture. We want the right to be different." The assertion of this right, Ms. Harris believes, will ultimately benefit the nation as a whole; from their own native peoples Americans can learn to appreciate a pluralistic world:

> By appreciating our differences—and there are 300 Indian tribes to appreciate—we will be better world citizens. We will learn to appreciate other cultures, like the Asian culture, the Latin, African, Middle Eastern cultures.[11]

The long and painful lesson of the past 300 years is that Indians are not white Protestants. Neither are blacks, chicanos, Jews, white ethnics, and the other minorities who have never completely assimilated to an ethic derived from the New England Puritans. The lesson taught by our treatment of the Indians is that a healthy society depends upon recognizing the differences between the groups which compose it. In 1949, Felix Cohen, a distinguished legal philosopher and a battler for Indian rights, compared the Indian tribe to the miner's canary: "When it flutters and droops we know that the poison gasses of intolerance threaten all other minorities in our land. And who of us is not a member of some minority?"[12]

THE BLACKS: IMPORTED VICTIMS

"We didn't land on Plymouth Rock, my brothers and sisters— Plymouth Rock landed on *us!*"[13] Malcolm X's observation is well borne out by the facts of American history. The oppression of Afro-Americans can be studied under three headings: legal oppression, economic oppression, and cultural oppression.

Legal Oppression

Blacks are America's only kidnaped minority. Snatched from their native land, transported thousands of miles—in a nightmare of disease and death—and sold into slavery, blacks were officially reduced to the status of cattle. The *Dred Scott* decision of 1857 declared them to be a species of "private property." The U. S. Constitution permitted the importation of slaves until 1808, solemnized the "right" of states to demand the return of fugitive slaves from other states, and, adding insult to injury, based congressional representation upon the whole number of free persons but three-fifths of the slave population.

The Civil War and the subsequent Reconstruction period gave many the hope that slavery and its legal vestiges would be abolished forever. The Thirteenth Amendment freed the slaves; the Fourteenth Amendment granted them citizenship, due process, and the equal protection of the laws; and the Fifteenth Amendment guaranteed their right to vote. Also passed during Reconstruction was a series of federal laws which spelled out these rights in more detail. One statute, passed in 1875, barred discrimination in the enjoyment of hotels, inns, restaurants, theaters, and other public accommodations. Another, passed in 1870, prescribed penalties against anyone trying to interfere with another's civil rights.

But even as these statues were being passed the Reconstruction era was drawing to a close. Southern whites, using every means from ballot fraud to Ku Klux Klan terrorism, had begun to regain control of Southern legislatures. By 1877, when the last federal troops had left the South, the nation had grown weary of protecting the civil rights of black people. There was little public outcry and only one dissent on the bench when the Supreme Court declared unconstitutional the 1875 statute which prohibited segregation in public accommodations *(The Civil Rights Cases,* 109 U. S. 3, 1883). The Court based its decision on a narrow reading of the Fourteenth Amendment, limiting its prohibition to state-imposed discrimination and preventing Congress from enacting any statutes except in pursuit of this specific prohibition.

In 1896, in *Plessy v. Ferguson,* 163 U. S. 537 (1896), a clear case of state-imposed discrimination was presented to the Court. The state of Louisiana had enacted a statute barring blacks from railroad coaches occupied by whites. Plessy, a one-eighth Negro, attempted to enter a white car and was forcibly ejected. He brought suit under both the Thirteenth and Fourteenth Amendments, claiming that compulsory segregation was a "badge of servitude" which stigmatized the black race and deprived its members of the equal protection of the law.

The Court rejected Plessy's argument and let the statute stand. Pointing to what it considered "the underlying fallacy" in Plessy's argument, the majority opinion rejected his "assumption that the enforced separation of the races stamps the colored race with a badge of inferiority." If this is the case, the Court concluded, "it is not by reason of anything found in the act, but solely because the colored races chooses to put that construction upon it."

In a spirited dissenting opinion, Justice Harlan, himself a Southerner from Kentucky, replied that everyone knew the real purpose for the enforced separation of the races in America: to degrade the black race. He prophesied, accurately as it turned out, that this decision would encourage more aggression against black people and reverse most of the progress made during Reconstruction.

> We boast of the freedom enjoyed by our people above all other peoples. But it is difficult to reconcile that boast with a state of the law which, practically, puts a brand of servitude and degradation upon a large class of our fellow citizens, our equals before the law. The thin disguise of "equal" accommodations for passengers in railroad coaches will not mislead anyone, or atone for the wrong this day done. . . .

By the turn of the century the plight of the blacks was the worst since slavery days. Lynchings occurred in unprecedented numbers. Black voting had been curtailed by grandfather clauses, selectively applied literacy tests, and poll taxes. Segregation, enforced by laws in the South and white public opinion in the

North, had worked its way into every area of American life: schools, neighborhoods, public accommodations, and transportation. Not for another forty years did the first cracks appear in the monolith of American apartheid.

In 1938 a lawsuit argued by attorneys for the NAACP compelled the state of Missouri to provide legal education to blacks on the same terms as that provided whites in the state (*Missouri ex rel. Gaines v. Canada,* 305 U. S. 377). The issue of whether this meant establishing a black law school or integrating the existing white one was not settled, however, because the beneficiary of the Court's decision suddenly and mysteriously disappeared, never to be seen again.

During the 1940s blacks began to make gains in winning back their right to vote and their right to live where they pleased. *Smith v. Allwright,* 321 U. S. 649 (1944), outlawed the white primary. A political party, the Supreme Court held, was not a strictly private club but an integral part of the state's electoral machinery. Thus, any exclusion on the ground of race was a violation of the Fifteenth Amendment. On the question of neighborhood segregation, *Shelly v. Kraemer,* 334 U. S. 1 (1948), held that restrictive covenants based upon race (agreements not to sell to blacks) were unenforceable in the courts.

Not until the 1950s, however, did the essence of *Plessy v. Ferguson* suffer a reversal. Desegregation came to postgraduate education by way of two cases decided by the Supreme Court in 1950, *Sweatt v. Painter* (law schools) and *McLaurin v. Oklahoma* (graduate schools).[14] Four years later came the momentous *Brown* decision—*Brown v. Board of Education of Topeka,* 347 U. S. 483 (1954). Speaking for a unanimous court, Chief Justice Earl Warren asked and answered the question which affected virtually every school district in the South and symbolized a whole way of life in America.

> We come then to the question presented: Does segregation of children in public schools solely on the basis of race, even though the physical facilities and other "tangible" factors may be equal, deprive the children of the minority group of equal educational opportunities? We believe that it does.

Harlan's dissent in *Plessy* had been based upon the *purpose* of segregation—to degrade the black race—but Warren's opinion avoided this line of argument, relying instead upon the evidence of contemporary social science to show that the *effects* of segregation are "feelings of inferiority" among blacks. Warren thus planted an ambiguity at the heart of the decision: Does racial separation per se cause feelings of inferiority, or only *compulsory* racial segregation? This problem will be explored later in the chapter.

To declare an end to legal segregation is one matter; to enforce the decision quite another. In 1955 the Court spelled out the means of implementation *(Brown v. Board of Education of Topeka,* 349 U. S. 483, 1955). *Brown II,* as it is sometimes called, ruled that the lower federal courts were to supervise the desegregation process, and school boards would have the burden of demonstrating to these courts that a "prompt and reasonable start" was being made. But many school districts took advantage of this proposed "period of transition" to invent sophisticated dodges for getting around the decree of *Brown I.* Others openly defied the Court. President Eisenhower finally sent troops into Little Rock, Arkansas, to escort black children to school through screaming mobs. A generation after the historic 1954 decision, *de jure* segregation (segregation with the sanction of law) was practically eliminated, but *de facto* segregation (segregation resulting from such facts as neighborhood residence patterns) remained in effect throughout the nation—more so, perhaps in the North than in the South.* In March of 1970 President Nixon outlined his administration's policy: *De jure* segregation must be eliminated at once, but *de facto* segregation does not violate the Constitution, and should not be eliminated at the expense of the neighborhood school or through any means which involve busing children beyond normal geographic zones. Even in areas of *de jure* segregation, however, the Nixon administration counseled caution and gradualism. On the one hand it was the first administration in history to sue an entire state—Georgia—to end school segregation. Yet in the case of Mississippi, the administration requested the courts to delay the desegregation of thirty school districts in the state. This was the first time an administration had ever formally asked for a slowdown in desegregation. The request was granted by the lower courts but reversed by the Supreme Court.

The *Brown* decision of 1954 marked the beginning in a series of steps taken to restore the full constitutional rights of black Americans. As the decade drew to a close Congress finally began to join in this effort, the first time since Reconstruction. The period 1957–1968 marked a new era of civil rights legislation. Five major bills, dealing with voting, housing, employment, and the right to use public accommodations, were passed during the period [see the chart on pages 101–102].

The new era of civil rights legislation came to an end with the election of Richard Nixon. He came to office in the wake of several devastating urban riots, of Black Panther shootouts with the police, and of charges of "reverse racism." In his presidential campaign of 1968 Nixon criticized the report of the National Advisory Commission on Civil Disorders for blaming the riots on the effects of white racism. In 1970 he opposed, as "regional legislation," congressional efforts to extend the Voting Rights Act of 1965 for another five years. (After its successful passage, however, he signed it.) The dominant view within the Nixon administration may have been summed up in the famous memo written to the President by Daniel P. Moynihan, a key adviser in domestic affairs. Moynihan wrote that "the time may have come when the issue of race could benefit from a period of 'benign neglect.' The subject has been too much talked about. . . . We may need a period in which Negro progress continues and racial rhetoric fades."[15] The question haunting many civil rights advocates, however, was whether Negro progress *would* continue under an administration which had so openly wooed Southern segregationists and had temporized even in clear-cut cases of deliberate discrimination.

---

* In New York City 80 percent of the black students attend majority-black schools. In Chicago's public schools almost 97 percent of the black students attend majority-black schools. Kenneth Clark, the psychologist and educator whose research was cited in the *Brown* decision of 1954, wrote in 1969: "In the 15 years since 1954, relative change has been unquestionably greater in the South than in the North. In fact, the South can look at the North with a certain ironic condescension in terms of the acceptance of rapid change toward a nonracist society." Congressional Quarterly, Inc., *Civil Rights: Progress Report, 1970* (Washington: Congressional Quarterly, Inc., 1971), pp. 49–50.

Major Civil Rights Statutes, 1957–1968

1 *The Civil Rights Act of 1957* prohibited any attempt to prevent persons from voting in federal elections and authorized the Attorney General to bring suit when a person was deprived of his or her voting rights. It also set up a Civil Rights Commission and a Civil Rights Division in the Justice Department. Except for these last two provisions, the act accomplished little, since resistance to black suffrage in the Deep South was massive and determined, more than a match for the case-by-case approach provided for by this act.

2 *The Civil Rights Act of 1960* strengthened provisions of the 1957 act for court enforcement of voting rights, and it required voting records to be preserved by state officials. It also contained limited criminal penalties relating to bombing and the obstruction of federal court orders, e. g., orders to desegregate schools.

3 *The Civil Rights Act of 1964* was the first serious response by Congress, at least since the time of Reconstruction, to the problem of segregation. By this time sit-inners had been beaten, civil rights workers killed, Martin Luther King jailed, and black children blown to pieces while attending Sunday school. The nation had watched some of these events with horror, including the infamous dogs and fire hoses of Birmingham, Alabama. These provided much of the impetus for the bill, which forced a reluctant Kennedy administration to take action. After Kennedy's death the bill was strengthened in Congress (with some Southern members of Congress voting for the stronger amendments in the mistaken belief that the bill would never pass with such amendments tacked onto it). Thanks in part to the legislative savvy of President Johnson, the bill was passed despite the determined efforts of Southern Senators, including a last-minute filibuster. The bill was roundly denounced by Senator Barry Goldwater, the Republican party's candidate for 1964, and this marked the beginning of the Republican party's partnership with the Deep South.

The key provision of the bill was its prohibition of discrimination in public accommodations—hotels, motels, restaurants, and the like. Thus the bill, in effect, revived the Civil Rights Act of 1875, which the Supreme Court had found unconstitutional in 1883 (see above, p. 98). This provision was later challenged on the same grounds, i. e., that it was trying to prevent a merely "private" discrimination, but it was sustained by the Supreme Court in *Heart of Atlanta Motel v. U. S.* (1966).

Other provisions of the bill included the prohibition of discrimination by unions and employers and the establishment of an Equal Employment Opportunity Commission. These last provisions have also become important to women's rights, because they prohibited employment discrimination by sex as well as race.

4 *The Voting Rights Act of 1965* was proposed by President Johnson in a speech culminating in his prediction that "we shall overcome." The appropriation of this language by a former Southern senator may have been the high water mark of civil rights during the sixties. The ensuing legislation finally broke the back of Southern resistance to black suffrage, because it authorized the Attorney General to appoint federal examiners to register voters in areas of marked discrimination. The effect was electrifying: For the first time since Reconstruction blacks began to win contests for local offices. White Southerners began a mass exodus from the Democratic party—"a nigger party," some called it.

5 *The Civil Rights Bill of 1968* prohibited discrimination in the sale or rental of housing. It also protected persons exercising such civil rights as attending schools and persuading others to assert their rights. But the bill also contained a rider, introduced by conservatives as the price for their support, making it a crime to cross state lines to "incite a riot." This riot-conspiracy provision was a reaction to urban riots and the "outside agitators," such as Rap Brown, whom conservatives believe to be the cause of riots. The so-called Rap Brown provision of this bill was reviewed in Chapter 1.

Economic Oppression

The progress made in eliminating official apartheid is small comfort to those black Americans who suffer the effects of economic oppression. Being able to go into any restaurant is a meaningless right if one cannot afford a meal. In 1934, W. E. DuBois resigned in disgust from the NAACP, the organization he helped to found, because it failed to pursue this problem of economic oppression.

World War II brought jobs to blacks in unprecedented numbers. Asked who his favorite white man was, Malcolm X once answered, "Hitler. He got us jobs." Even so, these jobs were usually the most menial ones. Blacks seeking employment in defense industries were embittered by policies like that of a West Coast aviation factory which declared openly that "the Negro will be considered only as janitors and in other similar capacities. . . . Regardless of their training as aircraft workers, we will not employ them."[16] Only when black labor leaders such as A. Philip Randolph threatened a march on Washington was something done about employment discrimination. President Roosevelt issued Executive Order 8802 creating a federal Fair Employment Practices Commission. Although it lacked enforcement powers, the FEPC set a precedent for treating nondiscriminatory employment as a matter of constitutional right. Despite this legal recognition of the right to work, economic oppression and its effects were still omnipresent facts of life a generation later.

Much of this economic stress resulted from lack of proper education and training—the heritage of discrimination in the past—but much of it also was a part of an ongoing discrimination against qualified blacks. The Civil Rights Act of 1964 contains a provision (Title VII) which prohibits employers from refusing to hire a person, or discriminating against him or her on the job, on account of race, religion, sex, or national origin. It also established an Equal Employment Opportunity Commission (EEOC) to work with state and local agencies and investigate charges of job discrimination. But EEOC has no enforcement powers. The Civil Rights Commission has characterized it as a "poor enfeebled thing," and its Democratic chairman resigned early in the Nixon administration, charging "a crippling lack of support."[17]

In one area, that of racial discrimination in unions, the Nixon administration at first appeared to move vigorously. In June of 1969 the administration announced a controversial plan for admitting larger numbers of racial minorities into federally assisted construction projects. Called the "Philadelphia Plan" for the city in which it first went into effect, it set "goals" for the number of nonwhite employees to be hired on construction projects financed by federal funds. It was immediately denounced by some labor leaders and members of Congress as a "quota system" which would do more harm than good. The Philadelphia Plan caused a split among advocates of civil rights. Some welcomed it, while others feared that it would needlessly divide labor and civil rights groups.

But those with misgivings about the Philadelphia Plan had no cause to worry. It was quietly abandoned at the start of Nixon's second term. Indeed, what troubled many civil rights advocates at the start of Nixon's second term was that *all* programs to increase minority hiring were being discouraged. By December of 1972 the Office of Federal Compliance in the Labor Department had become badly demoralized. All efforts to end job discrimination on federally assisted projects were being reversed by the higher levels of the Labor Department, so the staff found themselves with little to do except collect their salaries. "I am getting paid $28,000 a year to go out and feed the pigeons," one Compliance official in Washington complained.[18]

Much the same fate was suffered by President Nixon's "black capitalism," one of the key planks of his campaign platform in 1968. As early as March 1970, Senator Edward Brooke, the only black Republican in Congress, confessed his dismay "at the lack of momentum in the black entrepreneurship, which was something that Mr. Nixon spoke of in great depth during his campaign."[19] In Nixon's 1972 campaign the "black capitalism" theme was eliminated.

Despite a noticeable lack of encouragement from the Nixon administration, black Americans made some gains in the economic sphere between 1960 and 1971. The family income of nonwhites nearly doubled. The ratio of black and white family incomes also changed substantially, climbing from 53 percent in 1961 to 63 percent in 1971. (This was a long way from equality, but it did represent progress over the previous decade, 1951–1961, which had brought no changes in the ratio.) In 1973 Richard Scammon and Ben Wattenberg, whose bestselling book on *The Real Majority* (1970) had celebrated the virtues of "centrism" and "moderation," found something new to celebrate. Writing in the April 1973 issue of *Commentary,* they described the "huge amount of progress," the "real progress," the "enormous progress" made by blacks in the economic sphere.[20] Even in 1973, many critics found fault with Scammon and Wattenberg's use of statistics—their tendency to emphasize the rosy data while playing down the gloomy data.[21] But not until the following year was it really clear how premature the celebration had been. Scammon and Wattenberg had contended that black economic progress was not only "a massive achievement" (for which white liberals could take credit), but that "to all appearances it is here to stay." But statistics published in 1974 by the U. S. Bureau of the Census told a different story. After reaching a high—61 percent of white income— in 1969 and 1970, black income began slipping downward relative to that of whites. By 1973 it had fallen back to 58 percent—the same level as in 1966. This constituted an erosion in the "progress" toward income parity. The reasons for this erosion are less clear, although the policies of the Nixon administration and the advancing recession probably had much to do with it. Unskilled and semiskilled workers, who are usually "the last to be hired and the first to be fired," are the one hardest hit by recession. Black workers fall into that category in disproportionate numbers.

Cultural Oppression

Black Americans have preserved and developed a vital culture under the most difficult circumstances. In slavery days most were denied even rudimentary education because of their masters' fears that it might "spoil" them. With slavery's end, blacks were lucky to get a few years of schooling, and these segregated schools were invariably the ones with the least funds, the worst facilities, the poorest teaching staff, and the shortest duration. Even in the North black students were discouraged from setting their goals too high; there was no place for them in society except at the bottom.

Despite this lack of education, black culture in America has grown, thrived, and influenced the culture of America and the world. Blues, spirituals, and jazz, all of them unique products of black America, belong to the world and to the ages. Blacks in America have also developed a rich verbal tradition—concrete, dramatic, full of metaphors and puns—which has produced great poets, novelists, orators, lyricists, and playwrights since the days of slavery.

Yet the centuries of demoralization have also left their scars. The Coleman Report, the most famous survey of black and white achievement in recent years, found that in 1965 the average Northern black sixth grader was about 18 points behind his white counterpart in tests of verbal ability, reading comprehension, and arithmetic skills.

Hence a paradox. Despite the vitality of black culture, black children are behind their white counterparts in nearly every index of scholastic achievement. Emanating from this paradox are two contradictory solutions to the problem of low achievement in black students. *Integrationists* consider the problem of low achievement as connected with the isolation of the races in America. The solution, then, would involve a vigorous and deliberate mixing of the races in schools: busing, school pairing, and the like. Advocates of *black culture,* on the other hand, consider the problem of low achievement among blacks as resulting from *too much* contact with whites. The general line of argument is that white culture has demoralized blacks, deprived them of the kind of collective self-confidence which sharpens the appetite for learning. Let us examine each position more closely.

Integration Integrationists have won important victories in the Supreme Court in recent years. In *Swann v. Charlotte-Mecklenburg Board of Education,* 401 U. S. 1 (1971), the Court upheld a District Court's order to bus children from predominantly black schools in Charlotte, North Carolina, to predominantly white schools elsewhere in the area. In its opinion the Court took note of Charlotte's history of official segregation. In such cases, the Court held, it is not sufficient for a school district to revert to "color blind" pupil assignment plans. It must now actively integrate the races, using color as a criterion for achieving racial balance in the school. In a 1973 case, *Keyes v. School District No. 1,* the *Swann* ruling was carried even further. The Court required the city of Denver to redraw its entire school system's district lines for the purpose of integrating the races. The Denver school system had never embraced any official policy of segregation, but some of its attendance zones in the past had been drawn on the basis of ethnic criteria. This was sufficient for the Court to find the entire school system segregated, and to call for immediate steps to bring about racial balance in every district. Since most Northern school districts have done their share of racial gerrymandering in the past, the *Keyes* decision brought the entire nation, not just the South, closer to a showdown on busing.

Indeed, the showdown had already begun. George Wallace won the 1972 Democratic primary in Michigan—one of the most liberal states in the Union—on the strength of the busing issue. In the summer of 1972 Congress tacked an amendment to a higher-education bill, limiting the federal courts' powers to use busing to achieve racial balance. An even stronger bill was killed only when a minority of Senate liberals resorted to a device made famous by Southern conservatives—the filibuster. In 1974 another antibusing amendment almost passed; it was finally scuttled during the last few days of the Ninety-third Congress. There was also some support for a constitutional amendment banning busing. In 1973 the Senate Judiciary Committee held hearings on such an amendment, which stated: "No public school student shall, because of his race, creed, or color, be assigned to or required to attend a particular school."

In 1974 the probusing forces received a setback at the hands of the Supreme Court when it ruled, 5-4, that cross-county busing cannot be ordered by courts unless they first find a clear pattern of deliberate racial discrimination in all the counties involved. The case arose in the Detroit area, where a district court judge had ordered busing between the city of Detroit and its suburbs. Since American cities are becoming increasingly black as whites flee to the suburbs, city-suburban busing is a highly explosive issue. The Court defused the issue, at least temporarily, by sending the case back to the district court to determine whether deliberate segregation had been imposed by the cities and suburbs. The Court thus left the door ajar: *If* the probusing litigants can bring in empirical evidence showing that city and suburban officials have conspired to keep blacks out of predominantly white schools (or vice versa), then busing becomes an appropriate remedy, even if the buses must cross district, county and city lines.

While lawyers pondered the implications of the Detroit decision, violence erupted in the streets to another Northern city. In the summer of 1974 a district court judge, after finding a pattern of racial discrimination in the Boston public school system, ordered busing between black and white areas of the city. As the school buses carrying the black children rolled into the Irish working-class neighborhoods of South Boston, they were met with jeers, curses, and stones from mobs of parents and children. While blacks tended to view this reaction as one of plain racism, spokesmen for the Irish community insisted that the issues were more complicated. South Boston contained poor but viable neighborhoods with strong ethnic roots, which, the opponents of busing contended, would be destroyed by the sudden massive influx of black students. The whites of South Boston were also resentful because they saw themselves as victims of social engineering controlled by white liberals—affluent missionaries who themselves lived in the suburbs or who sent their own children to private schools. Of the judge who ordered the busing one woman commented: "I don't think he understands ethnic pride or what it means to be a working class person bearing the burden of the people [from outside] who use this city." Whatever the reasons—racial prejudice, ethnic pride, class consciousness—the confrontation in the streets of Boston was more than a local event. It was reported throughout the nation, argued and agonized over by commentators, and deplored by President Ford (who then added that he opposed "forced busing"). Blacks came into Boston from other cities to participate in marches against "white racism," and, as if to prove this analysis correct, the Ku Klux Klan began arriving from the south.

Developments of this sort have caused even some strong supporters of civil rights to wonder whether busing is worth the risks involved.[22] From the standpoint of scholastic achievements among black children it has produced no measurable results, although it may still be too early to judge fairly.[23] From the standpoint of race relations it has become a bitter and divisive issue.

Black Culture Among those opposed to busing and other means of deliberately integrating the races are those blacks who regard it as a confession of black inferiority and a threat to the autonomy of black culture. The Congress of Racial Equality began, like the NAACP, as an integrationist organization, but changed its policies and goals during the 1960s. In the spring of 1973, CORE joined the Nixon administration and the State of Virginia in urging the Supreme Court to reject a plan for busing children across city-suburban lines. In its legal brief, CORE charged that the integration plan would cause "disastrous consequences to black children by their being uprooted and placed in schools where estrangement may be their only find, as countless black parents expect." Victor Solomon, the associate national director of CORE, later told the press that the merged metropolitan district was "a testament to the belief of some blacks and some whites that blacks are inferior and can only learn in the presence of whites."[24]

America has apparently reached a crossroads* on the question of what it means to be "culturally deprived." Are black children culturally deprived when kept away from the American "mainstream"? Or is that mainstream itself so polluted that blacks and other ethnic minorities are better off removing themselves from it and rediscovering their own cultural roots? On the one hand the NAACP and other liberal organizations are pressing forward in the fight to integrate the nation's schools. On the other hand many blacks are demanding community control of neighborhood schools, black studies programs in high schools and colleges, separate dormitories and clubs.

Integrationists sometimes argue that black separatism plays into the hands of white racists, because it accepts segregation as a way of life. Black separatists reply by distinguishing between *separation* and *segregation*. Segregation, they say, is compulsory separation, ordered and controlled by whites for the purpose of degrading blacks. Separation, on the other hand, implies the voluntary association of blacks for the sake of preserving their own culture.

Brown v. Board of Education blurred this distinction between voluntary separation and compulsory segregation. "Separate educational facilities," in Chief

---

* In 1973 Roy Wilkins of the NAACP believed that the juncture had already been passed. "We do not discern any growing separatist philosophy. Rather, we think it is on the wane." Wilkins was also scornful of black studies programs. "After all, those young people have to face the world. Can you get a job with IBM by saying you majored in black studies?" *New York Post,* July 7, 1973, p. 2.

Justice Warren's opinion," are *inherently* unequal" (emphasis added). In 1965, when CORE was just beginning to consider the merits of black separatism, James Farmer (then its national director) commented on Warren's formulation:

> I am not a lawyer, but I think that the phrase "separate educational facilities are inherently unequal," which supports the philosophy of total integration, invites some misinterpretation. Separation need not be inferior in all cases and all places. What is crucial is the *meaning* the culture places upon the separation.[25]

Put another way, Farmer's condemnation of Jim Crow was not based upon its alleged *effects* on the "hearts and minds" of black children, but on its manifest *purpose*—keeping blacks "in their place." This, it may be recalled, was the approach of Justice Harlan's dissent in *Plessy v. Ferguson* back in 1896. For Harlan, the alternative to segregation was not integration but the *freedom* of blacks to join—or not to join—the company of whites. In retrospect, it seems a far simpler and more direct way to strike down Jim Crow than trying to show that racial separation inherently leads to "feelings of inferiority" in black children. Nearly seventy years after *Plessy*, James Farmer returned to the spirit of Harlan's famous dissent:

> What we wish is the freedom of choice which will cause any choice we make to seem truly our own. . . . Jim Brown, a thoughtful man and pretty good fullback, offended some people when he said that he personally wouldn't want to live with whites but that he damned well wanted to know that he could if he did want to. I think he represents the thinking of many Negroes.[26]

Having explored the oppression—legal, economic, and cultural—of black Americans, let us turn to the problems of another group of Americans, a group sometimes referred to as the "silent" or "forgotten" minority.

THE WHITE ETHNICS: "FORGOTTEN" VICTIMS?

The constant preoccupation with black-white relations in the communications media—newspapers, radio, TV, magazine, and books—during the sixties sometimes made it appear that blacks are the only oppressed minority in America. On this point many white ethnics* disagree. "I was born in Italy," the wife of a contractor told political analyst Samuel Lubell. "When I came here as a girl, I was called a wop and a dago. Companies wouldn't hire an Italian or a Catholic. Now the government makes them hire colored."[27] Is this bigotry, plain and simple? Or is it something more complex—a painful recollection of prejudice suffered in the past, coupled with a discovery that the same kind of snobs who sneered at Italians a generation ago have now become the patrons of blacks? The thrust of this woman's anger is not directed at "the colored" (an old-fashioned term, not a racist one) but at "the government," which doles out its benevolence with something less than impartiality.

"The government," to ethnics, usually means more than the official law-

---

* "White ethnics" is generally understood to have a religious, class, and regional meaning: lower middle-class Catholics whose parents or grandparents immigrated from southern or eastern Europe. The Irish are sometimes also included in this category, although they have lost most of their ethnic distinctiveness over the past two generations.

making organs of society. What is really meant is better expressed as "the establishment": the liberal, college-educated elites who occupy key positions in government *and* in the communications media, prestige universities, foundations, churches, and all the other institutions which structure and define our nation's social priorities. This "establishment," from the ethnic's standpoint, has either ignored or misunderstood the problems and point of view of white minority groups in America.

The Universities

Italians are the second-largest minority in New York City, but they constitute only a tiny fraction of the City University's faculty, and most of them are in the lower echelons. Of the 169 deans in the system in 1973, only 4 were Italian. Although Italian-American students constituted 25 percent of the student body, little financial or remedial help was available to them. One alumnus complained:

> Despite the fact that many of the students desperately need academic help and counselling, they are expected to make it on their own. As was true of their fewer predecessors, today's Italian-American students are expected to sink or swim alone while CUNY [City University of New York] devotes its resources to the needs of other ethnic groups—and does so with great publicity.[28]

This kind of double standard is not uncommon in American universities. Postgraduate schools have also tended to exclude ethnic minorities from special consideration. A black recruiter from the University of Michigan Law School told the author in February 1971 that the average black student in the school had a Law School Aptitude Test score of 475 and a 2.6 (C +) cumulative undergraduate grade average. For white students, including white ethnics, the required aptitude score was at least 600 and the grade point average in the range of 3.5 (B + to A −). Similar policies, or some variation of them, were followed by a number of other law schools.

In 1974 many white ethnics and other interested parties were carefully watching the progress through the courts of a suit brought by a young man named Marco DeFunis, a Jewish student, against the University of Washington Law School. The school had rejected DeFunis while admitting three dozen minority students with lower grades and test scores than his. DeFunis appealed his case to the United States Supreme Court, but the Court refused to rule on it on the grounds of mootness. The law school, it seems, had admitted DeFunis pending an outcome to the case, and by the time it reached Court DeFunis was about to graduate. Justice William Douglas, however, strongly dissented from the mooting of the case, and condemned the use of racial criteria for admission. Since Justice Douglas was one of the Court's most outspoken champions of civil rights, many law school officials sensed that the days of "affirmative action" based upon race were numbered. "That's kind of handwriting on the wall for the next time a case like this reaches the Court," an associate dean of a Midwestern law school admitted.

A widely held assumption among white liberals is that white ethnics don't need extra help in schooling or jobs because they have already "made it." This assumption is not borne out by the facts. About half of the Irish, Polish, and Italian households in the nation are involved in blue-collar work, and the average real wages of industrial workers with three dependents actually declined during the 1960s from $88.06 in 1965 to $87.27 in 1969. This is a long way from affluence, yet the same assumptions which go into the special help programs of universities are sometimes also applied to antipoverty programs. In 1969 Peter Schrag wrote:

> In Pittsburgh, where the members of the Polish-American organizations earn an estimated $5,000 to $6,000 (and some fall below the poverty line), the Poverty Programs are nonetheless directed primarily to Negroes, and almost everywhere the thing called urban backlash associates itself in some fashion with ethnic groups whose members have themselves only a precarious hold on the security of affluence.[29]

The Media

The communications media constitute another element of America's cultural "establishment." Here, too, ethnics complain that their problems have been ignored and that they themselves have been presented as clowns and fools. A worker in Chicago told a reporter:

> The liberals always have despised us. We've got these mostly little jobs, and we drink beer and, my God, we bowl and watch television and we don't read. It's goddamn vicious snobbery. We're sick of all these phoney integrated TV commercials with these upper-class Negroes. We know they're phoney.
>
> The only time a Pole is mentioned it's to make fun of him. He's Ignatz Dumbrowski, 274 pounds and 5-foot-4, and he got his education by writing in to a firm on a matchbook cover. But what will we do about it? Nothing, because we're the new invisible man, the new whipping boy, and we still think the measure of a man's what he does and how he takes care of his children and what he's doing in his own home, not what he thinks about Vietnam.[30]

The general picture of the white ethnic conveyed by the media is that of an Archie Bunker-type of bigot and reactionary.* Yet Father Andrew Greeley, a priest and a sociologist, has analyzed public opinion poll data on white ethnics and found them significantly more liberal on political and social issues than their WASP counterparts: more liberal even than Northern WASPs on matters of race relations, more likely to favor a guaranteed annual wage, to say they would vote for a black President, to be concerned about the environment. "In other words, if American liberals are looking for groups to support action on pollution, integration, welfare reform, and electing blacks to political office, it is precisely among Catholic blue-collar workers that they should look."[31] This suggests that the ethnic working class has not strayed very far from the reform alliance in which it played such a vital role from 1932 to the 1960s. Despite these findings, however, there can be little doubt that the New Deal alliance of minorities is under serious

---

* Even though Archie Bunker is formally a WASP, he bears a suspicious resemblance to the liberal's version of the Catholic working man: He lives in Queens, Long Island, has a pot belly, says "terlet" for toilet, pushes his wife around, and hates sex.

strain today. The last presidential campaign which combined the support of Indians, Mexicans, blacks, and white ethnics was that of Robert Kennedy in 1968, and after his assassination many of his ethnic supporters ended up voting for George Wallace.

CONCLUSION: TOWARD INTERGROUP COALITION

There are politicians and ideologues in this country who have a vested interest in racial polarization. They count on "negrophobia"[32] to hold together an alliance between the upper class and the lower middle class—a strange alliance from an economic point of view but one which feeds on ethnic fears and tensions. Unless these are resolved, it seems unlikely that any populist coalition of all the "plain people," regardless of race, can ever be assembled in America.

Such a coalition is long overdue. Very few blacks, reds, browns, or white ethnics enjoy the privileges, the tax breaks, and the political influence of the affluent. Most suffer from poor municipal services, air pollution, high medical costs and food prices. All of them are lied to by Madison Avenue hucksters, generals, politicans, and Presidential press secretaries. Poor and middle-class people of all races tend to favor tax reform, family income allowances, national health insurance, pollution control, increases in Social Security, and the avoidance of foreign military adventures. A coalescence of ethnic and racial groups could release a flood of reforms which most European countries instituted years ago.

What stands in the way of such a coalition? One factor has already been mentioned: the tendency of each group to ignore or misunderstand the claims of others. Like the characters in a Chekov play, each talks loudly and righteously to itself. When their positions collide, negotiable issues are translated into "nonnegotiable demands." Busing, for example, is now so tangled in confrontational rhetoric that it can only be resolved by the Supreme Court—or by a new amendment to the Constitution. But suppose instead that whites had made a greater effort to understand the position of black parents who pay taxes but must send their children to schools where conditions are unsafe and the environment is unsuitable for learning. Suppose, further, that blacks made more effort to understand the position of whites in not wanting *their* children bused into such schools. Instead of hardening their respective positions into constitutional absolutes, would it not have been more appropriate for both sides to negotiate solutions? A preliminary solution would seem to be some form of one-way busing—*out* of the ghetto—to those parents who request it. (A longer-range solution: better municipal services and police protection, combined with economic growth, job opportunities, and housing subsidies to help those who want to move.) One-way busing on the basis of individual option, which Northerners call "open enrollment" and Southerners call "freedom of choice," has apparently done little toward realizing the integrationist ideal of racially "balanced" schools. But if the basic goal is not salt-and-pepper but the freedom of black parents to find the best schools for their children, one-way busing seems the most practicable solution, and certainly the one least likely to produce a constitutional amendment banning busing.

Besides the factor of nonnegotiable confrontations, another impediment to intergroup coalition is the tendency for romantics to misunderstand the nature of politics. The kind of political "fraternity" being preached in this chapter has little to do with "brotherhood" in any sentimental sense. The assumption here is that people's choice of "brothers" is a purely social matter; the expectation here is that people as a rule will associate with "their own kind." In politics, however, people from completely different ethnic groups will want to stick together because of bread-and-butter issues (tax reform, for example) which cut completely across life-styles and ethnic preferences.

Groups get together in the political arena for the sake of mutual advantage. This astoundingly simple axiom is not always appreciated, especially by idealists. Writing on black power in 1967 Stokeley Carmichael and Charles Hamilton condemned the white middle class because "this class wants 'good government' *for themselves;* it wants good school *for its children.*"[33] But what is wrong with this? Later in the book the authors themselves argued for a politics of black self-interest. In defending black power they admitted, at least implicitly, that other groups also have the right to "take care of their own first."

> Irish Catholics took care of their own first without a lot of apology for doing so, without any dubious language from timid leadership about guarding against "backlash." Everyone understood it to be a perfectly legitimate procedure.[34]

But Irish Catholics did not accuse other groups of lacking "a viable conscience as regards humanity," nor did they promise "to modernize—*indeed to civilize*—the country."[35] To a vintage Irish politician this would sound suspiciously like WASP talk, that peculiar mixture of piety and arrogance which would make everyone over in the name of "civilization" and "humanity."

Democratic pluralism proceeds on the premise of "live and let live." It recognizes that all groups have legitimate self-interests, and tries to build majority coalitions when these interests coincide. The ingredients for a new reform coalition are scattered throughout America in the form of ethnic and racial minorities with common needs and grievances. An American writer proud of his Slovak heritage put it this way: "The inevitable coalition is between blacks and ethnics. To make a coalition, mutual love is not a prerequesite. Mutual respect, or even mutual need, will do."[36]

NOTES

1. Stokeley Carmichael, "A Declaration of War," in Massimo Teodori, ed., *The New Left: A Documentary History* (Indianapolis and New York: The Bobbs-Merrill Company, Inc., 1969), p. 281.
2. Congressional Quarterly, *Civil Rights: Progress Report 1970* (Washington: Congressional Quarterly, Inc., 1971), p. 45.
3. Peter Schrag, "The Forgotten American," in Michael P. Smith, ed., *American Politics and Public Policy* (New York: Random House, Inc., 1973), p. 317.
4. *The Democratic Prospect* (New York: Harper & Row, Publishers, Incorporated, 1962), p. 25.
5. The critical distinction between social prejudice and ideological racism is developed

in Hannah Arendt, *The Origins of Totalitarianism* (Cleveland: The World Publishing Company, 1958), passim.
6 James Truslow Adams, *The Founding of New England* (Boston: Little, Brown and Company, 1921), p. 348.
7 Jesse Lemisch, ed., *Benjamin Franklin: The Autobiography and Other Writings* (New York: Signet Books, New American Library, Inc., 1961), p. 133.
8 Clyde Warrier, "We Are Not Free," in Alvin M. Josephy, Jr., ed., *Red Power: The American Indians' Fight for Freedom* (New York: McGraw-Hill Book Company, 1971), p. 73.
9 Richard M. Nixon, "Message to Congress on Indian Affairs," in Josephy, ed., op. cit., p. 213.
10 Terri Schultz, "Bamboozle Me Not at Wounded Knee," *Harper's,* CCXLVI (June 1972), pp. 46–56.
11 *The Journal-News,* Rockland County, N. Y., June 21, 1972, p. 3C (Monitor News Service Dispatch).
12 Felix S. Cohen, "Indian Self-Government," in Josephy, op. cit., p. 28.
13 Malcolm X, *Autobiography* (New York: Grove Press Inc., 1966), p. 201.
14 *Sweatt v. Painter*, 399 U. S. 619 (1950); *McLaurin v. Oklahoma State Regents*, 399 U. S. 637 (1950).
15 Congressional Quarterly, op. cit., p. 24.
16 Quoted in *Report of the National Advisory Commission on Civil Disorders* (New York: Bantam Books, Inc., 1968), p. 223.
17 Congressional Quarterly, op. cit., p. 33.
18 *The New York Times,* Dec. 19, 1972, p. 24.
19 Congressional Quarterly, op. cit., p. 53.
20 Ben J. Wattenberg and Richard M. Scammon, "Black Progress and Liberal Rhetoric," *Commentary,* LV (April 1973), p. 36.
21 See "Letters from Readers," *Commentary,* LVI (August 1973), pp. 4ff.
22 Christopher Jencks, "Busing—The Supreme Court Goes North," *The New York Times Magazine,* Nov. 19, 1972, p. 125.
23 For a review of this research, see that of Nancy St. John in *Review of Education Research,* February 1970.
24 *The New York Times,* Apr. 19, 1973, p. 16.
25 James Farmer, *Freedom—When?* (New York: Random House, Inc., 1965), p. 116.
26 Ibid., p. 119.
27 Samuel Lubell, *The Future While It Happened* (New York: W. W. Norton & Company, Inc., 1973), p. 92.
28 Richard Gambino, "The Lonely Italian-American," *The Village Voice,* June 7, 1973, p. 29.
29 Schrag, op. cit., p. 318.
30 Quoted in Michael Novak, *The Rise of the Unmeltable Ethnics* (New York: The Macmillan Company, 1971), p. 60.
31 Andrew M. Greeley, "Political Attitudes among American White Ethnics," *Public Opinion Quarterly,* XXXVI (Summer 1972), p. 216.
32 Kevin P. Phillips, *The Emerging Republican Majority* (Garden City, N. Y.: Anchor Books, Doubleday & Company, Inc., 1970), passim.
33 Stokeley Carmichael and Charles V. Hamilton, *Black Power* (New York: Random House, Inc., 1967), p. 41.
34 Ibid., p. 51.
35 Ibid., p. 41.
36 Novak, op. cit., p. 257.

Part Two

Processes of Democracy

Chapter 4

Campaigns and Elections: Are They Worth the Bother?

Public cynicism about politics and politicians already runs high. If this is not cleaned up, the political system will come apart . . . with influence, dominance, and even control put up for sale to the highest bidder.

David Brinkley*

Something strange and sad has been happening to Americans since 1960: They have been losing their faith in the electoral process.

More and more of them are staying away from the polls. In 1960, some 64.3 percent of eligible voters showed up to vote, but the number declined steadily during the sixties and reached a low of 55.6 percent in 1972. (Voter participation rates in off-year congressional elections dropped from 46.3 percent in 1962 to 38 percent in 1974.) There may be a number of explanations for the declining turnouts, but one of the reasons is probably a growing sense of frustration, a feeling that "you can't fight city hall." Studies of variable rates of political participation suggest that those most likely to get involved in politics are those who possess a greater sense of mastery over "the system."[1] More and more people, it seems, are

---

* David Brinkley's preface to Robert N. Winter-Berger, *The Washington Pay-Off* (New York: Dell Publishing Co., Inc., 1972).

feeling that they have no such mastery, that they might as well stay home on election day because the politicians are going to do what they please anyway. Part of this sense of impotence is the feeling that there is really no meaningful choice between parties. In the wake of Watergate people were not just disgusted with Nixon, or with the Committee to Reelect the President (CREEP), or with the Republican party, but with the Democrats as well. A Louis Harris poll published in August of 1973 revealed that a 69–21 percent majority of those surveyed felt that "dirty campaign tactics exist among most Republicans and Democrats, and the Nixon campaign people were no worse than the Democrats, except they got caught at it." Americans have never thought highly of politics as a profession, but in recent years they have been giving it increasingly lower ratings. What is more alarming, Americans in greater numbers are pessimistic about the future of their country and more inclined to see the past as a better time than the present. (A wave of nostalgia swept the country during the early seventies: Americans appeared to be receptive to the suggestion that everything was better during the era of sock hops and rock 'n' roll.) All in all, a kind of collective sadness seems to have descended upon the nation, a sadness rooted in political frustration. One of America's proudest boasts—that we, unlike so many other countries, get our leaders by means of free elections—seems to have lost its appeal to many Americans.

Is voting a rational process in America? Or is it just a matter of blind lever-pulling? What about campaigning—is it mostly noise and hoopla? What do *we* get out of it? Are we really electing people who represent the majority of Americans? Or is our electoral system so tied up with big money, so shot through with corruption, so rigged against ordinary people, that it isn't worth bothering about? These are questions which trouble us in this post-Watergate era—questions which can all be boiled down to a central issue: Does our electoral process work the way it is supposed to work?

In theory, the democratic electoral process works like this. Those who aspire to govern in America must go out and campaign, during which time they must make it clear how they stand on issues, what their overall philosophy is, and what they would do to solve the problems facing the nation. Different candidates will have different ideas about what policies are best for the nation. They will present their competing ideas in the public arena, leaving it to the majority of voters to decide which they prefer. Democracy is "that institutional arrangement for arriving at political decisions in which individuals acquire the power to decide by means of a competitive struggle for the people's vote."[2]

But the competition is not just a hustle after votes; it is also a kind of dialogue in which everyone is enlightened in the course of the campaign. The quest for office thus becomes an extension of the discussion process, "the free trade in ideas," which makes democracy not just a ritual of counting heads but a process of stimulating what is inside the head. "If the spirit of discussion—which is the spirit of giving as well as taking, and of learning as well as teaching—is present from beginning to end, there is genuine reason for thinking that the opinion of the majority, intrinsically and inherently, will possess quality and value."[3]

Admirable and encouraging theory! But unfortunately, says the skeptic, the theory seems to have frightfully little to do with the facts of political life in America. The skeptic may not only have trouble remembering any political campaign in America which provided the voters with a coherent discussion of issues; he or she may even doubt whether the American voter is *ready* for a serious discussion of issues. Aren't voters rather easily conned? If they were rational to begin with, why do politicians spend so much money on nonsense, from spot commercials to free ball point pens and slogan-bearing shopping bags? And, speaking of money, where do the politicians get the money to spend on Madison Avenue humbug, and how much influence do these fatcats who provide that money have over our supposedly "democratic" electoral process? The skeptic has not forgotten the cash-filled suitcases that went flying around the country during the 1972 campaign, and suspects that whoever filled up those suitcases exerted more influence over candidates, issues, and outcomes than did the ordinary voter. In short, the skeptic has very serious doubts about whether our electoral process—the whole procedure by which votes are solicited and given—is working the way it is supposed to work in a democracy.

This chapter will not erase all the doubts about our electoral process; it may even create new ones. But by throwing a little light on the way our process works, it may help the reader to separate legitimate concerns from cheap cynicism. (The statement that "everything is fixed" is really just a cover for laziness and ignorance.) More important, the chapter may help to indicate the areas which need reform, and the kinds of reforms which seem most appropriate. If "everything is fixed," then reform is out of the question, but if *some* things are "fixed," then the point is to un-fix them. The worst effect of cynicism is that it leads to a paralysis of will. If all efforts to reform the electoral system are dismissed as futile, it becomes that much more difficult to alter the status quo.

This does not mean that the Doubting Thomases who shared their skepticism with us in the preceding paragraphs were necessarily cynics. Their questions, indeed, deserve serious treatment. The remainder of this chapter will be mainly occupied with the task of answering three questions:

1   How rational are American voters?
2   How rational are American political campaigns?
3   How equally are Americans represented in the electoral process—is it really "one man, one vote"?

Let us begin with the most basic of these three questions.

HOW RATIONAL IS THE VOTER?

There is not much point in considering the flaws in our system of voting and campaigning if the voters themselves are basically irrational. Yet it is exactly this suspicion which surfaces so often during classroom discussions of American voting. The suspicion is that Americans really do not know what they are doing when they go into the polling booth—or at least that they can be easily manipulated by "hidden persuaders" and Madison Avenue tricks. Joe McGinnis's *The*

Selling of the President, which became a best seller when it was published in 1969, fed this suspicion. It left readers with the impression that Richard Nixon won the presidency in 1968 through the cunning use of media technology. One of the media specialists who worked on Nixon's campaign was quoted as saying: "Voters are basically lazy, basically uninterested in making an *effort* to understand. . . . Reason requires a high degree of discipline, of concentration; impression is easier. Reason pushes the viewer back, it assaults him, it demands that he agree or disagree; impression can envelop him, invite him in, without making an intellectual demand. . . ."[4]

The notion that voters can be "enveloped" by media specialists may be tantalizing, especially to media specialists, but little empirical evidence exists to support it. Despite Nixon's intensive use of elaborately staged commercials ("spontaneous" question-answering before hand-picked audiences), Hubert Humphrey continued to close the gap between the two as the campaign progressed. Nixon won, of course, but no one has ever demonstrated that he wouldn't have won anyway. Two years later, three of the biggest media spenders, Richard Ottinger of New York, Howard Metzenbaum in Ohio, and Sam Grossman in Arizona, lost their elections. One of the largest firms of professional image-makers, Bailey, Deardouff and Bowen, could not show a single winner among its major senate and gubinatorial races. While TV viewers are frequently impressed by documentaries and news shows, they maintain a healthy skepticism when it comes to political ads—even benevolent ones like antismoking commercials.[5] The effect of television on viewer opinion remains a shadowy area in political research. Social scientists have not gotten very far beyond Bernard Berelson's modest conclusion of a generation ago: "Some kinds of communication, on some kinds of issues, brought to the attention of some kinds of people, under some kinds of conditions, have some kind of effects."*

Whatever their reservations about voter rationality, then, few serious students of society and politics are ready to agree that the American voter can be manipulated by media hucksters. Yet social science research into voting behavior has sometimes painted a gloomy picture of the voter's rationality. Some of the classic studies of voting behavior during the 1950s and early 1960s suggested that the voter's choices were largely based upon whim, fancy, and unthinking habit. In 1954 three social scientists studied the behavior of voters in Elmira, New York, and concluded that political preferences in the town were based more on sentiment than reasoned choice and were characterized "more by faith than convic-

---

* Cf. Harold Mendelsohn and Irving Crespi, *Polls, Television and New Politics* (Scranton, Pa.: Chandler Publishing, 1970): "Whether or not televised political commercials actually affect the voter directly in terms of altering his choices is open to question—a question to which serious researchers have yet to address themselves." But see Thomas E. Patterson and Robert D. McClure, "Political Advertising: Voter Reaction," paper presented at the Annual Meeting of the American Association for Public Opinion Research: May 17–20, 1973 (mimeographed). The authors analyzed voter reaction to a series of "Democrats for Nixon" commercials and found a significant number to be influenced by some of the ads. The authors, however, do not lend any support to the notion that the commercials succeeded through "image making." On the contrary, "political commercials are probably more persuasive for more voters when they communicate issue, rather than image, information" (p. 2).

tion."⁶ In 1960 another team of social scientists found the "causes" of the voting decision to lie in such variables as socioeconomic status, education, and parental party preferences.⁷ While the latter study avoided explicit value judgments, the impression which emerges from it is that the voter is a kind of marionette, pulled this way by parents, that way by teachers, perhaps another way by peers, business associates, neighbors, and so on. Occasionally the voter may be pulled in contrary directions at the same time, and is then "cross-pressured." The voter is a passive creature, responding to an almost infinite variety of pushes and pulls, but incapable of making independent judgments based on his or her own self-interest. These and other studies of the American voter conducted during the 1950s and the early 1960s seemed to lend support to the view that the mass of people are turbulent, capricious, and incapable of real deliberation. One eminent political scientist worried that when too many people get involved in politics, "emotion rises and reasoned discussion declines."⁸ Another insisted that democratic freedom depends upon a certain degree of *non*participation: "The price of freedom is eternal vigilance for some and a modest disengagement for others."⁹

More recent studies, however, suggest that voting behavior may be more rational than the earlier research has indicated. One such study was that of V. O. Key, published posthumously in 1966 and entitled *The Responsible Electorate.* "The perverse and unorthodox argument of this little book," Key said at the outset, "is that voters are not fools."¹⁰ Key classified voters into three categories: "standpatters" (those who voted the same party in two or more successive elections), "switchers" (those who changed their party preference from one election to the next), and "new voters" (those voting for the first time). Delving back through a generation of public opinion poll data, Key found a correlation between people's opinions on issues and their choice of candidates and parties. The evidence, in other words, did not indicate that people vote blindly, or out of habit, or because they are pressured in some unconscious way. On the contrary, Key's correlations suggested that people make conscious and deliberate choices when they go to the polls: They choose to stick with a party or switch from it on the basis of how it stands on issues which they care about.

More recent research tends to corroborate Key's optimistic view of voter rationality. In a 1971 study using completely different methodology and data, David RePass reached a somewhat similar conclusion. In examining "salient issues" (issues of deep concern to the public), RePass found that the public is able to perceive and sort out differences between the parties. "On most issues, more than 60 percent of the respondents perceived party differences."¹¹ The Democratic party, for example, was identified with such social welfare measures as Medicare, Social Security, and aid to the poor. After 1964 the Democratic party was also identified with civil rights and integration. The Republican party was linked with a harder line on communism, state's rights, and fiscal conservatism. In the words of RePass, "we have shown that the public is in large measure concerned about specific issues, and that these cognitions have a considerable impact on electoral choice."¹² In 1972 Gerald Pomper also found that voters were able to distinguish parties on the basis of issue orientation. Examining voter reaction to six items—aid to education, medical care, job guarantees, fair employment, school integration, and foreign aid—Pomper found that the majority of voters had become increasingly aware of party differences during the sixties and had come to conclude that the Democratic Party was more liberal on these issues.[13] All this suggests an electorate which is alert to party differences, aware of issues, and ready to make rational choices in the voting booth instead of merely pulling levers blindly.

Independent Voters: Rationality Rediscovered
Since the beginning of the 1960s there has been a great increase in independent voting, particularly among young people. A Gallup poll published in mid-1974 showed 33 percent of the respondents identifying themselves as independents—10 percent more than those who called themselves Republicans. On some Northern urban campuses, more than 50 percent of the students identify themselves as independents.[14] The voting studies conducted during the 1950s and early 1960s generally concurred that independents were even more irrational than party loyalists—less informed and interested, more likely to shift with the tides, and less likely to have any real convictions. The authors of *The American Voter* in 1960 describe them as follows:

> Far from being more attentive, interested, and informed, Independents tend as a group to be somewhat less involved in politics. They have somewhat poorer knowledge of the issues, their image of the candidates is fainter, their interest in the campaign is less, their concern over the outcome is relatively slight, and their choice between competing candidates, although it is made later in the campaign, seems much less to spring from discoverable evaluations of the elements of national politics.[15]

This conclusion has also been challenged by more recent studies. Key in 1966 found a correlation between party switching and disagreement with the party on issues.[16] In the 1971 study by RePass it was discovered that independent voters were able to recall specific issues better than any other group except strong Republicans.[17] A study published in 1972 by Walter DeVries and V. Lance Terrance tends to reinforce this picture of the maverick voter as a discriminating and thoughtful citizen. Focusing on the political behavior of ticket-splitters, the authors found them well ahead of straight-party voters in participation in elections, political news-reading, discussion of candidates, and in being consulted by others for political opinions. The ticket-splitter reads more newspapers than the party loyalist, and is more likely to watch news and documentary shows on TV.

Voter Rationality: Summing Up
In summary, while the studies of voting behavior in the 1950s and early 1960s tended to depict the voter as ill-informed about issues and party differences (with independent voters being even more so than party loyalists), more recent research has been tending in the opposite direction: Most voters have a reasonably good idea of what they are voting for, and independents may be even more alert and discriminating than party regulars.

Some researchers, like Samuel Lubell, have maintained all along that the voter is basically rational. Lubell's studies of the American voter, which go back to the 1940s, have led him to this conclusion: "Over the last quarter of a century, my surveys show the voters have been basically rational, in that sense of self-interest is their strongest single motivation. Ditchdiggers are as rational as college professors and newspaper editors. . . . "[18]

During the fifties, Lubell's conclusion found little support among the nation's most prominent political scientists. That was when it was fashionable to debunk the "civics book" model of voters—people who think for themselves and make up their own minds on the basis of rational self-interest. Now the debunkers are themselves being debunked by a new generation of political scientists (plus those of the older generation who never minded being unfashionable).* The "civics book" model is indeed an ideal, but not an unapproachable one.

For the ideal to be approached, however, we need a system of voting and campaigning which provides us with some kind of coherent debate, which clarifies issues instead of obfuscating them, which gives us a choice of policies and programs instead of competing banalities. It is here, and not in any inherent irrationality of the voter, that the weaknesses of our system are most apparent.

HOW RATIONAL ARE AMERICAN POLITICAL CAMPAIGNS?

In some of the studies reviewed earlier it was noted that voters are able to perceive differences between party outlooks and philosophies. If this is so, the voters perceive more than we have a right to expect of them, because they get little help during the campaign season.

In practically every presidential race since 1936 the candidates and their campaign workers have fuzzed over and talked around policy differences, preferring to deal in personalities, scandals, and everything else under the sun except issues. In the fifties we had a liberal anticommunist Democrat (Adlai Stevenson) running against a moderate-to-liberal anticommunist Republican (Dwight D. Eisenhower). In 1960 Kennedy and Nixon ran against each other with no substantive difference on any issue except perhaps the defense of Quemoy and Matsu,

---

* Why the discrepancy between the earlier and later voting studies? In part, the answer may be that different historical periods were being studied. Campbell, and the other researchers whose studies seemed to point toward a pessimistic view of voter rationality, were looking at voters during the fifties, when the two major parties hugged the political "center" so tightly that their positions were almost identical. Small wonder that the average voter had trouble telling the difference between them! Some of the more recent voting studies, on the other hand, have covered voting behavior from 1964 onward, when the Republicans and Democrats began shifting to the right and left, respectively (at least on domestic issues). The voters, having perceived these differences, could now be pronounced rational.

This is not the whole story, however, since the studies by Key and Lubell vindicating the voter's rationality also covered voters from the fifties. Could it be that what we are dealing with is a tendency for "empirical" researchers to ferret out the facts which support their own ideology? It is impossible to read Key's last book or the recent writings of Lubell without catching the note of populism which runs through them. The purportedly "value-free" research of the fifties avoided open polemics, but it was not very difficult to perceive the authors' overall point of view: that people, *en masse*, are rather stupid.

which was almost as obscure an issue then as it is now. In 1968 we had Richard Nixon, who had a secret plan for ending the Vietnam war (he couldn't discuss it because of "national security") versus Hubert Humphrey, who spent most of the campaign trying to satisfy both hawks and doves. In only two presidential elections over the past generation, those of 1964 and 1972, did there seem to be much difference in the philosophies of the two major-party candidates. Even here, "philosophies" is too grand a word to describe the differences, which were painted in such gaudy colors that the candidates could not recognize their own portraits. Barry Goldwater in 1964 fell victim to Lyndon Johnson's TV commercials, which depicted him as a character out of *Dr. Strangelove* (a testimony not to the power of Madison Avenue but to the inanity of Goldwater's own ad libs—he once joked about what fun it would be to lob an atom bomb into the men's room of the Kremlin). George McGovern in 1972 was colored shocking pink by his opponents, some of whom came from within his own party, and he was never quite able to shake off his "triple A" rating: the candidate of "abortion, amnesty, and acid." (This was a malicious and misleading characterization, but McGovern never corrected it by a coherent presentation of his real views.)

The conventional political wisdom, at least among those who consider themselves seasoned hands at the game of politics, is that there *should not* be a great deal of difference between the platforms of the candidates. Both times during this generation when there was such a contrast (or seemed to be a contrast), in 1964 and 1972, the result was not just a victory but a landslide for one of the candidates—which in turn puffed him up with arrogance and delusions of grandeur. But the real danger, warns the salty old observer of American politics, is not the danger of tyranny but the danger of see-saw policy making. Landslides, first by one side and then by the other, threaten to cause American policies to veer wildly back and forth, depending on who has gotten the landslide and what set of policies has been so enthusiastically approved (or denounced: Landslides tend to be *against* the policy positions of the loser).[19] Ironically, it is argued, all this fighting over "extreme" positions really goes against the grain of most Americans. Most folks in this great land of ours, it is said, prefer candidates who do not stray away from the political "center," who take "moderate" stands on issues instead of getting "radical" about them.[20]

One problem with the above analysis lies in its undefined terms. What is meant by the "center"? What is a "moderate"? Where *is* the "center," and how do we know when we are standing in it? The center, at least in America, seems to be constantly shifting. Yesterday's "moderate" has a way of becoming tomorrow's "reactionary."

If "moderate" has no fixed meaning in terms of substance, perhaps it has something to do with method. Perhaps it means "a disposition to avoid any use of force or violence to attain one's goal." But if that were the accepted definition, those who argue that the majority of Americans are moderates would not have an easy time proving their case. A majority of Americans polled after the 1968 Democratic convention approved of Chicago Mayor Daley's immoderate way of handling street demonstrators. (The demonstrators were not moderate either, but extremism checked by extremism does not equal moderation.) Suppose we try another definition of "moderation": "a tendency to favor only incremental changes in society; gradualism." That definition, too, is fraught with perils for those who believe that the majority of Americans are "moderates." Public opinion polls indicate that a majority of Americans are receptive to a number of substantial changes in the status quo: comprehensive tax reforms, national health insurance, gun control, and other more-than-incremental changes which our "moderate" politicians have yet to enact.*

It is quite true, of course, that large majorities of Americans were repelled by Barry Goldwater and George McGovern, two avowedly noncentrist candidates. It has yet to be shown, however, that these two "extremists" were rejected because of their platforms or positions on issues. Indeed, a good case can be made that it was not the substance of what they talked about as much as it was the *manner* in which they talked.[21] What were Americans to make of a candidate who proposed awarding a thousand dollars to every man, woman, and child in the land, while admitting he had no idea what it would cost—and who then turned around and repudiated this proposal later in the campaign? (Then there was McGovern's more famous turnabout, also involving the figure of a thousand: "I support Senator Eagleton 1,000 percent," he said of his running mate, only to dump him shortly thereafter.) Can we blame the American voters for seeing something frivolous in these two prophets? Were Goldwater and McGovern really "radical"? "Radical" comes from the Latin word for "root," which is what both of them seemed to be lacking—roots, depth, steadiness, and constancy.

In short, there are no legitimate grounds for believing that Americans prefer issueless campaigns, want only incremental changes, or have no taste for genuine debate. Indeed, it may even be argued that they are becoming increasingly frustrated because issues are *not* being clarified and genuine choices are *not* being given them when they go to the polls. After the 1972 presidential campaign one political observer became so disgusted that he recommended "voting by abstention"—refusing to participate in any future elections until politicians stop insulting our intelligence during their campaigns. Americans, he said, should lay down the following conditions before they return to the polls: "Quit lying. Quit hiding the truth, quit misrepresenting. Quit being all things to all people. Try, for a change, to be *some* things to *some* people."[22] Is it not possible that Americans *have* increasingly been "voting by abstention" since 1960? This is one way to interpret the increasing fall-off in voting since that year. If it is a correct interpretation, then the present mood of apathy and cynicism cannot be dispelled by new slogans or new faces. Hiring new public relations people will, if anything, make

---

* Of course, a fundamental revision of our tax code and other like reforms may not be considered "radical" by many self-styled "radicals." It must be conceded that the majority of Americans reject any "ism" which *sounds* radical: "socialism," "communism," "fascism," and so on. But once we get away from terrifying labels and down to the substance of concrete proposals, Americans are much more receptive to change and innovation than the "moderate" ideologists give them credit for. The student may wish to try an experiment: ask someone—anyone, an uncle, a cousin—for an opinion of "socialism." Then ask the same person whether the government should take over the oil companies if they persist in raising their prices while making high profits.

matters worse. The gloom will be dispelled—or at least the chances for dispelling it will be greater—when the politicians start giving Americans a taste of real debate on real issues, instead of commercials, name-calling, staged media "events," and other forms of trickery.

But if all the above is correct, we still must ask this question: What can we do to encourage candidates to "quit hiding the truth, quit misrepresenting" and "being all things to all people"?

One way of pinning down candidates on issues is to face them off against each other in broadcast debates. By themselves, such debates do not insure that issues will be clarified. Nixon and Kennedy faced each other in a series of TV debates in 1960 without clearly defining policy differences. The format of those debates, however, was very loose—it left little opportunity for rebuttal, cross-examination, or follow-up questions. A tighter format might have squeezed more substance out of the candidates. Even so, the debates of 1960 produced some remarkable effects upon many of those who watched them. Among the 80 million people who watched at least one of the debates—an astounding figure in a nation supposedly bored by politics—about half discussed the debates within twenty-four hours. One postdebate survey asked people how the debates might be improved and found 70 percent able to volunteer suggestions. The same study gave a sixteen-item information test to its respondents and found them able not only to recall at least some of what was said, but to recall it on a nonselective basis: Kennedy partisans were able to recall what Nixon said and vice versa. This "is an extraordinary finding, suggesting that the debates not only overcame the well-known tendency toward selective exposure (which insulates one from opposition arguments) but also—at least as far as information is concerned—the tendency to perceive and recall selectively."[23] It may be more than a coincidence that so many voters turned out to vote in 1960.

The 1960 debates between Kennedy and Nixon were possible only because Congress temporarily suspended the "equal time" provision of section 315 of the Communications Act—the provision which states that if the networks are to donate time for political speeches they must do it on an equal basis. (Without that suspension, the debates would have become a cacophony of voices as every minor candidate demanded equal time.) In 1964 President Johnson decided he had nothing to gain from debating Barry Goldwater, so he advised his legislative leaders not to seek suspension of section 315. A similar nonevent occurred in 1968. Former FCC chairman Newton Minow observed that "the tragedy of the 1968 campaign on TV and radio is that what we are getting is each candidate's own appeal (paid political broadcasts) without confrontation to draw a comparison."[24] In 1972 the tragedy was compounded when an incumbent President barely acknowledged the existence of an opponent.

What is needed, then, is a way of forcing candidates and incumbents out from behind the smokescreen of paid ads, but the only way in which this can be done is through some modification of section 315. Otherwise equal time would have to be allotted not only to serious candidacies but to those from a scatter of minor parties, some of them frivolous.

Yet repeating the practice of 1960 would be unfair to third parties with a large following, such as George Wallace's in 1968. One way out of this dilemma is the proposal made by the Twentieth Century Fund in 1969: not "equal time" but "voter's time." The federal government would purchase a block of time from the networks at half the usual charge and distribute it to the candidates. Six half-hour broadcasts would be allowed to the candidates of the major parties, while minor candidates on the ballots of three-quarters or more of the states and getting at least one-eighth of the popular vote in the preceding election would be allowed two thirty-minute programs. This would still be unfair to minor parties, especially those which had come into being since the last election, but the inequity might be corrected by permitting candidates who could obtain a certain number of signatures to be included in a second round of free air time. The principle, without trying to spell out all the details, is what Herbert E. Alexander calls "differential equality of access," the principle "that major candidates are equal to major candidates, that minor candidates are equal to minor candidates, and that the two are not equal to each other. If a group grows or at the outset looks significant, it can jump to major status."[25]

In 1970 Congress passed a bill which would at least have touched upon some of the objectives outlined above. The Political Broadcast Act of 1970 would have *(a)* repealed the "equal-time" provision of section 315 as it applied to the presidential race, *(b)* compelled broadcasters to charge candidates no more than the "lowest unit rate," and *(c)* set limitations on the amounts candidates could spend for broadcast time. The bill passed both houses of Congress but was vetoed by President Nixon. The following year a broader bill (which set limits on spending not only for air time but for newspaper and billboard ads as well, and which provided for campaign fund disclosure) was passed and signed by President Nixon. The 1971 act survived at the expense of the equal-time repeal, which was scuttled in the House of Representatives, reportedly because of pressure from the White House. But the impetus remains strong for some sort of arrangement which will permit Americans to watch presidential candidates face each other in open debate. Debates would amount to only one tiny step toward penetrating the humbug which surrounds our national campaigns. Another step might be to abolish spot commercials—those slick little TV dramatizations which let us watch the shirt-sleeved candidate strolling through the slums while a voice tells us, earnestly and in about thirty seconds, how the candidate will save Western civilization. The spot commercial is inherently mendacious, and if the FCC can ban misleading advertising without incurring the wrath of the American Civil Liberties Union, it should be able to ban misleading political ads.

Of course a certain amount of publicity must be given to candidates, especially the newer faces, in order that they become familiar to the public. But there are other ways to do it. Our news media should take the responsibility of seeking out potential candidates who have something worth saying, something new to offer, some important issue to discuss. Political parties can also assist by drafting platforms with substance in them, seeking out candidates with fresh ideas, and providing them with organizational support instead of forcing them to buy support from Madison Avenue.

By themselves, neither TV debates, nor the abolition of spot commercials, nor the cooperation of the media and the parties, can end all the noise pollution in our campaigns and get them centered on issues. But if the public itself shows that it demands more than slogans like "Trust Muskie," that it wants greater discussion of the grounds for trust, it might begin to get its way. This can be done in a number of ways: by writing letters to newspapers demanding that the candidates clarify themselves on issues, by supporting and working for candidates who do have something to say—and who are not afraid to say it. Naturally, we tend to support those with whom we agree, but perhaps candor itself deserves some sort of reward. When the English philosopher John Stuart Mill ran for Parliament in 1865, one of his opponent's supporters tried to put him on the spot at a public meeting. Mill recounted the incident in his *Autobiography:*

> In the pamphlet, *Thoughts on Parliamentary Reform,* I had said, rather bluntly, that the working classes, though differing from those of some other countries in being ashamed of lying, are yet generally liars. This passage some opponent got printed in a placard, which was handed to me at a meeting, chiefly composed of the working classes, and I was asked whether I had written and published it. I at once answered, "I did." Scarcely were these two words out of my mouth, when vehement applause resounded through the whole meeting. It was evident that the working people were so accustomed to expect equivocation and evasion from those who sought their suffrages that when they found, instead of that, a direct avowal of what was likely to be disagreeable to them, instead of being affronted, they concluded at once that this was a person whom they could trust.[26]

Mill won the election.

Earlier in this chapter we discussed the question of voter rationality and concluded, with V. O. Key, that "voters are not fools." If anything can be called foolish, we went on to contend, it is not the voter but the political campaign. We then looked into a few suggestions for bringing the spirit of discussion—"the spirit of giving as well as taking, and of learning as well as teaching"—into American campaigns.

There remains at least one more reason for the current cynicism about politics. This is the widespread suspicion that elites and special interests exert more power over elections than do the majority of voters. This brings us to the last of the three questions to be examined in this chapter.

IS IT REALLY "ONE MAN, ONE VOTE"?

In theory, democracy rests upon the principle of "one man, one vote." If one person literally were to cast two, three, or many ballots it would surely be scandalous. Such scandals have indeed occurred in American political history (one local political boss used to urge his followers to "vote early and often"), but they belong largely to our colorful past. More recent examples of weighted voting have taken subtler forms. It was not until the sixties that, thanks to the Supreme Court of Earl Warren, America began to eliminate another kind of weighted voting—which results from the unequal apportionment of voting districts.

Malapportionment

Nearly all members of Congress and state legislators in America are elected from geographical districts, each district being represented by one representative or legislator. So far so good. In many states, however, the population variation between districts has been tremendous. One district might be two, four, or even eight times as large as another in terms of population. The effect of this imbalance has been to give voters in less populated areas greater weight in Congress or the state legislatures than those voters in more populated areas. Putting it another way, those living in the more populated areas were being cheated out of the number of representatives they would have gotten if the legislative districts were drawn according to the principle of equal population. Typically, "malapportionment"—the creation or maintenance of unequal legislative districts—benefited rural, thinly populated areas at the expense of cities and suburbs.

As a result of a series of decisions by the Warren Court,[27] nearly every state in the Union was forced to redraw both its congressional and state legislative districts during the 1960s. November 1972 marked the first time in the nation's history that members of congress were elected from districts of nearly equal population. By that time the state legislatures had also been reapportioned in conformity with the principle of "one man, one vote."

Yet weighted voting is far from being abolished in America. True, the weighted voting which resulted from malapportionment has been significantly reduced, but another form of weighted voting continues to plague our electoral process. Color it green.

Money in Elections

All voters have one and only one vote to bestow upon the candidate of their choice, but some voters have something else to give: large chunks of money. The candidates, of course, are grateful to all the good citizens who voted for them—but do they not have special reason to be grateful to those who kept their campaigns afloat by their financial generosity? And aren't there some obvious ways for elected officials to express their gratitude? Senator Joseph R. Biden, Jr., Senator from Delaware, told of going to a coffee sponsored by a labor union which was considering giving $5,000 to either him or his rival. After a bit of small talk, the question was asked bluntly: "Well, Joe, had you been in the 92nd Congress, how would you have voted on the SST [the Supersonic Transport plane, strongly supported by the unions] and while you're at it, how would you have voted on bailing out Lockheed?" "Now," Biden later testified, "I may be a naïve feller, but I knew the right answer for $5,000." Later in the same campaign, a group of Delaware millionaires invited him over for drinks, and began cross-examining him about his support for tax reform. "One fellow leans over and sort of pats me on the knee in a fatherly fashion and, as if to say, 'It's just among us,' says to me, 'Joe, you really don't mean what you say about capital gains, do you?' Now I knew the right answer to that one for $20,000."[28] To Biden's credit, he failed to provide the "right answers" to these questions, but he had to mortgage his house to pay for the campaign, and he won by a mere 1 percent of the vote. We are expecting too much of human nature if we assume that all candidates for office will do as poorly on campaign quiz shows as Joe Biden did in 1972.

Every voter votes with ballots, which are usually distributed equally, but some people also vote with dollars, which are not distributed equally. "When a politician's success depends on a combination of dollars and votes, the Nation is clearly less democratic than it would be if a victory depended on votes alone," said Senator Philip A. Hart of Michigan during hearings on campaign financing.[29] "The weighting of voting according to one's wealth is hostile to our system of government," said Justice William O. Douglas in dissenting from a Burger Court decision which permitted large landowners greater representation in water storage districts.[30] Douglas's words might also be applied to the still unresolved problem of money in politics. "The weighting of voting according to one's wealth" is perhaps best exemplified by the enormous, often secret, campaign contributions from wealthy donors. A person does not have to be unduly suspicious to entertain the thought that these generous gifts will yield equally generous dividends for those who contributed them.

In the wake of Watergate, the public's suspicions were raised to new heights. Here are two cases out of many others which came to light:

The Milk Deal In the first few weeks of March 1971, the Secretary of Agriculture, "after careful review of the situation and the provisions of law," refused to raise price supports for the raw milk used in making butter and cheese. On March 22, a major dairy lobby donated $10,000 to Republican committees. The next day the President and Secretary of Agriculture met with sixteen dairy-industry leaders, who urged them to reconsider. The day after that, another dairy lobby put $25,000 more into Republican committees. The following day the Secretary of Agriculture announced that milk prices could go up, after all. Dairy groups later contributed $442,500 to the Nixon reelection campaign.

ITT Early in 1972 the columnist Jack Anderson published a memo purportedly written by Dita Beard, a lobbyist for International Telephone and Telegraph, stating that ITT's "noble commitment" of $400,000 for the Republican National Convention "has gone a long way toward our negotiations on the mergers eventually coming out as Hal [ITT President Harold S. Geneen] wants them." The merger in question was the attempt by ITT to take over the Hartford Fire Insurance Company, and Anderson alleged that the $400,000 contribution was the reason for the Justice Department's decision to settle its suit against ITT out of court. At the time Mrs. Beard claimed that the memo attributed to her was a forgery, and the administration denied any involvement in the affair. A year and a half later, however, a secret memo introduced into evidence at the Watergate hearings lent considerable support to the Anderson charges. Written by Charles W. Colson, a former White House adviser, the memo described pressures brought on the Justice Department to drop the case from Attorney General Mitchell, John Ehrlichman, the President's domestic adviser, Treasury Secretary John Connally, and Vice President Agnew.

One of George McGovern's more prophetic utterances during his ill-fated 1972 campaign was his contention that the Nixon administration was "the most corrupt in the nation's history." Yet the problems of big contributions—and the suspicion of favors in return—can hardly be said to have originated with the Nixon administration. It was under Presidents Kennedy and Johnson that the Democratic party began systematically cultivating its relationships with rich contributors through such devices as "The President's Club." Although membership in this elite financial constituency cost only $1,000, its object was to stimulate larger contributions from wealthy members. The club operated in an aura of secrecy, snobbery, and inside-dopesterism. It offered a variety of functions, from which the press was excluded, ranging from dinners and receptions with the President to special seminars chaired by high White House officials. Between 1961 and the end of 1966 the President's Club accounted for nearly one-third of all the funds raised by events at which either the President or the Vice President appeared.

Defenders of this form of fund-raising argued that it was nothing more than a harmless appeal to social one-upmanship, but critics pointed to instances of what appeared to be more tangible rewards for contributions to the President's Club. In 1966, for example, it was revealed that officers of Anheuser-Busch, the nation's largest brewery, contributed (with their wives) a total of $10,000 to the club: A few weeks later the Justice Department dropped an antitrust suit against the company. It was also discovered that Vice President Humphrey, together with the head of the Justice Department's antitrust division, was flown to St. Louis during the airlines strike in the company's private plane for the All-Star baseball game and a pregame luncheon at the President's Club. Another series of revelations which embarrassed the Johnson administration in 1966 concerned the awarding of government contracts to prominent contributors and members of the President's Club. In one case involving the Office of Economic Opportunity, the firm winning the contract was not even among those originally recommended by the staff of OEO. In another contract involving the Veterans Administration, the member of the President's Club who won it was also a member of the John Birch Society. A Bircher would not be likely to contribute to a Democratic fund-raising club because of ideological agreement with the party!

In congressional campaigns the role of big money has been even more extensively documented—and more candidly admitted. When a former Maryland congressman who had served as chairman of the Merchant Marine Committee was questioned about the heavy contributions he received from the maritime industry, he said, "Who in the hell did they expect me to get it from—the post office people, the bankers? You get it from the people you work with, who you helped in some way or another. It's only natural."[31] A member of the Senate Finance Committee, when asked why he sponsored several tax amendments that would favor a particular industry, answered simply, "That's the way we finance our campaigns. Hell, I wish there was a tax bill every year."[32]

The scandal of campaign financing, then, goes far beyond one administration, branch of government, or (in Nixon administration jargon) "point in time." It has deeper roots, connected with the rising costs of campaigning, the availability of big money, the increased power and prestige of government, the inadequacy of existing laws, and the lack of any serious intent to enforce them.

Rising Costs Campaign costs have sharply escalated in recent years. Part of the reason for the increases has to do with the growing size of the electorate, but the staggering rise in spending since 1952 is out of proportion to numbers of voters. The cost-per-vote varied considerably from 1919 to 1952—from a high of almost 32¢ in 1928 to a low of 10.5¢ in 1944—but after each rise the cost would drop down again. After 1952, however, the costs per vote have gone steadily upward. In 1964 a new record of 35¢ was reached only to be nearly doubled, to 60¢, in 1968 (even if George Wallace's expenditures are excluded, the cost still was 51¢ per vote). In 1972 the Republicans alone spent between $55 and $58 million to reelect President Nixon—about one and a half times the *combined* expenditures for Humphrey and Nixon in 1968. Even Maurice Stans, Nixon's indefatigable fund-raiser, was reported to be somewhat embarrassed over the total.[33]

Large Contributors   Where has this money come from? Disproportionately, it has come from "fat cats"—large contributors with plenty of money to give. The Democrats, as we have seen, courted the very rich when they occupied the White House, and the Republicans had their turn during the Nixon administration. In 1972 the President's top ten contributors gave more than $4 million, the top 100 $14 million.[34] One man, W. Clement Stone of Chicago, who gave Nixon $2 million in 1972, reported that the President had said to him on two occasions: "Clem, you and I know that I wouldn't be here if it weren't for you."[35] Stone later acknowledged that he gave Nixon a total of $4.8 million in unreported contributions since 1968; he added that he was prepared to make it $10 million.

Perhaps in most cases individual big contributors like Stone expect nothing in return but the chance to rub shoulders with the powerful and hear their praises sung. But government, today more than ever, has assumed enormous and far-reaching responsibilities. Its regulatory machinery can either benefit or crush the large corporate enterprises with which it comes in contact. Today's big money must know where its bread is buttered. Members of Congress have been known to set up "cinch" amendments imposing severe restrictions on certain types of business, which are then withdrawn after the appropriate contribution is received.[36] President Nixon's campaign staff drew up a list of corporations "who have problems with the government" in order to shake them down for contributions. (By the end of August 1973, American Airlines and five other large corporations had admitted to giving illegal contributions to the Nixon campaign fund after being approached by campaign staffers. Within the next month another dozen corporations made similar disclosures.) Sometimes these donors are later double-crossed—they don't get the favors they are paying for—but this has not noticeably slowed the flow of "protection money."

Laws Regulating Campaign Contributions
Since 1907 corporate contributions to federal campaigns have been outlawed, and in 1943 and 1947 this prohibition was extended to labor unions. "Prohibition" is indeed the right word, for these laws, like the others regulating campaign financing, have suffered the same fate as antiliquor laws: They have either been evaded or ignored. Among the imaginative ways used to avoid the ban on corpo-

rate contributions were the following: donation of company goods and services, program book advertising, raises and expense accounts to reimburse company employees for contributions, and the use of "fronts" to channel money.

Another statute governing campaign financing, which Lyndon Johnson once called "more loophole than law," was the Federal Corrupt Practices Act of 1925. This statute required disclosure of receipts and expenditures by candidates for the Senate and House (but not for President or Vice President) and by political committees which sought to influence elections in two or more states. As amended, the act also limited to $5,000 the total amount any individual could give to a single candidate or campaign committee in a year. It limited the amount Senate and House candidates could spend to $25,000 and $5,000, respectively, and set an overall limit of $3 million which a single campaign committee could spend. Finally, it imposed a progressive gift tax on any contributions in excess of $3,000 to a single candidate or committee in a year.

One loophole in this law was its definition of a "campaign committee" as one operating in two or more states. The $3 million spending limitation was bypassed merely by setting up committees on a one-state level. Another loophole permitted individual contributors to bypass the $5,000 contribution limit by giving to several different committees supporting the same candidate—one reason for the proliferation of "good government" and "citizens for" committees during election years.

But detailed study of the loopholes in the Federal Corrupt Practices Act is beside the point, because during its forty-seven-year history the act was almost never enforced. The reason: Enforcement was left mainly to the Justice Department—and Attorneys General have been reluctant to prosecute their own party donors and fearful of eventual reprisals if they were to prosecute those of the opposition.* The hypocrisy finally ended in 1971 when the law was repealed.

Federal Election Campaign Act of 1972

At the end of 1971 Congress passed the Federal Election Campaign Act. Among the major provisions of the act are these five:

1 Candidates for federal office were limited to 10¢ per eligible voter in the amount they can spend on radio, television, newspapers, magazines, billboards, and automated telephone systems. (This provision, however, was repealed in 1974 by a new campaign spending law which set limits on *overall* expenditures.)

2 For a specified period before elections the broadcast media may charge candidates no more than the "lowest unit rate"—the amount which they would charge their best customers.

---

* One student of the subject put it this way: "No administration is likely to vigorously enforce the campaign finance laws against its own party membership, nor will they enforce them against the other party for fear of reciprocal treatment when party control changes." "Comment—The Federal Election Campaign Act of 1971, Reform of the Political Process," *Georgetown Law Journal,* May 1972, reprinted in U.S. Senate, 93d Congress, *Hearings on Federal Election Campaign Act of 1973, Subcommittee on Communications, Committee on Commerce,* Mar. 7–13, 1973, p. 398.

3 A "Rockefeller clause": Candidates for President or Vice President may contribute no more than $50,000 to their own campaigns; similar limitations for Senators and Representatives are $35,000 and $25,000, respectively.

4 Corporations and unions with government contracts may not directly contribute to political campaigns.

5 Comprehensive disclosure requirements: Political committees for candidates must register with federal agencies, providing the names of principal officers, the scope of the committee, and other information. They must report the total cash on hand, receipts, expenditures, as well as the name, address, and occupation of everyone contributing more than $100, and make all such information available to the public as well as to appropriate federal officers.

The Federal Election Campaign Act was the most comprehensive reform legislation passed by Congress since the enactment of the Corrupt Practices Act of 1925. Since the old law had proven unworkable and had been largely unenforced, Congress repealed it at the same time that it passed the new bill, which was signed—and praised—by President Nixon in February of 1972. "By giving the American public full access to the facts of political financing," the President said, "this legislation will guard against campaign abuses and will work to build public confidence in the integrity of the electoral process."

In retrospect the words seem ironic. During the Watergate investigations it was discovered that top-level White House advisers, including Stans, Mitchell, Haldeman, and Ehrlichman, had instructed their congressional liaison to slow down the bill's passage so that Republican fund-raisers could raise more money. Nixon himself waited the full limit of ten days before signing the bill, and his reelection committee had already begun a strategy of maximum fund-raising between the expiration of the old law (March 10) and the effective date of the new one (April 7). The Finance Committee to Reelect the President organized a squad of four to six "pickup men" to rove the country and collect money. The result was a torrent of contributions, some of them arriving after the April 7 deadline. In one two-day period the Finance Committee's office, according to one of its secretaries, became a "madhouse."[37]

This cynical evasion of the disclosure requirements in the new law was challenged by Common Cause, a citizen's lobby. In September of 1972 Common Cause sued the Finance Committee under the disclosure provisions of the *old* law, demanding that the committee make full disclosure of the pre-April 7 money. Two months later Common Cause had won a partial settlement, and in July of 1973 a full victory: A Federal District judge ordered the committee to make a full disclosure of all its contributors up to April 7.*

---

* *New York Times,* July 25, 1973, p. 32. Common Cause also began monitoring the new law, and here it met stiff resistance from within Congress. One of those who failed to report his campaign finances on time was Democratic Congressman Wayne Hays of Ohio, chairman of the committee which drafted the new law. When Hays's delinquency was made public, he raised the price of Xerox copies from 10¢ to $1.00 per sheet—a price no citizen's group could afford. This was subsequently reversed by a court decision.

Besides the disclosure requirements in the new law, another key provision is the one making it

From the very date of its enactment, then, some rather frenzied efforts were undertaken to get around the spending and disclosure regulations of the Campaign Finance Law of 1971. The scandalous fact is that if it were not for alert citizens, our campaign laws, new and old, would have been serenely ignored by the very agency charged with enforcing them. In this respect Nixon's Justice Department was no more lax than any of its predecessors, nor is there any reason to expect that future Justice Departments will be any more vigilant. The danger, then, is that the Campaign Act of 1972 could eventually suffer the fate of the Corrupt Practices Act of 1925 by becoming another relic of transient concern, unenforced and nearly forgotten as the years go by.

Broadly, two different methods of dealing with this problem have been considered by Congress. More than methods, they involve two different diagnoses of the whole problem of campaign financing.

The first diagnosis contends that previous reform efforts have been meaningless because they failed to decisively strangle, once and for all, the flow of big money into campaigns. The easy availability of this sort of money is the root both of extravagance and of influence-peddling during the campaign season. Unless the nation shows an iron will to prohibit large contributions, the corruption which surfaced so dramatically in 1973 will continue to plague future campaigns. What we need, then, are tougher laws banning "fat cat" contributions, and tougher machinery for enforcing these laws. Contributions, from whatever source, in excess of a stipulated amount, should be banned: Stiff penalities should be meted out to those violating the law. And enforcement should not be left up to a politics-ridden Justice Department. What is needed is an independent, bipartisan, nonpolitical agency to superintend these laws, letting the chips fall where they may when it comes to punishing offenders.

The foregoing analysis might be characterized as the hard-line, or "stick," approach. The "carrot" approach, on the other hand emphasizes inducements to avoid "fat cat" money instead of prohibitions against receiving it. According to Herbert Alexander, who has been studying campaign financing since 1962, our campaigns are not so much overpriced as underfinanced. What is needed is some means of reducing the disproportionate weight of big money and encouraging grass-roots financial support. While Alexander supports the concept of public disclosure in the Campaign Finance Act of 1972, he opposes spending limitations on the grounds that they may be both unenforceable and unconstitutional. Instead, as a means of weaning our politicians away from large campaign contributors, he favors the use of public subsidies.[38]

Subsidies and Tax Check-offs: The Revenue Act of 1971

Probably few Americans realized it in 1973, but a form of limited subsidy had already been passed by Congress two years earlier. An amendment to the Reve-

---

a crime for anyone holding a government contract to give campaign contributions "directly or indirectly." After Common Cause successfully sued a defense contractor for violating this provision, the House of Representatives—swiftly and without benefit of public hearings—repealed the provision. After a flurry of indignant publicity, however, the repeal bill failed to pass the Senate.

nue Act of 1971 provided for both a tax credit and a check-off system. The first provision lets contributors claim a tax credit of 50 percent of their contributions to a campaign, up to a limit of $25 for a joint return ($12.50 for a single return). Thus a couple who give $25 to a candidate or party are given back $12.50 by the Internal Revenue Service in the form of a credit against taxes owed. The second provision proved to be more controversial. It permits taxpayers to stipulate that $1 of their tax money ($2 on a joint return) should go to the party of their choice, or to a neutral fund if they favor no particular party. The money is then appropriated for use in presidential campaigns in accordance with a formula which would provide roughly $20 million to major candidates and a fraction of that amount to minor candidates, depending on the number of votes they received in the previous election. Any presidential candidate choosing this method of financing would be prohibited from soliciting private donations.

The fund-starved Democrats endorsed this amendment, but it was almost unanimously opposed by the Republicans, including President Nixon. After it was attached to the Revenue Act of 1971 in the Senate, Nixon threatened to veto the entire bill unless it was withdrawn. At the last minute a compromise was reached. House-Senate conferences retained the amendment but delayed its effective date until January 1, 1973—too late for the fateful 1972 presidential election!

S 3044 (1974): Carrot and Stick

S 3044 (Senate bill number 3044), an otherwise untitled piece of legislation which cleared Congress and was signed by President Ford at the end of 1974, combined both the "carrot" and the "stick" strategies discussed above.

Public Financing: The Carrot S 3044 provides public financing of Presidential elections, primaries, and national conventions. Any Democrat or Republican who wants to enter the presidential primaries may receive as much as $4.5 million in public funds *provided* that the candidate first raises $100,000 in small private contributions ($250 or less) from at least twenty states. The candidate must also agree to hold down prenomination spending to $10 million. In addition, the law provides $2 million for each major party convention, presumably to induce them to avoid the ITT method of financing their conventions (see above, p. 128).

Limits on Spending and Contributions: The Stick Now for the stick. S 3044 sets strict limits both on spending and on contributions. It stiffens disclosure requirements. And it provides a special enforcement commission to insure that the law is not administered by the Justice Department—which, as we have seen, has a very shoddy history of enforcing campaign spending laws. Let us look at these three aspects of S 3044 more closely.

Besides the $10 million *total* spending for primary elections, which was mentioned above, the 1974 law sets limits on spending *per state*. Thus, a presidential candidate could spend no more on a primary in a single state than twice the amount a Senate candidate would be allowed to spend in a primary. And how much is that? Senate candidates, under S 3044, are allowed to spend no more than $100,000, or 8 cents per eligible voter, whichever is greater. Thus, in a sparsely populated state like Alaska, the candidates would adhere to the fixed limit of $100,000, but in a state like California the Senate candidates would be better off following the 8-cents-per-voter limit, which would allow them to spend over a million dollars for a primary in that state. The presidential candidate would thus be able to spend over two million dollars in a California primary, but only $200,000 in Alaska. The 1974 law also sets spending limits on House primaries, and on the general elections for President, Senate, and House, using formulas along the same lines as that just described—fixed ceilings for the small states and per-voter ceilings for the large states.

As for limits on contributions, individuals are limited to overall contributions of $25,000 in a single year and no more than $3,000 to an individual candidate—$1,000 each in the primaries, a run-off (if there is one), and the general election. Organizations are limited to contributions of $5,000 in each of the three possible races for one candidate.

Disclosure Requirements The law requires each candidate to establish one central campaign committee through which all expenditures must be reported. These reports must be made ten days before and thirty days after every election, plus once a year during nonelection years. Contributions of $1,000 or more received within the last fifteen days before election must be reported within forty-eight hours. Any organization which spends any money to influence an election, even if it does no more than publicize the voting record of a member of Congress, must file reports as a political committee. (In the summer of 1975 this last provision was found to be unconstitutionally "vague and overbroad" by a U. S. Court of Appeals.)

Elections Commission The law creates an eight-member, full-time Federal Elections Commission, with enforcement powers, to be responsible for administering election laws and the public financing program. Here, many observers feel, is the heart of the 1974 law. If the Elections Commission enforces the law with the same enthusiasm, or lack of it, with which the Justice Department enforced the campaign spending laws in the past, it will be a nullity. The hope is that this special commission will display more zeal.

Although S 3044 cleared both houses of Congress by large margins, it was criticized harshly by those who felt it did not go far enough, as well as by those who felt that it went too far. On the one hand, Senator Edward Kennedy of Massachusetts pointed to a "glaring deficiency" in the law: its failure to provide public financing of congressional campaigns. (The original Senate version of the bill had provided such financing for Senate and House races, but that provision had been deleted as part of a compromise worked out by House and Senate conferees.) Abuses of campaign spending, Kennedy contended, "do not stop at the other end of Pennsylvania Avenue."[39] Yet for Senator James B. Allen of Alabama and other conservative critics, public financing even of presidential races seems to be nothing more or less than a raid on the treasury.

Critics of the new campaign finance law, who ranged from Conservative

Senator James Buckley on the right to former Senator Eugene McCarthy on the left, took their case to court, charging, among other things, that the statute violated free speech by limiting the amount candidates could spend to express themselves in the political "marketplace." By mid-1975 they had carried their case to the U. S. Court of Appeals for the District of Columbia—and lost. The court, by a 6-2 margin, rejected their contention that the new law constituted a "massive intrusion" into the political process. Acknowledging the failure of past reform efforts, the court majority nevertheless insisted that "these latest efforts on the part of our Government to cleanse its democratic processes should at least be given a chance to prove themselves. Certainly they should not be rejected because they might have some incidental, not clearly defined, effect on First Amendment freedoms." The court also upheld the public subsidy provisions. The only part of the statute found unconstitutional was the one requiring detailed financial statements from any organization which spends money to influence an election; as noted above, the court considered this section "vague and overbroad."[40]

Whatever the eventual fate of S·3044, it certainly represents a bold attempt by Congress to come to grips with the problem of the big contributors, whose money makes them, in George Orwell's phrase, "more equal than others" in the American election process. Any form of public financing would have seemed visionary at the beginning of the seventies. Yet by that time the United States was the only mature democracy in the world in which election costs were not paid for by the government. It took the scandal of Watergate to jolt the nation's lawmakers into taking this unprecedented step toward eliminating, in the words of Senator Walter Mondale of Minnesota, "the profound, smelly, stinking corruption of money in politics."[41]

CONCLUSION

In *The People, Yes,* Carl Sandburg wrote the famous words: "Sometime they'll give a war and nobody will come."[42] An equally populist ideal might be expressed this way: "Sometime they'll give an election and everybody will come." But to the political scientists of the 1950s and early 1960s, this ideal was a dangerous one. Too many people involved in the political process meant, for them, a rise in fanaticism and unreason. As we noted earlier, one of them suggested that "the price of freedom is eternal vigilance for some and a modest disengagement for others."[43] Over the past decade or so, this kind of smug condescension has been gradually dispelled as more recent studies of political behavior have shown that voters "are not fools" and that "ditchdiggers are as rational as college professors."

So the problem of nonvoting, the "modest disengagement," is nothing to be complacent about. It is a scandal—there is no better word for it—when about 40 percent of eligible voters do not bother to show up at the polls to elect the most powerful officer of a supposedly "democratic" nation. What is more, the "modest disengagement" has become increasingly less "modest" since the early sixties: In 1972 they gave an election and almost half the voters never came.

Why? The thesis of this chapter has been that Americans have become disgusted with the election process. They have been sold so much snake oil—a New Frontier, a Great Society, an Unconditional War on Poverty, a New American Revolution, a Full Generation of Peace—that they are suffering from rhetorical indigestion. They want some hard analysis and straight talk, which never seem to emerge from the crazy atmosphere surrounding our campaigns. They have also witnessed a series of shocking scandals concerning money in campaigns, and this has deepened their suspicion that rich people and special interests have a few more votes than the rest of us.

In short, the confidence of the American people in the process by which they select their governing officials has been profoundly shaken. It is hard to imagine how a nation can continue to function democratically if a large percentage of its population continues to believe that the electoral process is a fraud.

This chapter has hinted at some methods of reform. Its general thrust has been that American voters should hear more debate and less monologue, should see more unrehearsed confrontations between candidates and fewer staged "events," should be subjected not to spot commercials and other kinds of slick nonsense but to an orderly discussion of issues. What is more, American voters should be reminded—and should remind themselves—that they don't have to be rich (or have rich friends) to run for office in America, that no man or woman has to "sell out" to special interests in order to get campaign money. Finally, it might help to restore some sense of proportion of we cut down on the amounts spent for campaigns. No one expects America to return to the year 1860, when Abraham Lincoln spend a grand total of $100,000 on his campaign, but surely we need no more repeats of 1972, when an incumbent President spent something like $60 million to get reelected. (We shall probably never know the exact amount spent on that election because of all the unreported contributions, laundered money, and suitcases full of cash which were used to finance it.)

We have examined some recent laws aimed at eliminating the causes of public disgust. Probably more laws, and refinements on existing laws, will have to be enacted before we get close to solving the problem. It is hard to resist the logic in Senator Kennedy's argument that if public financing is important for presidential elections it ought to be at least as important for congressional elections. The complaint of Senator James Buckley of New York is also worth considering: that the spending limits of the new laws discriminate against nonincumbents because the incumbent already gets free publicity simply by being in office. Perhaps the challenger should be allowed a higher limit than an incumbent, or perhaps he or she should get some form of free publicity denied to the incumbent.

But all the adjustments and extensions of existing campaign laws will be meaningless if the spirit of these laws is forgotten. If Watergate is seen only as a "nightmare" instead of as an object lesson, the temptation to forget about it will become irresistible, and the new laws will probably go the way of the old Corrupt Practices Act of 1925—toward the graveyard of unenforced legislation. How, then, do we keep the heat on, and not let the nation drift back into another period of illusory "normalcy"? There are no simple or easy answers to this question. But part of the answer may lie in joining some form of citizen's pressure group like Common Cause.

But that is a topic for another chapter—the next chapter, as a matter of fact.

NOTES

1. See, for example, Sidney Verba and Norman H. Nie, *Participation in America* (New York: Harper & Row, Publishers, Incorporated, 1972).
2. Joseph Schumpeter, *Capitalism, Socialism, and Democracy* (New York: Harper & Brothers, 1950), p. 269.
3. Ernest Barker, *Reflections on Government* (New York: Oxford University Press, 1958), p. 68.
4. Joe McGinnis, *The Selling of the President 1968* (New York: Pocket Books, Inc., 1970), p. 224.
5. M. Timothy O'Keefe, "The Anti-smoking Commercials: A Study of Television's Impact on Behavior," *Public Opinion Quarterly,* XXXV (Summer 1971), pp. 242–248.
6. Bernard R. Berelson, Paul F. Lazarsfeld, and William N. McPhee, *Voting* (Chicago: University of Chicago Press, 1954).
7. Angus Campbell, Philip E. Converse, Warren E. Miller, and Donald E. Stokes, *The American Voter* (New York: John Wiley & Sons, Inc., 1960).
8. Robert A. Dahl, *Who Governs?* (New Haven, Conn.: Yale University Press, 1961), p. 279.
9. Robert E. Lane, *Political Ideology: Why the Common Man Believes What He Does* (New York: The Free Press, 1962), p. 33.
10. V. O. Key, *The Responsible Electorate: Rationality in Presidential Voting, 1936–1960* (Cambridge, Mass.: The Belknap Press, Harvard University Press, 1966), p. 4.
11. David E. RePass, "Issue Salience and Party Choice," *American Political Science Review,* LXV (June 1971), p. 394.
12. Ibid., p. 400.
13. Gerald M. Pomper, "From Confusion to Clarity: Issues and American Voters, 1956–1968," *American Political Science Review,* LXVI (June 1972).
14. Walter De Vries and V. Lance Tarrance, *The Ticket-Splitter: A New Force in American Politics* (Grand Rapids, Mich.: W. B. Eerdmans Publishing Co., 1972), passim.
15. Campbell et al., op. cit., p. 143.
16. Key, op. cit., passim.
17. RePass, op. cit., p. 398.
18. Samuel Lubell, *The Future While It Happened* (New York: W. W. Norton & Company, Inc., 1973), p. 154.
19. Rita E. Hauser, "The Center Can Hold," *New York Times,* Dec. 11, 1973, p. 45.
20. Richard M. Scammon and Ben J. Wattenberg, *The Real Majority* (New York: Coward-McCann, Inc., 1970), passim.
21. "Champ Clark of *Time* found that 'Nixononians are not against change. I have yet to meet one who wants the U.S. to stay exactly the way it is. But they have in kindred spirit a sense of orderliness, of tidiness.

    "'Orderliness' is the key word. It is tempting to say that whereas the 1972 election did not represent a backlash of political conservatism, or of racism, it did represent a cultural backlash." Seymour Martin Lipset and Earl Raab, "The Election and the National Mood," *Commentary,* LV (January 1973), p. 44.

22 Theodore J. Lowi, "A 'Critical' Election Misfires," *The Nation,* CCXV (Dec. 18, 1972), p. 620.
23 Elihu Katz and Jacob J. Feldman, "The Kennedy-Nixon Debates: A Survey of Surveys," in William J. Crotty, ed., *Public Opinion and Politics: A Reader* (New York: Holt, Rinehart and Winston, Inc., 1970), pp. 421–422.
24 Quoted in Harold Mendelsohn and Irving Crespi, *Polls, Television, and the New Politics* (Scranton, Pa.: Chandler Publishing Company, 1970), p. 312.
25 Herbert E. Alexander, "Communications and Politics: The Media and the Message," in Robert Agranoff, ed., *The New Style in Election Campaigns* (Boston: Holbrook Press, Inc., 1972), p. 385.
26 John Stuart Mill, *Autobiography* (New York: Signet Books, New American Library, Inc., 1964; originally published in 1873), p. 199.
27 *Baker v. Carr,* 369 U.S. 186 (1962): *Gray v. Sanders,* 372 U.S. 368 (1962); *Wesberry v. Sanders,* 376 U.S. 1 (1963); *Reynolds v. Sims,* 377 U.S. 533 (1964); *Lucas v. Colorado,* 377 U.S. 713 (1964).
28 Quoted in Wade Greene, "Who Should Pay for Political Campaigns?," *Columbia Journalism Review,* XII (January/February 1974), p. 25.
29 U.S. Congress, Senate, Subcommittee on Communications, *Hearings on the Federal Election Campaign Act of 1973,* 93d Congress, 1st Sess., p. 79.
30 *Salyer Land Co. v. Tulare Lake Basin Water Storage District,* 410 U.S. 719 (1973).
31 U.S. Congress, Senate, *Hearings on Federal Election Campaign Act of 1973,* op. cit., p. 91.
32 Quoted in Herbert E. Alexander, *Money in Politics* (Washington: Public Affairs Press, 1972), p. 151.
33 Although Stans bragged about raising "the largest amount of money ever spent in a political campaign," he later claimed that he objected to budgetary "overkill" and urged H. R. Haldeman, "Let's just run this campaign with less money." J. Anthony Lukas, "The Story So Far," *New York Times Magazine,* July 22, 1973, p. 21.
34 See the testimony of John Gardner, U.S. Congress, Senate, *Hearings on Federal Election Campaign Act of 1973,* op. cit., p. 91.
35 *New York Times,* Aug. 4, 1973, p. 13; Aug. 4, 1973, Part V, p. 2.
36 Alexander, op. cit., p. 298.
37 Quoted in Lukas, op. cit., p. 18.
38 U.S. Congress, Senate, *Hearings on Federal Election Campaign Act of 1973,* op. cit., pp. 244ff.
39 Congressional Quarterly, *Weekly Report,* XXXII (Oct. 12, 1974), p. 2865.
40 *New York Times,* Aug. 16, 1975, pp. 1, 46.
41 *New York Times,* July 25, 1973, p. 32.
42 Carl Sandburg, *The People, Yes* (New York: Harcourt, Brace and Company, Inc., 1936), p. 43.
43 See above, note 9.

Chapter 5

"Special Interests" and the Public Interest

The masters of the government of the United States are the combined capitalists and manufacturers of the United States.

Woodrow Wilson

Many people complain about unfair taxes, but Bob Loitz did something about [them]. His petition drive calling for federal tax reform netted over 200,000 signatures and provided the impetus for setting up numerous citizen tax reform groups throughout the Mid-west. As Loitz explained in a letter that accompanied the petitions, "I think that most people will agree that the Congress responds not because they see the light but because they feel the heat."

People and Taxes (Tax Reform Newsletter)*

Benign or Sinister?
To most Americans the term "pressure group" probably has a sinister connotation. It conjures up the image of hard-sell operators using any means of forcing favorable decisions out of government officials. Political cartoonists from Thomas Nast to Herblock have drawn caricatures of potbellied lobbyists manipulating legislators on behalf of "trusts" or "special interests."

---

*Vol. II, no. 9 (September 1974), P.O. Box 14198, Washington, D.C. 20044. Public Citizen's Tax Reform Research Group.

Political scientists, at least since the end of the Second World War, have often treated these popular notions with scorn. In 1963 Lester Milbrath conducted a series of interviews with Washington lobbyists and concluded that they had, on the whole, been slandered by muckraking journalists. In one of the closing chapters of *The Washington Lobbyists,* Milbrath struck an almost Agnewesque note concerning the role of the press:

> The press plays up the unsavory and sensational aspects of lobbying, printing very few stories about the ordinary, honest lobbyist and his workaday activities—presumably because they would not "sell." Further, reporters often become victims of the public's, and their own, preconceptions of lobbying; they look for evidence to prove what they already believe.[1]

In the 1958 edition of *Parties, Politics and Pressure Groups,* V. O. Key also warned that the popular notion of "pressure" can be "quite misleading, for much of the work of these groups does not involve turning the heat on Congress." Nor, Key added, is it fair to assume that they invariably seek indefensible special interests; their objectives "spread over as wide a spectrum of good and evil as do the motives of mankind generally." Finally, the view that pressure groups "are pathological growths in the body politic is likewise more picturesque than accurate." The safer assumption is that "the group system developed to fill gaps in the political system."[2]

During the 1950s and the early 1960s there developed an extensive body of literature in political science which not only challenged the popular "sinister" view of pressure groups but articulated what might be called the "benign" view. Some political scientists doubted that pressure groups could be understood in any moral framework: "Special interests, like their agents, the lobbyists, are neither good nor bad; they just are."[3] Others regarded them as generally helpful to the democratic process, providing legislators with valuable factual data and points of view while at the same time helping to stimulate the public's interest in issues.[4] Finally, the dominant political outlook during this period was the "group" theory of politics, which denied the very existence of a general interest, hoping instead for a mutual and peaceful adjustment of the various special interests in the nation.

On the one hand, then, is the sinister view of pressure groups, derived from what V. O. Key called the "lurid folklore"[5] of American politics. On the other hand is the benign view, which sees the activities of pressure groups—or "interest groups," a term preferred by some political scientists because it seems more "value-free"—not only as inevitable in America but as necessary to the proper functioning of our democracy. Which of these points of view is closer to reality?

Before trying to answer this question, it might be better to look closer at the theory and practice of interest groups in America.

GROUP THEORY

Group theorizing is at least as old as the United States Constitution. The Founders often disagreed over specific plans and policies for government, but they all took pride in being patriots and citizens of a republic. As such, they professed concern over the danger of "cabals" and conspiracies which might destroy the unity of the nation. One of the most potent arguments for adopting the Constitution was that a large republic with divided powers was necessary to control "factions." This subject was treated at length by James Madison in *The Federalist Papers,* a series of newspaper articles published in 1788 which were written to urge ratification of the Constitution.

"Faction" Madison defined as "a number of citizens, whether amounting to a majority or a minority of the whole, who are united and actuated by some common impulse of passion, or of interest, adverse to the rights of other citizens, or to the permanent and aggregate interests of the community."[6] When it came to "curing the mischiefs of faction," however, Madison rejected the possibility of either crushing them out of existence or talking people out of them. The first alternative was undesirable and the second futile, for factions are "sown" in man's nature. "Ambition" in the bad sense of that word, the ambition to "vex and oppress" others, cannot be eliminated, but it can be contained by the right application of force and counterforce. "Ambition must be made to counteract ambition."

In Madison's time a kind of popularized version of Newton's physics was in vogue,[7] and its mechanistic principles were often extended beyond the confines of physical science. In religion, deism pictured God as the winder of a clock-universe in which the stars and planets were held in their places by force and counterforce; in economics an "invisible hand" of competition would hold wages and prices in line.[8] In politics, Madison argued, factions were to be held in their orbits by "checks and balances." Our large Republic could contain all kinds of factions, and our government of divided powers would prevent any of them from taking full control of its machinery. Each branch of the government, and each faction of society, would resist the encroachments of the others, preserving at once the liberty and the equilibrium of the society.

Madison's belief that factions can be used to neutralize each other has enjoyed periodic revivals in the course of American history. In the mid-nineteenth century John C. Calhoun built his theory of the "concurrent majority" on the need to balance "the various and diversified interests of the community."[9] A simple majority, Calhoun argued, is bound to ride roughshod over the legitimate interests of minorities. Calhoun, who was trying to preserve the economic and social system of the antebellum South against encroachments by a Congress which was filling up with representatives from the more populous Northern states, proposed a series of minority vetoes; the concurrence of every interest in America would be necessary before a decision can be made.

Early in the twentieth century group theory was carried to much greater lengths. In 1908 Arthur F. Bentley published *The Process of Government,* which served to inspire a later generation of group theorists. Bentley interpreted the whole political process in America in terms of the interplay of group interests. Any suggestion that there might be such a thing as an overall public interest was, for Bentley, little more than bombast. "Government by the people," he said, is "a slogan and a rallying cry for some particular groups at special stages of their activity."[10]

Modern Group Theory

It was the hardheaded and seemingly empirical quality of Bentley's book which appealed to David Truman, who quoted it copiously and even borrowed its title in his 1951 book, *The Governmental Process*. Truman saw society as a mosaic of interest groups. Government itself could be seen as a series of groups interacting with one another and with nongovernment groups. As for the values which legitimize government and serve as ideals for society—justice, fairness, equality, and so on—these, too, should be seen as "interests," and we can assume that they command the support of at least some "potential interest groups" in the society.[11]

Group theories such as that of Truman were enormously influential, especially in academic circles, during the fifties and the early sixties.[12] In one sense they represented an updated version of Madison's checks and balances. Unlike Madison, however, group theorists were unwilling to consider the activities of groups in moral or ethical terms. David Truman quoted with approval Madison's definition of "faction" as "a number of citizens . . . united by some common impulse of passion, or of interest . . . ," but left off the rest of Madison's definition, ". . . adverse to the rights of other citizens, or to the permanent and aggregate interests of the community."[13] Madison saw factions as ineradicable evils, emanations of a less-than-angelic human nature. Truman pictured interest groups in much more positive terms, as the essential components of the governmental process. For Madison the ultimate aim of government was to achieve justice ("Justice is the end of government. It is the end of civil society."). Modern group theorists were satisfied with "consensus" and "mutual adjustment."

Given the general spirit of the times, group theory offered at least two distinct advantages.

First, it seemed to provide a "scientific" and "value-free" framework for studying society. Society, after all, was composed of interest groups, and each doubtless could rationalize its interests as "good" for the entire society. But political scientists need not take such claims seriously; they need only study the various groups and note their behavior with the same disinterestedness as astronomers who study the behavior of stars and planets. Even the grand abstractions, such as "justice," can be reduced to manageable form and studied scientifically if they are regarded simply as "interests." One person may pursue a favorable tax clause, another may chase after justice; both are looking after their "interests." But is not the one being selfish and the other altruistic? Such judgments, Truman replied,"have no value for a scientific understanding of government or the operation of society."[14]

Second, group theory seemed to offer at once an explanation of and a rationalization for American society in the fifties and the early sixties. The New Deal, the majority coalition which Roosevelt had led, seemed to be decaying during this period, fragmenting itself into a series of skirmishes between interest groups. The more nostalgic political scientists were calling for a party realignment which would revive the majoritarian spirit of the previous decade, but the group theorists were more accurate, at least for the period from roughly 1945 to 1964, in describing the political process as the interplay of fragments. They were also more realistic in perceiving that the big ideological battles of the thirties—for instance, between those who advocated and opposed the idea of a welfare state—were nearly over. Under Eisenhower the Republican party had begun to take over some of the key programs of the Democrats and had even begun to accept their philosophy. With "issue politics" dormant, "interest politics" took over. In the game of interest politics the players are not concerned about winning great moral or ethical victories but with getting their own particular pieces of the action. Politics becomes a case of "who gets what, when, how."[15]

The group theory of politics not only described the politics of the fifties and early sixties, it also justified it. The period was pervaded by what C. Wright Mills called the "conservative mood."[16] The dominant public philosophy was "centrism,"[17] which stigmatized the advocacy of radical change as irresponsible and "extremist." Group theory fit this conservative mood because it depended for its successful operation on logrolling, compromise, and mutual accommodation. The interest-group approach, as one of its advocates freely admitted, militates against "sweeping programs of comprehensive and coordinated reconstruction."[18] It puts a premium on gradualism, since sweeping changes would disrupt the smooth functioning of the system and alienate those groups with a vested interest in the status quo.

Three Critics of Group Theory

Group theory, as both an explanation and a justification of the American political system, has come under increasing attack in recent years. Its major critics have included E. E. Schattschneider, Robert Paul Wolff, and Theodore Lowi.

E. E. Schattschneider: "Public" vs. "Private" Interests As early as 1960, E. E. Schattschneider questioned the failure of the group theorists to distinguish between "public" (common) interests and "private" (special) interests. "Is it possible," Schattschneider asked, "to distinguish between the interests of the members of the National Association of Manufacturers and the members of the American League to Abolish Capital Punishment?" The obvious factual difference, he answered, is that *"the members of the A.L.A.C.P. obviously do not expect to be hanged."* Schattschneider thus demonstrated that the distinction between self-interest and the interest of the community as a whole—a distinction which the group theorists had dismissed as value-laden and "unscientific"—was important to the study of pressure groups. To ignore the distinction, to pretend that all interests are special interests, "forces us into circumlocutions such as those involved in the argument that people have special interests in the common good." The argument can be made, perhaps, "but it seems a long way around to avoid a useful distinction."[19]

Robert Paul Wolff: Who Speaks for "the Whole"? Schattschneider also pointed to the upper-class "bias" of most pressure groups in order to demonstrate that pressure group politics fails to represent all segments of the community. This general approach was taken up and developed by Robert Paul Wolff in a 1965 essay, "Beyond Tolerance," and in Wolff's later book on *The Poverty of Liberalism*. In Wolff's opinion the trouble with interest-group theory is not only that it tends to ignore those lonely but prophetic voices who don't belong to established pressure groups, but that it fails to take account of the nation as a whole. Some social ills, Wolff contended, cannot be cured by the techniques of interest-group politics.

> For example, America is growing uglier, more dangerous, and less pleasant to live in, as its citizens grow richer. The reason is that natural beauty, public order, the cultivation of the arts, are not the special interest of any identifiable social group. . . . To be sure, crime and urban slums hurt the poor more than the rich, the Negro more than the white—but fundamentally they are the problems of the society as a whole, not of any particular group. That is to say, they concern the general good, not merely the aggregate of private goods.[20]

Theodore Lowi: Who's in Charge Here? This theme of the "general good" as opposed to "the aggregate of private goods" also figured prominently in Theodore Lowi's critique of interest-group politics, *The End of Liberalism* (1969). Lowi saw the central problem of his time as being the erosion of authority in government, and for this loss he found the interest-group ideologists largely responsible. They had, he argued, gotten the American people and their legislators so used to the idea that government is nothing more than the mutual accommodation of private groups that the whole sense of authority—the conviction that government acts legitimately and on behalf of all the people—had become dangerously weakened. Congress had delegated away its discretionary authority to administrators, and they in turn handed it over to private groups. As a contemporary example Lowi cited the operation of the Economic Opportunity Act.[21] Congress, through the blank check of "maximum feasible participation," had given away billions to administrators, who then subdelegated authority and money to "community action groups." The result, Lowi concluded, was not only confused administration but the systematic recruitment of racial separatists, accompanied by an increase in cynicism and militancy. Lowi's book cited other well-known cases of government agencies parceling out their lawmaking powers to private groups and thus delegating away their own authority. His solution: Our government should start using its authority instead of delegating any more of it away; it should draw up tight rules for administration instead of leaving it to the discretion of bureaucrats; it should start regulating private groups and stop the endless bargaining with them; it should assert itself and act like a lawful government instead of merely another interest group.[22]

The criticisms of Schattschneider, Wolff, and Lowi differ in important ways. Schattschneider's came from a New Deal perspective, Wolff's from that of the New Left, while Lowi's has a "law and order" ring. What the three criticisms share, however, is a common preoccupation with precisely the thing which the group theorists had dismissed as mere sham: the common good. The three critics seemed to agree that there is a good for the American people as a whole which transcends the particular "goods" desired by the various special interests in the nation. In certain cases it not only transcends them but may be opposed to them. The quality of our life, which Wolff alluded to, is an example. A more particular case is that of the environment. Since the end of the Second World War the pollution of our air and water has been a growing problem. Yet for thirty years none of the major pressure groups, business, labor, farm, veterans, and so on, ever considered pollution as a threat to its interests—indeed, the *prevention* of pollution was sometimes regarded as a threat, since it might cost money or jobs— so nothing was done about it. Since the American people as a whole had no effective lobby in Congress, the public interest was sacrificed by the very group process which satisfied all the private interests.

In this connection it might be well to recall the distinction proposed by the French philosopher Jean-Jacques Rousseau more than two centuries ago. In his *Social Contract* (1762), Rousseau distinguished between the "general will" and the "will of all." The general will, Rousseau said, "considers only the common interest," while the will of all "takes private interest into account, and is no more than a sum of particular wills." Each person in the community undoubtedly has his or her own private interest or particular will, "but take away from these same wills the pluses and minuses that cancel one another, and the general will remains as the sum of the differences."[23] This is Rousseau's answer to those who say that all communities are divided into special interest groups. Each person may have a side of him or her which considers only these special interests. But each person also has another side which wills a good for the community as a whole. When the various pluses and minuses of particular interests cancel themselves out, there still remains this sense of community, which each individual shares to some extent.

Summing up the point of agreement between the criticisms discussed earlier—a point with which this writer agrees—we might put it this way: The group theorists' central mistake was to ignore the communitarian side of people's nature and to glorify the selfish side. Their analysis of groups, vulgarized into a popular ideology, ended up as a justification for acquisitiveness, cynicism, and plain greed.

This excursion into theory still does not resolve the question whether pressure groups are benign or sinister forces in American life, but it does bring us further than we were at the beginning. In the first place it permits us to raise an eyebrow at the suggestion that pressure groups are useful because their representatives can supply lawmakers with valuable factual data. What Congress obviously needs is its *own* factual data, its own in-house capability for getting and processing them. (Its present facilities, the Library of Congress, congressional staff, and two computers, are hopelessly inadequate.) Second, and more broadly, the foregoing theoretical discussion suggests that "the public good" is not mere rhetoric but a meaningful standard against which to measure the claims of any group. Reasonable people may disagree over exactly what constitutes the "public good," but keeping it as a reference point provides a focus for orderly debate. To surrender it, to simply say that all points of view are "interests," is to surrender any means of judging group behavior. Without "value judgments," unscientific though they may be, the empirical study of pressure groups becomes directionless and thereby less fruitful.

Of course, there are vested interests and vested interests. Madison, in *Federalist 10,* noted that while property differences are the most "common and durable" source of faction, even "the most frivolous and fanciful distinctions" have been enough to divide people into factions. In *Gulliver's Travels,* Jonathan Swift's satiric novel, men fight over whether to crack their breakfast eggs at the big end or the little end. Big-Enders and Little-Enders form opposing factions, each furiously and righteously contending for dominance. People may not be quite so silly in reality, but the allegory should at least remind us that interests can take more subtle forms than those centered on such tangible rewards as economic gain. Here is where reformers and those who claim to represent "the public interest" must be on their guard. They always run the risk of developing a kind of vested interest in their own position, so that they cling to it without carefully considering whether it represents the general interest of society. Because they are not profiting from their position in terms of dollars and cents, they delude themselves into thinking that they have no other personal stakes in it. They forget that they may have invested large chunks of their egos in their particular campaign, which could get bruised by defeat. What appears to them to be the purest altrusim on their part may really hide a fear of humiliation.

The problem of unconscious vested interests is a serious one, and there is no easy solution to it. Perhaps the beginning of a solution is an acknowledgment of the problem. The unconscious tendency of people to identify their individual egos with the nation's good can probably never be rooted out, but perhaps it can be checked or tempered by a certain degree of humility. "In the bowels of Christ," Oliver Cromwell once exclaimed, "admit that you may be mistaken!" Unfortunately, Cromwell himself failed to heed this excellent advice.

There is another kind of unconscious vested interest, aside from the interest we all have in being right. This interest takes the form of an unconscious class or occupational bias. Take, for example, the issue of the environment. It is quite true that all people, rich and poor, doctors, lawyers, and hodcarriers, need clean air and water. But if you are an unemployed worker and a factory is coming into your town, you may decide to tolerate a higher *degree* of pollution than your environmentalist neighbor, who happens to be a college professor. If he or she tells you that everybody has an interest in clean air, you can reply that everybody also has an interest in eating. Many environmentalists belong to professions or enjoy incomes which free them from the daily struggle to wrench a living from nature. It makes sense for *them* to demand nothing less than 100 percent pure air and water—but can they claim to represent the *public* interest?

This is a serious question, but it does not have to be answered by abandoning the concept of the public interest. What it does is to challange those who claim to represent a public interest—in this case, the environment—to take a more inclusive view of the situation. If, for example, closing a particular factory will put people out of work, environmentalists (if they really want to represent the public interest) must include in their proposal to close the factory a plan to find new jobs for its employees.

Actually, the question in most environmental fights is not whether the factory should close but whether it should clean up its operations (by installing afterburners, sewage treatment plants, and the like). The question, in other words, is one of money, and the factory owner or strip miner is wont to say: "If you force me to restore the land or clean the air it'll cost you—I'll charge higher prices; better to accept a little trade-off, such as dirtier air in exchange for lower prices." But this implied threat might prompt us to ask whether it is really necessary for the consumers to pay, whether the industries themselves should not pay out of their own profits, whether they can afford to do so, what sort of profits they do make, what their accounting books look like, and other intrusive questions. In short, there is no inherent contradiction between a clean environment and full employment, but there may ultimately be a contradiction between a clean environment and "private" enterprise—"private" in the sense that its operations are free from public supervision. Other "public" interests, such as consumer protection and auto safety, involve the same considerations: What will they cost? Who can best afford to pay? What profits are sufficient? Who should be allowed to see their accounts and make such decisions? These questions cannot be explored here. All we can do is note that they touch the heart of America's hybrid economic system, a system which permits corporate enterprises to act like governments and receive government assistance while shielding themselves from government supervision.

Turning from theory to practice, and from the perplexities of the term "public interest" to the less subtle problem of special interests, let us see how the latter operate upon government. The most obvious place to start is the time-honored haunt of the "lobbyist," from whose lobbies the word itself is derived: the Capitol building.

INTEREST GROUPS IN CONGRESS

During every session of Congress pressure groups of all kinds converge on the Capitol. *Congressional Quarterly,* a periodical report of congressional activities, lists twelve different categories of lobbies: business, citizens, education, employee-labor, environment, farm, health, lawyers, state and local government, veterans, power, and transportation. A thirteenth category not listed but often discussed is executive lobbies. The President maintains his own congressional liaison, and executive-branch lobbies can exert a potent form of pressure. Among the President's resources in influencing Congress are his access to the media, appeals to party loyalty, and the ability to offer credible threats and punishments. Senator Charles Goodell of New York, a Republican dove, felt the wrath of President Nixon when Spiro Agnew came into his state to campaign against him in the 1972 election. (Goodell lost his seat to the first Conservative ever elected to the Senate, James Buckley.) President Johnson was skilled in using both the carrot and the stick, and President Kennedy had a skilled, professional staff of congressional liaison men known as the "Irish Mafia."

Business lobbies appear to have the largest number on Capitol Hill. In *Congressional Quarterly's* selected list of lobbies active in 1973, business lobbies numbered nineteen, as compared to seven for labor, eight for farm groups, and six for the environment. By themselves these figures tell us very little about the relative strength of these groups, since labor has large numbers of rank-and-file members and the environmental groups have a high percentage of articulate and activist members. But business, too, has its grass-roots affiliates (the Chamber of Commerce alone has 4,000 local organizations, 40,000 business firms, and an overall membership of 5,000,000), and its members rank among the highest of all groups in education and political awareness.

One well-known study of business influence in Congress, by Bauer, Pool and Dexter, concluded that business lobbies "were on the whole poorly financed, ill-managed, out of contact with Congress, and at best only marginally effective in supporting tendencies and measures which already had behind them considerable Congressional impetus from other sources."[24] The authors admitted, however, that the particular issue they examined, foreign trade policy, was not a "salient" one.[25] The business community was divided, uncertain, and often uninterested in the issue. (The authors could have also added that the rise of multinational corporations had by this time made it ludicrous to call low tariffs a "liberal" trade policy.) It ought not to be surprising that business lobbying *in this case* was without much focus or intensity. In other cases where the benefits to businesses are more clear and unambiguous, such as oil depletion allowances and corporate tax loopholes, business lobbying appears to be more effective. On November 1, 1973, the *New York Times* reported:

> Plans to bring up a tax-reform proposal in the House of Representatives this week were apparently thwarted today by strategists in two key Congressional committees, some of whom conceded that they were acting under pressure from the oil industry and other businesses.

According to the *Times* report, three members of the House Rules Committee, who had voted only the day before to allow major tax-reform amendments to be attached to a bill, suddenly announced that they intended to change their votes. The House Ways and Means Committee also began a drive to thwart the passage of the tax reform measures by pigeonholing it in their committee. The three members of the Rules Committee who changed their votes came from oil states, and their turnaround, along with the actions of the Ways and Means Committee, "came after half a day of intense activity by oil industry and other loblyists.[26]

Confessions of an Ex-Lobbyist

One resource that businesses, particularly large ones, have available is money. One ex-lobbyist, Robert Winter-Berger, places particular emphasis on this aspect of lobbying in his memoirs of lobbying days in the Capitol. Winter-Berger contends that lobbying can play four useful roles in the legislative process: informing the public, showing up weaknesses in bills, stimulating public debate, and forecasting the probable effects of a bill. "This is lobbying in its purest form." Unfortunately, he adds, "it is also lobbying in its rarest form."

> Most lobbying is underground, because more than opinions are exchanged. Money is exchanged: money for favors, money for deals, money for government contracts, money for government jobs.[27]

Winter-Berger's book is largely anecdotal, describing his own acquaintance with notorious lobbyists like the late Nathan Voloshen, who operated out of former House Speaker John McCormack's office. Toward the end of the book Winter-Berger concludes that nearly all lobbying ultimately involves "influence peddling" of one sort or another.

> Influence peddling generally occurs when some matter is too pressing to proceed through so-called normal channels. If the Congressman concerned cuts through red tape and acts on the matter, there is usually a payoff, whatever its disguise. It may be a donation to the Congressman's campaign fund or a donation in his name to his national committee; it may also be stock in a corporation, often issued in the name of a relative. Or perhaps a relative gets a good job in the company involved; perhaps the Congressman's house gets a new paint job or a new car in the garage. Maybe his family gets an unexpected trip to Europe, or the Congressman happily finds himself booked on a lucrative speaking tour. But in one form or another, there is a payoff.[28]

Lobbying Act of 1946

Winter-Berger's charges may be exaggerated and sensationalized. Lester Milbrath's extensive interviews which went into his book on *The Washington Lobbyists* produced a much more austere picture of the lobbyist's "workaday activities."[29] But the definitive study of what congressional lobbyists do to influence legislation has yet to emerge, and part of the reason is the lack of available data. As a means of forcing disclosure of at least some relevant data Congress passed the Regulation of Lobbying Act in 1946. The act required paid lobbyists to file quarterly financial reports and to register with the House and Senate. These reports were to list all contributions, expenditures, and the name and address of anyone who contributed over $500 or received payments. The purpose of the act was to remove the uncertainty surrounding the influence of lobbyists on legislation, and to make lobbyists' activities known to Congress and the public. The act was vaguely worded, however, and raised serious questions about freedom of speech. It was challenged on First Amendment grounds and upheld by the Supreme Court only at the expense of weakening its effectiveness. In *U.S. v. Harriss,* 347 U.S. 612 (1954), the Court construed the act to require registration only if the primary purpose of the group is to influence legislation and only if the lobbyist directly contacts a member of Congress. In consequence, many large organizations such as the National Association of Manufacturers do not register as lobbies because they contend that lobbying is not the principal purpose for which they collect and receive funds. Other lobbyists contend that their contacts with Congress are designed to inform, not influence, and thus do not constitute lobbying. Despite the Lobbying Act, then, there is no way to tell how much money is being spent to influence congressional legislation. "All that can be said with certainty," one student of the subject concluded, "is that the amount reported to Congress and the public is a very, very small fragment of the total."[30]

By themselves such figures would probably not be very meaningful anyway, since the amount spent for lobbying itself is only a small part of its total employment in influencing the legislative process. To be sure, lobbyists have spent impressive sums in dining and entertaining members of Congress, and this reportedly plays a role in softening up potential opponents and establishing congenial relationships with potential friends.* Of greater importance, however, is the amount of money spent not on direct lobbying but on campaign financing. The same coalition of dairy lobbies which gave President Nixon $422,500 in campaign contributions in 1972[31] also made generous contributions to the campaigns of key members of Congress. According to Nick Kotz of the *Washington Post*, they "concentrated their attention on senior members in key committees of Congress with jurisdiction over the price of milk, price supports, import laws and anti-trust issues, matters in which [the dairy interests] are now embroiled." In some cases the contributions were made after the elections, and to victors who were originally unsupported by the lobbies.[32]

Even these examples of venality do not go to the heart of the problem of special interests in Congress. It is not necessary for a special interest to deal in bribes and payoffs for it to be contrary to the general interest. In this context the lurid tales of money under the table may be less relevant than the theoretical criticisms of interest groups summarized earlier in the chapter. The problem with even the most honest special interests is precisely that they are *special:* They fail to consider, in James Madison's words, "the permanent and aggregate interests of the community." "The general interest" may be an elusive concept, but, say the critics of group theory, it must be seen as more than the sum of individual interests.

An excellent example of the dangers in equating the general interest with the sum of particular interests is Congress's decision in 1971 to provide a $250 million loan guarantee to the Lockheed Aircraft Corporation.

A Confusion of "Interests": The Lockheed Loan

Lockheed, the nation's largest defense contractor, has had its share of bad press in recent years. In 1970 Pentagon officials blocked a congressional probe of the corporation's finances when Lockheed's contract to produce the C-5A, a huge military transport plane, also produced a $2 billion cost overrun, long delays, and

---

*"A veteran staff member of a Senate subcommittee subject to intense lobbying pressures advised:

'Don't leave out the parties. They're damned important, especially with the new Congressmen. The new man arrives in town with his wife. They're both a little awed. And what happens? All of a sudden, they are invited to a little dinner party given by the Washington vice president for a billion-dollar corporation. They're impressed, but there's more to it than that.

'Let's say the Congressman is a liberal. He's suspicions of big business. What does he find? The big shot is a darned nice guy. He doesn't have horns and a tail. He charms the wife and he's deferential to the Congressman. They go away feeling a little differently. Maybe it doesn't affect the way he votes, at least not right away. But it's a softening process.'" James Deakin, *The Lobbyists* (Washington: Public Affairs Press, 1966), p. 8.

a final product with some disconcerting flaws. ("The wing continues to be one of the major problem areas on the C-5A," one official report concluded.)[33]

In 1971 Lockheed faced a new crisis. Rolls-Royce Ltd., the British manufacturer of jet engines for a civilian airliner being produced by Lockheed, declared bankruptcy and abruptly stopped work on the engines. Lockheed, already suffering the results of bad planning and mismanagement, insisted that without substantial loans the plane could not be completed and Lockheed itself might be forced into bankruptcy. The banks refused to make such loans without government guarantees, and the Nixon administration responded by sending to Congress a bill to guarantee $250 million in bank loans to the beleaguered corporation.

On its face there seemed little reason for Congress to comply. The plane in question was civilian, not military, so its production could not be justified on the grounds of national security. The corporation's reputation for reliability had already been compromised by the C-5A scandal a year earlier. Both left and right could object to the proposal—the left because it was, in Wisconsin Senator Proxmire's words, "a big business giveaway of the worst sort,"[34] and the right because such massive public assistance to private business seems to violate the spirit of "free enterprise." Yet Congress approved the loan. Why?

No convincing evidence of bribery or skullduggery has ever been unearthed. The evidence is rather that the major economic pressure groups and their congressional supporters accepted the administration arguments that the loan was necessary to their particular interests. "The failure of major business enterprises," then-Treasury Secretary Connally argued, "can have serious national and regional consequences, including the causing of substantial unemployment, as well as other business failures."[35] Connally claimed that Lockheed had 35,000 subcontracting companies, most of them small businesses, and these would go under unless the loan were approved. Labor was also concerned, as George Meany, president of the AFL-CIO, publicly announced his support for the loan. Labor unions took out ads and in one case threatened a boycott of Wisconsin products because of Senator Proxmire's opposition to the loan. In the end, a triumvirate of pressure groups—big business, small business, and labor—persuaded Congress to risk a quarter-billion dollars of taxpayers' money to support an inefficient corporation's plan to produce an airline of no demonstrable public purpose. The general interest of the nation had been sacrificed to a "consensus" of special interests, each of them acting honestly and in good faith to serve its particular constituents.

In his Farewell Address in 1961 President Eisenhower warned against the power and influence of what he called the "military-industrial complex." He said the impact was "felt in every city, every state house, every office of the Federal government" and posed serious dangers to democracy.[36] While the exact meaning of Eisenhower's warning is open to question,[37] his formulation of a hyphenated "complex" is relevant to the Lockheed situation. The Lockheed loan was favored by the generals since it concerned the nation's largest defense contractor. It was also favored by labor leaders interested in jobs and small businesses interested in subcontracts. A majority of Congress developed an interest in the Lockheed loan because of its economic benefits to particular states and congressional districts. "Our concept," Hayden and Pilisuk concluded in a long essay on the subject, "is not that American society contains a ruling military-industrial complex. Our concept is more nearly that American society *is* a military-industrial complex."[38] If this concept were strictly accurate it would be impossible to bring about reform in America, since no one could appeal to anything but the immediate economic interests of Americans. Reformers must assume that *homo Americanus* has two sides, one concerned only with immediate, selfish ends, and the other capable of a longer view. But the Lockheed case illustrates how difficult it is to make the longer view prevail in Congress.

Of course, the argument could be made that the Lockheed loan *did* serve the national interest. If the corporation went bankrupt, it would cause massive unemployment, loss of tax revenue, swelling welfare rolls, less purchasing power, more unemployment, and so on. In Long Island, New York, home of two major defense contractors, they have a saying: "When Grumman or Republic sneezes, Long Island gets pneumonia." Those who supported the Lockheed loan contended that the corporation was not just going to sneeze; it was about to go into convulsions.

But even if that were true, it does not follow that the government must bail out sick corporations. "Give us money," the corporation says, "or we'll die, dragging the economy down with us." Instead of acceding to this demand, the government has at least two other alternatives. First, it can let the corporation go under, but soften the economic impact by finding other jobs for its workers, if necessary hiring them for public service employment. (In the 1930s the government established the Works Projects Administration, which hired statisticians to compile reports, farmers to plant trees, artists to paint murals in post offices, and so on. At the end of 1974, Congress began, very tentatively, to revive the practice by creating a few hundred thousand temporary jobs; within the first few weeks of the program there were five applicants for every job.) Secondly, the government may decide that it needs Lockheed's products too much to let the corporation go under. If that were the decision, it would seem that the most direct way to implement it would be to take over the corporation. Perhaps that amounts to socialism, but the present system of government subsidy is also a form of socialism—a very strange form of socialism, which sends massive infusions of public funds into corporations without requiring them to submit to public direction. Lockheed's decision to produce a civilian airliner was its own business. Paying for it was ours.*

---

* The costs of providing public-service employment are very high, but so are the costs of subsidizing corporations. As for taking over corporations, government bureaucracies are often cumbersome, inefficient, wasteful, and corrupt, but so are corporate bureaucracies. The advantage of abandoning the fiction of "private" for corporations funded by the public—the advantage, in other words, of having the state take over these corporations—is that the public, at least in theory, can then exert control over decisions and priorities. (We can decide, for example, whether the nation really *needs* to produce another civilian airliner.) In practice, of course, "public" bureaucracies can be just as remote and irresponsible as private corporations, but least we have some laws (such as the 1966

INTEREST GROUPS AND THE EXECUTIVE

The influence of special interests in the executive branch presents a different problem. Over the past half-century, but particularly since World War II, the power and responsibility of this branch have grown enormously. The larger private interests, most notably corporate interests, have aggrandized themselves by sharing in this growth.

During the crisis of the Depression the Roosevelt administration invited a wide variety of special interests, from corporations to labor unions, to join in programs of industrial rule-making and self-policing. During the war years, when private industry was called upon to produce an unprecedented flow of war materiel, it was given a corresponding responsibility in establishing priorities and making policy, often in secret. By the cold war years, American business had gone far to refurbish its image, marred by the Depression, as a responsible and beneficent institution. The practice of government-business "partnership" was not only normalized and routinized but given a special dispensation by the ideological nature of the conflict. Since communism appeared to threaten both democracy and capitalism, it seemed plausible to many that patriotism meant an equal loyalty to both. The results of this merging of ideologies—democracy and capitalism—and merging of bureaucracies—public and private—continue to haunt the administrative process today. A relatively recent illustration of the problem in the administration of foreign policy: the case of The International Telegraph and Telephone Company (ITT), the Central Intelligence Agency (CIA), and Chile.

ITT, CIA, and Chile

On September 4, 1970, Dr. Salvatore Allende Gossens, the first self-declared Marxist to do so, won a plurality of votes (36.1 percent) in Chile's presidential elections. According to Chilean law, a runoff election must subsequently be conducted in the Chilean Congress by secret ballot. This was held on the following October 24, and confirmed Allende as the victor. Between the general election and the runoff, American officials expressed alarm over the fact that the installation of a Marxist President in Chile appeared to be imminent. At a press briefing on September 16, Secretary of State Henry Kissinger said: "I have yet to meet somebody who firmly believes that if Allende wins there is likely to be another free election in Chile." Kissinger predicted that Allende's election would present "massive problems for us, and for democratic forces and for pro-U.S. forces in Latin America, and indeed to the whole Western Hemisphere." The whole situation, he concluded, "is not too happy for American interests."[39]

Despite Kissinger's apprehensions about the future of free elections, Allende's Chile did hold a series of elections between 1970 and 1973. The most recent one—the last free election in Chile—was the congressional election of March 1973. Despite predictions by opposition parties that they would capture

---

Information Act) which force government agencies to open their files to members of Congress and citizens.

two-thirds of the vote and impeach Allende, the Marxist President's supporters actually gained several seats in Congress and won 7 percent more of the popular vote than Allende himself received in 1970.

This set the stage for the final event of Allende's presidency: his violent overthrow and the abolition of consitutional government in Chile. On September 11, 1973, the Chilean armed forces bombed the presidential palace, and Allende either committed suicide or was murdered shortly afterward.

What was America's role in these events, and what role in turn did American private interests play in the direction of American policy? These questions will not be answered definitively or completely for years, if ever. But even at this stage, thanks to a probe by a subcommittee of the Senate Foreign Relations Committee, there exist some data to help illuminate the relationship between International Telephone and Telegraph, the American-owned multinational corporation, and highly placed American policymakers.

As early as July of 1970, before the general elections, Harold Geneen, president of ITT, summoned William Broe, who headed the CIA's clandestine operations, to his hotel room, and offered him a "sum of seven figures" (the exact amount was never mentioned) to channel through the CIA to one of Allende's right-wing opponents. The contact was arranged by James McCone, former head of the CIA and now a director of ITT. McCone had set up the Geneen-Broe meetings through his friend Richard Helms, then-director of the CIA.

The meeting between Geneen and Broe ended inconclusively. Broe relayed Geneen's proposal to his superiors in the CIA, but it was turned down. (One of ITT's representatives in Chile wired back on September 1 that "most reliable indicators" pointed to a victory by the right-wing candidate, and the State Department may have shared this optimistic view.)

After Allende's plurality in the general election, however, the concern both of United States officials and ITT representatives sharply escalated. It was obvious, two ITT officials wrote to the senior vice president of the corporation, if Allende were elected, "existing business and financial links with the U.S. would be strangled." More particularly, ITT's fear was that it would be expropriated; the giant multinational corporation had a $152 million investment in Chile, and controlled the country's telephone system. Allende had complained about the company's high rates (which netted it an annual $13 million in profits) and its practice of installing phones only in the more affluent sections of the cities. ITT's strategy for preventing Allende from taking office included secret meetings with Allende's defeated opponents, pledges of financial support to them coupled with suggestions that they provoke the left in order to justify a coup by the military, financial support for *Mercurio,* a right-wing paper, and pressure on the U.S. Information Agency "to start moving *Mercurio* editorials around Latin America and into Europe."[40]

During this period ITT was confidentially briefed on United States actions by American officials in the area. Chilean army officials, according to the ITT memo quoted above, agreed that Allende "must be stopped," and had been "assured full material and financial assistance by the U.S. military establishment." The memo also noted that ex-President Frei of Chile was under "steadily increasing pressure from the U.S." to enter into a plan in which the elections would be declared invalid and Frei would be reinstalled by the Chilean Congress.[41]

On September 29, 1970, a second series of contacts between the CIA and ITT began. This time it was Broe, the CIA official, who did the proposing, and he did so with the full approval of his director. "He indicated," according to ITT's memo, "that certain steps were being taken but that he was looking for additional help aimed at inducing economic collapse." The plan was for all private companies to withdraw credits, technical assistance, spare parts, and other economic necessities. The CIA official praised ITT and promised full financial support for its participation in the plan. "I was told that of all the companies involved ours alone had been responsive and understood the problem. The visitor [Broe] added that money was not a problem"[42] After meeting with representatives from other American-owned companies in Chile, and finding little enthusiasm for the CIA plan, ITT concluded that it was unfeasible and rejected it.

During this period the Allende government had been negotiating with ITT over the terms of compensation to the corporation for its expropriation, but when word of these CIA-ITT conversations leaked into the American press, all negotiations were broken off and the company was seized without compensation.

The full story of how deeply involved the CIA and/or ITT were in the overthrow of Allende has not yet been told. What we do know, thanks to the investigative reporting of Seymour Hersh, is that the CIA channeled $8 million into Chile for covert operations during Allende's presidency, and that more than half of the $8 million was used to subsidize strikes aimed at his overthrow. The devastating strikes by truckers, taxi drivers, and shopkeepers, which played a critical role in Allende's downfall, were thus given subsistance payments by the CIA. Much more, obviously, needs to be told,* but what concerns us here is that high government officials were jointly invoved with a private interest in a scheme to disrupt a democratic election in another country—without either the knowledge or the consent of the American people or their Congress. More specifically, the following revelations emerge from the ITT-Chilean affair:

1 ITT was better briefed on American government policy in Chile than the United States Senate. Some of the confidential information circulated through the corporation came from its own observers on the scene, but a great deal of it was provided by executive officials—who withheld the same information from Congress! As Senator Frank Church remarked, "the executive branch or some part of it, in this case the CIA, obviously told the ITT a lot more about the policy toward Chile than this committee was ever told."[43]

2 ITT's close relationship to the executive branch was facilitated in part by

---

*A memo of October 16, 1970, from ITT's Latin American public relations director asserts that an impatient Chilean general was advised from Washington to delay his coup plans until "a later, unspecified date." The United States, the memo continued, gave him "oral assurance he would receive material assistance and support from the U.S. and others for a later maneuver." Memo from Hal Hendrix to E. J. Gerrity, Oct. 16, 1970, in U.S. Senate, Subcommittee on Multinational Corporations, *Hearings on Multinational Corporations and United States Policy,* 93d Congress, Part 2, p. 659.

an interchange of key personnel. John McCone, a high official of ITT, had been the director of the CIA for several years and remained a close personal friend of Richard Helms, then-director of the CIA. Jack Neal, the international relations director of ITT, had been a high State Department official for thirty-five years. John Connally, then-Secretary of the Treasury, had served as counsel to ITT shortly before taking office.[44]

3 Both ITT and the United States government were prepared to use each other to carry out their policies. ITT was ready to donate a million dollars for the government to channel through the CIA for preventing Allende's election. The government, for its part, asked ITT to conspire with other corporations to produce economic chaos in Chile. An identity of interest was thus created between a multinational corporation and the American government, a relationship so intimate that it sometimes was difficult to see where ITT left off and the government began. At one point Senator Fulbright asked the CIA representative, William Broe, whether "ITT in its actions or suggestions was attempting to implement the Government of the U.S. policy or was it pursuing and promoting its own corporate purposes?" Broe answered: "I have a hard time with that question, sir." After several attempts to elicit an answer, Fulbright tried to summarize: "In other words . . . ITT was [not] coming to you and saying, 'We would like to help the United States and promote its purposes,' that was not it, was it? It was there for its own corporate purposes. Is that correct?" But Broe's answer plunged the whole issue back into ambiguity: "Yes, I think that, they came and wanted to help support the United States and keep Allende out—to protect their interests."[45]

4 Democratic values were confused with economic interests. Jack Neal, the ex-State Department official who served as ITT's international director, justified the plan for preventing Allende's election on the ground that "we had an obligation to the Chilean people; they are great democrats," but in the next breath added, "I think we had a responsibility to our stockholders. . . . I think we had a responsibility to show the shareholders of ITT we were trying to do everything possible to protect our $165 million in Chile."[46] Throughout the hearings the Senators tried unsuccessfully to pin down ITT and State Department officials as to what they meant by "democracy" when the officials themselves had tentatively planned to subvert a democratic election. Harold Geneen, ITT's chairman, retreated in confusion when asked to defend his statement that American aid should be given only to "democratic" countries.

> Senator FULBRIGHT. You keep referring to our program of supporting democratic countries. The principal recipients of our aid are not democratic, are they? You would not consider Greece a democratic country, would you?
> Mr. GENEEN. Senator, I am a little lost on your question, I am sorry.
> Senator FULBRIGHT. You have said several times that our policy had been to support, foster, promote, and prolong democratic governments.
> Did you say that?
> Mr. GENEEN. Well, I was thinking primarily of Latin America and Chile when I spoke.
>   . . . .

Senator FULBRIGHT. Would you consider Brazil a democratic country? (Laughter)

It is the largest recipient of our aid, isn't it?

Mr. GENEEN. Well, Senator, I suppose you would have to add if you want to get into the background of this, democratic and friendly, and maybe put "or" in there.

Senator FULBRIGHT. What you really mean is non-Communist, I guess. Anything but a Communist, If they are Fascists it is perfectly all right. Is that correct?

Mr. GENEEN. Well, I don't want to get into an area that is not my background, Senator.[47]

"Incestuous" Relationships

The ITT-Chilean case may not be typical. Even if it were, the outcome of all the scheming between ITT and the CIA never produced an operational plan, since each rejected the other's pet scheme. Nor does the case offer any support to the vulgarized Marxist notion that business is a great monolith, since ITT was unsuccessful in trying to interest other American corporations in the CIA's plan to create economic chaos. But one or more of the four points discussed above do have a way of cropping up in other studies of the relationship between special interests and executive agencies.

At the close of the Senate hearings on the ITT-Chilean affair, Senator Frank Church voiced his concern about the "incestuous relationship" between the CIA and American corporations abroad. The "incestuous" label also applies to relationships between other corporations and executive agencies. Some examples of these may be explored in terms of the four features of the ITT-CIA affair in Chile.

1 Mutual Confidentiality ITT and the CIA were able to keep essential facts away from Congress and the press. Another major incident involving ITT and the government was the quiet, out-of-court settlement of an antitrust suit brought by the Justice Department against the corporation. Since the suit was dropped shortly after ITT gave a $40,000 campaign contribution to the Nixon reelection committee, and since an ITT memo (which got into the hands of columnist Jack Anderson) alluded to the role of this "noble commitment" in getting the suit dropped, Congress decided to investigate.

In the spring of 1972 the Senate Judiciary Committee began the probe and discovered that many of the crucial ITT documents had been shredded by the corporation. Since the Securities and Exchange Commission, an executive agency, had already begun its own investigation of the affair, a House subcommittee with jurisdiction over the SEC asked to examine the Commission's files in hopes of finding copies of the missing ITT documents. Acting on White House advice, however, the SEC chairman refused to comply, and, before the subcommittee could formally subpoena the files, had them trucked over to the Justice Department. Since the Justice Department was ostensibly conducting its own investigation of the affair, the effect of the transfer was to protect the documents against a congressional subpoena. By these methods ITT was protected by two executive agencies against the prying eyes of congressional investigators.

Confidentiality of this sort can be found in other executive agencies, notably those in the Defense Department. In the case involving Lockheed's cost overruns on the C-5A transport, which was discussed earlier in the chapter, Senator Proxmire's subcommittee asked the Government Accounting Office (an arm of Congress) to audit the books of the Lockheed Corporation in order to see whether its cost overruns were justified. When this alternative was refused by the corporation, the GAO asked the Defense Department for permission to see its records of the corporation's financial status. A representative of the Office of the Secretary of Defense refused, saying "it would constitute a violation of the confidential relationship existing between the Department and the contractor."[48]

2 Exchange of Personnel The "confidential relationship" between executive agencies and special interests is facilitated in part by an exchange of personnel. In the ITT-Chilean affair we saw that ITT's director was a former head of the CIA, that the corporation's international relations director had been a State Department official for thirty-five years, and that the Secretary of the Treasury had been special counsel to the corporation.

The corporate employment of former Executive Department officials is perhaps best shown in the case of ex-Army officers working for defense contractors. In 1969 Senator William Proxmire released a study showing that the 100 biggest defense contractors employed 2,072 former military officers above the rank of colonel in the Army or Air Force and captain in the Navy. This was about three times as many as those employed the last time a study was made ten years earlier.[49]

The shift of key personnel can also be in the other direction, from industry to government. At the end of 1972 President Nixon appointed Roy L. Ash, president of Litton Industries, to head the Office of Management and Budget. The appointment was made at the very time that Litton was engaged in a series of negotiations with the government over massive cost overruns and delayed production. Nixon also appointed Claude Brinegar, a senior vice-president of Union Oil, to head the Department of Transportation. Union's pipelines are regulated by the Transportation Department, but even this potential conflict of interest was less alarming to environmentalists than the fact that Union was one of the four companies involved in a major oil spill off the California coast in 1969, and the additional fact that Union had campaigned vigorously against diverting portions of the Highway Trust Fund to mass transportation.[50]

The exchange of key officers between industry and government is a frequent occurrence in regulatory agencies. Robert Sherrill claims that "there is so much shuttling between industry and government that it is sometimes difficult to see the line of demarcation between the regulated and the regulators."[51] William H. Tucker, a former chairman of the Interstate Commerce Commission whose rulings favored cutbacks in service by the Penn Central railroad, later left the Commission to become chairman of Penn Central.[52] In a study covering the years 1966–1968 Senator Gaylord Nelson found that twenty-four top officials of the Food and Drug Administration had left to take positions with drug firms.[53] In testimony before a congressional committee in 1970, Nicholas Johnson, Chairman of the Federal Communications Commission, spoke of a similar problem in the FCC: "The record number of FCC Commissioners and other staff who have left the agency to go to work for the very industries they were supposed to be regulating is not a fact to inspire confidence in the agency's performance."[54]

It can be argued that the expertise of business executives is essential if an administrative agency is to be run knowledgeably. In many cases, however, the business executives nominated or appointed are not experts but "generalists" with no special knowledge of the area. Claude Brinegar, the Union Oil executive appointed by President Nixon to head the Department of Transportation, admitted to having no background in transportation problems beyond taking airplane trips and "being bogged down in traffic on the harbor freeway getting to work."[55]

3 Protectiveness In the ITT-Chilean affair, the CIA was prepared to defend the corporation against meddlesome outsiders, in this case the Allende government. In less dramatic ways, other special interests have also cultivated client relationships with federal officials. In his book *The Politics of Consumer Protection*, Mark Nadel mentions a "low point" in the history of the Food and Drug Administration:

> One low point was reached in the late 1950s. A former FDA drug examiner testifying before the Kefauver committee claimed that the drug industry had more influence with the agency than its own medical officers. She testified that on one occasion, after she had urged the FDA to require a manufacturer to issue strong warnings about a tranquilizer to physicians, one of her superiors told her, "I will not have my policy of friendliness with the industry interfered with."[56]

Just as the drug industries have found their protectors in the FDA, defense contractors have found theirs in the Department of Defense. In 1972 the Navy Department tried to fire Gordon Rule, one of its leading cost-efficiency experts, after he criticized Litton Industries and the appointment of its president, Roy Ash, as Budget Director. Recalling former President Eisenhower's warning about a "military-industrial complex," Rule added that "old General Eisenhower must be twitching in his grave."[57] The next morning an admiral was at his door with resignation papers, and when he refused to sign, he was transferred to a minor assignment. Only after three months of bad publicity did the Navy Department restore Rule to his old post. A few years earlier, A. Ernest Fitzgerald, a management analyst for the Air Force, had been less fortunate. It was Fitzgerald who had alerted Congress and the public to the massive cost overruns on the C-5A transport plane being made by Lockheed.[58] After his congressional testimony in December of 1968, Fitzgerald was suddenly transferred to Thailand to review construction of a bowling alley, then discharged from the Air Force. A former presidential aide later supplied the reason: "He wasn't a team player."[59]

Executive agencies have not only protected special interests from the slings and arrows of criticism, they have also shielded them from the more impersonal forces of the marketplace. A $250 million loan-guarantee to Lockheed, which was discussed earlier in the chapter, at least had the approval of Congress, but other loans and grants have been given unilaterally by executive agencies. In 1972 the Navy provided loans totalling $36 million to the Grumman Corporation, another major defense contractor.[60] One of Grumman's subcontractors, the Gap Instrument Corporation, experienced an even more dramatic bailout in 1972 when the Navy purchased $1.7 million of Gap's stock, practically socializing the ailing corporation.[61]

The last point deserves emphasis. While remaining verbally faithful to the ideology of "private enterprise," our nation's largest corporations have gradually moved toward what Walter Adams has called "private socialism."[62] In 1966 H. L. Nieburg noted that "a kind of backhanded government planning, in which [corporations] participate and from which they benefit, has come to replace free enterprise."[63] Companies such as Martin Aviation, which does 99 percent of its business with the government, still regard themselves as "private" businesses, even though both their financial affairs and their bureaucracies are integrated with those of executive agencies.

4 Merging Ideologies What Senator Church referred to as the "incestuous" relationship between government and business is sometimes justified by the participants as necessary to protect "democracy." As we have seen in the ITT-Chile case, however, "democracy" can be confused with either anticommunism or profit making. This confusion is not uncommon in the history of American political thought, and probably has its roots in the belief that any interference with economic liberty is a move toward "regimentation."[64] This belief has provided special interests with an ideological weapon for fighting off threats of public ownership, control, or regulation. At the end of the forties the American Medical Association was able to beat back President Truman's proposal for public health insurance by launching a massive campaign against "this un-American excursion into State Socialism."[65] A similar campaign was conducted by the oil industry in the 1950s to defeat any meaningful government regulation of the industry. "Either the oil industry stays free," said the president of the American Petroleum Institute, "or one by one the lights of private enterprise will go out and the darkness of authoritarian government will settle over the land."[66] In the 1960s the aerospace industry and its supporters were also able to draw upon the amalgamation of democratic and "free enterprise" ideology in preventing an independent government review of the industry's cost estimates and production methods.[67]

Yet we have seen above that some of the largest special interests have become deeply involved with executive agencies—in getting grants and loans, in exchanging personnel and confidential information, in receiving a degree of protection from probers and critics. Since the Second World War a widening gap has opened between the ideology and practice of corporate interests in America. As this discrepancy becomes increasingly obvious, the basis for public acceptance of business rhetoric is correspondingly weakened.

The question of special interests in government cannot be compartmentalized into airtight categories of "legislative" and "executive" lobbying, although we have made such a distinction above for convenience sake. A third category, more basic than the other two, is grass-roots lobbying—lobbying the public.

INTEREST GROUPS AND THE PUBLIC

Since the 1920s corporations have become increasingly aware of the long-run advantage of favorable public opinion. Special interests have used a variety of slogans and appeals to integrate their goals with what they perceive to be public goals. We have heard that what is good for the country is good for General Motors and vice versa, that savings banks are people's banks, that progress is Westinghouse's most important product, that oil companies are deeply concerned about the environment. Businesses and other special interests are well aware that their strength ultimately rests upon public support, or at least public toleration. In the face of widespread hostility no pressure group, however wealthy it is or how cordial its relationship to legislators and executive-branch officials, can be very effective in the political process.

It is in the area of public acceptance that corporate interests have become vulnerable in recent years. The revelations over the past decade—revelations concerning unsafe vehicles in the auto industry, cancer-causing emissions in the chemical industry, "windfall profits" in the oil industry, cost overruns in the defense industry, illegal campaign contributions from just about every industry—have not been particularly helpful to corporate lobbyists and image-makers. Related to these revelations is an increased public concern about the environment, consumer protection, and honest government.

Citizens' Lobbies: Defenders of the General Interest

"Citizens' lobbies" have proliferated over the past decade, at once fostering and benefiting from these new national concerns. What makes the new national concerns different from those of the past (domestic communism, missile gaps, moon races) is that they cannot easily be accommodated to the concerns of large corporate interests. The new citizen lobbies have thus raised the question more pointedly than ever before: What is the *public* interest? The assumption that the public interest can be computed by adding up all the private interests has been shattered by the results of this "consensus": dangerous products, urban sprawl, a polluted countryside, unplanned growth, unnecessary products.

To aim at the public good is not always to aim accurately. Citizen lobbies are not always right, any more than special interests are always wrong. The distinction is rather along the lines suggested by E. E. Schattschneider earlier in this chapter: The members of the American League to Abolish Capital Punishment "do not expect to be hanged."[68] The benefits sought by citizen lobbies are not mainly self-serving and immediate, as they would be, for example, in the case of the American Petroleum Institute. In a sense, then, it is possible to call citizen lobbies *disinterested,* so that the term "interest group" may not be an accurate name for them. Of course, there is no sense pretending that public interest groups are concerned with nothing except what is good for everyone. "If men were angels," Madison remarked in *Federalist 10,* "no government would be necessary." Even the most public-spirited soul is likely to be tainted with the unconscious interests discussed earlier in this chapter—those growing out of fallen man's pride or modern man's tendency toward class bias. Those who claim to speak for the public as a whole always run the risk of being presumptuous. This should put us on our guard against self-righteousness, but it should not lead us to the conclusion that every interest is therefore a special interest, that those who want a clean environment are no different from those who want to foul it up for profit, that those who want consumer protection are the same as those who want to sell dangerous products, that those who work for tax reform are the same as those who have been fighting it off for the past half-century. "The public interest": People can always argue about the content of this ideal, and argue over whether a particular group is in fact representing it. But these are not good reasons for throwing it away.

Over the past decade a large assortment of groups claiming to represent the public interest have appeared, and old ones have been reinvigorated. A few of these may be examined briefly.

The Sierra Club is the best-known environmental group in politics. Founded in 1892, it remained relatively small and inactive until recently, when its membership climbed to 135,000 members in forty-one chapters throughout the United States. The club defeated an effort to dam the Colorado River (which would have flooded sections of the Grand Canyon), thwarted numerous efforts to develop wilderness areas commercially, and fought the trans-Alaska pipeline. In the late 1960s the club sacrificed its tax-exempt status to enter election contests.

Friends of the Earth is a hard-line preservationist organization created in 1969 after a split within the ranks of the Sierra Club. The organization, according to its founder, David Brower, wants "conservation to go on the attack, to . . . reclaim shopping centers, not swamps, cities, not mountains, polluted rivers, not free-flowing streams."[69] Although FOEs membership in 1973 was less than 15,000 it was rapidly growing.

League of Conservation Voters, originally an electoral arm of Friends of the Earth, became fully autonomous in 1972. The league represents the first environmental organization committed to a wholly political program. It has appraised the voting records of congressional candidates and presidential contenders, and raised money for campaign contributions to environment-minded members of Congress.

The Environmental Defense Fund was founded in 1967 with the motto, "Sue the bastards." The Defense Fund works through the courts, but its well-presented scientific testimony on the environmental effects of DDT, Alaskan pipelines, dams and stream channeling have been valuable in mobilizing public opinion.

Ralph Nader, since the publication in 1965 of his exposé of the automobile industry, *Unsafe at Any Speed,* has become the nucleus for a series of citizens' lobbies. His knack for dramatizing issues has won him support not only from the general public but from flocks of student volunteers. In 1969 a group of law students working under his direction put together a highly critical study of the Federal Trade Commission,[70] which was aired in the media and which led to a series of congressional hearings. The ranks of "Nader's Raiders" multiplied the following summer, and were given an institutional base with the establishment of the *Center for the Study of Responsive Law.* The center's full-time staff has produced a virtual torrent of muckraking books—on the Interstate Commerce Commission, the chemical industry, corporate air pollution, food adulteration, DuPont's influence in Delaware, the Bureau of Reclamation, design dangers in the

Volkswagen, private pension systems, and corporate power in America.[71] Nader has also helped organize four other consumer protection groups. The *Center for Auto Safety* attempts to prod members of Congress and industry and to require safer automobiles. The *Project for Corporate Responsibility* seeks greater accountability to the public by corporations. The *Public Interest Research Group* takes the government to court—and publicizes its actions—when the government seems to be acting in collusion with special interests; it also provides a public voice in administrative hearings. *Public Citizen* is a Nader-sponsored organization which directly supports six "action groups": Tax Reform Research Group, Retired Professional Action Group, Health Research Group, Citizen Action Group, Congress Watch, and Public Citizen Litigation Group. Each has a small professional staff which works with part-time students and volunteers on a variety of projects, such as petitioning the Food and Drug Administration to ban dangerous products, issuing reports on dangerous practices (the selling of flammable children's pajamas, irresponsible prescription of "morning-after" birth control pills and mind-affecting drugs), monitoring congressional actions and votes, suing federal agencies and the White House itself to release impounded funds, to open files for public inspection (one such suit helped expose the so-called Milk Deal), and forcing public hearings upon reluctant bureaucrats.

The Consumer Federation of America is a broad umbrella-type of organization set up in 1967 to help coordinate the lobbying activities of consumer groups throughout the nation. Among its approximately 140 member organizations are the *National Consumers League,* which was founded back in 1899, and *Consumers Union,* whose membership is drawn from the 1.3 million subscribers to the periodical *Consumer Reports.*

Common Cause, founded in 1970 and chaired by John Gardner, a former Secretary of Health, Education, and Welfare, has attracted some 200,000 people ready to pay its $15 annual dues and participate in a number of lobbying activities: for the Equal Rights amendment, against the Vietnam war, for eighteen-year-old voting, against the supersonic transport (SST), for congressional reform. Its most notable role has been in the area of campaign financing. First, it has monitored campaigns and publicized the names of those candidates and organizations who fail to make proper financial disclosures. Second, it has lobbied for ceilings on campaign expenditures and for public financing of campaigns. Third, it has gone the length of suing candidates and organizations for violating existing campaign finance laws. It was just such a suit, against the Committee to Re-elect the President, that raised the curtain on the "secret money" scandals of 1972.

Tax Action was formed early in 1973 by former Senator Fred Harris of Oklahoma. While the membership of Common Cause is generally from the more affluent, Tax Action spokesmen claim that its financing comes from the working class and the "silent majority." It seeks to unite both "liberals" and "conservatives" in a populist alliance against the unequal distribution of power and income in America. "Take the rich off welfare" is one of its slogans, and its literature has called attention to the tax loopholes and other advantages given to the rich. Appropriately, its national office is housed in a small and shabby loft in Washington.

These public-interest groups use a variety of tactics and lobby in a variety of settings, but the common thread running through them all is exposure and publicity. John Gardner of Common Cause contends that "effective communication is the most powerful single weapon of the public interest lobby." Quoting H. L. Mencken's definition of "conscience" as "the inner voice that warns us somebody may be looking," Gardner credits conservationists with having "persuaded literally hundreds of federal, state, and local agencies concerned with the environment that 'somebody may be looking.' "[72]

Getting the Public's Ear: Wide Publicity and a "Respectable" Message

Favorable publicity is partly a matter of getting good media coverage, but more basic is the ability to articulate views within the context of "Americanism." Americans tend to be suspicious of new "isms," especially if they seem to have a foreign flavor. The socialist movement in America failed in part because it was always on the defensive, always trying to explain that it would not put people in barracks or take away their religion. Special interests, we have seen, have been able to wrap themselves in the American ideology of "private enterprise," stigmatizing reform as "regimentation" and identifying the nation's interests with their own. The political strength of the newer public-interest groups lies in the fact that they have been able to "out-Americanize" corporate lobbies by packaging reform in traditional ideology. Instead of coming up with new "isms," they have fought special interests with the language of American conservatism. Ralph Nader, for example, has managed to associate corporations with violence—with cars that kill and maim, chemicals that poison, air that chokes.[73] He talks about "crime in the suites" and "corporate radicalism."[74] He appeals to the American tradition of self-help and invokes memories of New England town meetings.[75] Consumer groups in general proceed from an unarguable premise. As one congressional staffer put it, "Who isn't in favor of clean meat?"[76] As for conservationist groups, they can draw upon a native tradition of rural romanticism going back to Thoreau and Jefferson. In their successful fight to defeat a government-subsidized supersonic transport in 1970 they also enlisted the aid of a conservative economist to argue that the project was a step toward "socialism." In a similar way, Fred Harris's Tax Action turns the hated word "welfare" around to use on the privileged rich.

Despite this reliance upon conservative ideology, some of the reforms contemplated by the newer public interest groups are liberal and even radical. Tax Action calls for a redistribution of wealth, Common Cause champions subsidized elections, Friends of the Earth would "reclaim" the very center of suburban America, and Ralph Nader wants criminal sanctions of "maximum deterrence" used against offending corporations.[77] The paradox of Americans is that they seem willing to accept fundamental change as long as the change is justified in the context of tradition. Big business interests have long grasped this paradox, which enabled them to nudge the country toward a planned and socialized country in the name of "free enterprise." The new citizens' lobbies have discovered that America's old habits of thought can be just as potent in fighting corporations as they were in justifying them. Philosophically this may be absurd, but philosophers have seldom been effective lobbyists.

SUMMARY

    1 A valid distinction can be made between special interests and the general interest. This does not mean that lobbies purporting to represent the general interest are always right, nor does it rule out pragmatic alliances between them and special interests on occasion. The distinction turns rather on the fact that citizens' lobbies aim at all (citizens, consumers, breathers of air), while special interests are concerned primarily with their own group. Adding together, or even carefully "adjusting," all these special interests does not always produce a result consistent with the general interest.

    2 "Payoff," or the suspicion of it, continues to cast a shadow over the decision-making process in both the legislative and the executive branches. Outright bribery may be rare. But members of Congress receive campaign contributions from interest groups affected by legislation. And jobs are given to ex-administrators in the very industries they have been regulating.

    3 Aside from the grosser examples of special-interest influence, a continuing problem is the camaraderie and mutual protectiveness in the relationship between special interests and government. These "incestuous" relationships include the interchange of personnel, shared secrets, and merging ideologies.

    4 Despite these well-entrenched relationships, public interest groups have been making themselves heard and felt in recent years. The key to their success is publicity, which depends upon skillful lobbying, good organization, and favorable media coverage, but even more basically upon a supportive public opinion. The public-interest groups have gained this support by integrating reform with a familiar and traditional ideology.

Muckrakers and cartoonists have often pictured the special-interest lobbyist as a potbellied, cigar-chomping manipulator. Political scientists, perhaps just as often, have reacted with their own stereotype of "the ordinary, honest lobbyist" going about his "workaday activities."[78] Each points toward a partial truth. It is true that many good bills could not have been written without the assistance of lobbyists in providing information, sharpening issues, serving as vital channels of communication in the legislative process. It is equally true that the widespread suspicion of special-interest money is buoyed up from time to time by spectacular exposés. These aside, the more respectable forms of collusions involve a community of interest between government officials and special interests.

Yet these facts must not be allowed to obscure the more important fact that the American political process is responsive to counterpressure from citizens' lobbies. If the "Senator's helper" stereotype of the special-interest lobbyist can lead to complacency, the "manipulator" stereotype can lead to a wholly unwarranted cynicism. The experience of the past ten years suggests that public opinion can be mobilized by citizens' groups, special interests can be beaten at their own game, and politicians, by and large, do respond to pressure from the public, at least when it takes the form of serious and reasonable argument from large numbers of constituents.

Continued federal funding of Boeing's supersonic transport was considered a safe bet in 1970. It had been supported by three Presidents as well as by business and labor pressure groups. Yet a coalition of citizens and environmental pressure groups was able to defeat it. By means of ads, pamphlets, congressional testimony, lecture tours, and the recruitment of "name" opponents like Arthur Godfrey they were able to focus an intense flow of public pressure upon Congress. One Senator who changed his vote from support to opposition of SST probably spoke for many other politicians in citing the reason for his change of heart: "I read my mail."[79]

NOTES

1. Lester W. Milbrath, *The Washington Lobbyists* (Chicago: Rand McNally & Company, 1963), p. 298.
2. V. O. Key, Jr., *Politics, Parties and Pressure Groups,* 4th ed. (New York: Thomas Y. Crowell Company, 1958), p. 144.
3. James Deakin, *The Lobbyists* (Washington: Public Affairs Press, 1966), p. 38.
4. See, for example, Donald R. Matthews, *U.S. Senators and Their World* (New York: Vintage Books, Random House, Inc., 1960), chap. VIII.
5. Key, op cit., p. 152.
6. *Federalist 10.* The remaining Madison quotations are drawn either from *Federalists 10* or *51.*
7. Carl Becker, *The Declaration of Independence* (New York: Alfred A. Knopf, Inc., 1956).
8. Adam Smith, *The Wealth of Nations* (London: A. Strahan and T. Cadell, 1793).
9. John C. Calhoun, *A Disquisition on Government,* ed. by C. Gordon Post (Indianapolis, Ind.: The Bobbs-Merrill Company, Inc., 1953), p. 13.
10. Arthur F. Bentley, *The Process of Government* (Evanston, Ill.: The Principia Press, 1949), p. 455.
11. David B. Truman, *The Governmental Process: Political Interests and Public Opinion* (New York: Alfred A. Knopf, Inc., 1951), p. 34.
12. Other influential statements of "the group basis of politics" during this period included the following: Earl Latham, "The Group Basis of Politics: Notes for a Theory," *American Political Science Review,* XLVI (June 1952), pp. 376–397; Robert T. Golembiewski, "'The Group Basis of Politics': Notes on Analysis and Development," *American Political Science Review,* LIV (December 1960), pp. 38–51; Robert Dahl, *A Preface to Democratic Theory* (Chicago: University of Chicago Press, 1956). Texts and case studies written from the "group" point of view are too numerous to mention.
13. Truman, op. cit., p. 4.
14. Ibid., p. 38.
15. Harold Lassell, *Politics: Who Gets What, When, How* (Cleveland: Meridian Books, The World Publishing Company, 1958).
16. C. Wright Mills, *The Power Elite* (New York: Oxford University Press, 1956).
17. The term was apparently derived from an influential book published by Arthur

Schlesinger, Jr., at the beginning of the period, *The Vital Center* (Boston: Houghton Mifflin Company, 1949).
18 Robert A. Dahl, *Pluralist Democracy in the United States* (Chicago: Rand McNally & Company, 1967), p. 190.
19 E. E. Schattschneider, *The Semi-Sovereign People* (New York: Holt, Rinehart and Winston, Inc., 1960), pp. 24, 26.
20 Robert Paul Wolff, "Beyond Tolerance," in R. P. Wolff, B. Moore, and H. Marcuse, *A Critique of Pure Tolerance* (Boston: Beacon Press, 1965), pp. 49–50.
21 Theodore J. Lowi, *The End of Liberalism* (New York: W. W. Norton & Company, Inc., 1969), chap. 8.
22 Ibid., chap. 10.
23 Jean-Jacques Rousseau, *The Social Contract* and *Discourses,* ed. by G. D. H. Cole (New York: E. P. Dutton & Co., Inc., 1950), p. 26.
24 Raymond A. Bauer, Ithiel de Sola Pool, and Lewis Anthony Dexter, *American Business and Public Policy: The Politics of Foreign Trade* (New York: Atherton Press, Inc., 1963), p. 324.
25 Ibid., pp. 122, 119, 479.
26 *New York Times,* Nov. 1, 1973, p. 8.
27 Robert N. Winter-Berger, *The Washington Pay-Off* (New York: Dell Publishing Co., Inc., 1972), p. 38.
28 Ibid., p. 313.
29 See above, p. 1.
30 Deakin, op. cit., p. 23.
31 See Chap. 4, above, p. 128.
32 Reprinted in the *New York Post,* May 18, 1973, p. 4.
33 Quoted in *The Power of the Pentagon,* a Congressional Quarterly paperback (Washington: Congressional Quarterly, Inc., 1972), p. 88.
34 Ibid., p. 89.
35 Ibid., p. 87.
36 Robert I. Vexler, ed., *Dwight D. Eisenhower, 1890–1969* (Dobbs Ferry, N.Y.: Oceana Publications, Inc., 1970), p. 143.
37 See Arnold Rose's useful discussion of what Eisenhower did and did not mean. *The Power Structure: Political Process in American Society* (New York: Oxford University Press, 1967), pp. 36–37.
38 Marc Pilisuk and Thomas Hayden, "Is There a Military-Industrial Complex Which Prevents Peace?" *Journal of Social Issues,* XXI (July 1965), pp. 98–99. Emphasis added.
39 Background press briefing, Sept. 16, 1970, reprinted in U.S. Senate, 93d Congress, *Hearings on Multinational Corporations and United States Foreign Policy, before Subcommittee on Multinational Corporations of the Committee on Foreign Relations,* Mar. 20-Apr. 2, 1973, Part II, pp. 542–543.
40 Memo from Hal Hendrix and Robert Berrellez to Edward J. Gerrity, Sept. 17, 1970, reprinted in ibid., p. 615.
41 Ibid., p. 610.
42 Telegram from Edward J. Gerrity to Harold S. Geneen, Sept. 29, 1970. Reprinted in ibid., p. 627.
43 Ibid., Part I., p. 415.
44 Ibid., p. 40.
45 Ibid., p. 259.
46 Ibid., p. 80.

47 Ibid., pp. 485–486.
48 Quoted in *The Power of the Pentagon,* a Congressional Quarterly book, op. cit., p. 91.
49 *Congressional Quarterly,* Weekly Reports, Mar. 13, 1969, p. 451.
50 *New York Times,* Dec. 24, 1972, p. 39.
51 Robert Sherrill, *Why They Call It Politics* (New York: Harcourt Brace Jovanovich, 1972), p. 174.
52 Ibid. pp. 174–175. For citations of ten other instances involving former ICC commissioners, plus a longer discussion of the problem, see Robert Fellmeth, *The Interstate Commerce Omission* (New York: Grossman Publishers, 1970), pp. 15–22.
53 Sherrill, op. cit., p. 175.
54 Quoted in Morton Mintz and Jerry S. Cohen, *America, Inc.* (New York: Dell Publishing Co., Inc., 1971), p. 305.
55 *New York Times,* Dec. 24, 1972, p. 39.
56 Mark V. Nadel, *The Politics of Consumer Protection* (Indianapolis, Ind.: The Bobbs-Merrill Company, Inc., 1971), p. 97.
57 Quoted in Brit Hume, "Admiral Kidd vs. Mister Rule," *The New York Times Magazine,* Mar. 25, 1973, p. 38.
58 See above, pp. 151–152.
59 *New York Times,* Mar. 29, 1973, p. 12.
60 *New York Times,* Dec. 22, 1972, p. 1.
61 *New York Times,* Dec. 27, 1972, p. 1.
62 Quoted in Mark J. Green with Beverly C. Moore, Jr., and Bruce Wasserstein, *The Closed Enterprise System* (New York: Grossman Publishers, 1972), p. 3.
63 H. L. Nieburg, *In the Name of Science* (Chicago: Quadrangle Books, Inc., 1966), p. 195.
64 For a classic expression of this venerable ideology, see Herbert Hoover, *The Challenge to Liberty* (New York: Charles Scribner's Sons, 1934). Hoover was of course defeated by Roosevelt, but his strictures against "government dictation" are still effective rhetorical weapons in America.
65 Key, op. cit., p. 138.
66 Robert Engler, *The Politics of Oil* (Chicago: Phoenix Books, University of Chicago Press, 1967), p. 460.
67 Nieburg, op. cit., chap. XII.
68 See above, p. 8.
69 Quoted in Walter A. Rosenbaum, *The Politics of Environmental Concern* (New York: Frederick A. Praeger, Inc., 1973), pp. 77–78.
70 Edward Cox, Robert Fellmeth, and John Schultz, *The "Nader Report" on the Federal Trade Commission* (New York: Barron Publishers, 1969).
71 Fellmeth, op. cit.; James S. Turner, *The Chemical Feast* (New York: Grossman Publishers, 1970); John C. Esposito, *Vanishing Air* (New York: Grossman Publishers, 1970); Harrison Wellford, *Sowing the Wind* (New York: Grossman Publishers, 1973); James Phelan and Robert Pozem, *The Company State* (New York: Grossman Publishers, 1973); Richard L. Berkman and W. Kip Viscusi, *Damming the West* (New York: Grossman Publishers, 1973); The Center for Auto Safety, *Small—On Safety* (New York: Grossman Publishers, 1973); Ralph Nader and Kate Blackwell, *You and Your Pension* (New York: Grossman Publishers, 1973); Ralph Nader and Mark J. Green, eds., *Corporate Power in America* (New York: Grossman Publishers, 1973).
72 John W. Gardner, *In Common Cause* (New York: W. W. Norton & Company, Inc., 1972), p. 89.
73 Nadel, op. cit., p. 179.

74 Green et al., op. cit., Nader's introduction, p. vii.
75 Donald K. Ross, *A Public Citizen's Action Manual* (New York: Grossman Publishers, 1973), Nader's introduction, passim.
76 Quoted in Nadel, op. cit., p. 200.
77 Mintz and Cohen, op. cit., Nader's introduction, p. 18.
78 See above, p. 1.
79 Quoted in *The Washington Lobby,* a Congressional Quarterly paperback (Washington: Congressional Quarterly, Inc., 1971), p. 109.

Chapter 6

Parties: Remembrance of Glories Past

I belong to the increasing body of Americans who cannot forget that parties are instruments.

Felix Frankfurter*

Are political parties dying in America? Dr. Martin Peretz of Harvard has examined survey data which indicate "a steady and consistent number of people who are ready to throw both parties out."[1] *Newsweek* polled college students in the fall of 1969 and found that only 18 percent gave a favorable rating to parties, the lowest rating given to any American institution. Approximately the same rating emerged from a twelve-campus survey made by the *National Review* in 1971.[2] It has already been noted, in an earlier chapter of this book, that the ranks of independent voters have been growing steadily in recent years—they now outnumber Republicans by some 10 percent—and on some Northern campuses 50 percent of the students consider themselves independents.[3] Even assuming that the disaffection is only temporary, that the independents will eventually come "home" to Republicanism or Democracy, it seems likely that they will come home not as fervent partisans but as skeptics, ticket-splitters, voters for "the person (or the cause), not the party."

---

* Quoted in Morris K. Udall, "Where Do We Go from Here?" *New Republic,* CLXIX (Nov. 24, 1973), p. 16.

Accompanying the parties' loss of prestige is an almost catastrophic breakdown in organization. "Both of our parties," James MacGregor Burns noted in 1973, "are in disarray at virtually every level."[4] Local committees rarely meet anymore, and they deal with trivia when they do. Party organization has largely been replaced with personal organizations, loyal to their particular candidates but to no one else. And if one of these candidates is fortunate enough to get elected, these loyal retainers, not party leaders, will be the ones who will share the politician's power and enjoy his ear.

These reflections do not settle the question of whether our parties are dying, but they do raise an even more basic question: *Should* our political parties die? Are they worth keeping alive, or should we say, in the words of Gilbert and Sullivan, "they'll none of them be missed"?

They would be sorely missed, one answer goes, as an indispensable link between the people and their officials. Much concern has revolved around "the imperial presidency," an office cut off from the rest of the nation, its occupant surrounded by yes-men, its power dangerously personal, its operations shrouded in secrecy. It is noteworthy, the argument continues, that all of the nefarious operations collectively called "Watergate" were conducted without the knowledge of the Republican party leadership. Watergate was the work of political amateurs, insulated from the currents of party politics and loyal only to one man. Strong, vigorous parties, the argument concludes, can end the politics of *personalismo,* tie our officials to the public at large, and get the grass roots actively involved in the business of government.[5]

The pros and cons concerning the position of parties in America are therefore likely to combine elements of description, prediction, and prescription, such as the following:

"Are our parties dying?"

"Who cares?"

"*I* care. Without them we have apathy at the bottom and irresponsibility at the top."

"What, those hacks?"

"Those 'hacks,' as you call them, are what make democracy work. Sure, parties could use some reforms, such as—"

"Reform! Parties are anachronisms."

"Then they *are* dying."

"Who cares?"

But if it is granted that our political parties are worth saving, the next question is: Do they need "reform"? What sort of reforms? Minority quotas at conventions? More—or less—openness to the average, uncommitted voter? More—or less—media coverage? More—or less—party discipline? "Reform" toward what end, and for what purpose?

All these questions are pertinent to the study of parties in America today, but before we can even hazard some answers to them we must approach the subject more systematically. Let us begin with a more basic question: What *is* a political party?

"PARTY" DEFINED

There are many definitions of "political party." Some say too little (Disraeli defined "party" simply as "organized opinion"),[6] while others say too much: They load the definition with all sorts of functions which the definer *hopes* parties perform, or *wishes* them to perform. One writer defined a party as "an organization that activates and mobilizes the people, represents interests, provides for compromises among competing points of view, and becomes the proving ground for leadership. . . ."[7] But if parties "activate" people, why are so many people repelled by parties? If parties provide for compromise, why were the Republican national convention of 1964 and the Democratic conventions of 1968 and 1972 so uncompromising? If parties provide the proving grounds for leadership, why did the Republicans in 1952 pass over a seasoned party leader like Robert Taft to nominate General Eisenhower, a political neophyte? Obviously we need a definition of "party" which avoids question-begging, and while none is perfect, J. S. Coleman's may be the most useful for present purposes: "Political parties are associations formally organized with the explicit and declared purpose of acquiring and/or maintaining legal control, either singly or in coalition or electoral competition with other similar associations, over the personnel and the policy of the government of an actual or prospective sovereign state."[8]

Party, Pressure Group, Movement

Coleman's careful definition helps to distinguish parties from "pressure groups," which were discussed in the previous chapter. While both parties and pressure groups seek to influence governmental decision making, parties are organized for the express purpose of maintaining legal control over the society. American labor, for example, forms pressure groups to obtain favorable action from the government, but in England and other countries labor has sought to obtain legal control of the government, and thus has become a party. In becoming one, however, the Labour party lost some of its exclusiveness as a strictly workingman's organization. It learned that it must appeal to other elements of the population, including some of the middle class, in order to win elections.

A party, unlike a pressure group, plays a formal role in governing. Its name appears on ballots, its procedures for selecting candidates are likely to be regulated by the state. Its status is more public than private. It is akin to a political institution (such as a Congress or Parliament), and like such an institution it seeks to stabilize and perpetuate itself through formal rules and bylaws. This distinguishes parties not only from pressure groups but from *movements*. Movements, as the name implies, are more fluid than parties. They represent not things but ideas, hence need no organizational structure or bylaws. Movements place no value on stability—indeed, stability is usually the death of movements—and require no in-group loyalty in order to hold together. Their cohesion results from shared devotion to a doctrine or set of ideas rather than a loyalty to persons or obedience to rules. The distinction between parties and movements will become important later in this chapter, where we shall return to it.

AMERICAN PARTIES

In the definition of parties quoted earlier it was noted that parties acquire their power "either singly or in coalition or electoral competition" with other such associations. This provides a good starting point for distinguishing the American party system from that in other countries. American parties do not acquire power "singly" but in "electoral competition" with other parties—another way of saying that America is not a one-party system. In such countries as China and the Soviet Union one totalitarian party rules every facet of life and tolerates no opposition. Other one-party systems (such as in Taiwan and Egypt) are less totalitarian but no less intolerant of opposition parties. Still others, such as in Yugoslavia and Spain, permit only one party, but allow open factionalism within the party. Finally, there are de facto one-party systems which permit opposition parties to exist but govern principally through the dominant party. (India used to be the classic example, but in 1975 Prime Minister Indira Gandhi suddenly suspended civil liberties and jailed leaders of the opposition parties.) America fits none of these categories. Democrats and Republicans at once tolerate and compete[9] with one another; neither is assured lasting dominance on the national scene, and even locally one-party hegemony has eroded in recent years.

Party competition also sets American parties aside from those multiparty systems, most often associated with continental Europe, which rule through coalition. The American party system resembles Britain's in being a competitive bipartisan system. A closer examination, however, reveals important differences between the British and American party systems. Britain's party system, like that of Japan, West Germany, Australia, Sweden, and other countries, can be classified as a *distinct* bipartisan system, while America's bipartisanship is *indistinct*. The former systems are marked by a high degree of structure and discipline. Any member of Britain's Parliament who regularly and intentionally defied the party leadership would almost certainly lose the support of the party organization in the next election, and might be formally expelled from the party. American members of Congress, on the other hand, regularly defy the party leadership, as when Southern Democrats team up with conservative Republicans to defeat legislation favored by the Democratic leadership—and do so with impunity. Indeed, it is difficult to find the "leadership" of American parties. The President? But even the charismatic Franklin Roosevelt, fresh from his 1936 landslide, was unable to purge Southern conservatives from his party. Congressional party leaders? Their effectiveness turns almost entirely upon their individual personalities. One of the most successful of them, Lyndon Johnson, used wheeling and dealing, rather than rules or sanctions, for lining up votes, many of which were bipartisan. National party chairpersons? They are usually creatures of the party's presidential candidate. If the candidate loses, "his" party chairperson goes down with him; if he wins, the party chairperson becomes merely another adviser. The only disciplined party leadership in America has been at the local level, in the urban "machines" run by "bosses." This sort of party leadership, however, has scarcely been appreciated (except, perhaps, in romantic retrospect) by those articulate enough to write about it. Americans have always been suspicious of well-defined leadership structures or hierarchies. They like to talk about "rugged individualism," they have made folk heroes out of mavericks, and the very expression "party line" sounds alien and subversive to their ears.

A price has to be paid for this sort of individualism, and to many critics this price is unacceptable. Political leaders from Woodrow Wilson and Franklin Roosevelt to Barry Goldwater have chafed under the American party system. Wilson frankly wished America had adopted the British system, and tried his best to impose it. Roosevelt, according to Basil Rauch in *The History of the New Deal*, hoped to produce an "adjustment of party lines which would make party labels correspond with political philosophies."[10] Goldwater declaimed against "fuzzy" Republicanism and promised "a choice—not an echo" in 1964. By far, though, the greatest reservoir of discontent with American parties does not lie among practicing politicians but within the ranks of political scientists. In the late 1940s a committee of the American Political Science Association went on record favoring "a more responsible two-party system." Its report argued that parties ought to formulate more specific and comprehensive party programs, nominate candidates pledged to the programs, and see that their candidates stick to these programs when elected. In 1970 the APSA took a critical look backward at its earlier report, in effect reversing it, but the political science profession still remains the richest source of arguments for "responsible" parties.

"RESPONSIBLE" PARTIES: SOME PROS AND CONS

The case for "responsible parties"[11] is rooted in two considerations.

The *first* is a sort of political truth-in-packaging argument: The voters are entitled to know what they are voting for. Suppose they vote in a Democratic Congress. What do they get? Instead of a unified majority in Congress, they get a hodgepodge of shifting coalitions, some of them surely contrary to the mainstream of Democratic sentiment in the nation. Southern Democrats (who, thanks to seniority, have enjoyed disproportionate strength in Congress) often team up with conservative Republicans to defeat legislation sponsored by the Democratic leadership. (Republicans, at least those who claim to be "real" Republicans in the tradition of Taft and Hoover, have also cause to complain about mislabeling, since liberal Republicans like Jacob Javits and Charles Percy are often difficult to distinguish from Democrats.) Hence the charge of "irresponsibility"—and the proposed solution: Separate the sheep from the goats; let liberal Republicans become Democrats and conservative Democrats become Republicans; let them run on platforms which provide the voters with meaningful alternatives; then, make them implement these pledges so that what the voters see is what they get.

The *second* part of the "responsible parties" argument proceeds from a presumed need for "activism," the need to "get things done." James MacGregor Burns has complained about "government by fits and starts"—governmental paralysis, broken only by frantic bursts of activity when crisis appears. He argues that "responsible" parties can help solve this problem by setting the framework for sustained planning on the basis of a program approved by the voters. Unified and disciplined parties, parties which hold frequent conferences, formulate policy and platforms, punish violaters, and generally carry out their pledges, can go a long way toward ending "the deadlock of democracy."[12]

Opponents of the "responsible parties" model have raised a variety of objections to it: that it would destroy flexibility in policy making, discourage compromise, provoke divisiveness and extremism, lead to a multiparty system, force voters into simplistic either/or preferences, require an unhealthy centralization of parties and spell the end of intraparty democracy. Perhaps the most basic question raised by critics of "responsible" parties is whether such a system can be grafted onto a nation like ours. Our parties are not distinctively "liberal" and "conservative," the argument runs, because our people are not. Politics in America are too complex to fit neatly into such categories. Even in England the extent to which voters are clearly expressing "Conservative" or "Labour" preferences is open to serious question, but the bewildering variety of issues in contemporary America makes any such labels meaningless. Our constitutional system is at one with our political culture in discouraging such clear-cut choices. Unlike England's, ours separates the President from Congress, electing each from a different constituency and at different times. Congress itself is divided into two branches (England's House of Lords, once the "upper" house, has become largely ceremonial) and these branches are elected for different terms. To expect disciplined and united majorities to emerge from this constitutional framework is as unrealistic as expecting Americans to give up their individualism, their habit of improvisation, their suspicion of sharp ideological distinctions.

Both proponents and opponents of "responsible" parties can find grounds for satisfaction in the events of the past decade or so. Opponents may feel vindicated by election returns and public opinion polls. The nomination of "ideological" presidential contenders, by the Republicans in 1964 and the Democrats in 1972, ended in disaster for both parties at the hands of the voters. Senator Goldwater's declaration to the contrary notwithstanding, American voters apparently *do* consider "extremism" a vice and "moderation" a virtue. Americans seem to prefer a kind of hazy politics, with ideological and even party labels playing a minor role. While still serving as Democratic leader of the Senate, Lyndon Johnson was shrewd enough to play down his party identification. "I am," he wrote, "a free man, an American, a United States Senator and a Democrat—in that order."[13] When even party leaders mute their identities, how is the average voter to react to "responsible" parties?

Yet the advocate of "responsible" parties can also rummage through the events of the recent past and find grounds for vindication. A 1971 study by David Nexon suggested that Republican activists have always tended to be conservative ideologues. Democratic activists have been less ideological than their Republican counterparts, probably because they have been drawn more from the ranks of "professional" politicians, i. e., urban bosses and labor union leaders. This could change, Nexon speculated, if more amateur activists were to play a role in the Democratic nomination process.

> If the issues of the future rub the electorate as raw as Vietnam and, to a lesser extent, Black Power did in 1968, control of the Democratic Party may be wrested from the

decaying machines and the labor unions that have partially replaced them. Data for 1972 would then show high participation and greater "extremism" for activists in both major parties. . . .[14]

This, of course, is exactly what happened in 1972. While "extremism" may not be the right word—"issue orientation" is clumsier but more precise—the people who nominated George McGovern were certainly not pragmatic technicians unconcerned about programs or issues.

Nor has it been only the party activists who are attuned to differences in ideology. Studies cited in a previous chapter suggest that the average voter is also issue-oriented.[15] Whether, as the studies of V. O. Key suggested, the voters have always been aware of issues, or whether the awareness is of more recent origin, the point is that American voters can no longer be considered indifferent to programs and ideologies.

As if in response to this fresh evidence of public awareness, politicians everywhere seem to be changing parties to fit their ideologies. Senator Strom Thurmond, a former Southern Democrat, is now a major power broker in the Republican party. Former New York mayor John Lindsay, whose liberal brand of Republicanism was a constant annoyance to conservatives in his party, is now a Democrat. Former Los Angeles mayor Sam Yorty, a conservative Democrat, is now a Republican. Congressman Don Riegle (Michigan) and former Congressman Ogden Reid (New York), both liberal Republicans, have become Democrats. Former New York Governor Nelson Rockefeller, once the very symbol of liberal Republicanism, has publicly confessed the error of his old ways and shifted perceptively to the right. Without any formal party reorganization, then, the sheep and the goats have been separating *themselves.*

These developments may give comfort to the advocates of "responsible" parties. Yet their ultimate hope seems to be fading.

What is this hope? It pervades the whole argument for "responsible" parties; it is so obvious that it is sometimes not even stated. The hope is that programmatic parties, parties that "mean something," will energize people, engage them, get them involved in the political process.[16] Yet the "vast boredom with politics"[17] which James MacGregor Burns thought he saw in the America of early sixties has deepened—*despite the fact that parties have become more ideological.* In 1964, with Goldwater versus Johnson, Americans were given a more clear-cut choice of domestic alternatives than they had had any time since 1936—yet voter turnout declined from its high of 64 percent of eligible voters in 1960 to 62.9 percent. In 1968, American voters were given a choice of three well-known candidates, one of whom, George Wallace, sounded distinctly different from the others—yet voter turnout declined to 61.8 percent. In 1972 most voters were aware that McGovern and Nixon stood for distinctly different political philosophies—and voter turnout declined another 5 percent.

By 1973 the "vast boredom" which Professor Burns wrote about a decade earlier had turned into what pollster Louis Harris called a "rather deep cynicism."[18] This is not to say that political parties had caused the cynicism and apathy, only that they were powerless to prevent it. Parties, whether programmatic or not, do not seem to have much impact on the attitudes or behavior of the American public. The arguments pro and con over "responsible" parties have become academic, and even some of the academics are growing weary of it all. One article published in the *Journal of Politics* in 1971 was entitled "Toward a More Responsible Two-Party System? What, Again?"

Whether they provide choices or echoes, then, political parties seem to have lost much of their power to engage the voters and shape the political order. To speak of such a loss, of course, implies an obligation to explain *what* was lost and *how* it was lost. How did parties engage the attention of voters, and what effect did they have upon the development of American democracy? In order to see in perspective the low estate to which parties have fallen today, one must look back at the role of parties in American history. For it is not in the present but the past that the glory of American parties shines most brightly.

THE EMERGENCE OF AMERICAN PARTIES

Despite the enormous role parties were to play in the expansion of American democracy, their emergence was unheralded—and unappreciated—in the early days of the nation. Parties are nowhere mentioned in the Constitution. The Founders generally regarded them as another species of "faction": ineradicable, probably, "sown in the nature of man," but nothing to be proud of. Thomas Jefferson once declared that "if I could not go to heaven but with a party, I would not go there at all."[19] George Washington in his Farewell Address condemned "all combinations and associations, under whatever plausible connection, with the real design to direct, control, counteract or awe the regular deliberation of the constituted authorities."[20]

Pronouncements of this sort were typical in the eighteenth century. At the time they seemed almost truisms, beyond the realm of dispute. Like many other political truisms, however, they were ignored in practice by everyone, including their authors. Washington himself became the mainstay of the Federalists, our country's first national party, and it was not long before Thomas Jefferson was riding into the Presidency on the back of a rival party called the Republicans.

Washington's expressed aversion to political "combinations and associations" was by no means hypocritical. By the 1790s it was easy for the Federalists to forget that they were themselves a political "association." They originated as the party of the Constitution, and within a few years of its ratification the nation's new charter had become a kind of holy writ. Washington, the hero of the Revolution, was unanimously elected and was to become the very incarnation of national solidarity: He was grave, deliberate, "above politics," a figure of awesome dignity. But the increased drift of his administration toward East-coast, mercantile, and banking interests at the expense of rural, Western, and Southern interests made schism inevitable, and this split was given an ideological dimension by the different reception each side gave to the French Revolution and its aftermath. As republican France embarked upon a long series of wars with England, Americans divided into Anglophiles and Francophiles, the first accusing the second of anarchism and atheism, the latter responding with its own favorite epithet: "monocrat." The mercantile interests of the Eastern seaboard, who had by now appropriated the name "Federalist," generally favored the British, while the rural and Western interests tended to side with the cause of the French Revolution.

The Cabinet of George Washington became the crucible for these national divisions. By the mid-nineties Secretary of State Jefferson was the leader of "the French faction," as they were called by their enemies, or the "Republicans," as they preferred to call themselves. Alexander Hamilton, the Secretary of the Treasury, served as a brilliant, if abrasive, spokesman for the Anglophile Federalists. With Washington's retirement these divisions flared into open political warfare, and in 1796 the Federalists won their first battle by an ominously slim margin—71 electoral votes for John Adams (Hamilton was considered too extreme to win the nomination) to 68 for Jefferson. But four years later, in 1800, the score was approximately reversed: 73 votes for Jefferson and 65 for Adams. In a remarkable display of party unity, each Republican elector gave his second vote to Aaron Burr, Jefferson's running mate, producing a tie between the two and throwing the election into the House of Representatives. After Jefferson's final victory in the House, the Federalist party rapidly disintegrated, and, after 1816, ceased to exist.

In retrospect the extinction of the Federalists may seem to have been written in the stars. Preoccupied with the interests of the East Coast and openly disdainful of "the mass of the people," they had the misfortune to live in a nation which was rapidly expanding westward and increasing in numbers. Destiny aside, however, a more critical factor in the decline of the Federalists was their inability to bend, to compromise, to build coalitions. Jefferson, no less than Hamilton, sided with narrow class interests (he once described farmers as God's "chosen people"), but he knew how to forge alliances with others of quite different interests and temperaments. In 1791 he and his fellow Virginian James Madison journeyed into New York State, ostensibly on a "botanical" field trip, and helped to build an alliance with New York Republicans that paid off in 1800 when Jefferson and Burr carried the state.

This early success of the Jeffersonian Republicans in cementing alliances between disparate interests was repeated again and again in the history of emerging parties. In the 1830s and 1840s the flood of impoverished Irish immigrants found a home in the newly formed Democratic party, which managed to link them together in a victorious coalition with Western frontiersmen and Southern farmers. As the Civil War approached, the new Republican party (not to be confused with the old Jeffersonian Republicans) was created through an alliance of prairie farmers, some Northeastern manufacturers, native laborers, abolitionists, Free-Soilers, Barnburners, Know-Nothings, radicals, utopians, and bankers.[21] A period of Republican dominance continued almost without interruption until 1921, when the new immigrants from Southern and Eastern Europe were combined with Irish machine politicians, Southern rednecks, Northern blacks, university liberals, and many former Republicans to produce, in effect, a new Democratic party.

In surveying the sweep of party history, one quality of our parties seems particularly striking: their almost breathtaking opportunism. Irish immigrants barely off the boat were greeted with open arms by native American party bosses who must have despised everything about them—their poverty, their "popery," their accents, their manners—everything, that is, except their ability to cast ballots. Years later, the descendants of these immigrants would (with the greatest of reluctance, and, as it were, against their better judgment) share some of their power with the newer immigrants. They would also manage periodically to meet, nominate candidates, draft solemn platforms, and make private deals with people who hated *all* immigrants.

These are improbable coalitions; they may also seem irrational, unprincipled, or both. Yet from the standpoint of popular self-government America's opportunistic parties played an epic role. They helped bring a sprawling collection of people together in a republican experiment—not a perfect republic, of the kind demanded by philosophers and hommes de lettres, but a rough-and-ready, vernacular type of republic of continental proportions. More specifically, parties played three key roles in the development of American democracy.

SOME FUNCTIONS OF PARTIES

1 Bringing In the "Outs"

American parties exerted a powerful force for bringing the "outs" in. What was accomplished by violent revolt in the European continent was done loudly, rudely, sometimes crookedly, but more or less peacefully by political parties in America.

In the mid-nineteenth century a nativist writer in Philadelphia named John Hancock Lee complained about the rapid rise to power of immigrants "who had not been sufficiently long in the country to have lost the odour of the steerage." These "noisy and riotous" immigrants had proven to be "exceedingly active at the elections," it appeared, and their activism was "encouraged and applauded by party leaders and aspiring demogogues." The votes of the immigrants were secured with promises of minor offices, "all of which they were rapidly beginning to fill." And then, inexorably, the tragic chain of consequences:

> It so happened, however, that they were not altogether satisfied with petty positions; they began to feel their importance, and to make demands of those who had used them for tools, that excited some little alarm. The babe, that had lain quiet in its cradle, had grown up to manhood, and its gigantic body was no longer to be easily managed. The servant aspired to be master.[22]

Honest citizens "looked on aghast" and tried to stop the "threatening evils," but the party leaders "were helpless, and, like wretched gamesters, were daily increasing their stakes, with the desperate hope of getting 'even in the end.' They were playing a losing game."[23]

What offended the sensitive nostrils of John Hancock Lee and all the others like him was, we can see in retrospect, a happy event in the evolution of American democracy: a nonviolent transfer of power from a few insiders to a mass of outsiders. The WASP party leaders who had ridden the back of the tiger soon found themselves inside, but in the process the tiger was tamed. In seizing power an angry and disorderly proletariat learned the elementary grammar of political action as it carved out a place for itself in the political system.

"The newer races," as Boston's Mayor Curly called the immigrants and their descendants, were not the only "outs" in American history. Indeed, it was not long before the nativists themselves began to feel alienated. Their response was to form their own party, the American or "Know-Nothing" * party. The Know-Nothings at one point elected governors in six states, but split over the slavery issue in 1856, and their Northern wing was eventually absorbed into the Republicans.

Here was a recurrent pattern in our party system. A group or interest which felt itself "out," ignored by the regular parties, would form its own party. As soon as it began to show its muscles at the polls one of the two major parties would suddenly discover a sympathy for parts of the third party's platform. The third party, in the meantime, would begin to discover that its crusading zeal was not matched by tight organization. The loss of a charismatic leader or the onset of factional quarreling within the party would prove to be the last straw: The third party would disintegrate, with one of the major parties getting many of its members and one or two of its planks. The Populist party, or its majority faction, thus disappeared into the Democratic party after 1896, and the left wing of the Bull Moose Progressives joined the Democrats in 1916. In 1972 the Republicans inherited some of the planks and supporters of George Wallace's American party.

Third parties in America have been short-lived for a number of reasons, not the least of them being the fact that our electoral system discriminates against them.† But another reason, of particular interest here, is the loss of their platforms and members to one or another of our vote-hungry major parties.

Immigrants are thus not the only "outs" to find a home in one of our parties. The alienated, those who lost their status or their income, those who felt threatened, or ignored, or insulated by the political system would eventually find a home in the Democratic or Republican party. The primary motive for this hospitality—the relentless search for new voters—was certainly not the purest, but the end result was to make the political system sensitive to a variety of demands from a diverse and restless people.

2 Expanding the Circle of Participation

Besides providing a home for the alienated, parties helped to expand the circle of participation in politics. They did this through a variety of means, from their nominating machinery to the general air of excitement they used to generate.

Early in the 1760s John Adams indignantly described the activities of the Boston "caucus" in the following terms:

---

* The name derived from the party's obsession with secrecy during its formative period. When members were questioned about the party they invariably answered that they knew nothing.

† Our electoral system is generally one in which the winner takes all. In presidential elections the party which "carries" the state gets all the state's electoral votes; the losers, no matter how close their margin, get nothing. In congressional races the balloting is by districts; each district is represented by only *one* member of Congress, that of the winning party—the losers get nothing for their pains. This system is tough enough on a losing major party. It devastates minor parties.

> This day learned that the Caucus club meets at certain times in the garret of Tom Dawes, the Adjutant of the Boston regiment. He has a large house, and he has a moveable partition in his garret which he takes down, and the whole club meets in one room. There they smoke tobacco till you cannot see from one end of the garret to the other. There they drink flip, I suppose, and they choose a moderator who puts questions to the vote regularly; and selectmen, assessors, collectors, firewards, and representatives are regularly chosen before they are chosen in the town.[24]

Deep down inside it may have been the tobacco and "flip" that bothered Adams' Puritan conscience more then the practice of using preelectoral slates, because Adams himself was later picked by Federalist caucuses to be his party's standard-bearer in two elections. Prior to the development of the caucus, politics in America was largely the business of "notables," landowning elites, and those lucky enough to form "connexions" with them. The development of the party caucus permitted a professional class of politicians to bring the names of others, not necessarily economic or social elites, before the voters. This helped to dissolve the quasi-aristocratic system of elite politics which colonial America had inherited from the mother country.

In the early days of the nation presidential nominees were chosen by congressional party caucuses, but by the 1820s this practice was itself criticized as undemocratic. In 1832 the Jacksonian Democrats became the first major party to abolish "king caucus" and replace it with a nominating convention. From then on the convention system quickly triumphed, dominating the nomination process for the rest of the century. The convention system vastly extended the range of political participation, since it was composed of delegates from local parties throughout the entire nation.

It is worth pausing a moment to note the democratizing effect of these evolving mechanisms for nominating candidates. We may picture the historical stages in terms of a widening series of concentric circles. The center circle would correspond to the elite politics of "notables," which was transcended by the caucus system, represented by the second circle. A third circle, reached during the Jacksonian period, would be labeled "conventions." Each of these stages opened the range of those involved in the nominating process—both those eligible for nomination and those who were to do the nominating—to a still larger group of Americans. Before the end of the nineteenth century pressure began building to add a fourth circle, the primary system, which would expand the range still further. But discussion of this last circle must be deferred until later in the chapter, for it was not the work of our major parties but of forces basically opposed to them.

The role of parties in extending participation went further than the kind that can be illustrated by neat concentric circles. The move from caucus to convention was accompanied by a heightened spirit of suspense, drama, and general pageantry surrounding the nomination process, giving citizens throughout the nation some sense of vicarious, if not actual, participation in the making of political history. The age of torchlight parades and stump-speaking had begun—genuine American folk arts in the nineteenth century, and as much social as they were political occasions. The grand and gaudy age of party patronage had also commenced, giving greater numbers of the population a material stake in the outcome of elections. The prestige of parties swelled, and there began a period of vigorous competition between them. All this had its effect on the number of people attracted to the polls. In 1824 only 26.9 percent of eligible voters went to the polls, but in 1828 the turnout was over 57 percent and in 1840, 80.2 percent.[25] Democracy exists as a potential when the mass of people have the right to vote; it begins to take on real meaning when people exercise their right. Parties in their heyday—from the 1830s to the end of the nineteenth century—helped to turn the promise of participation into a noisy and boisterous reality.

3 Standing for (and against) Something

Parties not only whipped up the enthusiasm of rank-and-file voters, they gave them something to vote for: They simplified choices and made them intelligible to the average citizen.

American parties, always opportunistic, were never nihilistic. In spite of the remarkable diversity of groups contained in them, they stood for and against identifiable points of view. They linked together an amazing variety of interests, but they did so on the basis of commonality. The Jacksonian Democrats combined small businessmen, farmers, and laborers into a coalition against the big merchants and manufacturers of the East, and the ideological consistency of the Democrats was reflected in their policies and pronouncements: against national banks and other enterprises granting exclusive benefits to a favored few, against artificial barriers to advancement, for "equality of opportunity," for "the common man," the small entrepreneur, the wildcatter, the worker. In a similar way, the birth of the Republican party brought together an almost comically diverse collection of interests which were nevertheless united on one critical point: Slavery must not be extended into the new territories.

Although scientific opinion polling is of recent origin, Americans have probably always had a fair idea of what they have been voting for and against. For this the parties must be given a share of credit. They have given the voters slates of candidates more or less committed to certain positions: for or against labor unions, social welfare, and so on. The positions have seldom been spelled out in detail, sharp differences have usually been avoided (platforms and speeches always being well-greased with platitude), but the general thrust has been plain enough for average voters to understand. Without parties they would have had to study the voting record, political philosophy, and psychological profile of each and every candidate for public office—an impossible "civic duty" for people who work for a living.

Parties have been credited with other useful roles. Writers on parties sometimes stress the role of the party leader as an "honest broker." In bringing the "outs" together into a winning coalition, party leaders have had to smooth over differences between the various factions and get them to bargain with one another. Given the volatile mixture of peoples and races in America, the argument goes, this sort of mediation has played an invaluable role in preventing explosions. This argument has substance, but it also contains a flaw. It fails to take account of what the Marquis d'Argensen observed in the eighteenth century: "The agreement of two particular interests is formed by opposition to the third."[26] Parties have divided as well as united. Our nation's most profound schism, the Civil War, was hardly avoidable once the Republican party, itself a bundle of compromises, refused to compromise on the one issue which held all its factions together: the question of slavery in the territories. Successfuly party leaders have always known how to reconcile and unite, but they have also had to know what to oppose. (Or perhaps whom to oppose. Kevin Phillips, a Nixon strategist and author of *The Emerging Republican Majority,* called it "the whole secret of politics—knowing who hates who.")[27]

Another role often associated with parties has to do with the virtues of efficiency and cooperation. The separation of powers between President and Congress is tailor-made to produce deadlock, but parties, so the argument goes, have helped to set the stage for legislative-executive cooperation by giving the President and at least one party in Congress something in common—their party membership—and Presidents who have taken their party leadership role seriously have been able to bridge the gap between the two branches. This argument, however, overlooks the fact that parties have in some ways heightened and sharpened the separation of powers. The rise of the nominating conventions gave the President a new, nationwide base of power. This innovation, part and parcel of the expanding party system, helped to strengthen the Presidency,[28] but it did not necessarily contribute to efficiency, as the record of President Jackson's vetoes illustrates. In cases where the President comes from one party and the congressional majority from another, a strong party system tends toward dissonance, not cooperation, between the two branches.

But whatever disagreements there may be on particulars, the generally innovative role of parties in the evolution of American democracy cannot be denied. Parties turned elitist institutions like the electoral college into anachronisms.* They introduced newcomers to self-government, became levers for the discontented to tilt the "powers that be" without upsetting the whole constitutional system. They expanded the practice of self-government from the few to the many by involving the grass roots in the political process, simplifying choice, dramatizing politics, making it comprehensible to the head and heart of the average citizen.

---

* Article II and Amendment XII of the Constitution provide for the election of President and Vice President by means of an electoral college, with each state having a total number of electors equal to the combined number of its senators and representatives. The electors from each state, according to Article II, are to be selected "in such manner as the legislature thereof may direct"—which, historically, has been the method of popular election. In *theory,* the Framers expected these electors to use their own discretion in voting for President and Vice President, thus subjecting the popular will to the rational and sober direction of an elite body. By 1800, however, these rational and sober gentlemen had become party automatons, pledged to vote for their party's choice for President and Vice President.

Because the electoral college has not been formally abolished, which would require a constitutional amendment, we continue to go through a silly ritual every four years. Let us say that a majority of voters in California, which has forty-five electors, vote for Smith and Jones for President and Vice President. What the California voters have actually done is to pick a slate of forty-five Democratic or Republican electors (depending on which party Smith and Jones belong to); the electors take a junket to the state capital the following January and, to absolutely nobody's surprise, proudly cast their forty-five ballots for Smith-Jones.

Turning from past to present, however, generalizations become more difficult. Are parties still innovative? Do they continue to play a creative role in democratic development? We lack the perspective of hindsight to answer these questions with much assurance. What we do know is that parties have lost some of the key resources, both material and psychological, which had given them cohesion and élan—qualities without which no institution or association can be very innovative. A number of historical developments have contributed to the breakdown of party solidarity and the undermining of party spirit.

HISTORICAL DEVELOPMENTS UNDERMINING PARTY STRENGTH

Reduction of Patronage

One development tending to weaken party strength is that the power of parties to disperse patronage has been greatly curtailed since the rise of Civil Service employment.

The spoils system, defended as a positive good under Jackson and accepted as normal under Lincoln, became increasingly intolerable in the graft-ridden atmosphere of the Grant administration. But the scandal reached a climax when President Garfield was assassinated by a disappointed office-seeker. In 1883 President Arthur signed the Pendleton Act into law, creating a Civil Service Commission and providing for federal jobs through means of competitive examinations. During the next half-century the Civil Service concept worked its way throughout the federal bureaucracy and into state and local government as well. The parties were thus deprived of an important inducement for recruiting and retaining loyal party workers. For many people party zeal is a sufficient motivator, but for many others the prospect of a job—or of keeping a job already awarded—is a much more reliable guarantee of continued loyalty. Civil Service has not, of course, abolished patronage.*

Decline of Partisan Charity

The nationalization and professionalization of social services, combined with the upward mobility of the working class, stripped parties of another means of buying support: partisan charity.

Historically, our national parties have derived their strength from local party organizations, which in turn built their power not only on spoils—even in the halcyon days of patronage there were not enough jobs for everyone—but through their help to people in need. The widow got her free coal delivery and food basket through the personal intercession of her local ward-heeler; she and her relatives repaid this favor with a kind of gut loyalty which puzzled and annoyed middle-

---

* Patronage is still highly visible at the top and the bottom of the American political system. Every year thousands of presidential appointments are given to people with the right connections (although these are often highly qualified people who would have no trouble finding employment elsewhere). At the local level progress toward eliminating patronage has been the slowest. Since the nation contains 3,000 counties, 17,000 townships, and 18,000 special districts—producing about 1,500,000 jobs—the harvest of patronage plums is not inconsiderable. But the merit system has made inroads even here: Much federal grant-in-aid legislation requires that state and local employees paid in whole or in part with federal funds be placed under merit procedures.

As for the federal bureaucracy, 80 percent of the jobs are filled by Civil Service.

class reformers. But today the chances are that the widow herself has become middle-class. Even if she has not, her mite comes in the form of regular checks from an impersonal and distant Social Security Administration, and they are not charity but hers by right. She owes nothing to her precinct captain, and the latter knows it.

Advent of the Primary Election Primaries introduced an element of open divisiveness into the nominating process, lessened the room for maneuver and "deals," and weakened the leadership hierarchy of parties.

In the early nineteenth century the transition from legislative caucus to conventions greatly strengthened the hand of local party organizations, whose leaders were able to pick convention delegates. Convention choices were ostensibly arrived at by balloting, but the balloting was only the ceremonial surface of a series of deals worked out by party leaders, who then ordered "their" delegates to vote as instructed. There were convention fights, but these were eventually resolved by barter and horsetrade among party leaders. The stalwarts and wheelhorses of the parties, men of experience if not always wisdom, faced challenges at every turn, but they were certainly masters of their own house. Toward the end of the nineteenth century, however, this very mastery was decried as "bossism" by the Populist and Progressive movements. Insurgents in the regular parties, many of them disgruntled over having failed to get nominated, added their voices to those demanding "reform" of the nominating process.

The most logical reform seemed to be that of letting the voters themselves decide on who should be the party's nominee. But which voters? All voters, regardless of party? Seven states eventually adopted this method, called the *open primary*. Or only those registered in the party? Forty-one states adopted this method, or variations of it, called the *closed primary*. Two states, Alaska and Washington, have adopted a kind of wide-open primary, called the *blanket primary*, which permits the voter to pick candidates from both parties. This has been known less formally as the "free love" primary.

Primaries have reduced the range of rewards and punishments available to party leaders. In England a maverick Member of Parliament can be punished by his party leaders simply by being denied renomination. In America a candidate openly hostile to the party leadership could be nominated and renominated as long as he or she retained the confidence of the rank and file. Even before primaries, of course, American parties were not "disciplined" on the English model; mavericks were invariably tolerated as long as they could win elections. But primaries weakened even the initial power of party leaders to find candidates consistent with the general line of the party, and they opened up the possibility of a challenge by "outsiders" to a leadership-endorsed candidate. These challenges are often bitter ones, and the wounds sometimes fail to heal in time to fight the opposition party.

Influence of the Mass Media
The enormous increase in the power of the mass media since the turn of the century has undermined the mystique of parties.

When George Norris was growing up in rural Ohio in the 1870s, he later recounted in his autobiography, one of his neighbors ventured the opinion that a Democratic soul could not enter heaven.[29] This was the kind of atmosphere which produced rock-ribbed Republicans, and Senator Norris himself remained one until he went to Washington in 1903 and discovered that "the Republican Party was subject to influences similar to those I believed controlled the Democratic Party; and soon I learned there was no difference between the parties in this respect."[30] The same "discovery" was made simultaneously by reporters for the new "muckraking" newspapers and magazines. Mass-produced on cheap paper by rapid-fire presses, written in a lively, popular style, they purported to tell the "inside story" of politics in America. A common theme in muckraking journalism was that the two major parties were not competitors but collusive partners in graft and corruption. As if this bad press were not bad enough in itself, the muckrakers' lurid tales increased the pressure for primaries, third parties, and "nonpartisanship," draining more blood from the two parties.

The cruelest cut, however, was not so much the loss of reputation as the loss of an important function. Local party officials had once served as opinion leaders, but the print revolution turned people's attentions toward professional journalists as the source of facts and ideas. This trend was greatly accelerated by the development of radio in the twenties and television in the fifties. Today, Walter Cronkite, not the local ward heeler or party zealot, has become the authoritative source of news. It must be added that the perspectives of TV reporters and camera crews have not been very flattering to either party. If George Norris' theological neighbor of the 1870s were alive today, he might suggest that Republican souls are in as much danger as Democratic ones.

WEAKENING OF PARTY TIES: AN IRREVERSIBLE PROCESS

Independent voting, ticket-splitting, and other symptoms of party weakness are not, then, transient phenomena. They are not likely to disappear in the years to come, for the historical developments which undermined the strength of parties have become a permanent part of the American landscape. The weakening of party ties has been deplored by a number of writers, and on a variety of grounds: that it has led to the rise of extremist candidates,[31] that it has created a politics of "image" instead of substance,[32] that it has led to the rise of bureaucratic irresponsibility,[33] that it has abolished intermediary ties between the President and the people,[34] and that it has dampened our zest for politics.[35] All these points may be true,* but they often seem to be premised on nostalgia. It is sometimes forgotten that the social and political underpinnings for the old party system are irretriev-

---

*Some of them, however, especially the argument that party professionals are more likely to nominate "moderates" and amateurs to nominate "extremists," seem highly dubious. (See Rita E. Hauser, "The Center Can Hold," *New York Times,* Dec. 11, 1973, p. 45.) Democratic party professionals gave the nation Lyndon Johnson, who demonstrated his "moderation" by sending half a million Americans to the other side of the globe to fight the bitterest, most divisive foreign war in American history. Johnson's administration—brought to bay by amateurs—was followed by that of a Republican "moderate," also nominated by professionals, which featured political espionage and sabotage, orchestrated perjury, bribery, extortion, tax evasion, obstruction of justice, intimidation of critics, saturation bombing of open cities, and invasion of other countries.

ably lost. We can no more abolish primaries than we can abolish television or Social Security, or bring back torchlight parades, free coal deliveries, and Irish wakes. A return of vigorous parties would involve an impossible step backward into the past. Consider, for example, the logic of the "responsible parties" argument. For a party to be "responsible," it must exert "discipline" over potential mavericks. This in turn requires a leadership structure free from the pressure of meddlesome "outsiders." Judson James, an advocate of "responsible" parties, contends that television coverage of conventions has "gotten out of hand."

> The inflation and repetition of rumors give floor reporters a chance to create artificial drama and disrupt the efforts of delegates to deliberate. The need of the networks to provide "entertainment" rewards a coverage of conflict and division that is reinforced by publicity. Thus the interest of the networks are [sic] directly antagonistic to the party leadership's need to build up consensus and harmony.[36]

But what is the alternative? That the cameras be trained only to the rostrum, so that viewers can be treated to a succession of speeches which the delegates themselves largely ignore? The heart of the convention is "the efforts of the delegates to deliberate," and if the electronic media are not allowed to eavesdrop, speculate, and gossip about this, they might as well be barred from the convention—an unthinkable alternative, since parties today need television more than television needs parties.

PROGRESSIVISM: A PERENNIAL MOVEMENT

As a national party the Progressives lasted four years, from 1912 to 1916 (with a brief revival in the 1924 presidential elections), but as a movement it seems, if anything, to be growing. Richard Hofstadter, though critical of Progressivism, provided a useful sketch in *The Age of Reform,* of some of the key Progressive values by contrasting them with those of the immigrant.

> While the boss, with his pragmatic talents and his immediate favors, quickly appealed to the immigrant, the reformer was a mystery. Often he stood for things that to the immigrant were altogether bizarre, like women's rights and Sunday laws, or downright insulting, like temperance. His abstractions had no appeal within the immigrant's experience—citizenship, responsibility, efficiency, good government, economy, businesslike management. The immigrant wanted humanity, not efficiency, and economics threatened to lop needed jobs off the payroll. The reformer's attacks upon the boss only caused the immigrant to draw closer to his benefactor. Progressives, in return, reproached the immigrant for having no interest in broad principles, in the rule of law or the public good. Between the two, for the most part, the channels of effective communication were closed.[37]

Can it be said today that women's rights are "bizarre" to the grandsons and granddaughters of the immigrants? Or is it fair to say that citizenship and responsibility are meaningless "abstractions" to the descendants of the immigrants? Hardly. If such values are basically "Protestant," as Hofstadter insisted, then the nation has been largely "Protestantized." The reform movements attracted to Eleanor Roosevelt and Adlai Stevenson in the 1950s included large numbers of

Jews. The "amateur Democrats," as political scientist James Q. Wilson rather condescendingly called these reformers,* came straight out of the progressive tradition, emphasizing values of citizen participation and challenging the boss-controlled hierarchy of urban Democratic machines. At the other end of the ideological spectrum, the Conservative party—with Catholics prominent in its leadership—has also sounded a progressive note in its denunciation of "elitism," its support of referenda, its appeal to grass-roots involvement. The themes of progressivism were also pervasive in the "new politics" movements which rallied around Eugene McCarthy and George McGovern in the late sixties and early seventies, and these movements were by no means homogeneous in their ethnic-religious makeup.

The progressive ethos—toward citizen involvement, majoritarianism, open debate, impersonal tests of political merit—has worked its way deeply into the American mentality. It is held in esteem by every ethnic group, and across the ideological spectrum from right to left. Every seasoned politician now knows that he or she must pay lip service to it. Gone are the days when Tammany's most famous boss, William Marcy Tweed, could reply to his critics by asking: "What are you going to do about it?"† This does not mean that politicians *are* more honest and open than they were at the time of the Tweed ring, only that they must *appear* to be so. Hence the rise of public relations and "image-making" in politics, and, sometimes, a kind of more-democratic-than-thou moralism. Certain philosophies are not taboo in open forums. At the Republican Convention of 1952, Senator John Bricker made the mistake of defending his position on the seating of contested delegates in terms of venerable Whig principles: "Now, members of the convention, this is a republic in which we live. We govern ourselves through representatives and not by a democratic majority vote of the country."[38] Leonard Lurie, a journalist who was present, wrote later:

> It is hard to understand why "Honest John" was so candid with his fellow delegates about his political philosophy, but they quickly showed him he had made an error. There was heavy booing and Bricker was forced to fall back and praise God, the Constitution, and the country before they would allow him to continue.[39]

The 1952 conventions were the first to be televised—which may have had some-

---

* James Q. Wilson, *The Amateur Democrat* (Chicago: The University of Chicago Press, 1962). Although Wilson's book was written during the "value free" era of American social science, he did not succeed in hiding his own feelings toward Democratic reformers. He portrayed them as pseudo-aristocratic parvenus, combining naïvete with snobbishness. He characterized them as "consumers," rather than "producers" of culture, since so few of them had any publications to their credit (itself a rather snobbish comment). He saw them as being impressed with the mere appearance of culture, which they associated with aristocracy—hence their affection for Roosevelt and Stevenson—and he argued that it was this fascination with class and style which was the basic reason they fought the regular Democrats. Wilson's method was largely deductive, using selected quotes from selected members of the reform movements and deducing what the inner motivation was behind the remark. The book may reveal more about James Q. Wilson than his subject of study. See particularly, chaps. 1, 2, 12, passim.

† Tammany's last boss, Carmine DeSapio, was an altogether different breed of machine politician. He was so piously conscious of progressive ideals that Murray Kempton once called him "the Norman Vincent Peale of politics." Quoted in Warren Moscow, *The Last of the Big-Time Bosses* (New York: Stein and Day Incorporated, 1971), p. 41.

thing to do with this public display of democratic righteousness. Television, the "cool" medium, has been devastating to the prestige of conventions. High drama in the convention hall often appears farcical on the home screen, stirring speeches have a way of sounding like partisan bombast to the skeptical viewer, and all the accepted cliches ("The sovereign state of Wisconsin, home of sweet cream, proudly casts. . . .") become silly and dreary on TV.

A Progressive Goal: One Presidential Primary

TV has thus reinforced the progressive impulse in America. It has worked like a corrosive acid on the institutions and procedures of the old party system. Conventions are now widely discredited in America, with 72 percent of those polled in 1972 agreeing that they should be replaced by one national primary (a proposal once made by Adlai Stevenson).

Progressives tend to favor the one-primary approach to nomination because it seems to them more logical, efficient, and democratic. They point to the present apples-and-oranges system of state presidential primaries: Some merely indicate preference, others separate preference and delegate selection, others merely provide for the election of delegates, and so on. Nearly all such state laws have enough loopholes to permit organized minorities to exert disproportionate influence over the delegate-selection process. Advocates of a national primary also point to the time and expense of entering these primaries, and the inconclusive nature of the results. Opponents of such a national primary, however, contend that it would create more problems than it would solve. Specifically:

1 It might "create ill-assorted tickets and produce Vice Presidents who could not be trusted or prepared by the President for the possibility of succession."[40] After Eagleton and Agnew, both products of conventions, this argument has a slightly ironic flavor.

2 A national presidential primary "would eliminate the possibility of coalition building within each party."[41] Another piece of irony. Recent conventions (the Republicans in 1964, the Democrats in 1968 and 1972) have produced—what? Not coalitions but apocalyptic confrontations, with opposing factions girding themselves for Armageddon inside and outside the convention hall.*

3 The sudden-death nature of a single primary, combined with the enormous expense involved in it, would prevent unknown candidates like McGovern or McCarthy from developing their support in stages. But for people concerned about issues rather than the fate of particular candidacies this argument has little meaning. Taking Eugene McCarthy as an example, if Presidents had to be renominated in a primary every four years, would there have been a *need* for him?

---

* The irony in this argument was revealed most forcefully in the April 1973 issue of *Commentary*. Penn Kemble and Josh Muravchik had written an article in the previous December issue which denounced the McGovernites for taking over the 1972 Democratic convention, allegedly stacking the rules against their opponents, misrepresenting the sentiments of the Democratic grass roots, and generally acting like tyrants. Among the comments from readers, published in the April issue, was a letter suggesting that the best solution to all these alleged abuses of the convention would be a national primary. The authors replied that "parties facilitate the congealing of interest groups and bargaining and interaction among groups"—forgetting, apparently, the whole point of their article, which was the Democrats' *failure* to do these things in 1972!

Robert Kennedy's reticence in challenging President Johnson on the war issue stemmed in great part from his sense of its futility, since Johnson's renomination—in a boss-controlled convention—seemed a foregone conclusion.

Is it possible to compromise—to retain the convention while using the primary for the actual nominations? This raises the obvious question of what sort of purpose the convention could serve if it were not allowed to nominate candidates. Leonard Lurie, the journalist quoted earlier, believes that conventions could still be held every four years, but "their main function would now be to debate and illuminate the issues that separate the candidates."[42] It seems clear, however, that a nationwide primary would spell the death of the convention, since conventions have never been forums for debate and illumination. "The blaring of bands," Lurie says, "the bursts of gaity and lights . . . would all continue."[43] But people do not hire brass bands for debates!

The convention, in short, seems to have lost its essential "reason for being." It is so unreliable a means of building consensus that it may be doing exactly the opposite—polarizing and embittering the various wings of the party—and it is so far from eliciting "a high degree of popular participation in the high drama of democracy" * that almost three-quarters of the nation want it abolished.

Progressives versus Centrists

Early in this chapter we distinguished between *movements* and *parties;* somewhat later we went on to discuss progressivism, which began as a party but which was transformed into a perennial movement. The movements of the past two decades are new manifestations of what Richard Hofstadter called "the progressive impulse" in America. The rhetoric of the movements is strongly flavored with updated versions of the "abstractions" Hofstadter found in the progressive movement: Citizenship has become "citizen politics," efficiency is now called "modernization," responsibility means "one man, one vote," good government is defined in terms of "participatory democracy," and so on. The new movements cherish the same assumptions about the nature of people and government which the progressives cherished: individualism, rationalism, high idealism.

The new progressive is thus an easy target for the champions of "realism." The late Reinhold Niebuhr, a liberal but tough-minded theologian, once used the term "foolish children of light" to describe idealists who fail to understand the darker side of human nature.[44] Niebuhr's point was not merely that the incautious idealist fails to perceive greed and selfishness in others, but that he fails to see it in himself. He may thus be unaware of his own biases, his own personal

---

* The quotation is taken from a classic defense of presidential nominating conventions written by Pendleton Herring in 1940. (Pendleton Herring, *The Politics of Democracy: American Parties in Action* [New York: Rinehart & Co., 1940], p. 163.) A critic who had called conventions "idiocy" was described by Herring as "a cultured and sensitive man who evidently does not enjoy roughhousing. He would feel equally ill at ease at an American Legion convention or an enclave of the Elks." A sissy. By the 1970s, however, quite a large number of thoroughly virile Americans, especially the young, would feel "ill at ease" among Legionnaires or Elks. Such organizations have experienced difficulty in recruiting new members, and the reason is probably that they have the flavor of a bygone era of "roughhousing"—even the term is quaint.

stakes, in the seemingly altruistic goals he pursues.[45] Many critics of the new progressives would agree with this analysis and immediately suggest the perfect case study: the McGovern Commission and its progeny.

The McGovern Commission and the 1972 Democratic Convention

In 1968 the supporters of Eugene McCarthy's candidacy complained that they had been undemocratically excluded from the delegate selection process. Delegates were often handpicked by party bosses, and caucuses were closed to McCarthy supporters or were suddenly moved to new meeting places without prior notice. Many delegates were selected years before the convention, making them unresponsive to current issues and attitudes. The "unit rule" for selecting delegates in many states—which meant that the faction with a majority of votes at a convention or in a primary could claim all the delegates from the state—prevented McCarthy supporters from obtaining even a share of them. At the 1968 Democratic Convention a minority report of the convention's Rules Commission called for the abolition of the unit rule and for "all feasible efforts . . . to assure that delegates are selected through party primary, convention, or committee procedures open to public participation within the calendar year of the national convention."[46] The resolution passed by a vote of 1,350 to 1,206—the only victory by the McCarthy forces at the convention, but a highly consequential one. Under this mandate, Fred Harris, then chairman of the Democratic National Committee, appointed a twenty-eight-member Commission on Party Structure and Delegate Selection, to be headed by Senator George McGovern. After taking testimony and circulating drafts of its proposals, the McGovern Commission at the end of 1969 issued a series of guidelines for selecting delegates to the 1972 convention. These included:

> Abolition of the unit rule.
> Removal of all discriminatory fees, costs, and assessments on candidates.
> All delegates to be selected within the calendar year of the convention.
> The most controversial guideline: all states must "encourage participation" of racial minorities, women, and youth, "in reasonable relationship to the groups' presence in the state."[47]

Opinions have differed over whether the last guideline could be called a compulsory "quota system."* But what was obvious to any TV viewer in the summer of 1972 was that the whole makeup of the Democratic Convention had radically changed. The traditional coalition of big-city officials and union leaders had been, in effect, evicted. Only 10 percent of the delegates were union officials, less than a third had held any party or governmental office, and only 11 percent had

---

* McGovern himself was vague in summarizing the guideline for the readers of *Harper's* magazine in January 1970. His commission, he said, expected the states to take "affirmative steps, including specifically inviting black and brown delegates to party meetings." (George McGovern, "The Lessons of 1968," *Harper's,* CCXL [January 1970], p. 47.) Critics, however, have pointed out that the commission's later interpretations of its guidelines dropped the word "encourage," inserted the word "requirement," and made the absence of quotas a prima facie violation of the guideline. (Penn Kemble and Josh Muravchik, "The New Politics and the Democrats," *Commentary,* LIV [December 1972], p. 79.)

attended the 1968 convention. The representation of women, on the other hand, went from 13 percent in 1968 to 38 percent in 1972; blacks went from 5.5 percent to nearly 15 percent. And 27 percent of the delegates were under thirty.[48] Most symbolically of all, Chicago's Mayor Richard Daley, something of an arch-villain to the Democratic left since 1968, was barred from being seated as a delegate.

Critics of the McGovern Commission and its work charge that its chairman, consciously or unconsciously, was feathering his own nest under the guise of "reform" and "democracy." McGovern's guidelines, they contend, produced a stacked convention, filled with "new politics" types, who then proceeded to nominate the "new politics" candidate—George McGovern. Years ago Reinhold Niebuhr had contended that a subtle class bias "taints" even the noblest words and deeds.[49] By the end of 1972 the critics of the McGovern guidelines had what they considered tangible evidence of such bias: 39 percent of the delegates had done postgraduate work, as compared with 4 percent of the general population; 31 percent had annual incomes exceeding $25,000 and another 31 percent ranged from $15,000 to $25,000; Iowa, the corn state, had one farmer among its forty-six delegates; Chicago, an ethnic stronghold, had only three Poles and one Italian; New York, with more union members than any other state, had three representatives of organized labor (but nine Gay Liberation advocates).[50]

Part of the reason for this rather exotic mix was undoubtedly connected with the so-called quota system, which even McGovern later repudiated. But another reason is simply that the "new politics" types who dominated the convention were more energetic in taking advantage of the democratization effected by the McGovern guidelines. Primary elections for selecting convention delegates were used in thirteen states in 1968; in 1972, twenty-two states employed this method. The abolition of the unit rule permitted McGovern supporters to win at least a part of a state's delegation, where otherwise they would have been frozen out. The requirement that meetings be held at uniform dates and times prevented regulars from using last-minute changes and other tricks to confuse the insurgents. Part of the reason, then, why the McGovernites took over the convention of 1972 was that they took advantage of some eminently fair reforms. If the motto of the Jacksonian revolution was, "to the victors belong the spoils," the motto of the new progressive revolution might be, "to the energetic go the victories." The corollary: "to the lazy go the leavings." Lane Kirkland, secretary-treasurer of the AFL-CIO, revealed an important reason for the low labor representation in 1972 when he told an interviewer: "As a rule *we haven't made an effort* to put 'labor' delegates. We haven't had to, because the party structure in the past was run by professional politicians. And they would consult us."[51] Other critics of the McGovern guidelines complained that primaries give "an advantage to *energetic* minorities, since the masses of people do not vote in primaries."[52] Kirkland observed ruefully that "the whole world is run by a handful of people who are willing to sit until the end of meeting."[53] The lesson for union members, party regulars, "centrists," and all their supporters, is that they too must now find the energy to stay until the end of the meeting.

Shortcomings of the New Progressives

The progressives have some lessons of their own to learn. Their success in nominating McGovern became a Pyrrhic victory when the voters overwhelmingly rejected a candidate identified with "abortion, amnesty and acid." Part of this was the result of the bitter slander thrown by Humphrey's backers, but some of it resulted from the McGovernites' obsession with "style." Shirley MacLaine enthusiastically described her delegation, the second largest at the convention, as resembling "a couple of high schools, a grape boycott, a Black Panther rally, and four or five politicians who walked in the wrong door."[54] That this enthusiasm was not shared by the voters should be a powerful lesson to progressives: Their cultural perimeter may be narrower than they think. "Youth" may mean campus radicals to them; but many police officers and mechanics are also young. "Women" may be represented by Gloria Steinem and Bella Abzug, but Louise Day Hicks is also a woman. "Minorities" may mean blacks and chicanos to the progressives, but Poles and Ukrainians are also minorities. Ten years before the McGovern insurgency a Stevensonian liberal was quoted by James Q. Wilson as saying that he joined the reform movement after he entered a regular party headquarters and found "a lot of seedy types hanging around. This sort of hit me hard."[55] But possibly the American electorate contains a lot of "seedy types."

Another shortcoming of progressives is that they never seem to make it clear—probably because it is not clear in their own minds—what their overall goal is. Is their goal to reform parties—or to reform America? And what does "reform" mean? If it means "strengthening" parties, the parties might be better off without their help. If it means making parties more "responsible," that goal might better be reached without primaries and other "amateur" inputs.[56] Or is the goal to "reform" America? If so, what does this entail? Substantive reforms (such as clean air, a more equitable distribution of income, racial justice, safe streets, consumer well-being) or procedural reform (a greater democratization of the political process)? The Democrats' debacle in 1972 resulted in no small part from a fuzziness about goals. The McGovernites were accused of helping themselves under the guise of helping their party, but the truth is probably more complex and less sinister: They were trying to help their country and also believing, or half-believing, that they were helping their party. But with parties as with General Motors, what is good for them may not also be good for America. An arguable case could be made that the best thing that could happen to our parties would be for reformers to stay out of them, for primaries to be abolished, and for the good old days of patronage to be restored. But it would be hard to prove that these historical reversals would help the country.

THE FUTURE OF AMERICAN POLITICAL PARTIES

The large issue is whether parties may have lost their relevance to contemporary America. With primaries doing the nominating, television taking over the functions of opinion leadership, political socialization, and entertainment, civil service replacing the spoils system, what is left of parties? In groping for an answer it is difficult to avoid ambivalence.

On the one hand, parties will, for the foreseeable future, continue to cue electoral choice and to serve as repositories for different sets of beliefs and attitudes. A study of state voting in Nebraska, a state which permits no party designation on the ballots, concluded that the absence of such labels was associated with ignorant and inconsistent voting behavior.[57] The words "Democratic" and "Republican" continue to have meaning, at least to those who consistently vote for or work for one or the other of the two parties and, at least since 1964, these meanings have corresponded to liberal or conservative ideological preferences.[58] The words also have meaning to members of Congress. Despite all the talk about bipartisan coalitions in Congress, studies of roll call votes have found party to be the single most reliable indicator of congressional voting behavior.[59] As for third parties, they remain, as they always were, seasonal spectacles. The most recent third-party bombshell, that of George Wallace's American party, was defused in exactly the same way that all third parties were defused in the past: by the theft of some of its key planks. America, then, continues to have a stubborn two-party system that offers voters a choice of general points of view and responds to the pressure of malcontents.

On the other hand, parties have lost prestige, organizational strength, reliable voters, and reliable workers. The ranks of ticket-splitters and independent voters appear to be growing. Conventions are in massive disfavor. Nearly every big-city machine has fallen to pieces. Where parties once played an innovative role—in expanding democracy, abolishing slavery, instituting social welfare—today's parties seem more concerned with maintaining stability,[60] and even in this role they have not been very successful.

Since the campaigns of Adlai Stevenson in the 1950s, the two parties have experienced periodic floods of volunteers. The "amateur Democrats" James Q. Wilson wrote about in 1962 were followed by "amateur Republicans" two years later in the Goldwater campaign. These zealous souls have been cordially distrusted by the party regulars, and with good reason: They have been more concerned with particular causes and candidates than with the fate of the party, they have regarded the parties as no more than vehicles to serve the ends of movements organized outside of the party, and they tend to regard party regulars as hacks and moral compromisers.[61] The very vitality of these amateur Democrats and Republicans is a sign of ill-health in the parties.

In a book first published in 1952 Samuel Lubell described the relationship between the two parties in this way:

> Our political system . . . has been characterized not by two equally competing suns, but by a sun and a moon. It is within the majority party that the issues of any particular period are fought out; while the minority party shines in reflected radiance of the heat thus generated.[62]

Lubell meant that our two parties have seldom been equal in strength in any given period. Instead, long periods of Democratic and Republican dominance have alternated with one another: the Democrats from 1828 to 1860, the Republicans from 1860 to 1932, the Democrats again from 1932 to 1952. Since that time, however, the pattern has been much less clear. Which party was the sun in the fifties, sixties, or early seventies? Hefty presidential majorities for the Republicans in the fifties were counterbalanced by the loss of Congress to the Democrats. A paper-thin presidential majority for the Democrats in 1960 was followed by a Democratic landslide in 1964, a paper-thin Republican victory in 1968, and and a Republican landslide in 1972. Kevin Phillips, the Republican party strategist, predicted an "emerging Republican majority,"[63] yet Republican registration continued to decline, the party remained a minority in Congress, and most governorships were held by Democrats. Watergate was a crushing blow to the Republicans, but it may have hurt all incumbents.[64] There remained a serious question whether the Democrats would win a lasting majority from it. (They certainly won, and won big, in the congressional elections of 1974, but this was primarily a reaction to Nixon's misdeeds and Ford's ill-timed pardon of the former President; whether the victory would survive the demise of the Watergate issue remained questionable.) A Harris poll taken in December of 1973 showed Republican Gerald Ford running ahead of Democrats Henry Jackson and Edward Kennedy; by December of 1974 Ford's rating in the polls plummeted, Kennedy had formally announced his noncandidacy, and Jackson was no more appealing than he was twelve months earlier. No candidate of either party seemed very exciting to the voters.

By the mid-1970s, then, neither party seemed about to enter a new era of dominance. In Samuel Lubell's astronomy metaphor, neither party seemed likely to become a sun; *both* had become moons, pale reflections of the radiance outside them. That radiance had not been shed by parties but by movements. History has already recorded the achievements of the civil rights movement—the sit-inners with cigarette burns in their necks, the demonstrators who braved fire hoses, mobs, cattle prods and police dogs, the heroes and martyrs who shook the whole structure of racial oppression in America. What innovative roll did the parties play in the civil rights revolution? (As late as 1964 the Democratic national convention was still seating Jim Crow delegations as the "legal" representatives of Alabama and Mississippi.) As for the peace movement, we know about its epic struggle to end the nightmare of Vietnam, but what role did the parties play? (As late as 1968 the Democrats rejected even a mildly worded peace plank which would have called for an end to the bombing of North Vietnam.) Scammon and Wattenberg, strategists for the "centrist" faction of the Democratic party, put "Vietnam dissent" in the same category as "campus disruptions, drugs, pornography," and "the generation gap"—annoying problems they hoped would somehow go away. Vietnam protesters were "walking political catastrophes."[65] The litany of issues dodged, ignored, or finessed by the parties is a lengthy one. What did the parties have to say about ecology? What help did they give the consumer movement? How did they stand on the energy crisis? It was not parties but movements which seized upon these issues and used them as giant levers for changing the social landscape of America. Movements have not only mobilized opinion, but performed functions more specifically associated with parties: getting out the vote, putting issues on the ballot, even nominating candidates. (Was it not "amateur Democrats," political outsiders, who took over the Democratic convention in 1972?) In short, while parties may continue to exist, and even to play useful roles, it will likely be because they find some way of accommodating themselves to the movements instead of dismissing them as transient phenomena or condemning them as "extremist" factions. The movements are here to stay, and the likelihood is that they will steer the parties rather than be steered by them. At the Democrats' 1974 "issues convention" it was an old pro, Mayor Richard J. Daley of Chicago, who seemed to understand this fact better than the "centrist" intellectuals who write articles for *Commentary*. In agreeing to a compromise charter provision which preserved the principle of "affirmative" representation of women, blacks, and young people, Daley said: "I wasn't involved. I was not even consulted. But I recognize when power moves and I recommend the compromise."[66]

Yet those who consider themselves party "reformers" or "progressives" should not waste time in self-congratulation, especially when self-criticism seems to be so long overdue. The most serious "progressive" shortcoming was already mentioned above—a certain fuzziness about goals. It is not enough to win victories over party regulars or to secure representation for certain elements in the population. The real question is *why*: For what ends are these battles being fought?

CONCLUSION: PARTIES AS INSTRUMENTS

We cannot discuss substantive ends here, but when it comes to the question of procedure, all reformers worthy of the name—whether they consider themselves "left" or "right," whether they register as Democrats, Republicans, or whatever—implicitly agree on this goal: the broadest possible involvement of the public in the political process. For a long period in our nation's history our parties served this goal, but it is no longer clear that they still serve it. Since the beginning of the present century, many of these functions have been taken over by movements, which have operated separately from parties and sometimes in opposition to them. Movements have introduced new ideas, interrupted bureaucratic momentum, energized the oppressed, stung the consciences of the comfortable, and democratized American institutions.

It is not yet clear whether parties will recover their old vigor. It seems doubtful. Parties will certainly remain as nominating vehicles for some time to come, however, and this is the real point. From the point of view of this book, the goal is not so much to "reform" or "strengthen" parties but to *use* them. Parties are instruments, not ends in themselves,[67] and reformers should have no hesitation in using them, exploiting them shamelessly, to serve the purposes of the nation as a whole.

How would this irreverent, pragmatic approach to parties manifest itself in practice? It would not prevent reformers from working through parties, but it would mean, in the words of former Senator Eugene McCarthy, that if such an approach fails, "there may be a need to threaten from outside."[68] Such threats could include the threat to support the opposition, to form a third party, to ruin the election of party candidates by bad publicity. In making such threats, however, reformers should not pretend that they are helping "their" party. This is nonsense, and it lends substance to the charge of hypocrisy frequently leveled at reformers.* It would clear the air of cant if reformers were to recognize their

---

* In a book published in 1970 John Kenneth Galbraith provided a classic example of this nonsense. "Where, this autumn, a Republican of evident candor and honest mind is opposing a Democrat who is far gone with these flaws, it will be a service to the Democrats to support this

goals as being quite different from those of parties, though not always incompatible with them. They could then approach party regulars in a spirit of barter and exchange—which is the spirit party regulars have always appreciated—and address them thus: "Look, we have something to give (enthusiastic volunteers, contributions, possibly an attractive candidate) and you have something to give (a venerable line on a voting machine); we have something to threaten (horrible publicity—we're articulate, and the media love us), and you have something to threaten (no line on the voting machine). Now let us reason together."

NOTES

1. Quoted in John S. Saloma and Frederick H. Sontag, *Parties: The Real Opportunity for Effective Citizen Politics* (New York: Alfred A. Knopf, Inc., 1972), p. 334.
2. Cited in ibid., pp. 338–339.
3. See above, chap. 4.
4. James MacGregor Burns, "The Democrats' Opportunity," *The New Republic,* CLXIX (July 21, 1972), p. 18.
5. Ibid.
6. Quoted by Anthony King, "Political Parties in Western Democracies," *Polity,* II (Winter 1969), p. 113.
7. Roy C. Macridis in his introduction to Roy C. Macridis, ed., *Political Parties: Contemporary Trends and Ideas* (New York: Torchbooks, Harper & Row, Publishers, Incorporated, 1967), p. 9.
8. Quoted in James Jupp, *Policical Parties* (London: Routledge & Kegan Paul, Ltd., 1968), p. 4.
9. But see Walter Karp, *Indispensable Enemies: The Politics of Misrule in America* (New York: Saturday Review Press, 1973). It is Karp's contention that the major American parties are secretly in collusion with one another. Instances of such collusion certainly exist, and Karp rightly points out some of them. Karp's mistake—an egregious mistake—is to generalize these instances into a blanket assertion that American parties always and everywhere make deals to "throw" the election. This leads him to the edge of silliness: Al Smith was deliberately selected by the Democratic bosses because they knew his urban Catholic manners would alienate the South, George McGovern was secretly promoted by the Democratic regulars in order to lose the election—and so on.
10. Basil Rauch, *The History of the New Deal* (New York: Creative Age Press, 1939), p. 317.
11. See, for example, E. E. Schattschneider, *Party Government* (New York: Holt, Rinehart and Winston, Inc., 1942); American Political Science Association, Committee on Political Parties, "Toward a More Responsible Two-Party System," *American Political Science Review,* XLIV, Supplement (September 1950); James MacGregor Burns, *The Deadlock of Democracy* (Englewood Cliffs, N. J.: Prentice-Hall, Inc., 1963). Austin Ranney provides a useful summary and evaluation of various arguments for "responsible parties" in *The Doctrine of Responsible Party Government* (Urbana: The University of Illinois Press, 1962). Judson James, another advocate of "responsible" parties, would distinguish his position from that of the "party government" argument of Schattschneider and others. See Judson L. James, *American Political Parties in Transition,* MS., 1973, to be published as a revision of his *American Republican." Who Needs the Democrats?* (Garden City, N. Y.: Doubleday & Company, Inc., 1970), p. 68.

Political Parties (New York: Pegasus, 1969). James acknowledges that the difference between "party government" and "responsible parties" is in many ways "one of degree rather than kind," and that many writers "use the terms interchangeably" (p. 24). This writer is one of them.

12 Burns, op. cit.
13 Quoted in David S. Broder, *The Party's Over: The Failure of Politics in America* (New York: Harper & Row, Publishers Incorporated, 1971), p. 68.
14 David Nexon, "Asymmetry in the Political System," *American Political Science Review,* LXV September 1971), p. 724.
15 See above, Chap. 4.
16 This theme is particularly evident in Burns' writings, which have a kind of evangelistic flavor. See, for example, his introduction to Saloma and Sontag, op. cit.: "Once upon a time party politics nourished and quickened the very life blood of American democracy. . . . But today we sorely miss the vigor, the combativeness, and the pervasiveness of the populist party spirit that once animated our political processes at every level of government" (p. xi).
17 Burns, *The Deadlock of Democracy,* op. cit., p. 1.
18 "By 69-21 per cent, a sizable majority of the people feel that 'dirty campaign tactics exist among most Republicans and Democrats, and the Nixon campaign people were no worse than the Democrats, except they got caught at it.' " Louis Harris's syndicated column, Rockland County, N. Y., *Journal-News,* Aug. 6, 1973, p. 15A.
19 Letter to Francis Hopkinson, Paris, Mar. 13, 1789, in Edward Dumbauld, ed., *The Political Writings of Thomas Jefferson: Representative Selections* (Indianapolis, Ind.: The Bobbs-Merrill Company, Inc., 1955), p. 46.
20 J. D. Richardson, *Messages and Papers of the Presidents,* Vol. I (Washington: U. S. Congress, 1897), p. 217.
21 A contemporary Southern editorial provided an excellent profile—in caricature—of the new party: "What is it but a conglomeration of greasy mechanics, filthy operatives, small-fisted farmers, and moon-struck theorists?" Quoted in Wilfred E. Binkley, *American Political Parties: Their Natural History,* 4th ed. (New York: Alfred A. Knopf, Inc., 1962), p. 220. According to Binkley, Lincoln pasted this editorial in his campaign book. Ibid.
22 John Hancock Lee, *The Origin and Progress of the American Party in Politics* (Philadelphia: Elliot & Gihon, 1855), p. 14.
23 Ibid.
24 Quoted in William Nisbet Chambers, *Political Parties in a New Nation* (New York: Oxford University Press, 1963), pp. 4–5.
25 Cited in William Nisbet Chambers, "Party Development and the American Mainstream," in William Nisbet Chambers and Walter Dean Burnham, eds., *The American Party Systems* (New York: Oxford University Press, 1967), p. 12. Chambers, in turn, cited the research of Walter Dean Burnham, which was "based as far as possible on primary sources." Ibid.
26 Quoted in Jean-Jacques Rousseau, *The Social Contract,* G. D. H. Cole translation (New York: E. P. Dutton & Co., Inc., 1950), pp. 26–27. Rousseau tried to get around the difficulties in unity-through-mutual-enmity by opposing each interest to itself.
27 Quoted in Garry Wills, *Nixon Agonistes* (Boston: Houghton Mifflin Company, 1969), p. 265).
28 Theodore Lowi, "Party, Policy, and Constitution in America," in Chambers and Burnham, op. cit., p. 248.
29 George W. Norris, *Fighting Liberal: The Autobiography of George W. Norris* (New York: The Macmillan Company, 1945), p. 21.
30 Ibid.

31 Rita E. Hauser, "The Center Can Hold," *New York Times,* Dec. 11, 1973, p. 45. Cf. Committee on Political Parties, APSA, "Toward a More Responsible Two-Party System" (1950). Note the "fourth danger."
32 Burns, op. cit., passim; Saloma and Sontag, op. cit., chap. 8.
33 Walter Dean Burnham, "The End of American Party Politics," *Trans-Action,* December 1969, pp. 12–22; Broder, op. cit., sees "party reform" as one way of attaching responsibility to "the mess in Washington." See pp. 159–166.
34 Burns, op. cit., especially "The Democrats' Opportunity." Jupp, op. cit., writing on parties throughout the world, puts it more generally: "The alternative to party rule is either aristocracy or violent repression" (p. ix). See, further, the Committee on Political Parties, American Political Science Association, "Toward a More Responsible Two-Party System" (1950): "The second danger is that the American People may go too far for the safety of constitutional government in compensating for this inadequacy by shifting excessive responsibility to the President." Broder, op. cit., takes note of this warning (p. 245).
35 Burns, op. cit., Broder, op. cit., and, between the lines, practically all advocates of "strong" parties.
36 James, op. cit., p. 163.
37 Richard Hofstadter, *The Age of Reform* (New York: Vintage Books, Random House, Inc., 1955), p. 185.
38 Leonard Lurie, *The King Makers* (New York: Coward, McCann & Geoghegan, Inc., 1971), p. 93.
39 Ibid.
40 James, op. cit., p. 178.
41 Ibid.
42 Lurie, op. cit., p. 261.
43 Ibid.
44 Reinhold Niebuhr, *The Children of Light and the Children of Darkness* (New York: Charles Scribner's Sons, 1944).
45 This point is brought out forcefully by Niebuhr in *Moral Man and Immoral Society* (New York: Charles Scribner's Sons, 1932), chap. 2. (See particularly pp. 40f. in 1960 paperback edition.)
46 Quoted in Saloma and Sontag, op. cit., p. 14.
47 A Report of the Commission on Party Structure and Delegate Selection, Democratic National Committee, *Mandate for Reform* (Washington: Democratic National Committee, 1971).
48 Cited in James, op. cit., pp. 169–170.
49 Reinhold Niebuhr, *Nature and Destiny of Man*, Vol. I, *Human Nature* (New York: Charles Scribner's Sons, 1941), p. 194.
50 Cited in Penn Kemble and Josh Muravchik, "The New Politics and the Democrats," *Commentary*, LIV (December 1972), p. 83.
51 Harry McPherson, "Watergate Has Undone the Republicans, Right?", *The New York Times Magazine,* Sept. 9, 1973, p. 53. Emphasis added.
52 Kemble and Muravchik, op. cit., p. 82. Emphasis added.
53 McPherson, op. cit.
54 Quoted in Kemble and Muravchik, op. cit., p. 83.
55 James Q. Wilson, *The Amateur Democrat* (Chicago: University of Chicago Press, 1962), p. 61.
56 Murray S. Stedman, Jr., and Herbert Sonthoff, "Party Responsibility—A Critical Inquiry," *Western Political Quarterly*, IV (September 1951), 454–468.
57 Susan Welch and Eric H. Carlson, "The Impact of Party on Voting Behavior in a

Nonpartisan Legislature," *American Political Science Review,* LXVII (September 1973). Cf. James, op. cit., p. 393: "The party label provides the marginally involved citizen with a means of assigning responsibility for unfavorable government acts, or with a general response to the current administration, without his having to have a detailed knowledge of current political events. Political parties therefore compensate for the low level of information and interest of the average voter. Without them, voting choices and public policy would be far more random and irrational."

58 See above, Chap. 4, pp. 119-120, and studies cited.
59 Julius Turner, *Party and Constituency: Pressures on Congress* (Baltimore: The Johns Hopkins Press, 1951); David B. Truman, *The Congressional Party: A Case Study* (New York: John Wiley & Sons, Inc., 1959). Although these studies were made in the 1950s, there is no reason to believe that the Congress of the 1970s is any less responsive to party influence. If anything, the fifties were more closely associated with "bipartisanship" in the public's mind.
60 Theodore J. Lowi, "Party, Policy, and Constitution in America," in Chambers and Burnham, op. cit. It is Lowi's contention that American parties have served a "constituent" or "constitutional" function, and that the impact of this function since 1840 has been conservative, or anti-innovative. This writer would move the date closer to 1900.
61 Wilson, op. cit., passim.
62 Samuel Lubell, *The Future of American Politics,* 2d ed., rev. (Garden City, N. Y.: Doubleday & Company, Inc., 1956), p. 212.
63 Kevin P. Phillips, *The Emerging Republican Majority* (Garden City, N. Y.: Doubleday & Company, Inc., 1970).
64 Morris K. Udall, "The Democratic Party," *The New Republic,* CLXIX (Nov. 24, 1973), 16-19; McPherson, op. cit., pp. 38ff.
65 Richard M. Scammon and Ben J. Wattenberg, *The Real Majority* (New York: Coward, McCann & Geoghegan, Inc., 1970), pp. 285.
66 *New York Times,* Dec. 9, 1974, p. 44.
67 After being either ignored or vilified by American political thinkers for well over a century after the Revolution, parties finally won favorable recognition *because* they had justified themselves as instruments. Yet by the 1940s grudging admiration had turned into prepossession. Textbooks, courses, and "specialists" on parties proliferated, creating an academic vested interest in the survival of "our two-party system."
68 Quoted in Saloma and Sontag, op. cit., p. 17.

Part Three

Components of American Democracy

Chapter 7

Congress: The Abdication of Power

Come Senators, Congressmen
Please heed the call
Don't stand in the doorway
Don't block up the hall.
For he that gets hurt
Will be he who has stalled.

Bob Dylan*

Emmet John Hughes, a former speech-writer to President Eisenhower and author of *The Living Presidency,* was appearing at a symposium on presidential power. In discussing the question of how presidential power can be checked, someone asked the inevitable question: What about Congress? Hughes responded with the story about Moses and Jesus playing golf. Moses teed off and shot a perfect hole-in-one. Then Jesus teed off and sent the ball high in the air, where it was snatched by an eagle and carried the length of the course. While flying over the eighteenth hole the eagle was struck by lightning, and it dropped the ball right into the hole. Obviously nettled, Moses turned to his golfing companion and said, "Do you want to play golf or do you want to keep screwing around?" And that,

---

* *The Times They Are A-Changin'.* © 1963 M. Witmark & Sons. All Rights Reserved. Used by permission of Warner Bros. Music.

Hughes said, is what we would ask Congress: "Do you want to govern or do you want to keep screwing around?"

The notion that Congress is wasting time, "screwing around," seems to be a common one in America. A Harris poll taken in January 1974 recorded an overall job rating of 69 unfavorable to 21 favorable. This was even lower than the rating given to President Nixon, who—after his "year of Watergate"—received a 68 to 30 negative rating.[1] In 1948 President Truman coined the expression "do-nothing Congress," which elicited such a favorable public response that it may have helped him win reelection. A generation later, President Nixon, also concerned about his tenure in office, suggested that Congress might be suffering from an "energy crisis," and his press secretary, Ronald Ziegler, thought that the staff of the House Judiciary Committee "should perhaps work late into the evening" to get its impeachment inquiry over with. One year and one President later, Gerald Ford—who had served in Congress for twenty-four years, eight of them as House minority leader—derided his former colleagues in much the same tone. President Ford defended his sudden, unilateral raising of oil import fees on the grounds that Congress was "diddling and dawdling" too much.

These kinds of innuendos never do Presidents any harm among their fellow Americans. All too often, a member of Congress is pictured as an idler, a trifler, fond of speechifying but unwilling to get down to serious business. The cartoonist's senator, who has a string tie and a Southern drawl, spends his day delivering orations and sipping bourbon. His name is Senator Claghorn or Senator Phogbound or Senator Snort.

This stereotype is particularly misleading today. Most members of Congress are anything but idlers. Their day starts early and ends late. They are in their office in the morning answering mail, meeting constituents, rushing off to committee meetings. Their afternoons may be divided between their office (more constituents and mail to be confronted), the floor of Congress (to which they are summoned by bells), downtown Washington (for media tapings), the steps of the Capitol (for a picture with a high school class from back home). Evenings might involve paperwork at home, or an out-of-town flight for political fence-mending, or a meeting with a columnist from home. Members of Congress work a long day, often seven days a week. Meals are interrupted, the phone is always busy, family life is disrupted. The mad pace of congressional life has helped produce a wide range of personal problems, from divorces to skin rashes, among the nation's legislators. Far from being an idle one, the average day of the average member of Congress may not provide enough leisure for some to think about *what* he or she is doing. This point will be considered later in this chapter. For the present it should be enough to conclude that the work ethic is alive and well on Capitol Hill.

Why, then, the reputation of doing nothing, of "screwing around," of fiddling while Rome burns, or trifling with the nation's future? Suppose we suggest this answer: While the public is wrong in picturing the member of Congress as an idler, it is not so wrong to sense that Congress as an institution has somehow failed to keep up with the pace of modern America. Members of Congress keep themselves busy from dawn till well past dusk, but Congress collectively has fallen behind the times.

CONGRESS: THE ABDICATION OF POWER

SYMPTOMS OF DECLINE

1 Congress has failed to lead the country toward basic and elementary reforms, reforms long accepted as essential in other industrial democracies. In the 1940s, during the war against Hitler, Congress was still solemnly debating whether or not to pass an antilynching bill. In the 1950s, about a half-century after most European countries had already adopted some form of national health insurance, Congress failed to pass even the most modest health legislation. In the 1960s, a decade of assassinations and soaring crime rates, Congress failed to adopt meaningful gun control legislation, legislation which was favored by a large majority of Americans. In the early 1970s Congress could not bring itself to pass even a minimal program of family assistance, nor later reach agreement on a national energy program.

2 Congress has been gradually ceding its legislative power to other branches of government. During the 1950s many members of Congress, especially Southerners and conservatives, were upset when the "activist" Supreme Court of Chief Justice Earl Warren seemed to be "legislating" social reforms such as desegregation of public schools. But would this have happened if Congress had not abdicated its own responsibility in the area of civil rights? Power abhors a vacuum. If an energetic and vital movement fails to find a response in one organ of government, it turns to others. The Supreme Court, staffed with liberals, was the logical place for civil rights advocates to turn during the 1950s, when *neither* President nor Congress was especially interested in innovation.

Over the longer run, however, it has been the Presidency which has been the chief beneficiary of congressional sluggishness. By mid-century it was no longer unseemly to call the President "chief legislator," because Congress by then had grown to expect and even demand his leadership in lawmaking. Gone are the days when Congress could scold a Cabinet officer for having the "effrontery" to draft a departmental bill for submission to Congress, as it did to the Secretary of the Interior in 1908.[2] By Eisenhower's time a veteran chairman of a major House committee reportedly admonished an administration witness, "Don't expect us to start from scratch of what you people want. That's not the way we do things here—*you* draft the bills and *we* work them over." By the 1950s the positions of President and Congress had become reversed. The President had become the initiator of legislation and the Congress reserved the right to veto. By the mid-1960s many liberal intellectuals seemed to agree with Professor Samuel Huntington's belief that this is the way it should be.[3] Legislation, he said, "has become much too complex to be handled by a representative assembly." Huntington proposed instead that "urgent" legislation be handled by the three "houses" of the executive branch: the bureaucracy, the administration, and the President. Congress's role should be limited to a veto power "like that of the British crown."[4]

The liberals began having second thoughts about this doctrine after Congress went them one better by abdicating even its right of veto over a Presidentially declared war in Southeast Asia. The activist President who led Congress down the path to Vietnam later described his technique in terms familiar to any good cowboy or mule-driver:

> I sometimes felt that Congress was like a sensitive animal—if pushed gently it would go my way, but if pushed too hard it would balk. I had to be aware constantly of how much Congress would take and what kind of mood it was in.[5]

By this approach Lyndon Johnson, a former Senate floor leader, was able to corral the necessary votes for an extraordinary array of domestic reforms, but it also permitted him to coax Congress into accepting—and funding—the most disastrous war in the nation's history.

After Johnson came Nixon. The new President and his staff seldom concealed their disdain for an institution which seemed incapable either of acting or of resisting the actions of others. True, Congress was less tractable than it was during the early days of Johnson. It balked at the passage of new domestic programs. But Nixon's conservative constituency did not care much about legislative programs and, by 1972, neither did Nixon. It was in the areas of foreign policy and "national security"—the latter a highly elastic category under Nixon—that the new White House was to have the freest hand: freedom to invade other countries, to blockade foreign ports, to bomb cities over and over, to concoct schemes for punishing "enemies," to set in motion a chain of covert actions which culminated in the Watergate break-in and cover-up. Even as the Nixon Presidency began disintegrating in the summer of 1973, Nixon's adviser John Ehrlichman was arguing that the President had inherent power to commit burglary, and E. Howard Hunt, one of the Watergate burglars, felt let down because White House officials failed "to interpose themselves between the seven of us who were initially indicted and the severe penalties of the law that have been imposed on us. . . ."[6]

UNCHECKED POWER: WHO IS REALLY TO BLAME?

It is not enough to deplore the abuse of Presidential power under Johnson and Nixon, or the dangerous accumulation of it under previous occupants of the White House. The real criticism should be directed at the body which abdicated so much of its power to the President, which kept it under such weak restraints, and which raised so few questions about the manner of its use. If Vietnam had been given a thorough airing by Congress in 1960, or even in 1965, would the fateful "commitments" have been made? If Congress had taken it upon itself to end the war in 1968, would street demonstrations and the reactions to them have taken such an ugly turn? If Congress had kept close tabs on power in the White House, would Watergate and related "horrors" have occurred? Whether or not these questions have final answers, they are tempting to ask at a time when public confidence in both President and Congress is not very high. To some, the politically fatal effect of Watergate on the fortunes of Richard Nixon and his associates means that the danger of executive tyranny is over. But this is a negative and ultimately futile way to confront the problem of unchecked power. Power, we have already suggested, abhors a vacuum, and if both President and Congress are weakened, power will find a new home, perhaps in another area of government or even in the private sphere. "Power tends to corrupt," Lord Acton once noted. But power is essential if government is to perform the tasks we demand of it today—to regulate industry, to hold down inflation, to prevent economic and social chaos. The second part of Lord Acton's dictum is more to the point: "absolute power corrupts absolutely." Unchecked power, which feels no resistance from another power, which operates secretly, which does not have to submit to hard questioning by anyone: This is the power which corrupts. The remedy for the abuse of power is opposing power from another branch or arm of government. In *Federalist 51* James Madison, one of the framers of the Constitution, said that "ambition must be made to counteract ambition." Madison is often interpreted as arguing for a static, negative system of government in which each branch is so busy preventing the others from exercising power that it hardly has time to accomplish anything itself. But Madison does not have to be understood in this purely negative sense. The real lesson of recent American history is that power is checked by power, and that power in the proper sense consists in taking initiatives, not merely in saying "no" to someone else's initiatives. Putting it another way, if Congress is to reassert itself and win back the esteem of Americans, it will have to be more than a veto on presidential power. It will have to begin acting as a legislature, not merely as a nay-sayer.

How, then, is a legislature supposed to act? In any system of representative democracy this branch of government is likely to play a variety of roles: discussing issues, helping to inform the public, representing constituencies, keeping a wary eye on the administration, and of course passing laws. In this chapter and in a later chapter, two basic legislative roles will be examined: passing laws and overseeing their administration. Legislative oversight will be considered in Chapter 9 as we examine the various checks on presidential power. For the present we shall chiefly be concerned with Congress as lawmaker. How does it exercise this role, what are the obstacles to it, and what can be done to remove these obstacles? To answer these questions let us take a closer look at Congress as a maker of laws.

Although we read or hear about very few of them, hundreds of laws are passed during each session of Congress.* Most of this total volume of legislation is routine and noncontroversial ("sundry measures," in the language of the *Congressional Record*): private bills for the relief of individuals, minor amendments to previous legislation, and public works projects (less politely, "pork-barrel legislation") such as dams and irrigation ditches, which keep members of Congress right with their constituents. Only a small fraction of the bills introduced each year involve major modifications of the status quo, and these measures must go through a legislative minefield on the way to becoming laws. Suppose we take a walking tour through this minefield.

THE LEGISLATIVE ORDEAL

Bills can originate from several sources. A member of Congress may direct his or her staff to prepare one. Or the bill may come from the administration, from an ordinary citizen, or from an organized lobby. (The director of a famous liberal lobby did not hesitate to take credit for the basic outlines of a bill passed by

* A new Congress begins every two years, always on the odd year. The intervening even year marks the second session of Congress. Hence the first session of the 93d Congress began in January 1973. The second session of the same Congress began in January of 1974. The 94th Congress, first session, began in January 1975, and so on.

Congress in 1970. "The bill was written right on here," he told the author, patting his desk.) Whatever its point of origin, the bill must be drawn up in the precise legal form required of legislative measures, and it can be submitted only by a member of Congress. Bills can be introduced in either house, but any bill pertaining to revenue must originate in the House of Representatives. This is expressly required in Article I, section 7, of the Constitution, which followed the British precedent of allowing the "lower" house to initiate legislation affecting our pocketbooks.

The method of introducing bills in the House is simple enough. A member simply drops the bill into a hopper on the clerk's desk. It is then assigned by the Speaker to an appropriate standing committee. The House has twenty-two such committees, dealing with a variety of matters from the Armed Services to Merchant Marine and Fisheries. The most important by far are the fifty-member Appropriations Committee, and the Ways and Means Committee, which was chaired for fourteen years by Wilbur Mills of Arkansas. Mills's power was awesome, his mastery of complicated tax codes was probably unsurpassed, and his personal life was once considered uneventful, but it all came apart in 1974 as a result of a combination of causes: ill health (mental and physical), congressional reforms, and the shock waves loosed by "the Argentinian firecracker," a Latin stripper who dove out of Mills's car into the Potomac tidal basin after Mills was stopped for drunken driving. He was replaced as Ways and Means chairman by Congressman Al Ullman.

The House once had forty-eight standing committees, but the Legislative Reorganization Act of 1946 shortened the number to nineteen while cutting those in the Senate from thirty-three to fifteen. By pruning back the tangle of committees Congress sought to restore unity and simplicity to its operations. But committee specialization apparently is unavoidable, because the ultimate effect of the Legislative Reorganization Act was a proliferation of subcommittees. The mammoth House Appropriations Committee, to take the most conspicuous example, has no less than thirteen subcommittees. When the Speaker refers the bill to an appropriate committee, then, the chairman of that committee will likely pass it along to one of its subcommittees. A civil rights bill, for example, might be referred by the Speaker of the House to the Judiciary Committee, and its chairperson in turn would refer it to a subcommittee specializing in civil rights questions.

The Committee—Heart of the Legislative Process

It is in the arena of committees and subcommittees that the real work of Congress takes place. Woodrow Wilson once declared that "Congress in session is Congress on public exhibition, whilst Congress in its committee rooms is Congress at work," and these words may be truer today than they were in 1885 when Wilson wrote them.[7] A congressional session today is not even much of an exhibition. A visitor to the gallery of either house will probably be disappointed if he or she expects to watch a good floor debate. This is the more likely scene: A solitary speaker is droning something into a microphone. Only a few dozen members are in attendance. Some are clustered in the rear, engaged in conversation; others are walking in and out. A few are lounging in their seats, reading, writing, talking. One may be dozing. None is paying much attention to the person at the microphone, which bothers the latter not at all because the speech is for the *Congressional Record,* the official transcript of House and Senate proceedings, and will be mailed to constituents. Once in a while a lively debate does break out, more often in the Senate than in the House, but such occasions are just that—occasions. When a vote on a major bill is about to take place, the chamber fills up with members, but they melt away when the vote is over.*

The nitty-gritty of the legislative process takes place within the committees and subcommittees which work over a proposed piece of legislation. If the bill is controversial the subcommittee will usually hold open hearing on it, with proponents and opponents invited (subpoenaed, if necessary) to state their views and provide facts. (The number and proportion of opponents and proponents will often reflect the views of the committee's leaders. If the chairman is a strong supporter of a piece of legislation, he or she may "tilt" the balance of invited witnesses in favor of the bill.) Then comes the real work of the committee or subcommittee: the "mark up" session. This is when its members begin to go over a bill line by line, considering each word, striking or amending it as they see fit. They may decide to strike every word after the enacting clause ("Be it enacted by the Senate and House of Representatives of the United States of America in Congress assembled, That . . .")—in effect, to write a wholly new bill. The modifications may not be as drastic as that, but rarely is a controversial bill unchanged by the committees and subcommittees to which it is referred. Here it is interesting to contrast the legislative procedures of Britain and America. Parliament, like Congress, sends legislation through committees, but the parliamentary committee lacks any real discretion in changing the substance of legislation. Its function is merely to make the necessary refinements in form and language before sending the measure to the floor of Parliament. When it comes to modifying legislation the parliamentary committee acts more as a body of clerks than of sovereign lawmakers. The discretion left in the hands of congressional committees and subcommittees shows that Congress retains its independence of executive direction—at least when compared to Parliament, where the majority does the bidding of the cabinet—but it opens the door to a variety of irresponsible practices. A committee or subcommittee may cut the heart out of a bill while retaining its title, thus sowing the seeds of confusion that will be reaped when the bill reaches the floor. Sometimes the original sponsor of a bill ends up voting against it because it no longer resembles the bill he or she had in mind.

The congressional committee retains life-or-death control of legislation: It may simply decide to "kill" a bill by not reporting it out. For years this was the fate of civil rights bills referred to committees chaired by Southerners, and it still

---

* "Members are called to the floor for a quorum call as the afternoon's debate begins. Soon, nearly everyone arrives to answer his or her name. Most stay for a while, listening and chatting. Then, inevitably, the drift begins. Pages hurry up and down the aisles with sheaves of messages, calling a congressman to argue with an executive department on behalf of a constituent, or to tell a garden club delegation why he favors the Shasta daisy for the national flower." Congressman Clem Miller, *Member of the House: Letters of a Congressman* (New York: Charles Scribner's Sons, 1962), p. 52.

happens to legislation strongly opposed by the leadership of a committee. A committee can be forced to release a bill if 218 members (one-half plus one) of the House sign a *discharge petition,* but this is a rare event. As a matter of temperament, members of Congress are reluctant to break with the usual ways of doing things. As a matter of prudence, members of Congress are even more reluctant to make enemies of committee chairmen, who have been called the "feudal barons" of Congress. Since the chairman exerts a powerful leverage over the actions of his or her committee (deciding when and how often it will meet, arranging its agenda, chairing the meetings, controlling the staff), he or she can retaliate against enemies by killing any of their pet bills which get assigned to the committee. A committee chairman is also part of the congressional power structure, with connections to other leaders and chairmen, so a frown can be contagious.

If the bill, or some version of it, is approved by the subcommittee, it is then sent to the full committee. If the full committee also approves it, the bill is sent on to the next stage of the legislative process. In the House this is the Rules Committee.

House Rules Committee
The House Rules Committee, established as a standing committee in 1880, is supposed to sort out legislation, separate the more important from the less important bills, and assign specific rules for debate: when the measure is to be considered, how long each of its provisions is to be debated, whether it can be amended on the floor, and so on. The need for a permanent Rules Committee became evident in the post-Civil War years when the immense volume of legislation reaching the floor of Congress caused logjams at the end of every session. In the press of last-minute business important bills were either neglected or passed without proper debate. The purpose of the Rules Committee was to establish priorities, making sure that the more important and controversial bills be given enough time for consideration instead of being crowded out by minor bills. Each bill, when it is reported out by a committee, is assigned a number and put on a calendar (the House has separate calendars for public revenue bills, nonrevenue public bills, and private bills), but the Rules Committee can ignore the calendar order in assigning the dates for each to be debated by the full House.

Although the Rules Committee was meant to serve this entirely laudable purpose, and more or less does serve it, it has also, at least since early in this century, served a more dubious end: the blockage of legislation. One of its former chairmen summed it all up neatly when his colleagues asked him to send to the floor some bills that he opposed. "You can go to hell," he answered, "It makes no difference what a majority of you decide. If it meets with my disapproval, it shall not be done. I am the committee. In me reposes absolute obstructive power."[8] For years a succession of conservative Rules Committee chairmen used this power to prevent liberal legislation from reaching the floor. "My people didn't send me to Congress to be a traffic cop," said Howard Smith of Virginia, who turned the Rules Committee into a roadblock for civil rights legislation during his tenure as chairman during the fifties and early sixties.[9]

There exists a variety of alternative routes around this roadblock, none of them very effective. One of them is Calendar Wednesday. On Wednesday of each week, unless dispensed with by unanimous or two-thirds consent, the Speaker runs down the list of each standing committee in alphabetical order. When named, a committee may call up for floor consideration any bill which it has reported out and put on the calendar. This end run around the Rules Committee has seldom been used, however, because opponents of a bill can stall House procedings by a variety of dilatory tactics (demanding periodic quorum calls, for example), making it virtually impossible for the House to conclude the proceedings, as it must do, in one day. Another alternate route is the motion to suspend the rules. On the first and third Mondays of each month and during the last six days of each session, the Speaker may entertain a motion to suspend the operation of the regular rules, in this case to pass a bill bottled up in the Rules Committee. This motion requires a two-thirds vote, almost impossible to obtain against the Rules Committee. A third alternate route is the discharge petition, rarely used for the reasons already given.

In recent years the awesome negative power of the Rules Committee has been weakened. In 1966 its chairman, Howard Smith of Virginia—whose determination and ability to block liberal legislation had become legendary—was defeated in a primary, and the other committee members took advantage of his departure to pass new rules circumscribing his successor. Since then, the Rules Committee, while still a potential threat to bills which challenge the status quo, is no longer a major obstacle to their passage.

The Committee of the Whole

Our bill, let us suppose, has passed through the subcommittee, full committee, and Rules Committee. It is now scheduled for floor debate. If the bill deals with revenue, however, it must pass through one more committee—the Committee of the Whole House. As its name implies, this committee is not limited to a fragment of the membership but embraces the entire House, meeting in the House chamber. It is physically indistinguishable from a regular floor proceeding except for the removal of the mace (a sort of club which we inherited from the British House of Commons but which goes back to the time of the Roman Republic: a symbol of legislative authority) from the Speaker's desk. Under this procedure the House is able to act with more dispatch, since the formal rules for debate are abridged and it takes only 100 members to constitute a quorum instead of the usual 218. During debate, with ground rules set by the Rules Committee, amendments may be offered, and each member is allotted five minutes to speak on each amendment. If the bill is passed by the Committee of the Whole, the House then formally reconvenes in order to take its official vote on the measure. If accepted, the bill, with all its amendments, is printed or "engrossed," and delivered to the Senate.

Here the legislative ordeal is roughly similar: The bill must pass through subcommittee and full committee, where it may be killed or amended or rewritten. The Senate, unlike the House, does not require all legislation to pass through a Rules Committee, so one potential obstacle is eliminated.

The Senate Filibuster

A much more formidable device for delaying or killing legislation is the filibuster. The Senate, unlike the House, permits unlimited debate on any measure, and this privilege has been used by senators on a number of occasions to "talk a bill to death." By monopolizing the floor a senator—more often a group of senators—can not only prevent a vote on a measure but prevent *any* business from being conducted. Thus the entire workload of the Senate is blocked as long as the filibuster remains in effect, and this puts pressure on a bill's proponents to modify or abandon it.

To grind Senate business to a halt a senator need only remain standing and talking. What he or she talks about is irrelevant: In the 1930s Senator Huey Long treated his colleagues to recipes for "Louisiana potlikker." While members still retain the privilege of reading from telephone books if they like, filibusters are more respectable today. The monologues are usually related to the topic of the bill, and a little variety is brought into the time-killing process by introducing a long string of emasculating amendments. While individual senators with leather lungs and steel bladders have held the floor for marathon performances, the most effective filibusters have been organized affairs, the *filibusteros* spelling each other off until the less determined majority gives up in resignation, despair, or disgust.

Only a large and determined majority can put an end to a well-organized filibuster, by invoking *cloture.* The number of senators necessary to invoke cloture has been varied from time to time. Once it was two-thirds of the entire membership; later it was changed to two-thirds of all senators present and voting. In the spring of 1975 the Senate changed its rules to allow *three-fifths of the entire membership, or sixty senators,* to invoke cloture. After cloture has been invoked, debate is then limited to one hour per senator, after which the measure must be voted up or down.

If the bill has passed the Senate, it may or may not be ready for the President's signature. If it is identical with the House version, the bill is returned to the House, which authorizes it to be printed and sent to the President. If minor amendments are attached, the House will probably agree to them unanimously. If the Senate amendments are substantive or controversial, however, a conference with the Senate may be requested. If the Senate agrees, a *conference committee,* composed of members from both houses, is appointed to iron out differences between the two versions. If a compromise is reached by the conference committee members, and if that compromise is then agreed to by both houses, the bill is then printed on parchment for the President's signature. The President in turn has four options: He can sign the bill into law, let the bill become law without his signature (which it does automatically if the President takes no action within ten days), veto it by returning the bill to its house of origin with his objections, or exercise a *pocket veto.* If the President holds on to a bill, "puts it in his pocket," and Congress adjourns in the meantime, the bill is killed.

Thus our bill is either enacted into law (by the President's signature or acquiesence) or vetoed. If the bill is vetoed while Congress is in session, it will then be returned to its house of origin, where it will need a two-thirds majority in order to override the veto. It then goes to the other house for a similar two-thirds vote. If both houses override the veto it becomes law over the President's objections.

NEGATIVE CHECKS: PRO AND CON

This ordeal of the legislative process has been traced in order to highlight a central feature of our Congress: its wide variety of negative checks. Negotiating a bill through the congressional minefield is a hazardous business. It is hard to predict when or if an explosion will occur, but everyone knows the risks of death or dismemberment. Will a Senate committee suddenly take a hard look at a bill passed by the House? This happened to President Nixon's Family Assistance Program in 1970. Will a group of determined senators filibuster a bill to death? For years this was the fate of civil rights legislation. Will a committee simply pigeonhole a bill, without holding any hearings? Any bill closing tax loopholes runs this risk in the House Ways and Means or Senate Finance Committees. At any point along the legislative route a bill may strike a mine and be blown to pieces—or, to use a less violent metaphor, it may slip into a hole and never emerge. The plenitude of negative checks in Congress is one important reason why the United States lags behind other industrial democracies in domestic reform—in gun control, family assistance, health insurance, campaign regulations—and why America was so late in guaranteeing the most elementary civil rights, such as voting and sitting down to a meal where one pleases.

Those who defend our system of negative checks usually begin by noting that the checks are not absolute.[10] When a sufficient head of steam gets built up behind an issue, the necessary majorities can be mustered in Congress to override vetoes, quash filibusters, and discharge bills from committees. It takes time to build such majorities, of course, but the defenders of the system argue that it *should* take time. George Washington once defended our bicameral system by comparing it to a cup and saucer. Just as hot tea is cooled by being poured from one vessel to the other, so hot legislation and hot heads are cooled by being poured from one chamber to the other. The defense of negative checks simply extends Washington's argument: The purpose of all the congressional roadblocks is to make members of Congress think twice—or several times—before passing legislation. Transient majorities cannot force their will on the rest of the country. Only a solid majority, acting on settled convictions rather than passing fancies, can get laws passed. This, argue the defenders of negative checks, is what prevents Congress from passing hasty or ill-conceived measures.

One difficulty in the defense of negative checks is that it assumes the nation can wait indefinitely for an overwhelming consensus to develop. But time does not stand still outside the halls of Congress. Grievances unredressed can be as dangerous as hasty legislation. Economic and social chaos cannot wait forever for perfect remedies. Sometimes imperfect ones must be tried, and quickly. Nations can drift into wars and depressions while legislators vacillate. Former Senator Joseph Clark was surely right in observing that "to do nothing in the modern world may itself represent a decision as disastrous as any affirmative action."[11]

A second difficulty in the argument for our present system of negative checks lies in its apparent assumption that the checks stop the passage of *all* varieties of hasty legislation. Actually, at least since the beginning of the Second World War, Congress has routinely approved gigantic defense budgets with little or no debate, has appropriated funds for the CIA without even asking how they are to be spent, has sometimes given the FBI *more* money than it requested, has passed laws to jail people for the crime of burning a flag or a draft card, for making a speech or even for planning to make one. Some of these bills have been passed with much haste and little discussion, In practice, then, the operation of congressional roadblocks is quite selective. Traffic bearing the name "family assistance" or "health insurance" or "gun control" may be backed up for miles, but vehicles with "patriotism" or "national security" written on the side have been known to get through without delay. Why the double standard? To answer this question we must ask another one: Who has been operating the congressional roadblocks? And the answer which immediately comes to mind, an inadequate answer but a beginning, is: old men.

SENIORITY

In 1974 the median age of the American was 28.1 years. During that same year the median age of the member of Congress was 53.2 years old. (It is younger today because of the influx of 75 freshmen Democrats in the congressional elections of 1974.) But the average member of Congress does not necessarily represent the power structure of Congress. The heart of Congress, we have seen, lies in its committee system, and the heart of the committee is the chairman. These "feudal barons," we noted earlier, exert a powerful control over the legislation which passes through the various congressional committees. In 1974 the median age of committee chairmen was 64.2. Many of these chairmen first came to Congress during the Presidency of Harry Truman, and the heads of five key House committees (Banking and Currency, Appropriations, Agriculture, Ways and Means, and Armed Services) first came to Congress before Pearl Harbor.

These men got to be chairmen because of the *seniority rule,* which bases eligibility for the post upon years of continuous service on the same committee (not simply on years in Congress, as many suppose), and membership in the majority party of the chamber. The seniority rule has been called the "senility rule," because it has rewarded mere political longevity without regard to merit. A Congressman, any Congressman, knew that if he waited around long enough, and if his party had a majority in the chamber, he could move to the top of his committee's pecking order. But by the time a Congressman reaches the age of sixty-five or seventy, and has sat in Congress for twenty years or so, his creative energies may be spent. In part the problem could be a matter of geriatrics,* although some senior members are amazingly chipper and others are not even very old. The problem may not be so much biological as it is biographical. One

---

* "There are so many old men in Congress that we actually have a lot of emergency medical gear just to keep them alive. We have our own ambulance parked behind the Capitol, ready to go at a moment's notice. In the cloakrooms, just out of sight of the galleries, we have stretchers and oxygen tanks. Doctors are always on duty whenever the House is in session and they can rush to the floor in less than sixty seconds. Sometimes they have to. On one occasion, I saw a senior member have a seizure on the floor. Unable to breathe, he slumped down in his seat and his face turned white. The doctors arrived in time to revive him and get him to a hospital." Congressman Donald Riegle, *O Congress* (Garden City, N. Y.: Doubleday & Company, Inc., 1972), pp. 163–164.

junior Senator has complained about the "super-Senators" in his chamber, the chairmen of the big committees who also serve as subcommittee chairmen on each other's committees. ("It's like an interlocking board of directors.") The big problem is that "they all reflect the same way of thinking—the same way of life. They don't have to talk about it." The super-Senators, in this freshman's view, "are the products of their experience and their times—they just don't have a feeling for what's out there with the people now."[12]

Another complaint often voiced about seniority is that it has given a special bonus to geographical areas which experience the least political competition. Stagnant one-party states and districts which send their congressional representatives back to office for term after term—states and districts usually characterized by a low voter turnout and low levels of political awareness—are precisely the ones which exert the greatest influence over Congress. Well over 80 percent of all congressional seats are usually considered "safe," but safest of all, at least so far as the Democratic majority is concerned, are those from the South. A disproportionately high number of committee chairmen have come from this region, a region which has the lowest turnout and the least electoral competition.[13] The seniority system is one reason why Congress has been called "a Union army led by Confederate generals." It was more than a coincidence that the four committee chairmen stripped of their positions in 1975 by the House Democratic caucus happened to be Southerners: Wilbur Mills of Arkansas (Ways and Means),* F. Edward Hébert of Louisiana (Armed Services), W. R. Poage (Agriculture), and Wright Patman (Banking and Currency) of Texas. Replying to the charge that the revolt against these chairmen was an anti-South vendetta, Representative Thomas M. Rees of California said: "The South, with all its one-party districts, just has more chairmanships. Texas had seven chairmanships and California none."[14]

Revolt against Seniority

The revolt against seniority began as far back as 1971, at the start of the 92d Congress, when the House Democratic caucus decided that if ten or more members challenged the chairmanship of any member, his or her position would be subject to a vote by the caucus. This still left the burden on those challenging a chairman—always a risky business—so the Democratic caucus in 1973 was persuaded to vote for committee chairmen by secret ballot of the entire Democratic membership. As soon as secret balloting was put into effect there were signs that seniority was in trouble. Although every single Democrat who would have been in line for a chairmanship under the seniority rule was confirmed, six of them were opposed by more than 20 percent of the caucus members. Among the six were the three who were voted out two years later: Poage and Patman of Texas, and Hébert of Louisiana. Then, between 1973 and 1975, came the unraveling of Watergate, the resignation and pardoning of Nixon—and the Democratic landslide in the congressional election of 1974. The 75 freshmen Democrats who entered the 94th Congress in 1975 knew about the reforms enacted during the

---

* Technically, Mills resigned his chairmanship, but he did so with the certain knowledge that he would otherwise be removed.

past two Congresses, and they knew they had the votes to take advantage of them. So, for the first time in the history of Congress, every single committee chairman was summoned by the newly elected members of the House to appear before them and answer their questions. Chairman Hébert, aged seventy-four, got off on the wrong foot by addressing them as "boys and girls," but within a few days he was frantically shaking hands with every unfamiliar person near the House floor, including some who were not even members of Congress. Too late! The full Democratic caucus in the House overrode the recommendations of its Steering and Policy Committee (composed almost entirely of senior members), and voted to remove Hébert from the chairmanship. Poage and Patman got the same treatment, and every other House chairman got the message: hereafter, in the words of New York Congressman Jonathan Bingham, "Chairmen will recognize they are not serving by divine right, but as elected representatives of the caucus."[15] In the Senate, meanwhile, the Democratic caucus voted for the first time to select committee chairmen by secret ballot. Although the Senate is more traditional than the House in its procedures, it appeared to be starting down the road which the House began traveling in the early seventies: toward the abolition of seniority. But for the time being the Senate Democrats were content to assert only the principle of accountability. In practice, they unanimously elected their chairmen according to seniority.

The successful challenge to seniority is one sign of an increasing impatience, particularly among the newer members of Congress, with the ways of life which have prevailed on Capitol Hill for so long. But the old ways die hard, and some of them are still very much alive. Because the time-honored traditions, or "folkways," of Congress have helped to shape its institutional behavior, they deserve a closer examination.

CONGRESSIONAL FOLKWAYS

Congress operates in an atmosphere pervaded by the folkways,[16] rituals, and even the artifacts of the nineteenth century. The Capitol itself is a living museum. Built in sections over a seventy-year period but substantially complete by the time of the Civil War, its marble halls still echo the style and flavor of that grand epoch. In 1973 New York's Senator James Buckley, a freshman Conservative-Republican, described the Senate in these terms:

> It is a place where a senator is entitled to free haircuts (although he is expected to tip the barber a dollar) in a barbershop which keeps a shaving mug with his name on it. It is a place where on each desk there is a little inkwell, a wooden pen with steel nibs, and a glass bottle filled with sand with which to blot writing, and where on either side of the presiding officer's desk is a spittoon and a box of snuff.[17]

Quaintness of this sort is less tolerable to other first-term members of Congress. Senator Lawton Chiles, a former Florida state legislator, has complained about the antiquated procedures for information-gathering in Congress. "We had computers in the Florida legislature eight or nine years ago. Here, if I want to find out where a bill is we'd have to go find the clerk who'd pull down an old dust-covered ledger and tell me the number and where it was, and that would be just the start."[18] In 1969, when the executive branch had 4,600 computers, Congress had a total of three, mostly occupied with payrolls and the addressing of newsletters.* Today most experts believe that Congress will eventually adopt some sort of comprehensive data processing system, but it already lags years behind the executive branch, most state governments, and private businesses in this respect.

Another time-saving device long rejected by Congress is the electronic voting system. Although many state legislatures had been using them for years, it was not until 1972 that the House finally installed devices permitting its members to instantly record their votes instead of waiting for 435 names to be called. The Senate still has not adopted the system.

Why has Congress been so slow to adopt useful gadgets like computers and vote recorders? In part, the answer lies in a mixture of pride and politics. In the summer of 1969, when a House subcommittee invited the Senate to participate in a joint study of computer potential, the Senate did not even reply to the invitation. The reported reason: It came from a subcommittee chairman, not from the House leadership, and this offended the pride of Senate leaders. As for electronic voting, it threatened to speed up roll-call votes. Thirty-minute roll calls had permitted members to leisurely stroll from their offices to the House floor and gave House leaders a last-minute chance to change some votes.

On a deeper level than pique or politics, however, Congress has shied away from mechanical innovations for the same reason it has avoided other kinds of innovations, including innovations in its procedures. Anything newfangled, anything which breaks old precedents, opens up new departures, or threatens old ways, is suspect. Within both chambers of Congress an elaborate series of folkways governs the conduct of legislators. These range from the etiquette of floor debates (which prevents one from addressing a colleague by name: he or she is "the gentleman" or "the gentlewoman" from New York or "the Senator from Texas") to more substantive matters like "Senatorial courtesy," which prevents Senate confirmation of any administrative appointment opposed by a Senator from the nominee's home state. Most of these folkways stress quiet cooperation, cordiality, tolerance of one another and of the status quo. Most of these folkways are harmless in themselves, and some are even useful as a means of avoiding any more of the fistfights and canings which occasionally broke out in the early days of Congress. Overall, however, they have had a deadening effect on innovation, because their supreme touchstone has been: conformity. "If you want to get along," said Sam Rayburn, one of the most famous and successful of House Speakers, "go along." Senator Carl Hayden, who finally retired in 1969 at ninety-one, gave us the Senate version of the maxim. "There are two kinds of Congressmen," he remembered being told when he first came to Congress, "—show horses

---

* According to reporter Warren Weaver of the *New York Times,* the main reason computers were installed in the Senate was to avert a catastrophe in the mail room. "What happened was that the lead plates used to address senators' outgoing mail got so numerous and heavy that the mail room floor began to give way, so the secretary was forced to buy a light-footed computer to do the job on tape." Warren Weaver, *Both Your Houses: The Truth about Congress* (New York: Frederick A. Praeger, Inc., 1972), p. 162.

and work horses. If you want to get your name in the papers, be a show horse. If you want to gain the respect of your colleagues, keep quiet and be a work horse."[19]

Today congressional folkways are threatened as never before. More and more "show horses" are coming to Congress, unwilling either to "keep quiet" or to "go along," and this has been playing havoc with the old traditions. But their legacy remains. "This is still," one House member said in 1973, "the most enduring Oriental society in America."[20]

Let us pause for a moment to summarize. The question has been: Why has Congress gotten the reputation of "screwing around" instead of governing? The answer, we have suggested, lies not in any innate laziness of the average member of Congress but in the procedures of Congress. These procedures have:

1 Emphasized negative checks.
2 Rewarded mere longevity in office by means of the seniority system.
3 Discouraged potential innovators and breakers of tradition by perpetuating congressional folkways.

FRAGMENTATION OF AUTHORITY

Let us now add a fourth factor that hobbles congressional initiative: Congressional procedures have fragmented authority, tempting members to act irresponsibly. To see the problem concretely it might be helpful to examine an issue which came to a head in the early seventies: the issue of presidential impoundment.

Impoundment Controversy

One of the most serious threats to congressional power in recent years, especially to Congress's control of the purse, is presidential impoundment—the refusal by the President to spend money appropriated by Congress.

The practice of impoundment goes back to 1800, when President Jefferson refused to spend $50,000 for Mississippi gunboats. In recent years the practice has involved billions of appropriated dollars. Under President Nixon impoundment became a major issue after it was discovered that the President had withheld some $15 billion of appropriations since coming into office. In the past, Presidents had impounded mainly military funds, but Nixon withheld massive amounts in the domestic area, in some cases starving out whole programs mandated by Congress.

Congress reacted with indignation. The President is "making a monkey out of the legislative process," declared Speaker Carl Albert of the House of Representatives. Others were more grave. "This encroachment is the most dangerous thing I've seen in my thirty years in Congress," said one senior member. Another saw it as a threat to "Congress' very existence." Another cited his years of experience: "I have been in Congress under seven Presidents, both Republicans and Democrats, and never during this 44-year period have we been closer to one-man rule."[21]

In reply, Caspar Weinberger, Nixon's Secretary of Health, Education, and Welfare, argued that Presidential impoundment would be unnecessary if it were not for Congress' "antiquated and illogical" budgetary procedures.

> Nowhere among its 300-odd committees and subcommittees, each responsible for a small portion of the budget, is there one focal point where a goal or spending ceiling can be set or monitored to assure spending sanity.[22]

Even Nixon's severest critics acknowledged that Weinberger had scored a clean hit.[23] The fact is that the Congress of the United States, which was spending about $300 billion ever year, lacked what any delicatessen owner knows he must have—a budget. Congress had no unified organ for balancing debits against credits, for shaping spending priorities, for deciding what it can afford to buy.

In the early years of Congress the House Ways and Means Committee performed this task, but by the middle of the nineteenth century Ways and Means was limited to matters of revenue raising, with spending placed in the hands of appropriations committees. Thus began the confusion of getting and spending, in which the right hand—the spenders—knew not what the left hand—the money-raisers—was doing. Congress hoped to resolve this confusion in 1921 with the passage of the Budget and Accounting Act. This statute created within the Treasury Department a Bureau of the Budget, designed to coordinate executive requests for money, and thus to give Congress some sort of initial budgetary structure to start marking up. In 1939 the Bureau of the Budget was transferred to the Executive Office of the President, and in 1970 President Nixon, after renaming it the Office Of Management and Budget (OMB), sought to make it into a device for gaining undisputed control of the sprawling federal bureaucracy.

Every year Congress works and reworks the executive budget requests, authorizes its own projects, and later passes the necessary appropriations bills to pay for all of it. The scramble for "pork barrel legislation"—public works projects back in the home district—is usually intense. A freshman Congressman who was defeated in 1972 has remarked on "the tremendous drive that animates Congressmen to gain publicity. Every second, every minute, this thought is not far from the center of consciousness: 'Now, how can I get this little plum for my district, so that I can call my publicity man and have him get the word out?' "[24] Some years earlier an experienced House member said the same thing, only more bluntly: "The biggest thing in electoral politics, in Congressional politics, is boodle, and the reputation you get back home for being able to get boodle."[25] The end result of this scramble for "boodle" is a great shapeless mass of expenditures, which has become an irresistible target for cost-cutters in the executive branch. In 1972, after Nixon impounded an unprecedentedly large chunk of it, some $12 billion, the stage was set for another "constitutional crisis." Congress began work on a number of bills forbidding or modifying this Presidentially asserted power. It took President Nixon to court on the issue, winning its case in the District court. The House Judiciary Committee considered the impoundments among the several possible grounds for impeachment, although it later dropped the issue as it narrowed the scope of its investigation.

Yet the underlying problem, the failure of Congress to budget itself, still remained. Congressman Al Ullman of Oregon, now the chairman of the House

Ways and Means Committee, conceded as much: "If Congress doesn't set its own house in order, it can't be too upset about the executive moving in and setting priorities."[26] Ullman was cochairman (with Jamie L. Whitten of Mississippi) of a Joint Study Committee on Budget Control, which proposed a special budget committee for each house of Congress. The two committees would be provided with a single joint staff rivaling that of OMB, plus computers and all the other necessary hardware. The staff would be directed to develop tabulations "on a recurring basis" which show the effects on expenditures of existing and proposed legislation. The tabulations would also compare projected spending and federal revenue estimates. The committee could thus make recommendations for shaping a congressional budget.

Congressional Budget and Impoundment Control Act
By the summer of 1974 the Ullman proposals, after undergoing a number of revisions in both houses, were enacted into a new law, the Congressional Budget and Impoundment Control Act of 1974. Among its key provisions were these three:

    1   The establishment of House and Senate budget committees and a congressional budget office to coordinate the preparation of budget totals
    2   The establishment of a strict timetable for passing legislation which appropriates money or which authorizes its appropriation
    3   A requirement that Congress must agree to any presidential impoundments of funds appropriated by Congress

The measure was passed by large margins in both houses, with many senators and representatives calling it one of the most important acts of the century. Even President Nixon, whose unilateral appropriations it was designed to check, seemed enthusiastic about signing it, saying: "A major problem is overspending by government and with this bill we can help to hold down the cost of living."[27] The only scornful voice came from Republican Congressman H. R. Gross, the legendary cost-cutter from Iowa who retired at the end of 1974. "Yes sir, everything is going to be hunky-dory," Gross said sarcastically, then prophesied: "Don't you believe it for a minute! Members of this House will find ways very quickly to warp any rules you can lay down here today, and some of you will be part of it."[28]

We have been discussing the problem of fragmented authority in Congress. One aspect of this problem has been the lack of any agency or committee to coordinate the getting and spending of public monies, a problem which the Budget and Impoundment Control Act was designed to remedy. But the underlying problem of fragmented authority remains, and it manifests itself in a number of other areas. One of them lies in the confused tangle of committees, each scrambling for as much jurisdiction over as many areas as possible. (The more jurisdiction, the more powerful the committee; the more powerful the committee, the more important its members.) The result is a great deal of overlap, duplication of effort, and frequent jurisdictional disputes between committees. The former Congressman who was quoted earlier in this chapter told the author:

When I was in Congress a seven-man energy committee was proposed. (Perhaps it might have been some help today.) You never heard such spleen! Senior Congressmen were fighting it because it might eat into the jurisdiction of the Interstate Commerce Committee, the Merchant Marine Committee, the Government Operations Committee, and so on. The energy committee was never instituted.[29]

The point was well illustrated, in fact writ large, by the reception given to the proposals of the Bolling Committee by the House of Representatives in 1974.

Congressional Reorganization: The Bolling Proposals

In February of 1973, amid considerable fanfare, the House approved the creation of a bipartisan committee, headed by Representative Richard Bolling of Missouri, to study and make recommendations for the reorganization of the House committee system. Bolling, a long-time critic of the existing committee system, termed his assignment "an impossible task" but one which "must be done."[30] By the end of 1973 the Bolling committee, having taken seven volumes of testimony from members of Congress, political scientists, citizen activists, and administrators, prepared its own draft recommendations.

Although the Bolling proposals were detailed and complicated, their underlying purpose was simple: to prune away dead committees, redistribute the work load most efficiently among the live ones, and create new ones to meet new problems. Thus three committees whose work load had become too light were to be dropped or absorbed into other committees. One eclectic committee, Education and Labor, was to be split in half to make two new committees. A new committee, Energy and Environment, was to be fashioned out of a revamped version of the Interior Committee. Older committees that had acquired vast jurisdiction, such as Ways and Means, would lose some of it to other committees. Such practices as voting by proxy in committee would be abolished, and more committee staff positions would be allotted to the minority party.

The Bolling proposals, apparently noble in intent,[31] ran into a hail of opposition when brought before the House in April of 1974. Wilbur Mills, then chairman of the Ways and Means Committee, was reportedly incensed by the proposal to strip his committee of jurisdiction over Medicare, international trade, and revenue-sharing. Those chairmen whose committees would be abolished or divided were not very happy, either. This produced some odd alliances, in some cases uniting liberals and conservatives in opposition to the Bolling proposals. Several members of the Democratic Study Group, a liberal House organization formed largely to fight the seniority system, complained that the plan did not adequately protect their seniority. Members of the liberal Education and Labor Committee coalesced with the conservative Ways and Means Committee to try to kill the reorganization proposals.[32] Opposition also came from lobbyists who had developed comfortable relationships with the existing committee structure. Said one: "A form and structure that you've been used to is something that you want to live with. No one wants to start building contacts all over again."[33] The Bolling proposals faced a powerful opposition, so powerful that his original appraisal of his assignment—"a wholly impossible task"—did not seem so exaggerated.

As we can see from the difficulty of reorganizing committees and establishing a congressional budget, the problem is that of fixing responsibility among 435 representatives and 100 senators. Everyone is for reform—reform of the other fellow's committee. Everyone is for economy—economy in the other fellow's district.[34] In part the problem is one of sheer numbers. Unlike the President, Congress has always been a "they." When the member of Congress comes home to his district, he can always blame the shortcomings of Congress on "the others."* This ploy seems to work, because the overwhelming majority of the members of Congress get reelected despite the low marks which the public gives to Congress as a whole. Members of Congress, then, can run against Congress and win approval by excoriating the collective sins of their own chamber. What Congress lacks is a firm structure of legitimate and responsible authority. It is true that both House and Senate have party leaders. The Senate has majority and minority leaders, with "whips," or assistants, to help round up votes for measures backed by their party. In the House the chief majority leader is the Speaker, or presiding officer, who is not (like the British Speaker in the House of Commons) a neutral parliamentarian but a partisan leader. The House also has majority and minority leaders, whips, and other party functionaries. The power of these party leaders, however, does not go much beyond the realm of persuasion, since party "discipline" has never been much accepted in America, and in recent years even party organization has fallen on hard times (see Chapter 6). There are Democratic and Republican caucuses in Congress, but there are also liberal and conservative caucuses, a black caucus, a woman's caucus, and a black woman's caucus. Big-city machines were once able to deliver solid blocs of metropolitan votes in Congress, but these voting blocks have dissolved with the decay of the machines and the growth of the suburbs.

In summary, if Congress at times seems to be "screwing around" or doing nothing, this factor should not be ignored: Congress lacks a firm structure of leadership which can crack the whip to round up votes, formulate policies, and take the rap for what Congress does or fails to do.

Negative checks, seniority, congressional folkways, fragmented authority—all four factors have played their roles in preventing Congress from acting boldly and energetically. Let us now add a fifth and last one: errand-running, or casework, for constituents.

CASEWORK: MISSING THE FOREST FOR THE TREES

In the eighteenth century the British statesman Edmund Burke raised the question whether a legislator should let his constituents dictate the policies he votes for in Parliament. In a famous address to his Bristol constituents Burke conceded that the legislator must devote himself to those who choose him. "But," he maintained,

---

* "Members feel relieved of personal responsibility, losing themselves in the mass of 435 Representatives and 100 Senators. If there are no funds for schools, housing, transportation, the President can be blamed, and if funds are forthcoming, the Member can always point to a speech, a last minute vote, or his name on an early bill co-sponsoring the project. It is a riskless game that frustrates Constitutional intent." Sidney H. Scheuer and Russell D. Hemenway, Chairman and National Director of National Committee for an Effective Congress, newsletter, Jan. 8, 1973 (mimeo).

his unbiased opinion, his mature judgment, his enlightened conscience, he ought not to sacrifice to you, to any man, or to any set of men living. These he does not derive from your pleasure, no, nor from the law and the Constitution. They are a trust from Providence, for the abuse of which he is deeply answerable. Your representative owes you not his industry only, but his judgment; and he betrays, instead of serving you, if he sacrifices it to your opinion.[35]

To modern sensibilities Burke's position, or at least his formulation of it, may seem a trifle too pious.[36] A member of Congress who faces reelection every two years never tells constituents that his opinions are "a trust from Providence." Even senators avoid this sort of talk. Besides, there is no evidence to suggest that members of Congress are often torn between their own opinions and those of their constituents. The two are usually well-matched, or at any rate compatible.

The congressional member's real dilemma as regards the folks back home is not so much a matter of principle as of priority: How much time should be devoted to solving constituents' particular problems instead of making laws to deal with the problems of the nation?

In reviewing the hypothetical member's average day at the beginning of this chapter it was seen that he spends a good part of it dealing with constituents: answering their mail, meeting them, posing for pictures with them, trying to reach them through the media. Members of Congress put great emphasis on these activities, in part because they know that generosity reaps rewards on election day. One Congressman estimated that "at least one-third of our activities today are spent in working toward re-election. You know the saying, 'You can't be a statesman unless you get elected.' "[37]

But the case for taking care of constituents goes beyond the concern for self-preservation. Members of Congress seem to enjoy playing a role which is so essential to people in need. The member is often the last resort for citizens who have trouble of one kind or another—trouble getting their social security payments, trouble getting Veteran's Assistance or an FHA mortgage, or a job with the FBI, or a federal grant for a local health center, or . . . The list is endless, but the intercession of a member of Congress is often necessary to cut red tape or straighten out a snag. The member, then, plays an essential role in humanizing the bureaucracy, making it work for individuals who would otherwise be ignored or given the runaround. Congressmen are informal ombudsmen, and they take pride in this role. One experienced legislator put it this way:

When I first came here I was dumbfounded by the number of requests. I was inclined to think I didn't have time for legislation. My first reaction was, "Why don't they contact the executive agencies or the proper department with which these problems are associated? Why should they expect me to take care of them?" Gradually I came to realize that each of these problems is very important to the person writing me, and that it is important for me to treat them as significant. Many people are baffled by our bureaucracy and don't know where to turn for help. Eventually somebody says, "Why don't you write your congressman?" and they do. I now realize that one of my most important functions is to help these people. If they are entitled to go through a door they cannot find, it is my job to locate that door so they can go through.[38]

The only trouble is that ombudsmanship takes up an enormous amount of time—more today than ever before. The proliferation of federal programs enacted during the 1960s has had a multiplier effect on casework. Now whole communities depend upon members of Congress to iron out kinks in federally aided programs. More and more members have joined the "Tuesday-Thursday club," disappearing from Washington from Thursday night to Tuesday morning to handle problems in their home district, and even those who stay in the Capitol are besieged with increasing numbers of letters, telegrams, phone calls, and visits from their constituents. This makes it increasingly difficult for legislators to legislate, or at least to know what they are doing when they legislate. Sometimes a vote is based upon a last-minute consultation with a colleague, or a quick glance to see how a trusted colleague is voting, or on nothing at all except a herd instinct to "go along." All members of Congress receive some sort of staff assistance, the size and quality varying with seniority and size of constituency, but staffers also get tied up in casework, and periodically, reelection campaigns.

Some members of Congress like it that way (reasoning that their constituents are less interested in lofty programs for the nation than in personal favors for themselves),* but the more thoughtful are troubled by the terrible pace of the members day, which leaves so little time for study or reflection. Senator James Buckley has suggested that members of Congress be given at least a week of free time each month to collect their thoughts, to plan, travel, and establish "meaningful contact with their constituents."[39] The suggestion is worth considering, but the danger is that "meaningful" constituent contacts might simply turn into more casework. Others have suggested the creation of a separate Federal Office of Ombudsman, with representatives in each district to take care of the casework.[40] Aside from the difficulty of persuading congressional members to surrender such a politically rewarding "burden," the proposal is intrinsically flawed because it ignores the fact of power. Putting the matter in bluntest terms, a member of Congress can get results for constituents because Congressmen can issue credible threats to bureaucrats. The threat of a fund cut-off, a congressional investigation, or even a hell-raising speech on the floor of Congress can change an unfeeling bureaucrat into a solicitous public servant—at least for a moment, for a particular constituent of a particular member of Congress. What kind of threats could an ombudsman make? Where would the ombudsman's power come from? Unless the proponents of such a post can show how it could be at once independent and effective, their proposal must remain forever in the "wouldn't-it-be-lovely" file.

---

* "An old-time congressman told me the quickest way to get defeated is not to answer the mail or pay attention to constituents. They care less about your votes and attitudes than about whether you are interested in, and take care of, their individual problems." Anonymous congressman quoted in Charles Clapp, *The Congressman: His Work as He Sees It* (Garden City, N. Y.: Anchor Books, Doubleday & Company, Inc., 1963), p. 84. Cf. Riegle, op. cit., p. 143: "The men in power . . . usually don't see themselves as needing more staff. And to many other, less senior, members, the lack of committee staff just isn't a pressing concern. It doesn't relate directly to their re-election hopes. They'd much rather take the people they have on their personal staffs and direct them toward servicing their districts, performing chores for constituents. That's far more important to them and their long-term chances of becoming committee chairmen than digging into the intricacies of the federal budget or pending legislation."

SUMMARY AND CONCLUSIONS

In this chapter we have examined five factors which have crippled congressional initiative in this century:

1. Its proliferation of negative checks
2. The practice and spirit of seniority
3. The stifling folkways of Congress
4. The lack of unified leadership
5. The press of casework

Let us concede that these factors have not always impeded effective lawmaking. For example, congressional folkways, particularly when used by skilled leaders like Lyndon Johnson or Sam Rayburn, were helpful in rounding up votes. "If you want to get along, go along" does have its constructive side. By the same token, the influx of iconoclasts into Congress in recent years may not be an unmixed blessing. Iconoclasts also tend to be prima donnas, and this makes it difficult to build the stable majorities necessary to pass bills. Seniority may have had its uses too, and its abolition in the House could lead to some nasty infighting as members of Congress try to oust existing chairmen and then compete for vacant chairs. Nevertheless, when we take all five factors together, their minuses outweigh their pluses. The folkways and rituals of Congress have helped to produce cohesion, but they have also helped to make Congress a kind of Byzantine institution, so tied to complicated rituals and so lacking in spontaneity that it has been unable to respond effectively to new challenges and crises—one reason for its tendency to delegate away authority to the President. The cohesion has also been obtained at the price of remoteness from the American people. "What are they doing for their money?" is a question frequently asked about members of Congress. As for seniority, its formal abolition may lead to some friction and uncertainty, but probably not very much. Even the freshmen "rebels" of the 94th Congress allowed seniority to rule except in three cases of chairmen who were widely regarded as being either feeble or out of touch with the sentiments of the House majority. Friction and instability may actually have been lessened by their revolt, for, as Common Cause has noted, "more monkey wrenches have been thrown into the proper functioning of the Congress by wayward committee chairmen than by anyone else."[41]

The five factors listed above do not exhaust the reasons why Congress has fallen behind the executive in the vital area of lawmaking. In all probability it has also fallen behind for the same reasons other legislatures in the world have lost power to cabinets and prime ministers: because wars and domestic upheavals have put a premium on secrecy, swift response, and bold initiative, properties more often associated with executives than with legislators.

Yet perhaps we have reached a point in American history where we might reconsider the peculiar merits of legislatures. Legislatures can seldom act as quickly or as quietly or as boldly as executives, but they may be able to act more thoughtfully and openly. These old-fashioned virtues may be especially appreciated by Americans today, who have suffered so many deceptions, endured so much arrogant abuse of power, and become weary—and wary—of so much secrecy.

This does not mean that Congress necessarily *is* more open or thoughtful than the executive, only that it has the potential. Decision making in the White House takes place, all too often, in an atmosphere of unreality. Discussion is confined to the narrow circle of the President and his chief advisers. The relationships are extremely familiar, for all the discussants are part of a team who work closely together every day. Furthermore, each participant in the discussion is acutely aware of the one for whom it is intended—the President of the United States, Chief Executive, Chief of State, Chief of Party, Chief Legislator, and, not incidentally, their boss.

In Congress, on the other hand, the relationship is one between peers—equals—and not necessarily "team player" peers. Each member of Congress has an independent base in his or her state or district. Constituents are the only ultimate bosses, for only they have the power to dismiss a member. Unlike presidential advisers, members of Congress can pound the table, can mercilessly probe their colleagues' arguments, without fear of losing their jobs. If open, robust discussion is a prerequisite for thoughtful policy making, Congress would seem better suited to this end than the executive branch.

But only potentially. Actually the trading in ideas is seldom very heavy in Congress. In part this results from the heritage of congressional folkways, which makes such a virtue of quietly "going along" that some members of Congress are never moved to say much of anything.* (Old congressional proverb: "Remember, nobody ever lost an election for a speech he never gave.") The constant preoccupation with casework has also been a contributing factor in the lack of focused debate in Congress. Still another practice limiting the range of discussion, or at least preventing the public from hearing it, is that of holding "mark up" committee sessions behind closed door.

Ending Secret Committee Meetings

The "mark-up" stage of the legislative process is obviously a crucial one. It is here that the bill is gone over line by line, with key words added or stricken from the draft bill. Yet until recently nearly all these sessions were held in secret. Not until 1973, after considerable pressure from Common Cause and other citizens' lobbies, did the House of Representatives vote to open up all committee meetings

---

* Congressman Harold D. Donohue, seventy-two, next in line in seniority for the chairmanship of the House Judiciary Committee after Congressman Peter Rodino, is one who has mastered the art of taciturnity. "Few can recall the last time he said more than three words in succession in a legislative debate," according to James M. Naughton (*The New York Times Magazine,* Apr. 28, 1974, p. 29). When the House Judiciary Committee was considering the impeachment of Richard Nixon the pressures were particularly painful to Donohue. This conversation was overheard at a 1974 St. Patrick's Day party in Washington:

Harold Donohue: You gotta do something. My district's getting on me.
Peter Rodino: What do you mean?
Donohue: All these press people. They keep asking me for statements.
Rodino: Haven't you been getting the legal briefs and studies from the staff?
Donohue: No, no, I've got all that. But you gotta write out something I can say.

to the public unless the particular committee specifically votes otherwise.* The presumption, then, is for open meetings, although such important House committees as Ways and Means and Appropriations have been slow to accept the presumption. In the Senate, however, the opposite presumption rules: Unless a committee specifically votes to open its mark-up sessions, they are considered closed. Three Senate committees—Banking, Interior, and Government Operations—have already voted to open their sessions, but the most powerful Senate committees, like Armed Services and Finance, continue to operate in secrecy.

Other Recent Reforms

The movement to end secrecy is one of a series of internal reforms adopted in recent years. Besides ending secrecy in the House Congress has:

—shown that it means business about ending the practice of automatic seniority in the House by voting not to reappoint three of its chairmen. It paved the way for a similar happening in the Senate making chairmanships dependent upon a secret-ballot vote in the Democratic caucus. (See above, pp. 217–218.)

—adopted a subcommittee bill of rights in the House. In 1973 the House Democratic caucus voted to allow each member of a committee to have one subcommittee assignment of his or her choice, thus preventing senior committee members from hogging all the choice subcommittees.

—put an end to unauthorized executive impoundments and established congressional committees to develop a legislative budget. (Congressional Budget and Impoundment Control Act of 1974, above, pp. 222–223.)

—stripped the Democrats on the House Ways and Means Committee of the power to a twenty-four-member Steering and Policy Committee, which is elected by the Democratic caucus and chaired by the House Speaker. The effect of this was to reduce the power of the Ways and Means Democrats (who have generally come from the more conservative elements of the party) while increasing that of the party's elected leadership, thus making it more responsible.

These reforms stirred the hopes of many who had been working to make Congress into a more activist organ of government. As early as 1973, Common Cause was becoming enthusiastic: "Congress in 1973 has done more to make itself an effective and responsible institution than has any preceding Congress since the days of Speaker Cannon. . . . The overall changes are so far-reaching that the Congress—particularly the House—is at last in a position to recapture its role as a co-equal branch of government."[42]

On top of these reforms came the Watergate revelations, which may have played at least a negative role in strengthening Congress's will to live by sapping the strength of its adversary. † In the various confrontations between President

---

* Before being approved, however, this important change in House rules was weakened by two amendments. The first of these allowed a committee which votes to hold secret bill-drafting sessions to invite outside participants; this loophole allows administration lobbyists and military brass to be present at meetings which exclude the general public. The second amendment allows a committee to take only one vote to close a series of meetings, rather than having to take a separate vote each day—which might embarrass the members.

† Some critics of Congress—including members of Congress—feel that the opposite effect came from Watergate: It may have *reduced* the motivation of Congress to reform itself. Senator Adlai

Nixon and Congress in 1973–1974, Republicans joined Democrats in resisting impoundment, voting down funds for the bombing of Cambodia, passing a War Powers Act which set limits to presidential prerogative, subpoenaing executive documents, and reporting out an impeachment bill.

It seems premature, however, to conclude that the long drift toward executive domination of events has been reversed and the vigor of Congress suddenly restored. It was not until the summer of 1973, months after the Vietnam war was officially over, that Congress finally forced the Nixon administration to stop bombing Cambodia. As for impoundment, it was not until President Nixon had withheld about $40 billion in appropriated funds, cutting into pork-barrel appropriations favored by powerful committee chairmen, that Congress finally responded. Finally, the subpoenas and the ultimate move toward impeachment came only after a long series of extraordinary provocations by the President—evasions, insults, defiance—and a correspondingly long chain of Watergate revelations.

In any case, the lethal effect of Watergate on one President's power tells us little about the power of future Presidents, and still less about the prospects for congressional power. The Presidency as an institution has a remarkable ability to rise from the ashes of particular Presidencies. It survived Buchanan and gave us Lincoln, survived Grant to give us Theodore Roosevelt, survived Harding to give us Franklin Roosevelt. If the past is any guide, then, vigor will one day return to the White House, and this will provide a better indication of whether Congress has recaptured its role as a coequal branch of government.

The spectacular self-destruction of the Nixon administration which began in the spring of 1973 may have diverted attention from the roots of the Watergate crisis. How did an administration inherit such a degree of unchecked power as to lead its top officials into believing that they could with impunity authorize burglaries, sabotage election campaigns, intimidate critics, distribute hush money, obstruct justice?

In this chapter we have tried to suggest part of the answer. Congress contributed to what Arthur Schlesinger calls "the imperial Presidency" through a series of piecemeal abdications over the course of a half century. Congress either delegated away power, as it did by passing the Budget and Accounting Act of 1921, or accepted unilateral seizures of power by Presidents, as it did in the case of impoundment.

Congress had given away vital powers, or let them be taken from it, because it had lost the capacity to exercise them properly. It had lost this capacity because it had failed to modernize its procedures for making laws, had failed to develop a capacity for planning and for responsible leadership, had failed to meet the legislative needs of modern America. To reiterate: Power abhors a vacuum. On

---

Stevenson (D., Ill.) believed that Watergate engendered "a new complacency, because the President is weakened." Another reform-minded member of Congress, Les Aspin (D., Wis.), summed up: "The heat's off." Quoted in Elizabeth Drew, "Why Congress Won't Fight," *New York Times Magazine*, Sept. 23, 1973, p. 19. Nevertheless, it seems doubtful that Congress would have been emboldened to take the actions it did against a strong President, high on the public opinion polls, were it not for Watergate.

September 7, 1942, President Roosevelt, who had carried Presidential lawmaking further than any of his predecessors, demanded that Congress repeal forthwith a certain provision of the Emergency Price Control Act. Then he added: "In the event that Congress should fail to act, and act adequately, I shall accept the responsibility, and I will act."[43] With extraordinary candor Roosevelt laid bare an attitude toward Congress which came to be shared, at least implicitly, by every one of his successors (with the possible exception of Eisenhower). Paraphrased, it comes to this: "If Congress lacks the brains or will or guts to act when the moment requires action, then *I* must do it—even if it means defying, thwarting, and overriding Congress." Truman committed the nation to war and seized steel mills to settle a labor dispute during the war. Kennedy invaded Cuba in 1961 and blockaded it in 1962 without consulting Congress. He also maneuvered the nation into an overseas adventure which Johnson escalated into another major war. (Senator William Fulbright of Arkansas, who was chairman of the Senate Foreign Relations Committee during the period of deepening involvement, noted that the Pentagon Papers—the Defense Department's massive study of how America got involved—made no mention of Congress except "as an appropriate object of manipulation, or as a troublesome nuisance to be disposed of.")[44] Nixon claimed unilateral power in everything from war and peace to domestic surveillance and impoundment of appropriated funds.

It is not enough to deplore the arrogance of the executive, to declare with Speaker Carl Albert that the President is "making a monkey out of the legislative process." If, as seems evident, the growth of unchecked power in the executive branch has not been the result of some prolonged conspiracy but simply an accretion of powers abdicated by the legislative branch, then the remedy should be equally clear: in Representative Al Ullman's words, Congress must "set its own house in order."

Perhaps Congress *has* begun to set its own house in order. The optimist can point to the procedural reforms enacted during the 93d and 94th Congresses, the general level of maturity displayed by the Senate Watergate Committee and the House Judiciary Committee during the impeachment hearings, the new laws and resolutions limiting presidential power (such as the War Powers Act of 1973)* which Congress managed to pass over the President's veto, and the new blood infused into Congress by the congressional elections of 1974.

"Hot Breath of the Country"

But if Congress has made progress toward modernizing its procedures and checking the power of the President, a good deal of the credit should go to those forces outside of Congress which have goaded it to do so. By itself Congress has been all too inclined to settle into routines which keep its members busy without really grappling with the real problems of the nation. During those periods in this century when Congress has truly gotten down to business there has been considerable pressure upon it from someplace outside of its chambers. In 1969 legislative scholar Ralph Huitt suggested a causal relationship between public arousal

---

* The War of Powers Act of 1973 is discussed in Chapter 9.

and congressional energy. During the early years of Woodrow Wilson's and Franklin Roosevelt's administrations, Huitt noted, Congress felt the "hot breath of the country." These two periods witnessed the "most productive bursts of congressional energy in this century."[45] Today the situation is rather different. The major vehicle for piping the "hot breath of the country" into the halls of Congress is no longer the presidency but the various citizens' lobbies such as Common Cause. But Huitt's point is still valid: The impressive record of internal reforms enacted in recent years came at least partly in response to the concerted pressures of citizens' lobbies.

From the standpoint of the "hot breath" theory, the most significant of recent reforms may have been the opening up of committee sessions to the public. By pulling aside the veil of secrecy and mystery in the House, and at least permitting an occasional peek into Senate committees, Congress gave the public a chance to breathe even hotter upon their representatives. Some students of Congress would go even further and would open up the House and Senate floors to radio and television coverage.* The danger in such coverage of floor debates is that it might turn members into ham actors and their chambers into TV studios. The danger must be acknowledged, but the experiment may still be worth a trial. At present the House and Senate chambers are not TV studios, but they often resemble museums: Except during floor votes they are actionless and nearly deserted. The camera's eye might produce better attendance and perhaps even some meaningful debate. The American public, which has been so overexposed to "decision making in the White House"—and has already seen the sleazy side of that decision-making process—might learn to appreciate the drama of lawmaking in Congress. As for bad drama, or ham-acting, those who specialize in this art might find TV audiences far more critical and "cool" than the ones they meet on the stump.

Whether the cameras are actually wheeled into the House and Senate chambers, the point is that unless the American public can become more concerned about the operations of their Congress, Congress is unlikely to be concerned about itself. Ironically, the citizens' lobbies which sting and goad Congress are also helping to strengthen its powers vis-à-vis the executive branch. An efficient and responsible Congress is a powerful bulwark against executive encroachment, and a feeble Congress virtually invites the President's contempt. But Congress is not always so happy to be helped in this way. Pulling out of context the famous paradox of Jean-Jacques Rousseau, Congress sometimes must be "forced to be free."

---

* Warren Weaver of the *New York Times* (op. cit., p. 18) asks us to "imagine the possibilities" of such a development:

Midway through Tuesday afternoon's episode of "Secret Storm," a voice interjects, "We interrupt this program to take you to the Senate floor, where debate is closing before the final vote on the consumer protection bill." Will the housewives impatiently switch channels to "Another World"? Well, some of them will, but a portion won't, and that portion may gradually increase. We cannot expect that special events coverage of congressional highlights will ever rival the moon landings, but it cannot help but bring the processes of government closer to millions of Americans and, in turn, compel improvements in those same processes.

NOTES

1 *Journal-News* (Rockland County, N. Y.), Feb. 11, 1974, p. 22A. A Gallup poll conducted the following April gave Nixon a lower rating than Congress (Nixon, 25 percent, Congress, 30 percent). Both polls tended to agree on why the public rated Congress poorly. In the case of Harris, the pollster compared his findings with the "high point through the years for Congress," which was 1965 when it received a 64-26 percent positive rating. This was also one of the most productive years in terms of legislative output: It had just passed two major civil rights bills, a poverty program, and other important measures. As for Gallup's survey of April 1974, "the survey indicated that most of the criticism leveled at Congress involved 'playing politics,' 'foot-dragging' on key legislation and failure to override Mr. Nixon's vetoes." *New York Times*, Apr. 28, 1974, p. 27. In other words, Congress gets low ratings because the public perceives it as "screwing around" instead of legislating, but in those instances where Congress *is* productive, its rating goes up.
2 Quoted in John Bibby and Roger Davidson, *On Capital Hill: Studies in the Legislative Process* (New York: Holt, Rinehart and Winston, Inc., 1967), p. 5.
3 Samuel P. Huntington, "Congressional Responses to the Twentieth Century," in Theodore J. Lowi and Randall B. Ripley, eds., *Legislative Politics U. S. A.* (Boston: Little, Brown and Company, 1973), pp. 106–122. The various arguments for "party reform" usually assumed that the leader of these disciplined parties would be the President. See, for example, James MacGregor Burns, *The Deadlock of Democracy* (Englewood Cliffs, N. J.: Prentice Hall, Inc., 1963). Clinton Rossiter's famous book on the Presidency in the 1950s, *The American Presidency* (New York: Harcourt, Brace & World, Inc., 1956), lists "chief legislator" among the many roles he assigns to the modern Presidency. Both writers were enormously influential in shaping the textbook view of presidential power.
4 Huntington, op. cit., pp. 121–122.
5 Lyndon Johnson, *The Vantage Point* (New York: Holt, Rinehart and Winston, Inc., 1971), p. 451.
6 *The Watergate Hearings: Break-in and Cover-up*, ed. by the Staff of the *New York Times* (New York: Bantam Books, Inc., 1973), p. 668.
7 Woodrow Wilson, *Congressional Government: A Study in American Politics* (Boston: Houghton Mifflin Company, 1925), p. 79.
8 Warren Weaver, Jr., *Both Your Houses: The Truth about Congress* (New York: Frederick A. Praeger, Inc., 1972), p. 83.
9 Quoted in Weaver, ibid., p. 87.
10 Today most defenders of negative checks are ranged along the conservative side of the ideological spectrum, and their fondness for such roadblocks is simply based on their distaste for liberal legislation. In the past, however, many liberals also argued the case for negative checks on procedural grounds: that they would prevent hasty, transient majorities from trampling on the rights of others or otherwise acting foolishly. See, for example: Walter Lippman, "Minorities Should Not be Coerced," *New York Herald Tribune*, Mar. 3, 1949; Lindsay Rogers, "Barrier against Steamrollers," *The Reporter*, XX (Jan. 8, 1959), pp. 21–23; John Fischer, "Unwritten Rules of American Politics," *Harper's Magazine Reader* (Chicago: Bantam Books, 1953). William H. White's magnolia-scented tribute to the Senate, *The Citadel* (New York: Harper & Row, Publishers, Incorporated, 1957), makes both points: The slowness of the Senate is procedurally wise *and* it prevents bad legislation—like civil rights bills—from getting on the books.

11 Senator Joseph Clark, *Congress: The Sapless Branch* (New York: Harper & Row, Publishers, Incorporated, 1964), p. 147.
12 Senator Lawton Chiles (D., Fla.), quoted in John Omicinsky, Gannett News Service, "Senate Club Irks Novice," *Journal-News* (Rockland County, N. Y.), Mar. 18, 1974, p. 19A.
13 Raymond E. Wolfinger and Joan Heifetz, "Safe Seats, Seniority, and Power in Congress," *American Political Science Review,* LIX (1965), pp. 337–349. Barbara Hinkley, in *The Seniority System in Congress* (Bloomington: Indiana University Press, 1971), argues that "there is no evidence that application of this rule [seniority] results in regional bias." This seems to be an overstatement of her own findings, for a few sentences later she asserts: "Congressional seniority can help to explain Southern, but not Western, overrepresentation." Any defender of congressional seniority will find small solace in Hinkley's book. She admits that the system reinforces the conservative tendencies in Congress and adds: "The seniority system clearly strengthens the particularistic, centrifugal tendencies in the Congress. By multiplying centers of power down to the level of committe chairmen, it contributes to the fragmentation of power which frequently makes any attempt to form a governing majority impossible."
14 *New York Times,* Jan. 23, 1975, p. 24.
15 *New York Times,* Jan. 17, 1975, p. 29.
16 Donald R. Matthews, *U. S. Senators and Their World* (New York: Vintage Books, Random House, Inc., 1960), chap. 5.
17 James L. Buckley, "On Becoming a United States Senator," *National Review* (Feb. 2, 1973), p. 147.
18 Chiles, op. cit.
19 Matthews, op. cit., p. 94.
20 Quoted in Elizabeth Drew, "Why Congress Won't Fight," *New York Times Magazine,* Sept. 23, 1973, p. 18.
21 *New York Times,* Feb. 11, 1973, sec. IV, pp. 1, 11.
22 *New York Times,* Mar. 27, 1973, p. 47.
23 The *Times's* Tom Wicker, one of those listed on the President's "enemies list," conceded that Weinberger "made the Administration's most convincing argument." *New York Times,* Mar. 29, 1973.
24 Interview with author, Jan. 28, 1974.
25 Richard F. Fenno, Jr., *The Power of the Purse: Appropriations Politics in Congress* (Boston: Little, Brown and Company, 1966), p. 91.
26 Congressional Quarterly, *Guide to Current American Government,* Fall 1973 (Washington: Congressional Quarterly, Inc., 1973), p. 91.
27 *New York Times,* July 13, 1974, p. 6.
28 *New York Times,* June 19, 1974, p. 35.
29 Interview with author, Jan. 28, 1974.
30 *New York Times,* Feb. 1, 1973, p. 7.
31 Yet the resolutions, in the opinion of at least one commentator, are "short of a reformer's dream."
The Appropriations Committee and the Armed Services Committee have been consistently attacked in the press and by public interest groups as bastions of excessive power, but they remain unscathed in the resolution and there are reports that Bolling left them alone to buy support for his package. Taylor Branch, "The Approaching Struggle over Reform in the House," *New York Times,* Apr. 28, 1974, sec. IV, p. 1. Branch also charged in the same article that members with seniority were given a

"grandfather clause," which would allow them to carry their rank with them if they switched to another committee.

The noble intent of the Bolling resolutions was also questioned from another standpoint. Some members of Congress pictured it as a "power grab" by Bolling, an effort to strip Wilbur Mills and other key chairmen of their power.

32 Ibid.
33 *New York Times,* Mar. 30, 1974, p. 11.
34 One veteran member of Congress from Texas quoted by Fenno said: "I am for economy in Idaho and perhaps in Maine and a considerable amount down in Oklahoma. Then in the districts of some of my [Texas] colleagues, I am for economy over there unless it would injure and hurt my colleagues; but when you come to my district I am for "economy, but." Fenno, op. cit., p. 16.
35 Edmund Burke, *Speech of the Electors of Bristol* (1774), *Works, Vol. II, p. 12.*
36 See, however, Heinz Eulau, John C. Wahlke, William Buchanan, and Leroy C. Ferguson, "The Role of the Representative: Some Empirical Observations on the Theory of Edmund Burke," *American Political Science Review,* LIII (September 1959), pp. 747–756. In this study, involving interviews with state legislators from four states (California, New Jersey, Ohio, and Tennessee), the authors found that only 14 percent identified themselves as "delegates," i. e., representatives operating on the basis of instruction from their constituents, while 63 percent identified themselves as "trustees," or free agents voting for what they consider to be right. This study, however, tells us little about actual legislative behavior. Legislators can always talk like Burke in a confidential interview with a political science professor—perhaps they think that political science professors expect to hear them talk that way—but will they act as Burkean in the legislature, or repeat the performance of Burke when they talk to their constituents?
37 Charles L. Clapp, *The Congressman: His Work as He Sees It* (Garden City, N. Y.: Anchor Books, Doubleday & Company, Inc., 1963), p. 97.
38 Ibid., p. 61.
39 Buckley, op. cit., p. 145.
40 See, for example, James Boyd, "A Senator's Day," in Charles Peters and John Rothchild, eds., *Inside the System,* 2d ed. (New York: Frederick A. Praeger, Inc., 1973), p. 12.
41 Common Cause, "Editorial Memorandum on Why the Seniority System in Congress Must Be Changed," 1973, p. 12.
42 Common Cause, "Editorial Memorandum on Common Cause and Congressional Reform," 1973, p. 2.
43 Quoted in Edward S. Corwin, *The President: Office and Powers,* 1787–1957, 4th rev. ed. (New York: New York University Press, 1957), p. 250.
44 U. S. Congress, Senate, Subcommittee on Separation of Powers, Senate Judiciary Committee, *Hearings, Executive Privilege: The Withholding of Information by the Executive,* 92d Congress, 1st Sess., 1971, p. 23.
45 Ralph K. Huitt and Robert Peabody, *Congress: Two Decades of Analysis* (New York: Harper & Row, Publishers, Incorporated), p. 185.

Chapter 8

The President: Powers

Shall we have a King?

John Jay to George Washington, 1787

THE STRANGE CASE OF RICHARD NIXON

Among the items listed in the index of Arthur Schlesinger's 1973 book, *The Imperial Presidency,* under the heading "Nixon, Richard M.," are these: "his inflation of presidential authority . . . and trend toward veneration of the President . . . his view of perpetual crisis . . . his monarchical yearnings . . . and banishing of challenge from presidential environment . . . withdrawal from external reality . . . disdain for presidential press conference . . . dislike of the press . . . delusions of persecution . . . view of presidential supremacy over Congress . . . justification for his government's lawless actions . . . compared to Charles I of England (by Trevor-Roper) . . . lack of understanding of the sickness of his Presidency. . . ."[1]

It is hard to talk about the dangers inherent in presidential power today without talking about the dangerous man who occupied the White House from 1968 to 1974. True, Nixon's Presidency had its positive features: his opening to China, his attempt to reach arms agreements and establish détente with the Soviet Union, his attempt to reform the welfare system, his attempt to mediate tensions in the Middle East. But the good parts were outweighed by all the scandals that eventually came to be lumped together and called "Watergate":

Threats to civil liberties—burglaries, phone taps, enemies lists, bugs, harassment of critics and news media.

Secret wars and secret bombings, conducted while administration representatives were stoutly denying them before Congress and the public.

Misuse of government agencies, such as the Internal Revenue Service, the FBI, the Justice Department, the CIA, and the Small Business Administration, for political purposes.

Strong evidence of extortion. Raising milk price supports after receiving the promise of a campaign contribution from the dairy lobby. Trying to call off an antitrust suit against a conglomerate corporation which later made a campaign contribution.

Attempting to subvert the election process through a variety of means, including sabotage, surveillance, and illegally soliciting campaign contributions.

Offering the FBI directorship to a federal judge at the very time he was presiding over the trial of Daniel Ellsberg, whose conviction had become a high-priority goal of the Nixon administration. As one of Ellsberg's attorneys pointed out, he would be in jail if he had offered a prize job to the judge at such a time.

Obstruction of justice: failing to report crimes, perjury, suborning perjury, destroying evidence, covering up crimes, trying to prevent Congress and the courts from finding out the truth.

Two themes seemed to run through all these scandals. One of them was cynicism—cynicism about people and about laws. People, Nixon and his advisers seemed to think, can be manipulated, handled, "stroked," if only the right techniques are applied. People are gullible—they *want* to believe their President, and they will if his story is properly packaged. People are motivated more by fear than by love, more by the prospect of material reward than by honor. As for laws, they are made to suit the needs of the Chief Executive. All laws, from the Constitution's Fourth Amendment to the Internal Revenue Code, can be bent if they get in the way of a President's plans. A second thread which seemed to run through all the Nixon scandals was a "siege mentality," an obsession with "enemies" everywhere, from the jungles of Southeast Asia to the political hustings in America, and a corresponding compulsion to use every instrument of government, without scruple or hesitation, to augment the political fortunes of Richard M. Nixon and to punish his enemies. "I believe in the battle," Nixon told a reporter in 1973, "whether it's the battle of a campaign or the battle of this office, which is a continuing battle. It's always there wherever you go. I, perhaps, carry it more than others because that's my way." And behind the closed doors of the Oval Office he told John Dean: "Nobody is a friend of ours. Let's face it!"[2]

A case can be made that the mentality which Nixon brought to the White House was unique. Seasoned reporters could not remember an administration which was as consistently vindictive and hostile as the Nixon one or that used the term "enemies" to describe domestic critics and political opponents. Other observers, like Princeton historian Arthur S. Link, found something unique about the extent of corruption in the Nixon administration. "It is unprecedented. There is nothing analogous to it in the past, nothing," Link contended. "The peculations of the Harding and Grant Administrations . . . were sores on the body politic but not cancers in the body itself. They didn't subvert democratic processes. They didn't corrupt entire administrations."[3]

All this may be quite true. The purpose of the present chapter is neither to support nor to dispute the proposition that Nixon carried arrogance and corruption to unprecedented heights. The purpose is rather to show that the *makings* of arrogance and corruption were already there by the time Nixon entered the White House. A word of explanation is in order.

"Not an Aberration but a Culmination"

As the Watergate scandal began to close in on him, Nixon tended to fall back on the "I'm not the first one" line of defense: Johnson also secretly taped and bugged; Johnson also took advantage of tax shelters; Kennedy tapped phones; under Roosevelt the FBI started breaking into foreign embassies; Eisenhower claimed executive privilege. Some of the assertions were probably false, others were misleading, and the whole line of defense rested on the faulty premise that illegal or unethical conduct is justified if others did it before. And yet, whatever the casuistical weakness in this defense brief, it contained a kernel of truth. Under Kennedy and Johnson phones *were* tapped, not only the telephone of James Hoffa and various mafiosi but that of Martin Luther King. Under Eisenhower, Kennedy, and Johnson official lies *were* told to the press and the American people—lies about the mission of a secret spy plane shot down over the Soviet Union, lies about the Bay of Pigs invasion, lies about the build-up in Vietnam. (Arthur Sylvester, Kennedy's Assistant Secretary of Defense, even proclaimed the administration's "right to lie.") Under Johnson official lying was sustained long enough to introduce the term "credibility gap" into the language of American politics. Under Roosevelt the FBI *did* begin breaking into foreign embassies, acting much the same as the "plumbers" acted under Nixon. Under Johnson, and perhaps earlier, the CIA began spying on American citizens in their home country, in clear violation of its 1947 charter.

Did Nixon misuse the Internal Revenue Service? But Kennedy's associates tried to tamper with the IRS as soon as they came into office in 1961.[4] Did Nixon, in the words of Arthur Schlesinger, "harbor monarchical yearnings"? But Kennedy's administration was compared to the Court of Camelot! Was Nixon "imperial"? But surely it would be hard to top the imperial pretensions of Lyndon Johnson, which showed through in everything from his Vietnam policy to little incidents like this one: Johnson had just finished delivering an address at an army base and began moving back toward the Presidential plane when a soldier in his official escort shyly pointed out that he was about to get on the wrong plane. "Sir . . . Mr. President . . . *your* plane is over there on the other side, sir." "Son," Johnson answered, "I want to tell you something—just so you never forget. . . . All of them—those over here *and* those over there—are *my* planes."[5]

Perhaps Nixon and his associates carried arrogance to even greater heights—but the very office he inherited was charged with the potential for abuse; it had already become an inflated, imperial position in the American system of government. Despite his caustic views of Nixon the man, Arthur Schlesinger makes his most salient point when he admits: "Nixon's presidency was not an aberration but a culmination."[6]

By dwelling too long on the flawed personality of Richard Nixon we may forget what James Madison took for granted back in 1789: "Enlightened statesmen will not always be at the helm."[7] Madison's point was that we must build into the American system enough constitutional checks to counter the mischief of an occasional rascal, fool, or would-be tyrant in high office. The real questions to consider, then, are not psychological but political: Not what kind of presidential "personalities" have occupied the White House, but what kind of powers have our Presidents been inheriting in recent years? What kind of powers did Nixon inherit that *allowed* him to carry on as he did for as long as he did? Suppose Nixon did have fantasies about "getting" his enemies—what could have emboldened him to act them out? What kind of sword did he inherit? And what about "all the President's men"? Much has been made of the arrogance and cockiness of Nixon's aides. But what could have puffed them up so much? How could they have come to believe that burglary, perjury, bribery, and obstruction of justice were not crimes, or at any rate not punishable crimes, when committed in the service of the President? What sort of powers did the Presidency have which tempted so many?

CULT OF "ACTIVISM"

There was a time, not so very long ago, when many of the same people who now worry about "the imperial presidency" actually encouraged its growth. Liberal intellectuals in the fifties and the early sixties derided Eisenhower for not being enough of an "activist" President. John F. Kennedy was attractive to them because he promised "vigor" in the White House. They liked to quote Woodrow Wilson's famous maxim that "the President is at liberty, both in law and in conscience, to be as big a man as he can." In *The Imperial Presidency* Arthur Schlesinger admits his own role in this liberal "cult":

> American historians and political scientists, this writer among them, labored to give the expansive theory of the Presidency historical sanction. Overgeneralizing from the prewar contrast between a President who was right and a Congress which was wrong, scholars developed an uncritical cult of the activist Presidency.[8]

During the fifties and early sixties liberals tended to favor a strong Presidency combined with a passive, tractable Congress. In domestic policy they inverted the traditional role of Congress and President. It was the President who should, in effect, "legislate," while the Congress should be limited to veto. In foreign policy even this congressional check seemed too much like meddling. The *New York Times* and the *Washington Post,* liberal professors, columnists, and politicians were vigorous supporters of the President's right to withhold evidence from congressional committees, to wage war without congressional consent, to send troops anywhere at his discretion. But what about the Constitution? Doesn't it give Congress, not the President, the power to declare war? "When it comes to action risking war," political scientist Richard E. Neustadt told a Senate committee in 1963, "technology has modified the Constitution." As late as 1964, Louis Koenig, another political scientist, wrote an article in the *New York Times Magazine* entitled, "More Power to the President (Not Less)."[9]

In the early sixties Neustadt's book on *Presidential Power* was all the rage among liberal political scientists and historians. (Schlesinger called it "the most brilliant and searching essay on the Presidency that we have had for a long time.") Neustadt's theme, which he stated at the outset, was "the personal power of the President and its politics: what it is, how to get it, how to keep it, how to use it," or "how to be on top in fact as well as name." *Presidential Power* was in part a "how to" book for Presidents, teaching lessons in how they might bolster their "prestige," their "professional reputation," and their control over the bureaucracy. (It won its author a job in the Kennedy administration.) But Neustadt also had some "do's" and "don'ts" for the voters: Don't elect overly modest people who concede powers to other branches of government, or who lack the instinct for power. Do elect people like Roosevelt, who "had a love affair with power." The book's underlying assumption was that the strong President will always be a good President. The strong man's contributions to the national good will emerge "as by-products of his search for personal influence." Indeed, "in a relative but real sense one can say of a President what Eisenhower's first Secretary of Defense once said of General Motors: what is good for the country is good for the President, and *vice versa.*"[10]

Ah, Camelot! Back in those days what was good for the President was good for the country. But when Nixon came into office, the same liberals who had enthusiastically endorsed this notion were now appalled by it, especially when it became clear that Nixon's aides had turned it into a living faith. What the liberals once called the "activist Presidency" they now called "the imperial Presidency." Of course, they had begun reconsidering their commitment to "activism" even before Nixon came into office, but even so the question remains: Was it on the basis of a genuine concern about the danger of a runaway Presidency—or was it simply that a particular President was not doing what they wanted him to do? Suppose liberal sentiment had not turned against the Vietnam war, a war many liberals once fervently supported. (In 1963 the *New York Times* chided Kennedy for calling Vietnam "their war," meaning a war for the Vietnamese to fight; no, it was "our war—a war from which we cannot retreat and which we dare not lose.")[11] Or suppose Johnson had not been so persevering, had pulled out of Vietnam when the liberals wanted him to. Suppose Humphrey, or better still Eugene McCarthy, had been elected in 1968. Suppose McGovern were elected in 1972, or some other candidate favored by the liberals were to win in 1976 or 1980. Would liberals still be worried so much about "the imperial presidency"? Or would they, perhaps, return to the old themes of "vigor" and "activism"? Does not the memory, or myth, of Franklin D. Roosevelt still help to shape the liberal's thinking about the Presidency? Does there not still remain among liberals a wistful hope for a new FDR, a Moses who "might yet lead us out of the wilderness"?[12]

Underlying this chapter is a very simple assumption. That assumption is that great amounts of unchecked power are dangerous in any President's hands, whether he uses those powers for good or for ill, and whether he is motivated by noblesse oblige or greed and malice. The assumption is basically the same as James Madison's assumption in *Federalist 51:* Men are not angels, and angels do not govern men. Presidents, like the rest of us, are mortal beings with all the failures and shortcomings which humans possess. The exalted office they occupy may bring out some of their nobler qualities, but it may also magnify their faults.

The object, therefore, is not to analyze the personalities of various Presidents, or to yearn for a leader with the right combination of "positive" qualities but to take an inventory of the powers possessed by the modern President and see whether we have sufficient checks upon them. If this seems a somewhat negative way of looking at things, we can reply that we have already seen the danger of too much positive thinking: The "can do" attitude in both the Johnson and the Nixon administrations brought the nation to depths of cynicism and despair. And if it is said that too much concern about the dangers of presidential power disregards the need for presidential leadership, we can reply that leadership in a democracy must come from several sources, including the Congress and the people themselves. The nation has had entirely too much leadership from only one power center. What we really need to do is to take account of the powers possessed by the person at that center, with a view toward making them more accountable to the citizens of the nation.

What are the President's powers, and from what do they derive? Let us start with what seems to be granted to the President by the United States Constitution.

CONSTITUTIONAL PROVISIONS

In Article I, section 8, the Constitution lists eighteen separate areas of congressional power, culminating in the famous "elastic clause": "To make all laws which shall be necessary and proper for carrying into execution the foregoing powers, and all other powers vested by this Constitution in the Government of the United States, or in any Department or officer thereof." The extended listing of congressional powers, culminating in this sweeping language, is all the more impressive when set beside the rather spare and miscellaneous assortment of powers granted to the President in Article II, sections 2 and 3:

1 "The President shall be Commander in Chief" of the armed forces, but—and this is sometimes glossed over by defenders of the President's war powers—only "when called into the actual Service of the United States." The President leads the armies, but does not declare war, nor does he have the power under the Constitution to raise and support armies, or to make rules for their governance, or to call out the militia to suppress insurrections or repel invaders (all of which are explicitly granted to Congress in Article I). Among the framers of the Constitution, Alexander Hamilton was the most outspoken advocate of "energy in the executive"—at the Constitutional Convention he candidly proposed an elected monarchy—but even Hamilton left no doubt that the President's power as Commander-in-Chief was to be "much inferior" to that of the British monarch:

It would amount to nothing more than the supreme command and direction of the military and naval forces, as first General and Admiral of the Confederacy, while that of the British king extends to the *declaring* of war and to the *raising* and *regulating* of fleets and armies—all of which, by the Constitution under consideration, would appertain to the legislature.[13]

2   The President "may require the opinion, in writing, of the principal Officer in each of the executive Departments, upon any Subject relating to the Duties of their respective Offices." Although there is no mention of the word "cabinet" in the body of the Constitution, its existence is implicit in this article. The executive departments, however, must be created by Congress.

3   The President "shall have Power to Grant reprieves and pardons for Offenses against the United States. . . . " The President's pardoning power has been used in a variety of imaginative ways. President Lincoln used it to provide a general grant of amnesty to an entire region of the country at the close of the Civil War. More recently, President Ford used it to "pardon" former President Nixon, even though Nixon had not been convicted, or even indicted, for "offenses against the United States," and never admitted committing them.

4   "He shall have Power, by and with the Advice and Consent of the Senate, to make Treaties, provided two thirds of the Senators present concur." Obviously the framers intended that the Senate share the President's power in the area of diplomacy. Not only the consent but the *advice* of the Senate is provided by this article.

5   He "shall appoint Ambassadors, other public ministers and consuls, Judges of the supreme court," but here again, only with "the Advice and Consent of the Senate," although in this case only a majority vote is required.*

6   The President is given a series of rights and duties in relation to Congress. He can veto legislation, but his veto can be overridden by a two-thirds vote in both houses; he can fill vacancies which may exist in the Senate during its recess, but the terms of his appointees will expire at the end of the next session; he can convene special sessions of Congress, but Congress has full power over its agenda once convened; he can adjourn Congress if its two houses cannot agree on the time for adjournment, but this occasion has never arisen. He must "from

---

* On one occasion President Nixon seemed to forget that Senate approval is an integral part of the President's appointment powers. The occasion arose when the Senate was considering the appointment of G. Harrold Carswell, a Nixon nominee to the Supreme Court. The administration was still smarting over one setback, Senate rejection (the first in forty years) of Nixon's previous nominee to the position, Clement Hainsworth, whose Circuit Court decisions had offended civil rights groups. When Senator William Saxbe (later Attorney General) wrote Nixon to ask his views on the Carswell nomination, Nixon replied:

What is centrally at issue in this nomination is the constitutional responsibility of the President to appoint members of the Court—and whether this responsibility can be frustrated by those who wish to substitute their own philosophy or their own subjective judgment for that of the *one person* entrusted by the Constitution with the power of appointment. [Quoted in Barber, op. cit., p. 427. (Emphasis added.)]

But as we see, the President is very clearly *not* the "one person" entrusted with the power of appointment.

time to time" give Congress information on "the State of the Union" and recommend measures which he considers "necessary and expedient."

7 He shall commission executive officers and "take care that the laws be faithfully executed."

Thus the sum total of powers granted to the President by the Constitution: to enforce the laws, to make treaties and appointments (but only with the advice and consent of the Senate), to command the armies (but only when called into actual service by Congress), to greet diplomats, to ask his Cabinet members' opinions, to exercise a qualified veto over legislation, to report to Congress "from time to time," and recommend legislation. Alexander the Great or Napoleon, looking over this list, would probably not be very impressed. Yet this list is at the root of the President's ability to exercise power and influence far beyond any that Alexander or Napoleon ever wielded. It has been the chrysalis for the modern Presidency, with its awesome powers in foreign affairs, its influence over every other branch and organ of government in the land, its capacity to affect the very tone and spirit of national life.

Without changing a letter of these constitutional provisions, strong Presidents—and even some not-so-strong ones—have been able to shape them to the dimensions of a vastly enlarged office. Often the Congress and the courts have cooperated or acquiesced in this enlargement, but even when they have not the process of presidential growth has continued relentlessly. At his second inauguration, Franklin Roosevelt was later to recall, "When the Chief Justice read me the oath and came to the words 'support the Constitution of the United States,' I felt like saying: 'Yes, but it's the Constitution as *I* understand it, flexible enough to meet any new problem of democracy—not the kind of Constitution your Court has raised up as a barrier to progress and democracy.'" The statement sounds arrogant (less than forty years later Nixon was accused of acting it out), yet it contains a germ of political truth: The parchment Presidency which emerged from the Convention of 1787 left history and experience to fill in its meaning in practice.

Presidential Roles: Three "Hats"

To study presidential power, then, we must examine it in practice, in the context of the historical precedents, court decisions, congressional statutes, and popular expectations which have shaped it over the past two centuries. A convenient and often used way of examining the President's powers is to consider some of the "hats" he wears. Some of them derive directly from the Constitution, while others have simply grown out of custom or exigency. In the 1950s Clinton Rossiter provided us with what may be the definitive inventory of presidential "hats." The President is at once Chief Executive, Chief of State, Chief Legislator, Commander-in-Chief, Chief Diplomat, Chief of Party, and Manager of Prosperity. We have already considered his role as Chief Legislator in Chapter 7. Let us take a closer look at three more of these roles—the three which have raised the most questions in recent years about "the imperial presidency": Commander-in-Chief, Chief Executive, and Chief of State.

THE PRESIDENT AS COMMANDER-IN-CHIEF

One of the reasons for the tapping of news reporters' telephones in 1969 was to find the source of an embarrassing leak to the *New York Times*. The paper had printed accounts of the Nixon administration's secret bombing of Cambodia, a neutral country. Congress had not declared war against Cambodia, nor was Congress any more aware of the bombing than was the rest of the country. Indeed, at the very time administration witnesses before congressional committees were declaring that the administration was determined not to expand the war into Cambodia.

The secret bombing of Cambodia was one incident among many in Nixon's handling of the war in Southeast Asia which was patently illegal. Although under the Constitution only Congress is authorized to declare war, and although the President is to be Commander-in-Chief only when troops are "called into actual service" in wars declared by Congress, Nixon unilaterally conducted and expanded an undeclared war in Southeast Asia. In 1970 he sent troops into Cambodia, ostensibly to flush out Communist "sanctuaries," although the sanctuaries were never discovered. Throughout the period 1969–1973, as he gradually reduced American troop commitments, he sharply escalated the bombing of North Vietnam, Cambodia, and Laos. At first conducted surreptitiously or justified as "protective reactions," the bombing of North Vietnam was openly resumed in the spring of 1972 when a series of Communist offenses routed the armies of the South. At the same time Nixon also mined Haiphong harbor and other North Vietnamese ports. Both operations were conducted without the approval or even the prior knowledge of Congress. When Congress in 1971 finally attached to a defense procurement bill a mildly worded amendment urging withdrawal from Vietnam "at a date certain," Nixon signed the bill but declared that the amendment "will not change the policies I have pursued." At the end of 1972, four months after Secretary of State Henry Kissinger declared that "peace is at hand," Nixon ordered an intensive bombing of Hanoi. Even after the peace accords were signed and the American troops had returned home, Nixon was still bombing Cambodia. Since Nixon's rationale for bombing had been the protection of American troops, a State Department official was asked how it could now be justified. "The justification," he answered, "is the re-election of President Nixon."[14]

It was under Nixon that Congress finally got its back up. Its threat to cut off funds for the Cambodia air war in 1973 forced Nixon to stop the raids. Over his veto Congress passed a War Powers bill, intended to limit the President's power to involve the nation in war without a congressional declaration. For a time the House Judiciary Committee considered listing the secret air war in Cambodia among the grounds for impeachment. Defense bills came under increasing scrutiny, as did administration requests for continued support of the Thieu regime in South Vietnam. Congressional doves and other opponents of presidential wars could perhaps be grateful to Richard Nixon: He pushed the President's power to make war so far that he stirred Congress into passing countermeasures.

Yet the powers had already been pushed pretty far. It hardly needs to be recalled that President Nixon was not the first President to conduct an undeclared war. He inherited the Vietnam war from Lyndon Johnson, who inherited it from John Kennedy. Johnson and Kennedy inherited it from Eisenhower, who inherited it from Truman. Yet the longest war in American history was conducted without a declaration of war by Congress. It was a presidential war, conducted by different Presidents of different parties and ideologies, but gradually escalating until it made a quantum leap under Johnson. Each President had played a role in the escalation through a series of "commitments." What was largely a moral commitment under Truman became a political and economic commitment under Eisenhower and a paramilitary commitment under Kennedy. Under Johnson (who had campaigned with the promise not to have "our American boys do the fighting for Asian boys") it became an American war of major proportions, involving over half a million American troops and more bombs than were dropped by all sides in World War II.

How did these Presidents justify their war? The grounds tended to shift. Sometimes it was our SEATO commitment, sometimes the Geneva Accords of 1954, sometimes our obligations under the United Nations.* The closest thing to a congressional authorization for the war was the so-called Gulf of Tonkin resolution, passed by the Congress in the fall of 1964, which authorized the President to take "all necessary measures to repel any armed attack against the forces of the United States and to prevent further aggression." But this resolution was passed on the basis of false information. Representatives for the Johnson administration told Congress and the public that two American destroyers on routine patrol far from the shores of North Vietnam were attacked by North Vietnamese torpedo boats. Actually the patrol was not innocent but provocative (the ships were loaded with electronic equipment for scrambling North Vietnamese radar), it was closer to the coast than claimed, and the "torpedo" reports, the task force commander cabled back, may have been the result of "FREAK WEATHER EFFECTS AND OVEREAGER SONAR-MAN." On the basis of this incident, or nonincident, the Gulf of Tonkin resolution was rushed through both houses of Congress, paving the way for the full-scale war that began in 1965. Later it was discovered that the resolution had been prepared by the Johnson administration months before the alleged incident in the Tonkin Gulf. All that was needed was an excuse for introducing it.

Long before Nixon, then, undeclared wars and faits accomplis had been brought about by Presidents eager to flex the nation's military muscle. In 1965 Johnson invaded the Dominican Republic, allegedly "to protect American lives"

---

* The Southeast Asia Treaty Organization (SEATO) was formed in 1955 at the initiative of the United States. Its members are Australia, France, New Zealand, Pakistan, the Phillipines, Thailand, the United Kingdom, and the United States. By a protocol to the treaty, SEATO extended its protection to Laos, Cambodia, and South Vietnam. The treaty declares the intention of its signers "to resist armed attack" and prevent subversion from without. In the event of subversion, however, which is what Johnson claimed the Vietnam situation was, the parties only agreed to consult with one another. Johnson engaged in no such prior consultations before involving the United States in Vietnam. In fact, the whole invocation of the SEATO treaty appears to have been an afterthought by the Johnson administration. As late as 1965, in a press conference explaining "why we are in Vietnam," President Johnson never even mentioned SEATO. The Geneva Accords of 1954 were the agreements ending the French occupation of Vietnam, signed by the French and Vietminh delegates and agreed to by the Chinese, British, and Soviets. The United States refused to formally associate itself with them, but took "note" of them and agreed to respect them.

during a revolution. The trouble was that he sent 22,000 American troops, about one hundred times more than were necessary for this limited purpose, and they were soon fighting alongside the established government against the rebels. The real reason, Johnson later disclosed, was his fear that the "Communists" might take over the Dominican Republic. Cold war tensions underlay a number of other unilateral military actions, covert and overt, under Presidents Kennedy, Eisenhower, and Truman. Kennedy authorized an invasion of Cuba in 1961 and an armed blockade during the "Cuban missile crisis" of 1962; in neither case was Congress even consulted beforehand. (It was Kennedy's unilateral blockade which was the occasion for Professor Neustadt's contention, referred to earlier in this chapter, that "technology has modified the Constitution.") Eisenhower sent U-2 spy planes over the Soviet Union, used the CIA to overthrow the governments of Iran (1953) and Guatamala (1954), and laid the groundwork for the invasion of Cuba. Congress was not informed of these moves. Truman committed the United States to a major land war in Korea without a congressional declaration; he did not even meet with congressional leaders until two days after he began the commitment. Undoubtedly one reason why the House Judiciary Committee in 1974 agreed to omit Nixon's secret bombing of Cambodia from its bill of impeachment was the realization that every other cold war President had been involved in acts which in one way or another bore some resemblance to the Cambodia bombing—in undeclared wars or covert operations, in ignoring Congress, or lying to it, or manipulating it. The *Pentagon Papers,* whose publication Nixon tried so hard to suppress, made Nixon's secret bombing look unexceptional beside all the similar acts of his predecessors.[12]

Repelling "Sudden Attacks": Presidential Warmaking

Indeed, long before Vietnam and the cold war, history records several instances when Presidents fought wars, or miniwars, or quasi-wars without benefit of congressional declaration.* (Presidents have also taken it upon themselves to risk war by sending troops abroad without any formal declaration of war by Congress: of 150 cases where American troops were sent abroad since 1798, Congress

---

* Jefferson spent unappropriated funds to arm American ships against British attacks, arguing later that he could not wait for congressional approval; Monroe did not consult Congress before authorizing Andrew Jackson to invade Florida, at that time a Spanish possession; Polk sent American soldiers into territory claimed by Mexico, provoking the Mexican War—which was later recognized but never formally declared by Congress; Lincoln committed the nation to suppress the South's rebellion by a variety of acts which were the exclusive prerogative of Congress, such as enlarging the size of the armed forces and drawing money from the treasury without statutory authorization; McKinley unilaterally sent 5,000 American troops to China to besiege Peking and suppress the Boxer Rebellion; Theodore Roosevelt invaded South American countries on his own authority and installed provisional governments; Wilson sent American forces into places as close as Mexico and as distant as Siberia without congressional authorization; as the nation drifted toward World War I, Wilson denounced "a little group of willful men" in the Senate who filibustered to death his bill to arm merchant ships—and then armed them himself. Congress at least declared World War I, but Wilson's Fourteen Points, which influenced the war and subsequent peace, were entirely a presidential initiative.

These examples are only a few of the many United States hostilities conducted without benefit of congressional declaration. In 1973 Senator Barry Goldwater cited 199 such actions abroad. (See the *Congressional Record,* 93d Congress, 1st Sess., July 20, 1973, pp. S14174–84.) The actions ranged from the 1798–1800 Naval War with France to the 1970 Cambodia invasion.

declared war in only 5 cases—the War of 1812, the Mexican War, the Spanish-American War, and the two World Wars.) Most of these actions were justified as defensive in nature—repelling attacks by Indians, pirates, rebels, Mexican outlaws. This has always been the strongest argument for the President's power to make war; it was supported by one of the most cautious framers of the Constitution, James Madison. During the discussions at the Constitutional Convention, Congress's power to "make" war was amended to "declare" war after Madison argued the need of "leaving to the Executive the power to repel sudden attacks."[15] This seems like sound common sense, but the difficulty with the doctrine of defensive war is that it can be stretched to cover so much. While still a Congressman, Abraham Lincoln made this observation in reference to the Mexican War: "Allow the President to invade a neighboring nation, whenever *he* shall deem it necessary to repel an invasion . . . and you allow him to make war at pleasure. Study and see if you can fix *any limit* to his power in this respect."[16] Lincoln's point has a contemporary ring. The presidential interventions in Korea, Vietnam, and Cambodia were all justified as necessary to "repel attacks." Once the American sphere of influence was extended to the borders of the "free world," the President's warmaking powers became correspondingly inflated.

Yet we must ask ourselves whether Madison's point is invalid simply because it has been misapplied. Are there not occasions which do require instant response to "sudden attack"? It is noteworthy that the same Congressman Lincoln who worried about the scope of presidential power in the Mexican War pushed the President's war powers to unprecedented lengths after he entered the White House. This was not necessarily inconsistent, for the two situations were quite different. Lincoln faced a genuine attack when the Confederates began firing on Fort Sumter in April of 1861, and Congress was not in session.

But that is the point. The nation may again face a genuine emergency, not a contrived or imaginary one. Is there some way of recognizing the President's right, indeed his duty, to repel sudden attacks without giving him license to conduct another Vietnam war? Congress labored mightily with this dilemma and brought forth the War Power Act in 1973. Whether this succeeded in resolving it is a question which must be left to the next chapter.

In summary, the President's power as Commander-in-Chief has grown by an accretion of precedents which, at least since the end of World War II, have largely gone unchallenged. In part this has been because of the atmosphere of continuous crisis and emergency during the cold war years.

Emergencies aside, however, the President's power to conduct war has also steadily grown by its close association with the President's power in the making of foreign policy.

Treaties: Partnership with the Senate?

In theory the President's power to make treaties is supposed to be with "the advice and consent of the Senate." In practice the word "advice" has been a nullity almost from the outset. In August of 1789 President George Washington walked into the Senate with the draft of an Indian treaty in his hand. He wanted the Senate's advice. But the treaty's seven headings, as one Senator reported later, "were so framed that this could be done by aye or no." When some senators objected to this take-it-or-leave-it approach, "the President of the United States started up with a violent fret. *'This defeats every purpose of my coming here'*, were the first words that he said." Although he cooled "by degrees"[17] and met once more with the Senate to discuss the treaty, he never returned, nor has any President again journeyed to the Senate to consult with it about a treaty. The remaining Senate power over treaties is mainly negative: It can veto them. Even then, however, a President can often work his will over the opposition of Congress by a means we shall now examine.

Executive Agreements: Getting Around the Senate

Presidents have found a way around the need for Senate consent: *executive agreements,* bilateral understandings with foreign governments which are not submitted to the Senate for approval. The executive agreement, which Arthur Schlesinger has called "one of the mysteries of the constitutional order," began creeping into use early in the nineteenth century, and Congress accepted it without qualm since it was used almost exclusively for minor and uncontroversial matters. Not until the time of Theodore Roosevelt did it become a major, and potentially provocative, instrument of foreign policy. Roosevelt, for example, concluded a secret agreement with Japan giving American approval to its military occupation of Korea. Thirty-five years later Franklin Roosevelt concluded a more portentous agreement—the famous "destroyer deal." In one of a long series of unilateral actions which brought the nation to the brink of war with Germany,[18] Roosevelt announced on September 3, 1940, that the United States had entered into an agreement with Great Britain to exchange fifty reconditioned destroyers for the use of naval bases in the British Caribbean. Edward S. Corwin has commented:

> Although the transaction was directly violative of at least two statutes and represented an exercise by the President of a power that by the Constitution is specifically assigned to Congress, it was defended by Attorney General, later Justice, Jackson as resting on the power of the President as Commander-in-Chief to "dispose" the armed forces of the United States, which was ingeniously, if not quite ingenuously, construed as the power to *dispose of* them.[19]

We have discussed the making of treaties and executive agreements, but these specific features still do not describe the full extent of the President's powers in the international sphere. Even a conservative Supreme Court in 1936 portrayed the President as "the sole organ of the federal government in the field of international relations."[20] Since George Washington in 1793 took it upon himself to declare America's neutrality in the Anglo-French war, Presidents have claimed the power (as Alexander Hamilton put it in defending the Neutrality Proclamation) to "establish an antecedent state of things."[21] They have recognized other governments and broken off relations. They have successfully claimed to be the sole conduit for diplomatic exchange. They have, through their travels and gestures and speeches, set the very climate of United States foreign policy. When this power was blended with that of Commander-in-Chief during an era of cold war, when continuing "crisis" was the order of the day, it was almost inevitable that Presidents should claim the power to conduct undeclared wars and covert actions with little thought about Congress except, in Senator Fulbright's rueful words, "as an appropriate object of manipulation, or as a troublesome nuisance to be disposed of."[22]

THE PRESIDENT AS CHIEF EXECUTIVE

Turning from the foreign to the domestic sphere, let us take a closer look at another presidential hat: that of Chief Executive. The President heads a massive bureaucracy, numbering almost three million people, which implements the laws of the federal government. Needless to add, this far-flung bureaucracy, which is spread over continents and which climbs from the local post office to the highest reaches of the federal pyramid, is an awesome source of power. Neither Congress nor the Supreme Court has anything like it at its command; the bureaucracy is unmatched as a source of expertise, "know-how," and sheer workforce for getting things done. Indeed, it has permitted the Chief Executive to seize the initiative even in areas which were once considered the proper sphere of Congress. One of the reasons Professor Rossiter considered the President as "Chief Legislator" is that the modern Presidency has the staff, the experts, and the technology—all of them subject to one person's authority—to shape and coordinate a legislative program. Congress, on the other hand, has lacked this machinery for long-range planning and coordination; it has struggled piecemeal with legislation, and has thus become increasingly dependent on the President for some sort of program to accept, reject, or amend. If the bureaucracy has enabled the President to move confidently into the area of lawmaking, how much more confidently does it enable him to wear the hat we are concerned with here, that of Chief Executive. (It can also set limits to his powers, a role of the bureaucracy which we shall study in the next chapter.) It has played a significant role in expanding the very meaning of the term "Chief Executive," enabling the President not only to execute what Congress has legislated but, to a great extent, to execute what he wants to execute, depending on what he thinks is good for the country.

What does it mean "to take care that the laws be faithfully executed"? The most obvious meaning is that the President has the job of enforcing statutes passed by Congress. But Congress has passed so many laws since 1789 that the executive faces a bewildering array of statutes to enforce.[23] Theoretically, the question of whether a statute should be enforced does not turn upon presidential discretion. But in fact, as Edward S. Corwin observed in 1957, "any particular statute is but a single strand of a vast fabric of laws demanding enforcement," and in the nature of things they cannot "all be enforced with equal vigor, or with the same vigor at all times." Consequently "the President's very *obligation to* the law becomes at times an authorization to *dispense with* the law."[24] As a case in point Corwin cited the antitrust laws, which from their enactment at the turn of the century have been enforced indifferently when they have been enforced at all. From what is known of President Nixon and ITT, the example is apt.

Nixon and ITT The ITT story has been recounted in an earlier chapter. It suffices here to recall the following: President Nixon and his close associates exerted considerable pressure on Justice Department career officials to drop an antitrust suit against the giant conglomerate. Nixon did succeed in getting a delay in the government's litigation of the case, during which time an out-of-court settlement was reached and the possible precedent of a successful antitrust action avoided. Had Nixon done it because he was bribed? The $400,000 which ITT donated to the Republican convention before the settlement raised this suspicion, but nothing was ever proven. Nixon's own explanation was that he had interceded on ITT's side because of philosophical considerations: He did not believe that bigness per se violated the antitrust laws, and he also worried about what a massive ITT divestiture would do to the stock market and the nation's balance of payments.[25] The explanation, if true, is still an admission of how much a President's political and economic philosophy can affect the manner in which he will "take care that the laws be faithfully executed." Nixon, the "law and order" President, opted for permissiveness in the execution of the antitrust laws against ITT.

Other Presidents and the Antitrust Laws

It must be immediately added that Nixon was not the first President to inject his philosophy into the enforcement of these laws. For more than a decade after the passage of the Sherman Antitrust Act of 1890 the Justice Department made no serious attempt to enforce it; Richard Olney, Attorney General during the second Cleveland administration, simply dismissed the law as being "no good."[26] The Clayton Antitrust Act, passed in 1914, was quietly shelved by President Wilson when he found that he needed the monopolies to help prepare for World War I. His successors were not disposed to revive the antitrust crusade.

Presidents have been known to selectively enforce the antitrust laws, to use them as a club to obtain concessions from corporations. When United States Steel raised its prices in 1962, and was followed by four other steel corporations, President Kennedy was furious over what he considered a violation of an implicit understanding his administration had negotiated between industry and labor for mutual restraint in wages and prices. Over the next seventy-two hours the Kennedy administration engaged in a flurry of activity, which included nocturnal visits to news reporters by FBI agents and a request to a New York District Court to empanel a special grand jury. An antitrust official described this last step as "routine." "Nevertheless," Grant McConnell wrote later, it was "remarkable that this particular price increase received such prompt consideration from a division whose pace has often been measured if not stately."[27]

Tax Laws: Their Political Use

Another area subject to discretion in enforcement are tax laws. What deductions should be allowable? What organizations should be tax-exempt? Whose returns should be specially audited? The opportunities both for favoritism and for harassment are immense, but since 1952—when tax scandals during the last months of the Truman administration provided the Republicans with campaign fodder—the Internal Revenue Service of the Treasury Department has tried to keep itself free from politics. One of the most serious charges against President Nixon was that he tried to politicize the IRS in violation of his duty to "take care that the laws be faithfully executed."

Among the confidential memos saved from the shredder during the Watergate investigations were some which revealed the annoyance of Nixon staffers at the obstinacy of the IRS. One written by White House Counsel John Dean in 1971 complained that the IRS Commissioner had been "afraid and unwilling to do anything with I. R. S. that could be politically helpful." Nevertheless, and despite a disclaimer to this effect in the Dean memo, Nixon staffers were not completely unsuccessful (to quote the memo) "in placing R. N. supporters in the I. R. S. bureaucracy."* For what purpose? Apparently the tax liabilities of both the friends and the foes of the President were much on the minds of Nixon's close aides. Friends: When the IRS began auditing the returns of the Reverend Billy Graham, who was a close friend of the President, Chief of Staff H. R. Haldeman received a note from a subordinate asking: "Can we do anything to help?" "No," Haldeman replied, "it's already covered."[28] Charles R. Rebozo, another Nixon intimate, was also thought to have benefited from his close association with the President. And, once again, ITT surfaced in the investigations of tax favoritism when it was disclosed that the IRS in 1969 had issued a ruling of nontaxability for ITT's acquisition of the Hartford Fire Insurance Company. The ruling, which reportedly saved ITT between $35 million and $50 million, was issued just seven days after the company applied for it—a record speed. Enemies: Much of this has been discussed in Chapter 1, but a few points bear repeating. Several different "enemies lists," including more than 600 names, were compiled and transmitted to the IRS with suggestions that their taxes be examined. (Among those audited by the IRS, under pressure from White House aides, was Lawrence F. O'Brien, chairman of the Democratic National Committee.) In 1969, after receiving a memo from the White House suggesting a concerted campaign against "activist" organizations—mainly antiwar groups—the IRS established a special unit which collected files on 11,000 such organizations and individuals.†

Yet politicizing the IRS (or repoliticizing it, if we take into account the scandals of the Truman administration) apparently did not begin with the Nixon administration. Bob Kuttner, Washington editor of the *Village Voice* and one who cannot be considered a Nixon apologist, has lent support to the assertion of Nixon aides that the IRS was politicized in 1961.

* The administration attempted to install, first John Caulfield, then G. Gordon Liddy, as chief of the IRS Office of Alcohol, Tobacco and Firearms. After the IRS rejected both men as unqualified for the job, administration officials removed the ATF from the IRS and made it a separate bureau in the Treasury Department—with Caulfield as chief of enforcement. The administration also installed Roger Barth, another "R. N. supporter" with no visible background in tax law, as Deputy Chief Counsel to the IRS. Barth, who quickly became known among career officials as a "political commissar," began forwarding sensitive tax information on individuals to John Ehrlichman, White House Domestic Advisor. He also involved himself in tax rulings outside his jurisdiction, and in forcing the resignations of uncooperative career officials. See Bob Kuttner, "The Taxing Trials of I. R. S.," *New York Times Magazine,* Jan. 6, 1974, pp. 8ff.

† ITT and IRS were not the only areas in which favoritism, bribery, and other forms of corruption were alleged to have been committed with the knowledge and approval of President Nixon. The so-called milk deal, in which milk companies were allegedly permitted to raise their prices in exchange for campaign contributions, has already been discussed in Chapter 5.

It was the Kennedy Administration that initiated the system of "X-checks," authorizing the I. R. S. to provide the White House with information on potential appointees, and the Kennedy Administration that foreshadowed the campaign against ideological organizations by asking the I. R. S. to investigate tax-exempt, far-right hate groups.[29]

There are, of course, questions of degree, and it seems obvious that the erosion of objective standards in enforcing the tax laws were beginning to reach landslide proportions under Nixon. Nevertheless, in this as in so many other areas, the words of Arthur Schlesinger must be recalled: "Nixon's presidency was not an aberration but a culmination."

Inherent Powers

We have been discussing the President's power to enforce statutes passed by Congress. What about cases where no statute exists? Suppose the nation faces a grave domestic emergency not covered by congressional law. Must the President wait for one? Or does there exist some residuum of inherent powers in the presidency which would let him act on his own?

Many TV viewers in the summer of 1973 were shocked to hear John Ehrlichman, who had been Nixon's chief domestic adviser, contend that the President had "inherent constitutional powers"[30] to authorize a covert break-in of a psychiatrist's office—nay, to go further if he felt it warranted. At one point the following exchange occurred:

> SENATOR TALMADGE: Now, if the President could authorize a covert break-in and you do not know exactly what that power would be limited [sic], you do not think it could include murder or other crimes beyond covert break-ins, do you?
> MR. EHRLICHMAN: I do not know where the line is, Senator.[31]

Thus did the man President Nixon considered one of the "finest public servants it has been my privilege to know" reduce the doctrine of inherent powers to absurdity. Yet the doctrine has a long history, going back to that most Whiggish of philosophers, John Locke.

John Locke (1634–1704) was widely read by the framers of the Constitution, and some of his phraseology found its way into the Declaration of Independence. He is best remembered as an advocate of legislative supremacy, but he also left room for what he called "prerogative" in the executive branch. "Prerogative" he defined as the "power to act according to discretion for the public good, without the prescription of law *and sometimes even against it.* . . ." His reasoning was that extraordinary crises might arise which require quick resolution, and in some of these cases the existing law is either silent, or—"if executed with an inflexible rigor"—actually harmful in these particular occasions.[32] In such cases the executive may take it upon himself to prescribe solutions and hope that the public will later approve them.

The framers of the Constitution, though deeply influenced by Locke, made no mention of prerogative in Article II (perhaps because prerogative is extralegal by its very nature), though it is possible that they may have intended to recognize it implicitly. Some commentators on the Consitution have called attention to the opening grant of power in Article II: "The executive power shall be vested in a President of the United States of America." In contrast, the beginning of Article I, on Congress, reads: "All legislative powers *herein granted* shall be vested in a Congress of the United States" [Emphasis added]. Does the absence of "herein granted" in the Executive aritcle mean that the President's powers are not limited to those granted by the Constitution? Does the fact that he is entrusted with *"the"* executive power imply a broad grant of power transcending the specifics of the Constitution?

These questions might prompt debate among constitutional scholars, but Presidents have been inclined to settle the matter by fiat. When the Civil War broke out, President Lincoln increased the size of the army and navy, disbursed public funds, closed the Post Office to "treasonous correspondence," and suspended the writ of habeas corpus* in various places—measures which the Constitution delegates to Congress but not to the President. True, Congress was not in session when war broke out, but as the war progressed Lincoln assumed even bolder unilateral powers while Congress *was* in session. He emancipated the slaves, suspended the writ of habeas corpus in places far removed from the actual fighting, and began to put his own plan of reconstruction into operation. In justifying these moves, Lincoln conceded the possibility that they might not be "strictly legal," but he insisted that they were necessary to save the Union. Defending his violation of the habeas corpus clause, Lincoln compared himself to a surgeon who must cut off a limb to save a life. He asked: "Are all the laws *but one* to go unexecuted and the Government itself go to pieces lest that one be violated?"[33]

"Steward of the People"
Sitting Presidents have seldom doubted the answer to Lincoln's rhetorical question. Presidents Hayes and Cleveland dispatched federal troops either to quell violence during labor disputes or to break up strikes—in at least one case over the vehement protest of a state governor—using broad and unspecific language to defend their actions: "to protect the property of the United States," "to preserve the peace and restore order," "to remove obstructions to the United States mails." President Theodore Roosevelt, who had a talent for turning a phrase, defended what he called the "Jackson-Lincoln" theory of the presidency by coming up with his own "stewardship" theory: "that is, that occasionally great national crises arise which call for immediate and vigorous executive action, and that in such cases it is the duty of the President to act upon the theory that he is the steward of the people."[34] A generation or more later, Franklin Roosevelt echoed this theme several times while serving his own twelve-year stewardship. The boldest assertion of it was his message of September 7, 1942, part of which was already quoted in the previous chapter: Roosevelt demanded that Congress

---

* Habeas Corpus, literally "You should have the body," is derived from the first words of an ancient writ commanding a jailer to produce the prisoner in order that the latter may receive a fair trial. Article I, section 9 of the Constitution, which is concerned with limitations on *congressional* power, states that "The privilege of the Writ of Habeas Corpus shall not be suspended, unless when in Cases of Rebellion or Invasion the public Safety may require it." Thus even congressional power to suspend such writs is only in exceptional cases; the President's power is nil.

repeal a section of a statute—or else "I shall accept the responsibility, and I will act."[35] Arthur Schlesinger still considers this threat justified, on the ground that "these were genuinely tough times."[36] But John Ehrlichman made the same claims when it came to the burglary of Daniel Ellsberg's psychiatrist—the country was in a turmoil, there were grounds to suspect Ellsberg was a spy, etc., etc.[37] To modern Presidents, times are always tough.

Court Rulings on Inherent Powers

The fact that Presidents have invoked "inherent powers," or even gotten away with using them, does not mean that the doctrine is constitutionally sound. In our system the question of constitutionality is ultimately decided by the Supreme Court. What has the Court said about "inherent powers"?

The answer is that it has said a number of things, not all of them quite compatible with one another. During the Civil War, in the famous *Prize* cases,[38] the Court held that the President, by virtue of his power as chief executive and Commander-in-Chief, was entitled to consider an insurrectionary region as enemy country and thus strip all its inhabitants of their constitutional rights. Three years later, though, the *Prize* ruling was qualified if not explicitly reversed in the case of *ex parte Milligan*,[39] which confined the President's power to suspend the ordinary operation of the courts "to the locality of actual war."

Yet later, other court decisions seemed to recognize the President's inherent powers even in the absence of war or domestic rebellion. One leading case was *in re Neagle*,[40] decided by the Court in 1890. The factual background invoved a member of the Supreme Court, Justice Field, whose life was threatened by a resident of California named Terry. To protect Justice Field, the Attorney General of the United States appointed an armed bodyguard, Neagle, to accompany him while he traveled circuit in California. Terry, true to his threat, tried to assassinate Field and was killed by Neagle, Field's bodyguard. Neagle was then taken into custody by California and charged with homicide. The issue before the Supreme Court was whether Neagle was entitled to release on a writ of habeas corpus under a federal law which authorizes a writ in cases where the prisoner is jailed "for an act done or committed in pursuance of a *law* of the United States" [emphasis added]. The problem was that Neagle was not acting in pursuance of a "law" but on an order of the Attorney General, issued presumably in the President's name. Was the President's order the same as a law? In this case, yes, said the Court. There is "a peace of the United States" which the President has the duty to enforce even in the absence of an express grant of power.

In re Neagle and other turn-of-the-century cases gave the doctrine of "inherent powers" judicial recognition. But it has suffered setbacks in more recent years. In *Youngstown Sheet and Tube v. Sawyer*[41] the Court declared unconstitutional President Truman's seizure of steel mills to settle a labor dispute during the Korean war. Conceding that Truman's seizure of the mills was not pursuant to any statute, the President's lawyers had argued that his authority to do so was derived from his inherent powers as Commander-in-Chief and Chief Executive to insure uninterrupted steel production during a wartime emergency. By 6 to 3 the Court rejected the government's claim, although its reasons for doing so were not altogether clear—each member of the majority insisted on writing his own opinion, and at least two of these opinions suggested that there might be cases where the President could legitimately act in the absence of an authorizing statute. Justice Jackson, for example, admitted that there might exist a "zone of twilight" in which the President and Congress have "concurrent authority," though he denied that Truman's seizure occupied this zone.

A more recent case touching on the question of inherent powers is *U.S. v. U.S. District Court*,[42] which denied to the Attorney General (then John Mitchell) the right to tap phones in domestic "internal security" cases without a court order. The government had tried to argue that the Safe Streets Act of 1968, which authorized wiretaps of suspected criminals provided a warrant could be obtained, had implicitly recognized the President's power to wiretap in "national security" cases *without* a court warrant. The Court denied this claim. What is remarkable is that Ehrlichman revived it during the Watergate hearings, and even escalated it by claiming that the Safe Streets Act implicitly recognized the President's inherent powers not just to wiretap but to commit burglary and—for all he knew—murder!

So we come to full circle on "inherent powers," from John Ehrlichman to John Locke and back again. Nothing seems very conclusive about it, except that strong and popular Presidents, acting in times perceived by the public as genuine domestic crises, have gotten away with asserting it. President Nixon and his aides pushed it, as they did so many other precedents, too far. But the doctrine has a venerable history, having been invoked by some of the nation's most beloved Presidents. And this is why, said John Locke, "the reigns of good princes have always been most dangerous to the liberties of their people."

> For when their successors, managing the government with different thoughts, would draw the actions of those good rulers into precedent and make them the standard of their prerogative . . . it has often occasioned contest, and sometimes public disorders, before the people could recover their original right to get that to be declared not to be prerogative, which truly was never so. . . .[43]

Before concluding this discussion of the President's responsibility to enforce the law, we can hardly ignore the role of President Nixon in relation to the Watergate cover-up.

The Watergate Cover-up

The White House tapes have provided some revealing glimpses into how the Nixon White House "faithfully executed" the laws in relation to Watergate. To begin with, the President apparently did not consider either the break-in or Donald Segretti's "dirty tricks" as anything other than peccadillos.[44] The newspaper revelations about Watergate he regarded as part of an orchestrated plot by his liberal opponents, disgruntled over his success in foreign policy and at the polls.[45] White House Counsel John Dean admitted to him that "I have been a conduit for information on taking care of people who have been guilty of crimes," but Nixon went on, unfazed, to discuss various means of keeping "the cap on the bottle," "taking care of witnesses," keeping people from testifying, cutting investigators "off at the pass" putting "the fires out," getting "the damn thing nailed down till past the election." [46] When told that White House aide Egil Krogh had lied to a grand jury, Nixon commented: "Perjury is an awful hard rap to prove." In contemplating the appearance of his aides before another grand jury, Nixon advised them on how to avoid a perjury charge: "Just be damned sure you say I don't remember. I can't recall." He wanted his aides "to stonewall it . . . plead the Fifth Amendment, cover up or anything else. . . . "[47] He discussed means of distributing hush money to the original Watergate defendants, and joined John Dean in envying the Mafia's expertise in laundering money.[48] Nixon asked Dean how much it would cost to buy the defendants' silence and was told it would cost a million dollars. Nixon: "We could get that." Later Nixon asked Dean whether "your immediate thing," about which there was "no choice," the thing Dean "damn well better" get done, was to distribute hush money to the defendants. Dean agreed. Whereupon Nixon said "Well, for Christ's sakes, get it. . . . "[49] Then came the final bombshell, the tape released after Nixon lost his court battle to retain possession of it, showing Nixon to be fully aware of White House involvement in the Watergate break-in as early as June 23, 1972—six days after it occurred—and actively plotting with Haldeman to keep the FBI from investigating.[50]

It is impossible to find any precedent for these kinds of conversations between a President of the United States and his chief advisers; but since Nixon was the first President to release, or be forced to release, transcripts of such horrifying tête-à-têtes, we cannot be entirely sure the Nixon conversations were unique in their candid contempt for the law. What we know *for sure* was unique about this particular President was not that he engaged in such conversations but that he provided us with a record of them.

In any case, the effect was electrifying. Even conservative Republican newspapers like the *Chicago Tribune* and the *Omaha World-Herald* called for the President's resignation. All aside from the legal implications of Nixon's conversations, it was the moral sleaziness of them which shocked many Americans. Columnist Joseph Alsop, who was usually friendly to Nixon, described the atmosphere as that of "the back room of a second-rate advertising agency in a suburb of hell."[51] Walter Cronkite told a group of friends: "You know what I think? I think we ought to take Lysol and scrub out the Oval Office."[52] The feeling was a common one, and it cut across the lines of party and ideology, that Nixon had not merely committed political or legal misdeeds, he had soiled the office of the Presidency, violating the trust given to him as the nation's official leader and representative.

This leads us to consider a third presidential role. It is hard to pin down juridically. It is not spelled out in the Constitution, nor has it ever been the subject of a court case. Yet no discussion of the American presidency can be complete without some consideration of the President's role as Chief of State—the ceremonial head of the United States government.

THE PRESIDENT AS CHIEF OF STATE

In some democratic countries—for instance, Great Britain and Japan—the political leader of the nation and the chief of state are not the same person. In England, for example, the Queen plays the role of official greeter, is escorted about in pomp and ceremony, serves as the living symbol of the nation's unity and the law's authority (". . . in the name of the Queen"). Yet the English monarch has no political power, having been reduced to a figurehead over the course of centuries. What purpose, then, does the Queen serve? The observation has often been made that she serves as a kind of lightning rod, attracting and safely grounding all those primitive, antidemocratic instincts which drive people to worship rulers. By bestowing their adulation on an impotent chief of state, a people can reserve their more critical faculties for judging the performance of their political leaders.

This is not the case in America. The American President is more than an executive, more than a commander-in-chief, more than a political leader. "He is, as it were, a republican king," said Clinton Rossiter admiringly,

> the figurehead as well as the working head of the government of the United States, "the personal embodiment" (in the words of President Taft) of the "dignity and majesty" of a mighty nation.[53]

As Chief of State the President has become a moral exemplar and national symbol. Franklin Roosevelt contended that the Presidency "is preeminently a place of moral leadership." His cousin Theodore had put it more succinctly: "The presidency is a bully pulpit." The President preempts air time for his addresses to the nation, he lectures, preaches, warns and reassures. He defines the tone and mood of the nation: "The Roosevelt Years," "The Eisenhower Period." For generations American schoolchildren have dreamed of becoming President. The office is full of history and legend; the modern President walks in the footsteps of semimythical figures like Washington and Lincoln.

The White House itself has become a national shrine. During John Kennedy's second full day as President, he invited his brother Edward and an aide, Paul Fay, to inspect the Oval Office. Spinning around in his swivel chair, the new President asked Fay how he felt. "I feel," Fay answered, "any minute somebody's going to walk in and say, 'All right, you three guys out of here.' "[54] Yet it did not take Kennedy long to adjust to the aura of the White House—indeed, to augment it by his style, his good looks, his quick wit, his glamorous family. His assassination added still another emanation to the reverential air of the White House.

It does not seem altogether equitable, then, for Arthur Schlesinger to dwell upon the "monarchical" trappings of the Nixon administration, especially in view of his own past service to the court of Camelot. The monarchical trappings were already in place by 1968. True, Nixon added his own touches: He dressed up White House police officers in costumes copied from the Belgian royal guard, he had himself announced by a flourish of silver trumpets, he gave up talking to reporters, preferring unilateral "addresses to the nation" to the give-and-take of press conferences, he surrounded himself with aides whose loyalty bordered on fanaticism. But here again it appears that Nixon's Presidency was more culmination than aberration. It was George Reedy, former press secretary not to Richard Nixon but to Lyndon Johnson, who wrote that "the life of the White House is the life of a court."[55] In *The Twilight of the Presidency* (1970), Reedy described the atmosphere of sycophancy and "pimpery" that surrounds the man in the White

House, the "camouflage" which the Presidency provides "for all that is petty and nasty in human beings," and which "enables a clown or a knave to pose as Galahad and be treated with deference."[56]

It is hard not to suspect that Reedy was recalling life in the Johnson White House, yet he insisted that his observations had a much wider application. One former Roosevelt aide, he said, listened to his stories about his days with Johnson and exclaimed: "Don't worry! That's the way is has been and that's the way it will always be!"[57]

This may be an overstatement. Before the time of Roosevelt, presidential power—and the prestige that goes with power—had ebbed and flowed. Periods of presidential dominance alternated with periods of congressional dominance. It depended, at least in part, on what kind of personality occupied the office of President. After thirteen years of Roosevelt, however, it seemed that part of his personal charisma had adhered to the office itself. Congress, for its part, seemed to have lost the will or the capacity to make a comeback, resigning itself to a passive, negative role in postwar America. It was the Presidency which was the center of action and drama. It had a kind of grandeur about it, and the belief became widespread that the office somehow elevated and ennobled anyone who occupied it. The belief, of course, did not spread by itself. Books, newspapers, magazines, radio, television, all played a great role in the selling of the Presidency.

During the fifties and early sixties a number of writers, mainly journalists and professors, fostered a kind of literary mystique of the Presidency. From their labors emerged "the textbook presidency," as Thomas E. Cronin called it.

> The student learns that the Presidency is "the great engine of democracy," the "American people's one authentic trumpet," "the central instrument of democracy," and "probably the most important government institution in the world." With the New Deal Presidency in mind, the textbook portrait states that Presidents must instruct the nation as national teacher and guide the nation as national preacher.[58]

Richard E. Neustadt taught that the strong President is the good President.[59] Theodore H. White glamorized both the office and the race for it in his *Making of the President* series.[60] Clinton Rossiter reassured his readers: "170-odd years, 34 Presidents—and still no gross abuse, and no likelihood of a gross abuse, of the confidence of the American people or the terms of their Constitution." The "screening process of nomination and election," Rossiter explained, "keeps such men as Thaddeus Stevens, Huey Long, and Joseph McCarthy far from the White House, and opens the way only to what Hamilton described as 'characters preeminent for ability and virtue. . . .' "[61]

Even the doctored transcripts of President Nixon's White House conversations disprove Rossiter's thesis. But the pertinent question is not whether Richard Nixon's character was notable for its virtue but why the intellectuals of the fifties and early sixties expected Presidents to be extraordinary human beings. (The roots of their faith must have gone deeper than the facile argument suggested by Rossiter—that surviving the nomination and election process in America somehow makes for decency and honesty.) In looking back over the unexamined assumptions of liberal intellectuals during the period in question, we can distinguish three factors.

First, as Thomas Cronin has pointed out, the memory of Franklin D. Roosevelt left a "halo-effect"[62] around the Presidency. Many of the leading writers on the Presidency during the fifties and early sixties had grown up during the Depression and served in the armed forces or government during World War II. The memories of FDR's strong but benign leadership during this period strongly influenced their view of the presidential office. Seen in the image of FDR, the Presidency was not only a progressive but a heroic institution which apotheosized its occupants.

Second, Congress seemed to be an indolent if not comatose institution to many American intellectuals. Professor Huntington's proposal to let the executive branch play the active role in lawmaking (discussed in the last chapter) did not seem shocking because it was already regarded as a fact of life in America. The Presidency seemed to be the real center of action and responsibility, the place where "the buck stops," as President Truman had put it, and this added to the prestige of the office—especially among reform-minded intellectuals anxious to "get things done."

Third, liberal intellectuals of the fifties believed that the greatest threat to American freedom came not from the top but from the bottom. States and localities appeared to be the true breeding grounds for racial bigotry and political intolerance. The dangers of an "imperial Presidency" seemed remote compared to those of Southern mobs and Northern red-hunters. Traumatized by the specter of right-wing populism,[63] the liberal intellectuals of the period tended toward elitism.[64] In this respect Congress was rated higher than local government because it was further removed from the rabble. But it was not high enough: During the McCarthy period the tides of fanaticism had invaded the chambers of the national legislature. Only the top of the pyramid had held fast: The Eisenhower administration finally fought back and helped destroy the Senator from Wisconsin. Hence the liberal's belief that some sort of filtering process must be at work to insure that only decent men made it to the top.

By the mid-1970s these three sources of the liberal's faith in the Presidency had been badly shaken. The "halo" of FDR had fallen from the President's head somewhere between Vietnam and Watergate. The President now seemed even less interested in domestic reform than Congress had been in the past. Finally, the same nomination and election process that had kept Huey Long and Joe McCarthy away from the White House had produced a President who coached his subordinates on how to beat perjury "raps," urged them to pay hush money, and conspired with them to obstruct justice.

In his role as Chief of State, President Nixon's main contribution to democratic government may have been this purely unintentional one: He let the air out of the Presidency. The aura of reverence which once surrounded the President was dissipated by the time Nixon left office. (The new President, Gerald Ford, enjoyed what must have been the briefest honeymoon of any President in history. Within a month his pardon of Nixon had caused his ratings in the polls to plummet; the editorial writers and commentators no longer had Nixon "to kick around," but they had a substitute.) By the mid-seventies the reverential aura which surrounded the Presidency in the fifties and early sixties had been blown away. Would writers on the Presidency ever again pump so much wishful thought into an office occupied by a fellow mortal? Whatever the future brings, we know now (even if we forget tomorrow) how foolish it was. "Enlightened statesmen will not always be at the helm": Never before, at least not in recent memory, has Madison's warning seemed so pertinent to the nation's highest office. The preoccupation now is with the task of finding enough checks to contain presidential power.

One danger is that the reformers may overdo it: Instead of merely setting limits to the President's power, they may fatally weaken it—prevent it from performing the tasks it is *supposed* to perform. Power abhors a vacuum. As was pointed out in the last chapter, the President acquired excessive power at least in part because Congress began to abdicate its own responsibilities. The same could happen to the President's executive power. If this is weakened beyond a certain point, executive power may accumulate elsewhere: among bureaucrats, corporate executives, military officers, or any other group willing to carry the burdens and enjoy the fruits of power. The need for a strong executive cannot be wished away. The President is elected every four years; generals, bureaucrats and business executives are not. The alternative to a strong President is a strong something-else.

The next chapter will study some of the existing checks on the President in order to see where they have slipped and how they might be tightened—without strangling.

NOTES

1. Arthur Schlesinger, Jr., *The Imperial Presidency* (Boston: Houghton Mifflin Company, 1973), pp. 491–492.
2. *New York Times,* Mar. 7, 1973, p. 22: *The White House Transcripts, New York Times* ed. (New York: Bantam Books, Inc., 1974), p. 108. Hereinafter cited as "Edited Transcripts."
3. Quoted in the *New York Post,* May 18, 1973, p. 18.
4. See below. pp. 251–252.
5. Quoted in Emmet John Hughes, *The Living Presidency* (New York: Coward, McCann & Geoghegan, Inc., 1972), p. 17.
6. Schlesinger, op. cit., p. 417.
7. See *Federalist 10.*
8. Schlesinger, op. cit., p. 124.
9. Cited in Schlesinger, op. cit., pp. 166, 170.
10. Richard E. Neustadt, *Presidential Power* (New York: John Wiley & Sons, Inc., 1960), pp. vii, 161, 185.
11. Cited in Schlesinger, op. cit., p. 374.
12. James David Barber, *The Presidential Character: Predicting Performance in the White House* (Englewood Cliffs, N.J.: Prentice-Hall, Inc., 1972), p. 454.
13. See *Federalist 69.*
14. *New York Times,* Mar. 28, 1973.
15. See Emmet John Hughes, *The Living Presidency* (New York: Coward, McCann & Geoghegan, Inc., 1972), p. 37.

16 Abraham Lincoln, *Collected Works,* R. P. Basler, Ed. (New Brunswick: Rutgers University Press, 1953), I, pp. 451–452.
17 Quoted in Edward S. Corwin, *The President: Office and Powers, 1787–1957,* 4th rev. ed. (New York: New York University Press, 1957), pp. 209–210.
18 See the twenty different incidents cited by Corwin. Ibid., pp. 202–204.
19 Ibid., p. 238.
20 *U.S. v. Curtiss-Wright Corporation et al.,* 299 U.S. 304 (1936).
21 Alexander Hamilton, *Works* (Hamilton, ed.), VII, 76.
22 See Chap. 7, n. 44.
23 Political scientist Theodore H. Lowi has proposed a "tenure-of-statutes Act." "Congress should on principle limit every statute and program to a life of no more than ten years." Theodore H. Lowi, ed., *Legislative Politics U.S.A.,* 3d ed. (Boston: Little, Brown and Company, 1973), p. 371.
24 Corwin, op. cit., p. 122.
25 *New York Times,* Jan. 9, 1974, p. 1.
26 Harry J. Carman and Harold C. Syrett, *A History of the American People,* Vol. II (New York: Alfred A. Knopf, Inc., 1957), p. 149.
27 Grant McConnell, *Steel and the Presidency, 1962* (New York: W. W. Norton & Company, Inc., 1962), p. 90.
28 *New York Times,* June 14, 1974, p. 19.
29 Bob Kuttner, "The Taxing Trials of I. R. S.," *New York Times Magazine,* Jan. 6, 1974, p. 66.
30 *The Watergate Hearings: Break-in and Cover-up, New York Times* ed. (New York: Bantam Books, Inc., 1973), p. 519.
31 Ibid., p. 521.
32 John Locke, "The True End of Government," in Ernest Barker, ed., *The Social Contract: Locke, Hume, Rosseau* (New York: Oxford University Press, 1962), p. 95.
33 Quoted in Corwin, op. cit., p. 230.
34 Theodore Roosevelt, *An Autobiography* (New York: Macmillan Publishing Co., 1913), p. 357.
35 See above Chap. 7, p. 231.
36 Schlesinger, op. cit. p. 34.
37 Schlesinger could reply that these claims were total nonsense—and that Ehrlichman knew it even as he made them. The evidence gathered by the House Judiciary Committee during its impeachment hearings in 1974 included notes made by Ehrlichman during a meeting between the President and his top aides a month after the publication of the Pentagon Papers. Ehrilichman's notes show that the Secretary of Defense told the White House that 98 percent of the documents could have been unclassified. The notes also have Nixon saying that "espionage" was "not involved in the Ellsberg case." Nixon added: "Don't think in terms of spies." (*New York Times,* July 23, 1974, p. 27.)

The White House tapes reinforce the conclusion that "national security" in the Ellsberg case was a wholly deceptive claim. In a meeting with top aides in July of 1971, Nixon expressed the fear that leaks about the SALT talks might compromise national security. "This does affect the national security—this particular one. This isn't like the Pentagon Papers." (*New York Times,* July 19, 1974, p. 14.)

But even if the publication of the Pentagon Papers was a phony "national security" crisis, Nixon inherited the knee-jerk disposition to invoke the claim of "national security" from the Roosevelt White House of World War II. Roosevelt's use of "national security" as an excuse for high-handed actions may not have been as cynical as Nixon's, but it was sometimes just as frivolous. For example, did the war emergency really justify the mass evacuation and interment of Japanese-Americans? Did they really represent a threat to the security of the nation?

38 *Prize cases,* 2 Black 635 (1863).
39 *Ex Parte Milligan,* 4 Wall 2 (1866).
40 *In re Neagle,* 135 U.S. 1 (1890).
41 *Youngstown Sheet & Tube v. Sawyer,* 343 U.S. 579 (1952).
42 *U.S. v. U.S. District Court,* E. D. of Mich., S.D., 92 S. Ct. 2125 (1972).
43 Locke, op. cit., p. 98.
44 "People break and enter, etc., and get two years. No weapons! No results! What the hell are they talking about?" Edited Transcripts, p. 158. On Segretti: "But, nevertheless, what the hell did he do? What in the (Characterization deleted) did he do? Shouldn't we be trying to get intelligence? Weren't they trying to get intelligence from us?" Ibid., p. 88.
45 "The establishment is dying, and so they've got to show that the *[sic]* despite the successes we have had in foreign policy and in the election, they've got to show that it is just *[sic]* because of this. They are trying to use this as the whole thing." Ibid., p. 120.
46 Ibid., pp. 154, 148, 143, p. 154; *New York Times,* July 14, 1974, sect. 4, p. 1.
47 Edited Transcripts, p. 148, *New York Times,* June 21, 1974, p. 16; July 14, 1974, sect. 4, p. 1.
48 Edited Transcripts, p. 146.
49 Ibid., p. 147; *New York Times,* June 21, 1974, p. 16.
50 *New York Times,* Aug. 6, 1974, pp. 14–15.
51 Quoted in R. W. Apple's introduction to Edited Transcripts, p. 3.
52 Quoted by Shana Alexander in Donald W. Harward, ed., *Crisis in Confidence: The Impact of Watergate* (Boston: Little, Brown and Company, 1974), p. 46.
53 Clinton Rossiter, "President and Congress in the 1960s," in Marian D. Irish, ed., *Continuing Crisis in American Politics* (Englewood Cliffs, N.J.: Prentice-Hall, Inc., 1963), p. 90.
54 Quoted by Theodore C. Sorensen in *Kennedy* (New York: Harper & Row Publishers, Incorporated, 1965), p. 249.
55 George E. Reedy, *The Twilight of the Presidency,* (New York: New American Library Mentor Books, Inc., 1970), pp. 17–18.
56 Ibid., pp. xii–xiii.
57 Ibid., p. xiv.
58 Thomas E. Cronin, "The Textbook Presidency," in Charles Peters and John Rothchild, eds., *Inside the System* (New York: Frederick A. Praeger Inc., 1973), p. 7.
59 See above, p. 240.
60 In his *Making of the President* series White suffered a steady decline in his ratings among liberal journals. *The Making of the President 1960* won unstinting praise in the *New York Times, The New Yorker,* and other organs of the Northeast establishment. But by the time *The Making of the President 1964* was published, liberal reviewers were becoming somewhat cool both to the style and to the substance of White's writing. By *1968* and *1972* White's antipathy to the New Politics and his reevaluation of Richard M. Nixon correlated with increasingly bad reviews in liberal journals. A *Village Voice* reviewer called him a "power groupie." His best reviews were now in the *Chicago Tribune* and the *Dallas Morning News.*
61 Rossiter, in Irish, ed., op. cit., p. 92.
62 Cronin, op. cit., p. 12.
63 A number of books were written on this theme during the fifties and early sixties.

One of the best known was Richard Hofstadter, *The Age of Reform: From F. D. R.* (New York: Vintage Books, Random House, Inc., 1955).

64 For an elaboration of this point, including citations, see my article "On Hannah Arendt—Politics: As It Is, Was, Might Be," *Salmagundi,* Fall, 1969-Winter, 1970, pp. 105–107.

Chapter 9

The President: Limits

Sits he on never so high a throne, a man still sits on his bottom.

Montaigne

At the end of an unusually hot summer in 1787, the Constitutional Convention had just wound up its business. In a preairconditioning age its members had met with doors and windows shut; they also agreed that there would be no transcripts of their proceedings and no leaks to the press. For a group of men who had met merely to "revise" the Articles of Confederation, they seemed inordinately concerned about secrecy. Outside, suspicions were aroused. Memories of George III were far from dead. What kind of government had been fashioned behind those closed doors and windows? When Benjamin Franklin, the oldest member of the Convention, returned home, his landlady could contain herself no longer. "Well, Mr. Franklin," she asked, "what have you given us, a republic or a monarchy?" "A republic," Franklin answered,"—if you can keep it."[1]

Franklin's laconic answer prompts these questions: How *do* we "keep" our republic? What sort of checks do we have to prevent it from turning into a monarchy? How well do they work? In the light of Watergate, do we need any new checks on the powers of the President?

Suppose we begin by examining the time-honored check upon monarchical ambition: the legislature.

CONGRESS AS A CHECK
The Power to Act: Legislation

The most obvious congressional check is the power to pass laws. In theory, a determined Congress, if it has the votes and if it keeps within the framework of the Constitution, can put the President in his place or tug and haul him where it pleases. A little over a century ago, President Andrew Johnson fumed as a "radical" Congress passed a series of statutes over his veto—including one which almost led to his undoing. (See below, pp. 273–274.) Closer to our own era, the "do-nothing" Congress which President Truman roasted in his campaign speeches managed to pass the Taft-Hartley Act (qualifying the power of labor unions) over his veto in 1947. A more recent example of Congress's power to check the President by legislation occurred in November of 1973. It was then that Congress managed to pass the War Powers Act over President Nixon's veto.

The War Powers Act The purpose of the War Powers Act was to resolve the truly frightening question raised in the last chapter: How do we prevent the President from pushing us into an undeclared war without stripping him of the power to repel sudden attacks on our country? The act sought to resolve the problem by allowing the President to fight wars in certain situations, for certain periods of time, and through the adherence to certain procedures.

The *situations* in which the President could send troops into hostilities were limited to these: when Congress declares a war, or authorizes it by statute, or when "a national emergency" has been created "by attack upon the United States, its territories or possessions, or its armed forces." The *time periods:* In the last two cases the President may conduct the war for sixty days, no more, unless Congress has declared war in the meantime. *But* the act provides for an additional thirty days' extension if the President declares that "unavoidable military necessity respecting the safety of the United States armed forces" requires continuing military action in the course of withdrawing our troops. The *procedures:* Within forty-eight hours of hostilities the President must submit a written report to the House and Senate setting forth his justification for the troop commitment, his statutory and constitutional authority for doing so, and his estimate of how long the war will last. He must answer any questions about the war which Congress raises, and must submit periodic progress reports on the war.

The act obviously enjoyed wide and bipartisan support, since it passed both houses over the President's veto, but it also had its share of critics. Roughly speaking, these critics divided into two camps, who opposed it for diametrically opposite reasons. Hawks, like Senator Barry Goldwater, felt that it weakened the nation's defenses and usurped the President's power to make war. Congress's right to "declare" war, Goldwater contended, "means nothing except to declare; and if you look it up in the dictionary, it is a very weak word."[2] Dovish critics of the act saw it not as usurpation but abdication, in this case an abdication of Congress's power to declare war—which in *their* dictionaries was not a weak word at all. In the past, Presidents had fought undeclared wars at their own risk. Now, they contended, the President had been handed a sixty-to-ninety-day hunting license,* during which time he could conduct a public relations blitz under the guise of complying with the act's requirement that he justify his actions.

It is not difficult to find flaws in the drafting of the War Powers Act. But perhaps the act's real significance was more symbolic than juridical. By passing it over the President's veto the Congress was serving notice, in very large print, that it wanted no more presidential quagmires, no more ten-year wars without congressional declarations. It was also telling the President that it wanted to be fully informed, not manipulated, concerning the President's military policies abroad. Finally, the passage of this and other legislation over Nixon's veto† hinted at a new spirit in Congress, a willingness to limit the President's power and to protect the power of Congress.

Even so, it is hard to imagine a sudden rebirth of congressional initiative. As we pointed out in Chapter 7, Congress in the twentieth century has not been particularly distinguished for taking the lead in lawmaking. It usually waits for the President to propose in order that it may dispose. In discussing congressional checks, then, the observation made by Clinton Rossiter in 1956 is probably still valid: "The real power of Congress over [the President] is essentially negative in character."[3] The refusal to pass a law, to approve a treaty, to confirm an appointment—all remain effective means to check the ambitions of a high-flying President.

The Power to Say "No"

The negative power of Congress was demonstrated a number of times during the Nixon years. Not since the inauguration of Zachary Taylor in 1849 had a President entered office facing opposition majorities in both houses of Congress, and this initial hardship was worsened by the often clumsy efforts of administration lobbyists. ("I suppose they're bright in their way," one Senator said. "But they

---

* Senator Thomas Eagleton, one of the original sponsors of the War Powers Bill in the Senate, was appalled at the final product which emerged from the Senate-House conference committee. Eagleton's original version of the bill spelled out in detail four conditions under which the President may fight a war, and limited the war period to 30 days without congressional approval. The House version was more loosely drawn as to conditions, and permitted the President to carry on his war for 123 days. The Senate-House conference committee split the difference by agreeing on the 60-to-90-day time period, and loosening up the conditions for fighting presidential wars. The result, Eagleton said, was "a horrible mistake" because it gave the President "unilateral authority to commit troops anywhere in the world for 60 or 90 days." Eagleton worried about some President turning the Middle East into another Vietnam, this time with permission of Congress. "How short can memories be? My God, we just got out of a nightmare." *New York Times,* Nov. 8, 1973, p. 20.

† Another bill passed by Congress over Nixon's veto, a $24.7 million water pollution control bill passed in 1972, was not only significant in itself; it also had a significant chain of consequences. In November of 1972, a month after the override, the administrator of the Environmental Protection Agency announced that the President had directed him to impound some of the funds. This turned out to be one impoundment too many for Nixon. It finally galvanized Congress, interest groups, and state governments together in a fierce resistance to presidential impoundments. David Levin, chairman of Florida's Pollution Control Board, told the Associated Press that as far as he could see, "Congress might as well not have overridden [Nixon's] veto. . . . I always thought we had three branches of government" (*New York Times,* Nov. 30, 1972, p. 43). Members of Congress, as we have seen in Chapter 8, were even more outspoken in condemning the impoundments, and, translating words into actions, began considering a series of measures ranging from anti-impoundment legislation to the adoption of a legislative budget. Nixon's impoundments were also challenged in the courts and overturned.

just don't understand this body. They just haven't figured out any way to communicate effectively."4) One notable defeat for President Nixon occurred in 1971, when Congress discontinued funding the development of a supersonic transport plane (SST) which the administration had strongly backed. In 1973 the negative power of Congress as a check on the President was demonstrated more pointedly when an impending cutoff of funds forced Nixon to stop bombing Cambodia.

Aside from saying "no" to the President's requests for laws or money, Congress can also naysay his nominations. The Constitution requires Senate confirmation of the President's nomination of Supreme Court justices, ambassadors, and other executive officers. In 1969, for the first time in forty years, the Senate refused to confirm a President's nominee to the Supreme Court. Nixon had nominated Clement F. Haynesworth, a South Carolina Circuit Court judge, but questions about Haynesworth's business dealings and their connection with his court decisions led the Senate to reject the nomination. Less than a year later, Nixon's second nominee for the position, G. Harrold Carswell, also was turned down by the Senate, this time because of his record on civil rights. Two consecutive rebuffs: the most embarassing of Nixon's defeats, until Watergate dwarfed them all.

And in fact the Watergate worm-can began to open wide during another confirmation hearing in the Senate, that of L. Patrick Gray as FBI Director. Gray had been serving as Acting Director since the death of J. Edgar Hoover in May of 1972. In February of 1973 Nixon nominated Gray to be permanent Director, and Senate hearings on the nomination began at the end of the month. For thirty-six days, under increasingly sharp questioning by increasingly suspicious senators, Gray made a series of damaging admissions: that he had supplied Presidential counsel John Dean with the FBI's files on Watergate, that he had conferred with Dean, that Dean "probably lied" in claiming that Watergate burglar E. Howard Hunt had no office in the White House. In the end, Gray was abandoned by the White House, allowed to "twist slowly in the wind," in John Ehrlichman's famous phrase, and his nomination was formally withdrawn on April 5. But by then the lid was off the can.

The Gray hearings before the Senate Judiciary Committee bring to mind another means by which Congress can check the President, or at least check up on him: investigations.

The Power to Investigate

The investigatory power, while not explicitly listed in the Constitution, is one of those implied powers long accepted as "necessary and proper" for carrying out Congress's delegated powers. Congress can undertake investigations through its regular standing committees or by means of special, "select" committees convened for a limited duration. The first of these met in 1793, after General St. Clair's military expedition against the Indians ended in disaster. Some members of Congress wanted to leave the investigation to President Washington, but the House of Representatives decided to take matters into its own hands and voted the investigation. Since that time, Congress has repeatedly undertaken investigations into a variety of subjects. Among the famous, in some cases notorious, investigations were Senator Nye's probe of the munitions industry in the 1930s, Senator Truman's investigation of waste in the military during World War II, and Senator McCarthy's investigations of alleged Communist influence during the 1950s.

The Watergate Committee

The "grand inquest" of 1973 was the Watergate investigation conducted by the Senate Select Committee on Presidential Campaign Activities, chaired by Senator Sam Ervin of South Carolina. Although the Watergate Committee met from May 17, 1973, to July 13, 1974, most Americans will probably best remember its televised hearings in the summer of 1973. During these three months the hearings played a crucial role in exploring the full range of the scandal, from the burglary itself to the activities of the "plumbers" in the ITT affair, the Ellsberg break-in, and the fabrication of fake cables, plus the enemies lists, the misuse of the IRS and other government agencies, the laundered money, and the overall philosophy of the Nixon White House. The hearings also afforded TV viewers a close look at "all the President's men," or a good number of them, some of whom had only recently occupied the highest positions of power.

The key witness was John Dean, a former Special Counsel to the President. Dean described a series of conversations he had had with the President from September 1972 until April of 1973, which, in his version of the conversations, indicated that the President and his chief aides conspired to cover up the Watergate break-in and pay hush money to the defendants. When a skeptical senator repeatedly pressed Dean on the details of these conversations, Dean said: "My mind is not a tape-recorder, Senator." At that time neither Dean nor any of the senators realized that there *was* a hidden tape recorder present during the conversations. This was disclosed in public for the first time when Alexander P. Butterfield, a former Presidential appointments secretary, told it to the committee on July 16, 1973, setting in motion a chain of events with momentous consequences.

Rights of Witnesses As anyone who watched the Watergate hearings might have gathered, a congressional investigation is a sort of combined trial, educational forum, and legislative hearing. Witnesses can be subpoenaed to testify, sworn in, and cross-examined; and the atmosphere sometimes becomes accusatory. "It's a great trial being conducted up here," John Mitchell remarked sarcastically after being grilled by Senator Ervin. Yet a congressional investigation lacks the procedural rigor of a trial: Witnesses may be accompanied by lawyers, but they have no routine right to cross-examine others; hearsay evidence is admitted; TV and radio coverage is permitted at the discretion of Congress. Technically, of course, no one is on trial, and the hearings can provide an opportunity for broad public education when carried by radio and TV. Even before the electronic age Woodrow Wilson contended that the "informing function" of Congress was to be preferred to its legislative function.[5] But here is where the danger lies: The hearings can degenerate into congressional "circuses," with members of Congress hamming it up at the expense of a witness's rights. Wild and reckless charges, bullying, and defamation were the hallmarks of many red-hunting investigations during the fifties. In 1957, in *Watkins v. U.S.*,[6] the Supreme Court ruled that no committee has the power to "expose for the sake of exposure," and that "no inquiry is an end in itself; it must be related to, and in furtherance of, a legitimate task of Congress."

Was the *Watkins* decision honored by the Watergate committee? The reader must judge on the information available. The committee's authorizing resolution carefully delineated the scope of the investigation, relating it to the study of whether there was need for "new congressional legislation to safeguard the electoral process."[7] This seemed to meet the *Watkins* rule of furthering "a legitimate task of Congress." And, true to its promise, the committee concluded its investigation by offering no less than thirty-five proposals for new legislation governing political campaigns. Yet it was clear from the outset that the committee's chairman saw its job in far broader terms—including the exposure of wrongdoing in the Nixon administration to as wide an audience as possible. Even if its proceedings interfered with the criminal trials of the defendants, Senator Ervin said, "it was more important that the American people get the truth than that a few people go to jail."[8]

Executive Privilege: The President's Countercheck

We can hardly discuss Congress's investigatory power without considering the President's countercheck: executive privilege.

The right of the President to withhold information or witnesses from the other branches of government is nowhere found in the Constitution, although President Nixon's lawyer argued—and the Supreme Court seemed to agree—that such a privilege is implied by the separation of powers. The term "executive privilege" was apparently never invoked until Attorney General William Rogers did so in 1958.[9] But Presidents have at various times refused to supply documents to one or another house of Congress. In 1796 the House of Representatives, investigating the background of the Jay treaty, asked President Washington for papers relating to the controversial negotiations. Washington refused, claiming that the House had no right to request such papers on the ground that he had already supplied them to the Senate (which, unlike the House, is the President's partner in treaty-making). This initial precedent for the President's refusal to supply information was not based upon a blanket claim of privilege but on the narrow grounds of the President's relationship to the Senate.

Over the next century or more, presidential attempts to withhold information from Congress were rare. Only in recent years has executive privilege been invoked as a general principle. When the House Un-American Activities Committee in 1947 demanded the security files of a physicist serving in the Truman administration, the President responded by reserving the right to determine whether disclosures would serve "the public interest." (Among the most ardent critics of Truman's claim was a young congressman named Richard M. Nixon.) An even more sweeping assertion of the President's right to withhold information was contained in a letter of President Eisenhower which was read before Senator McCarthy's investigating subcommittee during the Army-McCarthy Hearings of 1954. Eisenhower claimed that "it is not in the public interest that *any* of their conversations or *any* documents or reproductions [relating to what McCarthy was investigating] be disclosed."[10] Liberal newspapers like the *New York Times* and *Washington Post* defended Eisenhower's claim, letting Joe McCarthy stumble into the role of prophet:

> The question is, how far, how far can, I'm not talking about the present occupant of the White House, but we got a tremendously important question here, Mr. Chairman. That is, how far can the President go? Uh, who all can he order not to testify? The, any President, we don't know who will be President, 1956, 1960, 1964, any President. . . . Any President can, by an executive order, keep the facts from the American people. . . .[11]

"How far can the President go?" By 1973 the best answer to Senator McCarthy's question seemed to be: very far indeed. By then Nixon had invoked executive privilege on twelve different occasions in response to congressional requests for information concerning the ITT affair, the ouster of A. Ernest Fitzgerald,[12] and the Watergate scandal. In a policy statement of March 1973, Nixon broadened the scope of executive privilege to cover not only documents but testimony from any "member *or former member* of the President's personal staff."[13] Yet even this assertion did not bring the claims of executive privilege to their high-water mark. That was to occur the following month when Attorney General Richard Kleindienst, speaking on the President's behalf, told a Senate committee that the President's claim of executive privilege applied not just to top aides but to all 2.5 million employees of the federal government! But as the unfolding Watergate scandal drained his political strength, Nixon retreated. He did not protest when former top aides were subpoenaed to testify before the Watergate committee, and he allowed other aides still employed by the executive branch to provide testimony and submit to cross-examination. He agreed to the appointment of a Special Prosecuter within the Justice Department and promised him cooperation.

Nixon and Executive Privilege Once the existence of the White House tapes became known in July of 1973, however, the stage was set for a new confrontation over executive privilege—a confrontation which culminated a year later in a historic Supreme Court decision: *United States v. Richard M. Nixon.* We shall summarize the events leading to this decision in an endnote;[14] suffice it to say here that the case involved the Special Prosecutor's demand for tapes on the grounds that he needed them in the forthcoming trial of former Attorney General John Mitchell and others.

By an 8-0 decision the Supreme Court flatly repudiated the President's claim of an "absolute power" to withhold information. (Justice William Rehnquist disqualified himself because he had once worked for Mitchell in the Justice Department.) Instead, speaking for the Court, Chief Justice Warren Burger propounded a balancing test: Courts may weigh the President's need for confidentiality against other considerations. Three such considerations were held to be relevant to this case: (1) Even the President did not contend that these tapes contained military or diplomatic secrets; (2) The tapes were needed in the prosecution of criminal offenses; and (3) Provision was made for prior screening by a District

Court judge. Against these considerations the President offered "no more than a generalized claim of the public interest in confidentiality." This was not sufficient to tip the scales in his favor.

U.S. v. Nixon did not directly answer Joe McCarthy's question of "how far can the President go" in withholding information from Congress. But the very ingredients considered in its balancing test would seem to suggest that the Court—or at least its Chief Justice—would not be so receptive to congressional subpoenas of confidential documents held by the President. The opinion emphasized the need for the tapes in the upcoming criminal trials and suggested that "due process of law" would be violated if the tapes were denied. Congress could make no such claims. The Court repeatedly noted that the District Court must first screen the tapes. Congress has no similar mechanism. Finally, the Court agreed with an Appeals Court ruling of the previous fall that the President's conversations with his aides are "presumptively privileged," i. e., assumed to be confidential unless a strong case is made for disclosure.

It is difficult to make hard-and-fast generalizations about executive privilege as it relates to Congress. But out of the mixture of old precedents and more recent events we can perhaps make these observations:

1 Although the term "executive privilege" was not officially used before 1958, various Presidents have asserted the right to withhold information from Congress. Until Watergate, Congress has acquiesced.

2 Even during Watergate, Congress has been remarkably unaggressive in its demand for executive documents. The Watergate committee declined to appeal two District Court rulings upholding the President, and even during an impeachment inquiry the House Judiciary Committee did not take the President to court for his refusal to honor a subpoena (though it did vote to list this refusal among the grounds for impeachment).

3 Presidents have generally conceded the right of Congress to question close aides about activities with third parties which might be criminal in nature.[15]

4 Every President, save Nixon, to address himself to Congress's power to obtain information from the executive during impeachment hearings, has conceded Congress's absolute power in this area.[16]

5 In nonimpeachment cases the few lower court decisions we have are inclined toward upholding the President's claim of executive privilege as regards Congress.[17] Implicitly, the Supreme Court seems similarly inclined, although it has ruled that the President's claim is not "absolute."

Try as we may, it is really impossible to draw the bounds of "executive privilege" with precision. For 180 years, Arthur Schlesinger has noted, its bounds were determined by the political process, "with responsible opinion considering each case more or less on merit and turning against whichever side appeared to be overreaching itself."[17] It was not a tidy system, but at least it worked.

We have now considered three congressional checks on the President: the power to act; the power to refuse; the power to investigate. Let us conclude this section with a consideration of the legislature's ultimate weapon, the power of impeachment.

The Power to Remove: Impeachment

What is this weapon called *impeachment?* In 1956 Clinton Rossiter, quoting Henry Jones Ford, described it as a "rusted blunderbuss." After noting the Constitution's definition of impeachable offenses as "treason, bribery, or other high crimes and misdemeanors," Rossiter added:

> I predict confidently that the next President to be impeached will have asked for the firing squad by committing a low personal rather than a high political crime. . . .[18]

By 1974 some observers might have concluded that Rossiter's jest was prophetic. Watergate, the "third rate burglary," as the President's news secretary called it, seemed to lack the grandeur of a "high" crime. It had to do with low and sordid acts like bribery, burglary, extortion, lying, digging up dirt on enemies, "screwing" them, sabotaging campaigns, destroying evidence, covering up crimes, cheating on income taxes.

After all these scandals were unearthed the primary question in many minds could be reduced to five words: Was the President personally involved? The impeachment of Richard Nixon came to resemble a whodunit mystery, with his opponents leaking clues to the press and his supporters challenging them to produce the "smoking pistol"—the one conclusive piece of evidence linking the President to actual crimes. On August 5, 1974, the White House itself supplied the missing evidence. Having lost his court battle to retain possession of certain White House tapes which had been subpoenaed by Watergate Prosecutor Leon Jaworski, Nixon had no alternative to surrendering them. Since it was only a matter of time until the impeachment panel would also get hold of the tapes, Nixon decided to release transcripts of them to the public. The evidence in the transcripts turned out to be more than a "smoking pistol"; it was, in the words of columnist George Will, nothing less than a "smoking howitzer."

The transcripts showed that six days after the Watergate break-in Nixon was fully aware that John Mitchell and two former White House consultants, E. Howard Hunt and G. Gordon Liddy, had been involved in the break-in, even though Hunt and Liddy had not yet been arrested. He was told by Haldeman that "the F. B. I. is not under control" and that agents were tracing money found on the burglars to the Committee to Re-Elect the President. Nixon immediately began plotting the cover-up with Haldeman. They agreed that Haldeman should tell the FBI to, in Haldeman's words, "stay to hell out of this" because the break-in was a CIA operation, and exposure would compromise the CIA's intelligence activities. Nixon explicitly ordered Haldeman to tell the FBI to "lay off," and "don't go any further into this case, period!" When he released these extraordinary transcripts, Nixon admitted that "this additional material I am now furnishing may further damage my case." This proved to be one of the greatest understatements of Nixon's political career. "Devastating—impeachable," said New Jersey Congressman Charles Sandman, one of Nixon's most outspoken defenders on the House Judiciary Committee, and within hours he and the rest of Nixon's last-ditch defenders on the panel had changed their votes to "aye" on the question of his complicity in the cover-up. A day later Republican leaders in the House and Senate met with him and told him the grim arithmetic, which added up to an almost certain—and overwhelming—vote for impeachment in both houses of Congress. Senator Barry Goldwater later summed it up tersely to his colleagues: "Nixon should get his ass out of the White House—today!"[19] The thirty-seventh President of the United States missed Goldwater's deadline by three days, but on Friday, August 9, 1974, after tearfully bidding goodby to the remaining White House staff, he walked across to the lawn to take a one-way ride on the Presidential helicopter.

Let us suppose, however, that the last piece of evidence, the conversations which indicated what was clearly criminal behavior on Nixon's part, had not been found. For a time, indeed, it seemed as if the "smoking pistol" or "smoking howitzer" never would turn up. During that period before August 5 the President's defenders on the Judiciary Committee argued that the committee's charges against Nixon were lacking in "specificity"; that is to say, while the charges might indicate unwise, unstatesmanlike, or even immoral behavior on the President's part, they failed to specify—because they could not prove—specifically criminal acts committed by Nixon. The defenders of Nixon seemed to assume that a President must be a proven felon before he can be impeached, and that an impeachment panel must act strictly as a court of law if it is to perform its proper function. Dean Burch, Counsel to the President, described the impeachment proceedings as "one of the black spots in jurisprudence."[20] Ronald Ziegler, the President's press secretary, called the Judiciary Committee a "kangaroo court."[21]

But is an impeachment committee supposed to be a "court," kangaroo or otherwise? Are its proceedings matters of "jurisprudence"? Or is impeachment a *political* process, a means by which Congress can remove a President for grave offenses against the public good—grave but not necessarily criminal? Let us consider three factors: the logic of the Constitution, the relevant precedents, and the intentions of the framers.

Constitutional Logic At first glance the impeachment process prescribed in Article I, sections 2 and 3, of the Constitution resembles nothing so much as a criminal prosecution. The House acts like a grand jury, bringing charges against the President by majority vote. If the majority does vote the charges, the President is then "impeached," or formally accused. The Senate tries the case, with the Chief Justice of the Supreme Court presiding, and if two-thirds of the Senate vote agreement with any of the charges brought against the President, he is convicted.

But the Constitution goes on to state that punishment for impeachment "shall not extend further than to removal from office" and disqualification from occupying any other federal office. This is not criminal punishment. Furthermore, it states that the party convicted in an impeachment proceeding shall "be liable and subject to Indictment, Trial, Judgment and Punishment, according to Law." If impeachment were a criminal proceeding, would this not constitute double jeopardy, in violation of the Constitution's own Fifth Amendment?

Precedents Andrew Johnson was the only President ever to be impeached. Johnson suffered this fate in 1868 even though no indictable offense had been charged. But Johnson's impeachment is a dubious precedent. Many historians share the view of Samuel Eliot Morison that it was "one of the most disgraceful episodes in our history."²² Johnson was charged with defaming Congress by a series of inflammatory speeches and violating the Tenure of Office Act.

The statute in question, passed in 1867 over Johnson's veto, prohibited the President from firing certain executive officers without the advice and consent of the Senate. When Johnson went ahead and fired his Secretary of War, the House voted articles of impeachment and the Senate came one vote short of the two-thirds necessary for conviction. Although recent scholarship has cast doubt on whether Johnson can be regarded as a blameless victim of a "radical" vendetta,* it is generally agreed that the Tenure of Office Act was an unconstitutional statute. It was repealed by a subsequent Congress, and a 1926 Supreme Court case, *Myers v. U.S.*,²³ upheld the President's right to dismiss Cabinet members.

Other impeachment precedents have been concerned almost entirely with the removal of federal judges. Impeachment has been moved fifty times in the House since 1789, and the House has impeached twelve individuals. Of these twelve cases to reach the Senate, two were dismissed for lack of jurisdiction, six resulted in acquittals, and four were convicted and removed from office. In one case a senile and drunken judge named John Pickering was convicted on a variety of charges (including "loose morals and intemperate habits") unconnected with criminal behavior on the bench. Another judge was convicted for bringing his court "into scandal and disrepute," which in itself is not indictable. Still another was convicted of five different offenses which were serious but probably not indictable.²⁴

The Framers' Intentions "High crimes and misdemeanors" has been called a "term of art," which means that its definition must be understood in terms of its origin and usage at the time it was incorporated into the Constitution. Impeachment had long been used by Parliament as a means of removing Crown officers whose exalted station put them beyond the reach of ordinary courts. The expression "high crimes and misdemeanors" thus came to stand for political offenses, offenses against the public by officers of the state. These were understood in the broadest sense. By 1757 the English jurist Blackstone, writing on "high misdemeanors," considered the "first and principal" one to be "the mal-administration of such offices, as are in the public trust and employment."²⁵

The framers of the Constitution, while inclined toward a tighter construction than Blackstone's, nevertheless followed the general broad understanding of their English forebears. When George Mason of Virginia proposed that "maladminis-

---

* Michael Les Benedict, *The Impeachment and Trial of Andrew Johnson* (New York: W. W. Norton & Company, Inc., 1973). Benedict reminds us that the so-called radicals were only a minority in the Congress which impeached Johnson. He contends that it was Johnson's own actions which finally "forced the issue," causing moderates, however reluctantly, to join the radicals on impeachment. Benedict (p. 49) details a long series of provocations by Johnson, including the undermining of Congress's Reconstruction program:

The President's course, none of the elements of which clearly violated law, had a staggering effect on the South. He converted a conquered people, bitter but ready to accept the consequences of defeat, into a hostile, aggressive, uncooperative unit. He restored to them political and economic power and through that power domination of the men and women they had recently held as slaves. He had set back the work of Reconstruction, as it turned out, two full years and had ensured that Southerners would resist the Process instead of cooperating. To a large degree, the failure of Reconstruction could be blamed alone on President Johnson's abuse of his discretionary powers.

tration" be included among the grounds for impeachment, James Madison objected that this was "so vague as to be equivalent to a tenure during the pleasure of the Senate." Mason then limited his proposal to the addition of "high crimes and misdemeanors against the State," and this was adopted without discussion. But Madison himself construed impeachment in terms broad enough to include "negligence or perfidy of the Chief Magistrate." In the Virginia Ratification Convention Madison almost seemed to be anticipating some of the charges against President Nixon when he contended that a President can be impeached if he "be connected, in any suspicious manner, with any person, and there be grounds to believe that he will shelter him." Another Madisonian contention which was to become timely in the wake of Watergate was that a President could be impeached "if he suffers [his appointees] to perpetuate with impunity high crimes or misdemeanors against the United States, or neglects to superintend their conduct so as to check their excesses."[26] Madison made this contention during the First Congress.

Alexander Hamilton, who of all the members of the Convention may have been the most fervent champion of a strong Presidency, was also the coauthor (with Madison and John Jay) of the *Federalist,* the most authoritative commentary on the Constitution. In *Federalist 65* Hamilton addressed himself to the subject of impeachment:

> The subject of its [the Senate's] jurisdiction are those offenses which proceed from the misconduct of public men, or, in other words, from the abuse or violation of some public trust. They are of the nature which may with peculiar propriety be denominated POLITICAL, as they relate chiefly to injuries done immediately to the society itself.[27]

After examining these three sources—the logic of the Constitution, the weight of precedent, and the common understanding of "high crimes and misdemeanors" at the time the Consitution was framed—it seems reasonable to conclude that impeachable offenses need not be indictable ones, although they must constitute flagrant, grave abuses of power which seriously harm the public order.[28] In July of 1974 the House Judiciary Committee seemed to agree with this formulation. It voted to impeach President Nixon on three counts: obstruction of justice (covering up Watergate crimes), abuse of authority (using the IRS, the FBI, and other agencies to violate the rights of citizens), and failure to comply with the Committee's subpoenas for tapes and documents. Only the first of these three charges concerned an indictable offense, and even here the President's defenders were probably right to contend that it was too loosely drawn to hold up in a court. But the House of Representatives is not a court.

If the President's defenders mistook a political determination for a judicial verdict, their error was at least understandable. As long ago as the 1830s, Alexis de Tocqueville, a French visitor to Jacksonian America, noted that the people of this country tend to translate all their political issues into judicial ones.[29] It should not be surprising, then, that the judiciary has played a major role in curbing presidential ambition. Let us now turn from congressional checks to judicial checks on the President's power.

THE JUDICIARY AS A CHECK

"It is emphatically the province and duty of the judicial department to say what the law is." These famous words of Chief Justice John Marshall in 1803[30] laid down a principle which has become central to the American understanding of constitutional government: Federal courts, and ultimately the Supreme Court, are entrusted with the power to interpret both congressional and constitutional law. Given this responsibility, the judiciary can check a President by declaring his acts to be illegal or unconstitutional.

And yet, a parable: When Joseph Stalin and Franklin Roosevelt met at Yalta, Roosevelt reportedly demurred to one of Stalin's proposals on the ground that it might offend the Pope. Narrowing his already narrow eyes, Stalin replied: "And how many divisions has the Pope?" The Court's military capability is somewhat skimpier than the Pope's, since it has no Swiss Guard. The President wields the sword in America, and the Court must rely on his good will to carry out its decrees. What seems at first to be an American version of Stalin's Yalta remark was the (possibly apocryphal) explosion of President Jackson when he heard that Chief Justice Marshall had ruled in favor of the Cherokee Indians and against the state of Georgia: "John Marshall has made his decision:—now let him enforce it!"[31]

When we look at President Jackson's statement (or alleged statement) in its proper context, however, we see that he was not really defying Chief Justice Marshall, or even threatening to do so. The decision which Jackson would "let him enforce" was not a decision against the President but against the state of Georgia. Despite the Court's want of a sword, no President has ever defied a Supreme Court decision. Why not?

Perhaps the best answer is that what the Court lacks in physical power it makes up for in *authority*. We shall say more on the subject of authority in the next chapter. Suffice it here to note that the ability to command obedience does not always depend upon sheer might. Any good teacher or parent knows as much, but we might put the matter in a larger framework. Despite Stalin's rhetorical question, in fact even as he was asking it, one frail man, Pope Pius XII—who had no armies, no bombers, no extensive territories to call his own—commanded the allegiance and the obedience of millions throughout the world. Of course, if the Pope were regarded by his subjects as nothing more than an ascetic man wearing exotic clothes, his authority would be nil. But Catholics, at least during the days of Pius XII, saw the Pope as being God's earthly deputy, whose pronouncements on faith and morals were authentic expressions of the divine will.

The Supreme Court, in an analogous way, also enjoys a special status in the American tradition. Even the nation's Commander-in-Chief does not defy the nine unarmed men who comprise it. He does not defy them because he knows that Americans regard them not merely as a group of black-robed politicians, but as the final, authentic interpreters of the nation's highest law. "It is emphatically the province and duty of the judicial department to say what the law is." John Marshall's proposition struck a responsive chord in the hearts of his fellow citizens. In vain did Jefferson and other critics of the Court argue that judges are no different from other people, having "the same passions for party, for power, and the privilege of their corps." The American people have accepted the Court's claim to be the ultimate arbiter of all constitutional questions. "A very dangerous doctrine," said Jefferson. Dangerous or not, this widely accepted doctrine has enabled the Court to challenge, and on occasion check, the powers of the President. Its only weapon is its authority—the respect which it enjoys as the final interpreter of the Constitution.

But authority has its own limitations. If it lacks the physical force to back up its commands, it must rely upon the people's disposition to obey. This can be strained or even destroyed if it is pushed too hard or too far. Prudent authority figures must know how far and when their subjects will submit to authority. May it not be said that even popes must know when to stand firm and when to give way, when to be assertive and when to practice self-restraint? Whether or not it is proper to raise such a question concerning the Supreme Pontiff, it certainly can be raised when we turn to the Supreme Court.

The Court itself seems to be aware that authority has its limits. The authority of the judicial robe can inspire awe, but so can the sword of a popular President. The Court thus seems at times to temper its authority with a measure of prudence—especially during wartime, when the President's sword is bright with use. In *ex parte Milligan,* which was discussed in the last chapter, the Court vigorously repudiated Lincoln's claim that the President can suspend parts of the Constitution during a grave crisis like the Civil War. But the *Milligan* case was decided a full year after the war ended. The *Prize* cases (1863), decided when the war was in full swing, upheld the President's power to act without congressional authorization. Edward S. Corwin has noted that "the controlling opinion in the Prize cases squints one way, that in *ex parte Milligan* the other."[32] The Court's shifting eyes may be connected with the presence and absence of a major war. This impression is fortified by the experience during World War II, when the Court (including some of its most liberal justices) averted its face from the Bill of Rights in the so-called Japanese exclusion cases.[33] In three separate cases the Court upheld the right of President Roosevelt and the military to uproot American citizens of Japanese descent from their homes on the West coast and move them into concentration camps ("relocation centers," many of them patrolled by guards with machine guns) in the Rocky Mountain states. During the Korean war the Court did stand up to the President in the steel seizure case (discussed in the last chapter), but steel production was related only indirectly to the President's power as Commander-in-Chief. (It may also be not entirely unworthy of note that President Truman's popularity rating at that time was 23 percent, a point lower than Nixon's during the darkest days of Watergate.) During Vietnam the Court returned to its usual posture of deference to the executive during wartime. It refused to review an appeal of *Orlando v. Laird,* in which a Court of Appeals had denied a claim by an enlisted man that he need not go to Vietnam on the grounds of the war's illegality. The Appeals Court found that the Gulf of Tonkin resolution and continued congressional funding for the war were tantamount to a declaration of it. But even after Congress had repealed the Gulf of

Tonkin resolution the higher courts still refused to declare unconstitutional President Nixon's bombing of Cambodia. In 1973 a suit against the bombing was brought by Congresswoman Elizabeth Holtzman of Brooklyn and four Air Force officers. Although they won in District Court, the decision was overturned in the Court of Appeals, and the Supreme Court declined to review it.

In purely domestic affairs, even those categorized as "national security" cases, the Court has been less tolerant of unilateral initiatives by the President. While it has at times recognized the doctrine of "inherent" presidential powers during emergencies,[34] the Court has drawn sharp lines on the applicability of this doctrine. The President has been ordered to return seized steel mills,[35] prohibited from wiretapping without court warrant,[36] and told that newspapers may publish "top secret" documents.[37] And in areas where not even the President has claimed "national security," such as the impoundment of congressional funds or the withholding of tapes and documents from criminal investigators, the President's sword inspires the least awe in the hearts of judges.

But suppose a President kept everyone guessing as to whether he would obey a Supreme Court ruling? Might not the Court think twice before ruling against him? These questions were not academic ones during the season of Watergate. In July of 1973, when it first seemed possible that the President's claim of "executive privilege" might be tested in the Supreme Court, Nixon's deputy news secretary said that the President would abide by a "definitive" decision of the Supreme Court. A year later, however, when the tape controversy did reach the Court, White House representatives pointedly refused to say whether the President would obey *any* ruling, "definitive" or not, by the nation's highest court. Whether this was a subtle means of reminding the Court of its vulnerability ("John Marshall has made his decision:—now let him enforce it!"), or, as the President's lawyer claimed, simply a prudent refusal to comment on a pending case, the silence of the White House did not prevent an 8-0 decision against the President. The Court is not easily intimidated, at least not by an unpopular President during peacetime, because what it lacks in power it makes up in authority. Americans aspire to "a government of laws, not of men," and some of this veneration has rubbed off on the people who interpret the laws. To repeat: No American President has ever defied a Supreme Court decision.

Yet it takes a long while for a case to reach the Supreme Court, and only the most exceptional ones ever make it. Are there any unexceptional checks on presidential power—checks that operate without rising to the level of constitutional crises?

One of the most important day-to-day checks on one-man rule was never even considered by the framers. It has no place in our Constitution or in any classical American theories of checks and balances. Yet in modern times it has galled and frustrated many an ambitious President. I refer, of course, to the executive bureaucracy.

THE BUREAUCRACY AS A CHECK

The executive branch of the national government is not at all tidy. The Chief Executive presides over a sprawling collection of agencies and bureaus that includes three million employees, thousands of whom are in key policy-making positions.

In a posthumous work published in 1920 the German sociologist Max Weber discussed the nature of bureaucracy. In the first place, he noted, "there is the principle of fixed or jurisdictional areas, which are generally ordered by rules, that is, by laws or administrative regulations."[38] In America, even though its bureaucracy is not as well developed as that of European countries, there exist elaborate and detailed rules of administrative procedure which govern the bureaucracy, and not even the President can disregard them. Nixon, for example, tried his best to turn the Internal Revenue Service into an obedient machine for rewarding his friends and punishing his enemies. He made some inroads, but he never really succeeded in his aims, because there were too many IRS regulations which proscribed such a crass personal use of the agency. The bureaucracy thus imposes an administrative "rule of law" upon the President; there are certain things he may and may not do even in dealing with "his" own branch of government and "his" subordinates. When a bureaucracy performs its duties, Weber found, "the authority to give commands required for the discharge of these duties is distributed in a stable way. . . . " The rules spell out everyone's proper sphere of authority, so that the person at the top may not usurp the authority which properly belongs to lower officials. In the famous, or infamous, conversation of June 23, 1972, H. R. Haldeman complained to Nixon that "the F. B. I. is not under control." The agents of the Bureau had begun investigating the Watergate break-in and "their investigation is now leading into some productive areas. . . . " If the President exercised absolute control over the bureaucracy, he would not have to make excuses—he would simply have to tell the Bureau to stop—but Nixon and Haldeman spent a good part of that day rehersing a cover story to give the FBI. The story was calculated to appeal to the bureaucratic sense of "proper" jurisdiction: The FBI should "stay to hell out of this" because the break-in was a CIA operation. But blaming it on the CIA only got Nixon into more trouble; the intelligence bureaucrats saw their agency as being above mere partisan politics, and they resented being used as scapegoats for a dirty little operation against the Democrats.

Another characteristic which Weber found in bureaucracy:

> Methodical provision is made for the regular and continuous fulfilment of these duties and for the execution of the corresponding rights; only persons who have the generally regulated qualifications to serve are employed.[39]

Bureaucrats take pride in being "experts," especially career bureaucrats, who have reached their positions by means of qualifying examinations and the steady, methodical climb up the bureaucratic ladder. They can be subjected to a variety of humiliating punishments for not toeing the administration's line, but they cannot be easily dismissed, since they enjoy Civil Service status. Nixon's attempt to thrust his own lieutenants into the bureaus never got very far, and those "political commissars" he did manage to place were regarded with disdain by their nominal subordinates.

Thus the great, sprawling federal bureaucracy is a stubborn check upon the powers of the President. Even though the President directly controls the appointment of more than 2,000 top-level bureaucrats, he cannot be certain that their decisions will reflect his opinions. Presidents have trouble mastering even those departments where their nominal control is absolute—Cabinet departments, for example. Even a forceful President like Franklin Roosevelt confessed his frustrations:

> The Treasury is so large and far-flung and ingrained in its practices that I find it is almost impossible to get the action and results I want—even with Henry [Morgenthau] there. But the Treasury is not be to be compared with the State Department. You should go through the experience of trying to get any changes in the thinking, policy, and action of the career diplomats and then you'd know what a real problem was. But the Treasury and the State Department together are nothing compared with the Na-a-vy. The admirals are really something to cope with—and I should know. To change anything in the Na-a-vy is like punching a feather bed. You punch it with your right and you punch it with your left hand until you are finally exhausted, and then you find the damn bed just as it was before you started punching.[40]

Some years later Harry Truman echoed these sentiments as he reflected on his own experiences and predicted Eisenhower's: "He'll sit here," Truman said in the summer of 1952, "and he'll say, 'Do this! Do that!' *And nothing will happen.* Poor Ike—it won't be a bit like the Army."[41] One check on the President, then, is simple bureaucratic inertia. In one of the White House tapes Nixon stated the problem pithily: "Nobody follows up on a God damn thing."[42] By this time Nixon had already tried a variety of devices to correct this problem. He reorganized the old Bureau of the Budget as the Office of Management and Budget (OMB) and gave it the job of bringing the various Cabinet agencies under closer White House supervision. He organized a small "supercabinet" of trusted aides. After his reelection in 1972 he demanded the written resignations of hundreds of bureau heads—to be accepted at his discretion. None of these devices worked very well: the demand for resignations weakened morale and made recruitment difficult, the supercabinet was disbanded because of congressional opposition—which the post-Watergate White House lacked the strength to combat—and OMB, though it helped fill the vacuum in Presidential control after Watergate, simply could not keep all the bureaucrats in line. "There is no White House," one said as the crisis deepened. "There is no White House anymore."[43]

Besides bureaucratic inertia there is bureaucratic pride, especially if a bureaucrat has powerful friends on Capitol Hill. As Director of the FBI, the late J. Edgar Hoover was the nominal subordinate of the Attorney General, but Hoover built his own empire under eight different Presidents. None dared discharge, or even try to push around, this living symbol of law 'n' order. Hoover's obsession with communist conspiracies and his reluctance to protect civil rights did not endear him to American liberals, but before his death he made one important contribution to civil liberties: Though the President of the United States had approved the notorious "Huston plan" for domestic espionage, break-ins, mail checks, and surveillance, Hoover's objections aborted it. If Huston's memos are to be believed, Hoover stood alone against this insane police-state plan: He was "the only stumbling block," the one person who made "life tough in this area."

Huston complained about Hoover's "concern that the civil liberties people may become upset," and concluded that "He's getting old and worried about his legend."[44]

To inertia and pride we might add professionalism as another bureaucratic check on the President. The Justice Department and the Internal Revenue Service resisted attempts to politicize them during the Nixon years because they contained large numbers of career officials. It was at their insistence that the Justice Department went ahead with an antitrust suit against ITT despite the most intense White House pressure to drop it. At about the same time, career officials in the IRS were struggling valiantly against White House efforts to infiltrate the Service and use it as a partisan weapon. These bureaucrats had developed a feel for objective standards and a spirit of impartiality which helped shield their agencies against politicization. Their behavior seemed to demonstrate the accuracy of Max Weber's observation: "The political official—at least in the fully developed modern state—is not considered the personal servant of the ruler."[45] In this respect their civil service status also helped. As two students of the subject have put it: "Presidents come and go, the bureaucracy stays."[46]

As if Presidents have not had enough trouble with ordinary, chain-of-command bureaucrats, Congress over the past century has compounded the problem by creating a new class of "independent" bureaucrats.

Independent Regulatory Commissions

Beginning in 1887, Congress has created a series of independent regulatory commissions. Among the major ones: the Interstate Commerce Commission (ICC), the Civil Aeronautics Board (CAB), the Federal Communications Commission (FCC), the Federal Power Commission (FPC), the Federal Trade Commission (FTC), and the Securities and Exchange Commission (SEC). These commissions combine legislative, executive, and judicial functions. The Interstate Commerce Commission, for example, can adjudicate disputes between different railroads or trucking companies, set standards, establish new policies, and act as a watchdog to make sure the carriers are following them. Serious questions have been raised about how well the independent regulatory commissions have performed these tasks, but their relative freedom from presidential control is a matter both of law and of fact. In 1937 the President's Committee on Administrative Management, a study group, contended that the commissions constituted a "headless 'fourth branch' of the Government, a haphazard deposit of irresponsible agencies and uncoordinated powers. . . . "[47] The acts establishing the commissions provide that the President can remove commissioners only for incompetence or similar reasons, not because of policy differences, and in *Humphrey's Executor v. United States* the Supreme Court affirmed the constitutionality of this limitation on the President's removal power.[48] The President can (subject to Senate approval) appoint his own men and women to the commissions when the terms of the old members expire, but since the terms range from five to fourteen years he may have a bit of a wait.

Because of frequent resignations and the tradition that the chairmen serve at the pleasure of the President, Nixon succeeded in making a considerable impact on the makeup of the commissions. In slightly over four years he appointed new chairmen in six of them and succeeded in filling twenty-eight of the thirty-eight positions. Yet one President's meat is the next President's poison. Nixon's appointees tended to be conservatives with a strong "free enterprise" bent. Nixon's successors must live, at least for a time, with many of these appointments, whose policies may be sharply at variance with their own.

In arguing against the right of Special Prosecutor Leon Jaworski to sue the man who appointed him for refusing to release the White House tapes, President Nixon's lawyer characterized the Special Prosecutor's office as "a constitutional anomaly."

> We have only three brances, not three-and-a-third or three-and-a-half or four. There is only one Executive Branch. And the executive power is vested in a President.[49]

The Supreme Court rejected this argument on the grounds that the Special Prosecutor had been given "unique authority" by the Attorney General, including the authority to contest any assertion of executive privilege.[50] But can we not reply to the argument on more basic grounds? If the Special Prosecutor was an "anomaly," so are the independent regulatory commissions. The fact of the matter is that the tripartite separation of powers is not absolutely watertight in America. We may not have "three-and-a-third or three-and-a-half" branches, but since 1887 the President has had to contend with "a headless 'fourth branch' of the Government."

We have discussed the role of Congress, the courts, and the bureaucracy in checking a runaway Presidency. What other checks are available?

POLITICAL PARTIES AS A CHECK

The opposition party can needle the President, expose wrongdoing, and mobilize opposition at the polls. But in America "partisanship" is a bad word, so the effort can boomerang. During the impeachment proceedings against him, President Nixon apparently hoped to profit from the negative connotation of "partisan politics." If the whole impeachment movement were seen as a partisan vendetta by liberal Democrats seeking to reverse the 1972 election results, it would surely founder if it ever came to the floor of the House. These hopes were dashed, however, when as many as seven of the seventeen Republicans on the House Judiciary Committee joined the Democrats in voting impeachment.

Indeed, as the Watergate scandal unfolded, the most effective party pressures on President Nixon came not from the Democrats but from members of his own party: Republican congressional leaders, threatening defection, helped force the President to scale down his claims of "executive privilege" and retreat from his "stonewall" strategy. Democrats, for their part, generally refrained from blaming the Republican party for the scandals of a Republican administration. It was amid growing signs of bipartisanship in Congress that the impeachment movement gained momentum, and when the votes on the House Judiciary committee were taken, seven of the seventeen Republicans on the committee joined the Democrats in voting out one or more articles of impeachment. (Once the transcripts of the incriminating June 23 tapes—the so-called smoking pistol—were made public, the remaining Republican holdouts changed their votes to "aye" on the first article of impeachment, making the committee's verdict unanimous.) At the very end, it was not liberal Democrats but conservative Republicans like Representative Charles Wiggins and Senator Barry Goldwater who sealed Nixon's fate by calling for his immediate resignation. James MacGregor Burns continues to argue that "reconstruction and strengthening of our two party system"[51] is one of the best means of keeping the President in line, but if Watergate were cast into a partisan framework it would have produced deep and bitter division in our society and, possibly, might have failed to retire the President who was ultimately responsible for it.

THE PRESS AS A CHECK

The press occupies a peculiar position in the American political system. In a sense it is part of the system, which has earned it the title of "fourth branch of government." Its freedom is guaranteed by the First Amendment, and its influence has grown enormously over the past two centuries as a result of consolidation and professionalization of news reporting, the virtual revolution in communications technology, the growing appetite of Americans for "the latest news," and the ability of the American media to present it in a form which appeals to a mass audience. Today our politicians know that a "bad press" can threaten their plans or even their careers, and no press coverage at all is nearly as bad. Consequently, the ladies and gentlemen of the press are found everywhere in government, often as the invited guests of those who do the governing. They are courted by politicians, deluged with press releases, treated to "background briefings," and made the beneficiaries of high-level "leaks."

The cordiality of government officials poses obvious dangers to the independence of the press. If it is to perform its role as a check upon government power, the press must be *in* government but not *of* it. It must resist the temptation to cozy up to government officials or to act as if it were itself part of the governing establishment.

During the Nixon years the press was given very few such temptations. The relationship between President and press was lustily adversary, and the press's role as critic, watchdog, gadfly, and whistle-blower was demonstrated on a number of occasions: when it printed the Pentagon Papers, when it revealed the secret bombing of Cambodia, when it goaded the President with tough questions during news conferences, to cite a few of these occasions. The most prominent example, however, was Watergate. Nixon himself at first praised the role of "a vigorous free press" in exposing the scandal. But as the exposure continued, Nixon's acknowledgments became increasingly rueful. He complained that "a constant barrage—12 to 15 minutes a night on each of the three major networks for four months—tends to raise some questions in the people's minds with regard to the President."[52] As he neared the end of his political career, Nixon blamed his loss of public support on the "leers and sneers of commentators."[53] Whether or not Nixon was actually subjected to leers and sneers by members of the fourth estate, his relations with them were unprecedentedly bad; to get some idea of how bad they were, we only have to look back a decade or so to the days of Camelot.

John F. Kennedy had wooed news reporters since his days as a member of Congress, and by the time of his Presidency it was clear that his love was not unrequited. Everything about the man seemed to be designed to the tastes of the college-educated news reporters who followed him around: his youth, good looks, verbal agility, Harvard education, his dry, mildly cynical wit, his whole air of gracefulness and classiness. Kennedy inspired feelings of camaraderie among members of the press, which served him well when he entered the White House. If his weekly news conferences were virtuoso performances, some credit must go to the supporting role of the assembled news reporters. The mood was respectful, the questioning gentle, the Kennedy wit heartily appreciated. There was little of the combative atmosphere or the needling, follow-up questions which emerged during Nixon press conferences. With both President and press sharing many of the same cold war assumptions, Kennedy's hawkish line in foreign policy and his increasing involvement in Vietnam received little critical analysis. When the *New York Times* received advance information that Kennedy was planning an invasion of Cuba, he talked its editors out of printing it by appealing to their patriotism. (Later he admitted that it would have been better if the *Times* had printed it—it might have aborted the ill-fated venture.) It is hard to imagine Nixon enjoying such immunity. In general, Kennedy's strategy was to give reporters and editors the sense of joint participation in the high drama of government: He and they were not to be adversaries but colleagues. He even met with a group of editors and proposed a "constructive dialogue," in which both sides would cooperate in preventing what his Special Counsel, Theodore Sorensen, was to call "harmful disclosures."[54] Though nothing came of the plan, the very fact that it could be proposed during the days of the Kennedy administration tells us a great deal about the relationship between the President and the press at the time. According to Sorensen, Kennedy had to suppress his "surprise and indignation"[55] when the assembled editors and publishers failed to see the need for this scheme of self-censorship during peacetime—a scheme which Nixon would never have dared to propose.

Preparing the way for the changed climate of press relations in the seventies was the experience of the Johnson administration. Lyndon Johnson lacked what Theodore White called "the light touch" of John Kennedy. His attempts to manage the news were sometimes comically heavy-handed, and his habits of dissembling were so ingrained that he would tell lies about the most trivial matters, lies which could easily be disproved. ("My great-great-grandfather died at the Alamo" sent reporters off to the genealogical records, to discover that no such martyr existed among Johnson's ancestors.)[56] By 1968 Johnson's "credibility gap" had already reached canyonlike proportions. It remained for Nixon to turn alienation into a continuous, bitter confrontation.

Nixon's twenty-year history of battling reporters, his personal aloofness and inaccessibility, his orchestrated campaign against the media (discussed in Chapter 1), his choice of press liaison—young men like Ronald Ziegler, with no experience in dealing with reporters, no understanding of the way they work, and no compunctions about misleading them—all these factors contributed to a press relationship which was worse than any which veteran reporters could remember. Hugh Sidey of *Time* magazine observed that under previous administrations "you could talk, write about, or disagree" with administration officials, "but at the end of the day you could have a drink with them." Not so under Nixon.

> This crowd came in like an occupying army. They took over the White House like a stockade, and the Watergate, and screw everybody else. They have no sense that the government doesn't belong to them, that it's something they're holding in trust for the people.[57]

Of Nixon himself Walter Cronkite said in 1973: "He has never been able to sit down with newsmen, put his feet up, get out the bourbon bottle and say, 'Come on, gang, let's have a drink; you guys sure laid it into me today.' "[58]

This prompts a question: Is it a healthy relationship when President and press gather round the bourbon bottle at the end of the day? The question must be raised, because repression is not the only enemy of an independent press. Collusion can also interfere with the press's duty to pull no punches when it reports the facts and examines the policies of the White House. A case can perhaps be made—the thought should at least be considered—that charming, cordial, and very accessible Presidents like John Kennedy pose greater dangers to a free press than stiff, aloof, pugnacious Presidents like Richard Nixon. Whatever else Nixon did, he certainly put the press on guard against the abuse of power in the White House. The press responded by doing what it was supposed to do—muckraking—and doing it much more vigorously than it had ever done during the previous two administrations. Under Nixon, some of our leading news commentators worried about the rape of a free press, but if the last fifteen years or so provide any lesson, it may be that seduction poses the real threat to this important check upon the powers of the President.

THE BALLOT BOX AS A CHECK

One check on the abuse of presidential power is so obvious that it is sometimes overlooked: *the ballot box.* Americans can always exercise the option of "throwing the rascals out," and in this respect the Constitution provides a double check: The President must be elected every four years, and (thanks to the Twenty-second Amendment) he can serve no more than two terms.

The other side of the coin from throwing a rascal out is putting a good candidate in, and in this respect our electoral system imposes upon us the burden of choice. But how to choose? The platforms of competing candidates are often hard to distinguish from one another. Their campaign speeches seldom depart from the accepted American pieties. Their promises are usually kept as vague as possible; nor do we have any assurances that they will be kept. How, then, can we predict in advance how a candidate will behave once he gets into the White House?

Political scientist James David Barber is convinced that "personality" holds the key to predicting presidential behavior, so that by picking the "right" kinds of personalities for the Presidency and rejecting the "wrong" kinds, the American voters can exert a large measure of control over their political future when they go to the polls.[59]

The three "wrong" kinds of personality in Barber's classification scheme are the "passive-positive" type (who likes politics, or at any rate people, but is inclined toward doing nothing, letting events control him: William Howard Taft), the "passive-negative" type (who hates politics and does little: Dwight D. Eisenhower), and the "active-negative" type (who has no real love for politics but works feverishly: Herbert Hoover, Lyndon Johnson, Richard Nixon).

The people to elect, Barber believes, are "active-positive" types like Harry Truman, Franklin Roosevelt, and John Kennedy, who worked hard but genuinely loved it, found it fun.

Barber seems to assume that "personality" is the primary determinant of behavior, or at any rate that it can be examined in isolation from the other factors which influence a President's course of action. For example, what about the influence of ideology? Could it not have been William Howard Taft's view of the Constitution, more than his personality, which made him a do-little President? A President's performance might also be influenced by an event or a series of events over which he had little control. Would Hoover have been so "negative" if it were not for the terrible Depression, which occurred during his Presidency but which he certainly did not cause? True, he did not end the Depression, but neither did FDR. It was Hitler and the Japanese warlords, far more than the "active-positive" personality of Franklin Roosevelt, who set in motion the series of events which got America out of the Depression. Besides ideology and events themselves, the ambience of public expectations can also affect the behavior of a President. Suppose there were no cold war mentality in America—would LBJ have ever gotten us caught up in Vietnam?

It is hard not to suspect that much of Barber's analysis of presidential "personality" consists of Monday-morning quarterbacking. LBJ might have emerged as a second FDR (the President he tried to pattern himself after) if it were not for Vietnam. Many observers found Johnson zestful and "positive" about his job until Vietnam turned him sour, "negative." The same souring might have been the fate of FDR if his futile effort to end the Depression were not suddenly transformed by the onset of World War II. Then what? He might have ended up being classified with Herbert Hoover as another "negative" President. "If the end brings me out wrong," Abraham Lincoln observed, "a thousand angels swearing I was right will make no difference." We know how the end "brought out" every past President; what we do not know is how to convert this knowledge into a means of choosing future Presidents.

In any event, picking the right President is not the same as controlling him. Important as they are, quadrennial elections do not check the actions of a President *between* elections. They may even have lulled Americans into a false sense of security. Arthur Schlesinger has warned of a "plebiscitary presidency."[60] Many Americans think they have performed their duties as citizens by going to the polls every four years, then letting whoever wins run the country without further interference. This tempts the President to justify illegal or unconstitutional behavior on the grounds of the popular "mandate" he received one day in November—possibly four years earlier.* In this respect our presidential system has been compared unfavorably with the parliamentary model which exists in Great Britain and other countries. There a government may face an immediate test at the polls if it pursues an unpopular policy or becomes immersed in a scandal of Watergate proportions. In such cases new elections are called so that the voters can "throw the rascals out" without waiting years to do so.

The parlimamentary system has another feature which our system lacks: collective responsibility. One feature of the American Presidency which has troubled some observers is that, within his own sphere of government, the President has no peers. None of his advisers ever tells him to go soak his head, because none is in a position to do so. All are "the President's men," appointed by him, serving at his pleasure, doing his bidding. Of course the congressional and judicial branches of government can stand up to the President, but the problem here is the time lag. Congress and the judiciary usually find out what the President has done only after he has done it—after he has invaded Cuba, or bombed Cambodia, or seized the steel mills. The parliamentary system, on the other hand, provides timely checks on the Prime Minister: his colleagues. He must carry the majority of the Cabinet with him before making a major decision. All then become collectively responsible to the national legislature.

Today few serious students of American government would advocate that America change over to a parliamentary system. A metamorphosis of that kind would require such radical changes in our party system, our Constitution, our deepest traditions and mores, that it hardly seems worth discussing. But some critics of the Presidency have suggested that we adopt certain features common to parliamentary systems.

SOME PROPOSED CHECKS

1 One suggestion is that we adopt a *plural presidency*. Michael Novak has proposed that we give to two different persons the presidential functions of Chief Executive and Chief of State.[61] It was pointed out in the last chapter that Chief of State is the President's "monarchical" role: our official greeter, our moral leader, our ceremonial head of government. Novak's idea is to turn this role over to some likable type—a Dwight Eisenhower or a Margaret Mead—but make sure that the real power goes to a separate Chief Executive. This would demonarchize the executive by finding a separate, harmless outlet for popular adulation: a politically impotent king or queen, much like Britain's, except that this person would

---

* Or six years, if one "reform" were adopted. Sponsored by Senators Mike Mansfield and George Aiken (and favored by Richard Nixon), the six-year Presidency would supposedly take the office "out of politics" by eliminating the prospect of a second term and the need to campaign for it. This totally misconceives the problem of the modern Presidency, which is that it is not political *enough*. True politicians do not and cannot cut themselves off from abrasive voices. They must deal, haggle, persuade, negotiate, above all *listen* to others. The Presidency has already become too far removed from this humbling process. The six-year Presidency would remove the President even further, keeping him for six years in the rarefied atmosphere of a "nonpolitical" White House—an atmosphere calculated to foster a Byzantine mentality in even the humblest of people.

also "articulate public morality" and "be the Government's futurist, dreamer, proposer."

Novak's proposal seems to assume that unchecked power in the Presidency is a result of glamorization. Actually, it probably goes the other way around: Americans have glamorized the Presidency, especially since 1945, because they have seen it as the focus of such awesome powers and responsibilities—the place with the red telephone and the hot line, the place where the big decisions are made. To try to transfer this glamor to the person of a completely impotent Royal Dreamer would not be a political reform but a public relations venture with dubious prospects of success.

Barbara Tuchman's version of the pluralized Presidency has the merit of addressing itself to the source of the President's glamor: his power. She would divide the Presidency not in two but six.

> We could substitute true cabinet government by a directorate of six to be nominated as a slate by each party and elected as a slate for a single six-year term with a rotating chairman, each to serve for a year as in the Swiss system. The chairman's vote would carry the weight of two to avoid a tie.[62]

The framers considered and rejected a number of proposals for a plural executive along the lines suggested by Tuchman. One of the main reasons for sticking with one President was ably stated by James Wilson: A single magistrate would impart the "most energy, dispatch and responsibility."[63] Hamilton and Jefferson, despite their differences on so many questions, both seemed to agree that a plural executive would pose the danger of deadlocked and irresponsible government. Tuchman's proposals should be scrutinized in the light of these concerns. Her six-member cabinet would include departments ranging from foreign affairs to "Human Affairs, including H. E. W., Labor and the cultural endowments."[64] Who would coordinate all these departments? Who would mediate squabbles and decide priorities? The pluralistic Cabinet system works in countries with strong party discipline, which America lacks. A plural executive combined with a weak party system would do more than check the President's power. It would enfeeble it.

One of the themes running through this book is that power needs to be checked—but that we need power. Government today must deal with highly volatile crises in foreign policy, with our complex domestic economy, our enormous industrial plants, our unresolved social problems. For this it needs power. To do the reverse, to weaken the executive branch in the face of these challenges, would be to let drift determine the nation's direction. Surely this is not to be America's answer to "the important question" raised by Alexander Hamilton in *Federalist 1*: "whether societies of men are really capable or not of establishing good government from reflection and choice, or whether they are forever destined to depend for their political constitutions on accident and force."

The real question, therefore, is not how to reduce power in the executive but how to make it responsible and accountable. "The President," Clinton Rossiter observed in 1956, "is not a Gulliver immobilized by ten thousand tiny cords, nor even a Prometheus chained to a rock of frustration. He is, rather, a kind of magnificent lion who can roam widely and do great deeds so long as he does not try to break loose from his broad reservation."[65] By the seventies the problem was that the lion had somehow escaped the reservation. The task is to put him back— not to pin him down or destroy his power, but to keep him within bounds. The old lion is still capable of "great deeds," but they must be accountable deeds, performed in the light of day, with plenty of spectators watching. It is more or less in this spirit that other proposals have been suggested:

2 Senator Jacob Javits of New York has proposed that Congress require the President to report to it annually what steps he had taken to carry out laws and resolutions passed in the last session; the President and his Cabinet heads would then submit to questioning by a new joint committee of both houses, and the Congress would later vote on whether or not it was satisfied with the President's actions. The vote would not bind the President to anything, but it would, as it were, send him a message.

3 Senator Lloyd Bentsen of Texas has proposed that the highest positions in the Justice Department, including that of Attorney General, be closed to anyone who has held any position, paid or unpaid, in the President's campaign. The intention here is to prevent another former campaign manager like John Mitchell from using the Justice Department as a partisan instrument. Perhaps this proposal contains a rather naïve "antipolitical" bias,* but at least it attempts to eliminate crass partisanship in Justice without (like some other proposals) divorcing the Department from the President's control.

4 Senator Gaylord Nelson of Wisconsin has proposed that Congress ban any form of wiretapping or bugging without a court order. In a related proposal Senator Henry Jackson of Washington submitted a bill to require complete accounting to Congress by any agency conducting any kind of political surveillance.

5 Benjamin V. Cohen, a former legal adviser to President Roosevelt, has suggested an "executive council," composed of citizens "of highest public standing" (nominated by the President and confirmed by the Senate) to monitor the executive departments. This form of "executive council" bears too close a resemblance to a plural executive, but another version of it, suggested a generation ago by Edward S. Corwin, does seem worth considering. Corwin proposed *"that the President should construct his Cabinet from a joint Legislative Council to be created by the two houses of Congress and to contain its leading members"* [66] (emphasis Corwin's). This proposal would not require a constitutional amendment and would not formally abridge the separation of power since the Cabinet has only advisory powers. Yet, as Corwin pointed out, "there are advisers *and* advisers."

---

* Theodore Sorensen, former special counsel to President Kennedy, has criticized this proposal for its assumption that "political" types cannot be trusted to administer justice fairly. Yet Sorensen's own proposal seems to contain the same assumption: "The names of top civil servants at the department should no longer be submitted for political clearance. United States attorneys and marshalls should be career men and women appointed by the Attorney General, not brief beneficiaries of political patronage." Theodore C. Sorensen, "Justice Department Reform," *New York Times,* July 1, 1974, p. 28.

The proposed Cabinet would comprise men whose daily political salt did not come from the presidential table, whose political fortunes were not identical with his, who could bring presidential whim under an independent scrutiny. . . .[67]

6 One loophole in the Corwin proposal was shown during the Nixon administration. What if the President's Cabinet tends to become window dressing? Nixon largely ignored even a Cabinet of his own choosing, giving real authority to a group of intimates whose appointments were not confirmed by the Senate. To close this loophole of nonaccountability, Senator Walter Mondale of Minnesota has proposed legislation which would require Senate confirmation of every important officer within the executive branch.

These proposals are suggested not as an exhaustive list of reforms but as recommendations to be debated by Americans as they ponder the future of the Presidency in the seventies. Perhaps they are not necessary in view of all the other checks considered in this chapter. Although the old checks failed to prevent either Vietnam or Watergate, they did begin to take hold in the aftermath of the scandal. Congress limited the President's war powers, the Supreme Court qualified his power of executive privilege, the executive bureaucracy itself seemed less in awe of him than any time in recent memory, the Congress was getting ready to impeach, and the press merrily muckraked. Those critics whose chief worry is the "mystique" of the White House could also take heart. Nixon's behavior destroyed the myth of the virtuous President, and Nixon's defenders demythified the office by their constant repetition of the refrain: "Nixon was not the first!"

In the long run, keeping Clinton Rossiter's "magnificent lion" on its reservation depends less upon specific reforms than on the public's willingness to involve itself in the governing process. The President is elected every four years, but citizens can play a role in moderating his behavior between elections. This was demonstrated most dramatically in the aftermath of the "Saturday night massacre"—Nixon's dismissal of the first Special Prosecutor, Archibald Cox; the resignation of Attorney General Elliot Richardson; the firing of William Ruckelshaus, deputy Attorney General, for refusal to dismiss Cox—when a spontaneous burst of citizen wrath forced the President to appoint a new Special Prosecutor (Leon Jaworski) and hand over some tapes to Judge John Sirica. A Presidential spokesman called it a "firestorm."

THE LAST BEST CHECK: THE PEOPLE

Occasional firestorms are fine, but the Republic would probably be better served by the steady application of heat *by the people themselves.* Has not the paternalistic Presidency grown in part from a slackness in the public sector, an excessive faith in "experts," a preoccupation with private instead of political concerns, a willingness to delegate responsibility to others? What would happen if more "ordinary people" could bring themselves to write their congressional representatives about the issues that concern them, to prod them into the passage of timely legislation, to let them know that they will not tolerate corruption and abuse of office, to demand investigations when they seem warranted? In far fewer words

Benjamin Franklin seemed to be asking and answering both these questions when, on a hot September afternoon two centuries ago, he told his landlady that America was to be a republic—"if you can keep it."

NOTES

1. *The American Heritage History of the Presidency* (New York: American Heritage Publishing Co., Inc., 1968), p. 24.
2. *Congressional Record,* CXIX (July 20, 1973), P. S 14186.
3. Clinton Rossiter, *The American Presidency,* rev. ed. (New York: Harcourt, Brace & World, Inc., 1956, 1960), p. 54.
4. Congressional Quarterly, *Current American Government,* Spring 1973 (Washington: Congressional Quarterly, Inc., 1973), p. 40.
5. Woodrow Wilson, *Congressional Government* (Boston: Houghton Mifflin Company, 1925), p. 303.
6. *Watkins v. United States,* 354 U.S. 178 (1957).
7. Cited in *The Watergate Hearings: Break-in and Cover-up,* New York Times edition (New York: Bantam Books, Inc., 1973), p. 131.
8. Quoted in ibid., p. 7.
9. Arthur M. Schlesinger, Jr., *The Imperial Presidency* (Boston: Houghton Mifflin Company, 1973), pp. 158–159.
10. *U.S. News and World Report,* May 28, 1954. Emphasis added.
11. Emile de Antonio and Daniel Talbot, *Point of Order!* (Verbatim excerpts from Army-McCarthy Hearings of 1954) (New York: W. W. Norton & Company, Inc., 1964), pp. 63–64.
12. This is discussed in Chapter 6.
13. *New York Times,* Mar. 13, 1973, p. 16. Emphasis added.
14. Both the Watergate committee and Special Prosecutor Archibald Cox asked for tapes of key conversations between Nixon and his aides in order to test the truth of John Dean's assertions. Nixon refused both requests, and the matter was tried in the District Court of Judge John Sirica. His decision fully satisfied none of the parties. The Watergate committee's subpoena was rejected, and the Special Prosecutor was granted only a partial victory: Judge Sirica himself would screen the tapes and decide which parts could be heard by the Special Prosecutor. The Senate Watergate committee acquiesced in the decision, but both the President and Special Prosecutor appealed. The Circuit Court of appeals sustained the decision.

    The rest of the story is complicated and melodramatic. Nixon offered to let a friendly Southern Democratic Senator, John Stennis of Mississippi, hear parts of the tapes, and on the strength of this offer felt justified in ordering Cox to drop his appeal. When Cox refused, he was fired, but not before Attorney General Elliot Richardson resigned (rather than dismiss the man to whom he had promised "the greatest degree of independence") and Deputy Attorney General William Ruckelshaus got himself fired for refusing to transmit the dismissal order. The "Saturday Night Massacre," as it came to be called, set off a tremendous public furor, which caused Nixon to retreat still further from his "stonewall" approach by appointing a new Special Prosecutor, Leon Jaworski, and surrendering the disputed tapes to Judge Sirica. (But some tapes turned out to be missing and others contained mysterious gaps, later determined by a team of electronics experts to be caused by a series of five to nine erasures.) Nixon's new retreat emboldened the Watergate committee to subpoena 500 more tapes and documents, a demand which the committee later pared down to five tapes. The subpoena was turned down by the District Court, and the decision was not appealed by the committee.

By this time the House Judiciary Committee had begun serious consideration of the President's impeachment. The Committee subpoenaed Presidential tapes and documents. So did the new Special Prosecutor, on the grounds that he needed them in the upcoming trial of former Attorney General John Mitchell and others. The President responded to these subpoenas by making public some 1,200 pages of edited transcripts, replete with notations like "expletive deleted," "inaudible," and "material unrelated to Watergate deleted." By a narrow vote the Judiciary Committee declared itself unsatisfied with this arrangement, but declined to press it in the courts. (It was later discovered that the transcripts differed in a number of places with the tapes in the Committee's possession, and omitted some highly damaging remarks by the President.) The Special Prosecutor did press the matter in the courts, however, and after winning in District Court asked the Supreme Court to rule on the question directly, in special session. The case of *United States v. Richard M. Nixon* was decided by the Supreme Court on July 24, 1974.

15 President Truman allowed congressional committees to question top officials in the Internal Revenue Service concerning possible favoritism in the application of income tax rules. President Eisenhower allowed Congress to question Sherman Adams, his closest aide, concerning his receipt of a mink coat from a New Hampshire industrialist.

16 "A series of Presidents, from Washington through Polk and Buchanan to Mr. Nixon himself, have recognized the paramountcy of the Grand Inquest of the Nation. Polk put the matter most forcibly: given an inquiry into executive misconduct, the 'power of the House' . . . would penetrate into the most secret recesses of the Executive Departments.'" Raoul Berger, "Mr. Nixon's Refusal of Subpoenas: 'A Confrontation With the Nation,'" *New York Times,* July 8, 1974, p. 29. Cf. Berger's book, *Executive Privilege: A Constitutional Myth* (Cambridge, Mass.: Harvard University Press, 1974).

17 Schlesinger, op. cit., p. 396.
18 Rossiter, op. cit., p. 53.
19 This quotation and the previous quotations from Congressman Sandman, Haldeman, Nixon, and columnist George Will are taken from *Time,* Aug. 19, 1974 pp. 15A–20.
20 *New York Times,* July 22, 1974.
21 *New York Times,* July 23, 1974.
22 Samuel Eliot Morison, *The Oxford History of the American People* (New York: Oxford University Press, 1965), p. 721.
23 *Myers v. United States,* 272 U.S. 52 (1926).
24 Some of these precedents are admittedly shaky. At least one of them, the Pickering conviction in 1804, had partisan overtones, since Pickering was a Federalist judge whose removal was sought by a Republican President and Congress. In an even more partisan attack on another Federalist judge in the same year the House impeached Samuel Chase, Associate Justice of the Supreme Court. Chase was later acquitted in the Senate. Even if, as Professor Raoul Berger has argued, Chase deserved to be convicted, the exceedingly broad definition of impeachable offenses advanced by his accusers—which included the holding of "dangerous opinions"—would surely have jeopardized the independence of the judiciary. For Berger's argument, see his *Impeachment: The Constitutional Problems* (Cambridge, Mass.: Harvard University Press, 1973), chap. 8.
25 Quoted in Raoul Berger, "Impeachment for 'High Crimes and Misdemeanors,'" *Southern California Law Review,* XLIV (1971), p. 622.

26 Quoted in George F. Will, "Loose Talk about Strict Construction," *The Skeptic,* May/June 1974, p. 43. The other Madison quotations are from Berger, op. cit., p. 641.
27 Alexander Hamilton, John Jay, and James Madison, *The Federalist* (New York: The Modern Library, Inc., 1941), pp. 423–424.
28 This still does not resolve the problem of definition. What is "flagrant," what is "grave," and how do we measure degrees of harm? President Nixon's defenders warned that someday a liberal Democrat in the White House might be charged with such offenses, perhaps frivolously, by a conservative Congress.

If it does happen it will not be the first time conservatives made reckless use of impeachment. In 1970 Representative Gerald Ford, in words which were to dog him when he became Vice President, said that "an impeachable offense is whatever the House of Representatives considers it to be at a given moment in history." *Congressional Record,* CXVI (April 15, 1970), H 3113–14. (The occasion was a proposal to impeach a liberal Supreme Court Justice, William O. Douglas, reportedly in retaliation for the Senate's rejection of two Nixon nominees to the high bench.) Three years later, Attorney General Richard Kleindienst carried loose construction to the edge of nihilism when he told Senate committee members that if they didn't like Nixon's use of executive privilege they could always impeach him. How, he was asked, could they impeach the President if they were not allowed to subpoena witnesses from the executive branch? "You don't need evidence to impeach a President," he answered, "only votes." (The atmosphere was "so unreal," one Senator later said, "I wondered if it was really me—if I hadn't parted from my senses.") *New York Times,* Apr. 15, 1973, I A, p. 2. The danger that the Ford-Kleindienst approach might someday prevail in Congress had led some students of the subject to argue that impeachment should be reviewable in the courts. Court review seems contrary to the language of the impeachment article, which says that "the Senate shall have sole power to try all impeachments," but its proponents reply that in *Powell v. McCormick,* 395 U.S. 486 (1969) the Supreme Court invalidated the House's expulsion of Representative Adam Clayton Powell despite the Constitution's assertion that "each House shall be the Judge of the . . . Qualifications of its own members." See Berger, op. cit., pp. 650ff. Nevertheless, once we admit Hamilton's characterization of impeachment as a "POLITICAL" process, it is hard to accept the idea of court review, which would not only prolong a painful process but involve the judiciary in an area which lacks clear-cut judicial standards.
29 Alexis de Tocqueville, *Democracy in America* (New York: Vintage Books, Random House, Inc., 1945), I, p. 290.
30 *Marbury v. Madison,* 1 Cranch 137 (1803).
31 Quoted in Henry J. Abraham, *The Judicial Process* (New York: Oxford University Press, 1962), p. 298.
32 Edward S. Corwin, *The President: Office and Powers,* 4th rev. ed., (New York: New York University Press, 1962), p. 298.
33 *Hirabayashi v. United States,* 320 U.S. 81 (1943); *Korematsu v. United States,* 323 U.S. 214 (1944); *Ex parte Endo,* 323 U.S. 283 (1944).
34 *In re Neagle,* 135 U.S. 1 (1890); *In re Debs,* 158 U.S. 564 (1895). The *Neagle* case was discussed in the previous chapter.
35 *Youngstown Sheet & Tube Co. v. Sawyer,* 343 U.S. 579 (1952).
36 *United States v. United States District Court,* 407 U.S. 307 (1972). This case is sometimes cited as the "Keith decision," after District Judge Damon J. Keith, who made the original decision.
37 *New York Times Company v. United States,* 403 U.S. 714 (1971).

38 Max Weber, "Bureaucracy," in H. H. Gerth and C. Wright Mills, eds., *From Max Weber: Essays in Sociology* (New York: Oxford University Press, 1946), p. 196.
39 Ibid.
40 Quoted in Marriner S. Eccles, *Beckoning Frontiers* (New York: Knopf Publishing Co., 1951), p. 336.
41 Quoted in Richard E. Neustadt, *Presidential Power: The Politics of Leadership* (New York: John Wiley & Sons, Inc., 1962), p. 9.
42 *New York Times,* July 19, 1974, p. 14.
43 *New York Times,* June 7, 1974, p. 1.
44 The memo from which these quotations are taken is reprinted in *The Watergate Hearings: Break-in and Cover-up* (New York: Bantam Books, Inc., 1973), pp. 752–755.
45 Weber, op. cit.
46 Peter Woll and Rochelle Jones, "Bureaucratic Defense in Depth," *The Nation,* CCXVIII (Sept. 17, 1973), p. 231.
47 President's Committee on Administrative Management, *Administrative Management in the Government of the United States* (Washington: Government Printing Office, 1937), p. 36.
48 *Humphrey's Executor v. United States,* 295 U.S. 602 (1935).
49 *New York Times,* July 9, 1974, p. 25.
50 *New York Times,* July 25, 1974, p. 20.
51 James MacGregor Burns, "Keeping the President in Line," *New York Times,* Apr. 8, 1973, p. 15.
52 News conference, San Clemente, Calif., Aug. 22, 1973. Reprinted in the Watergate Hearings, op. cit., pp. 726–727.
53 *New York Times,* Sept. 5, 1973, p. 1.
54 Theodore C. Sorensen, *Kennedy* (New York: Harper & Row, Publishers, Incorporated, 1965), p. 321.
55 Ibid.
56 David Wise, *The Politics of Lying* (New York: Vintage Books, Random House, Inc., 1973), chap.2.
57 Quoted in ibid., p. 360.
58 "Playboy Interview: Walter Cronkite," *Playboy,* XX (June 1973), p. 90.
59 James David Barber, *The Presidential Character: Predicting Performance in the White House* (Englewood Cliffs, N.J.: Prentice-Hall, Inc., 1972).
60 Schlesinger, op. cit., pp. 254–255. See also Schlesinger, "What If We *Don't* Impeach Him?," *Harper's* CCXLVIII (May 1974), p. 12 and passim.
61 Michael Novak, "Dividing Presidential Functions," *New York Times,* May 9, 1974, p. 43.
62 Barbara W. Tuchman, "Should We Abolish the Presidency?," *New York Times,* Feb. 13, 1973, p. 37.
63 Quoted in Schlesinger, op. cit., p. 383.
64 Tuchman, op. cit.
65 Rossiter, op. cit., pp. 72–73.
66 Corwin, op. cit., p. 297.
67 Ibid., p. 298.

Chapter 10

Democracy and Judicial Review

Though she bends him she obeys him,
Though she draws him yet she follows. . . .

Henry Wadsworth Longfellow

This chapter will consider several aspects of the Supreme Court and the federal judiciary, but one central question runs through it like a red thread: Is judicial review compatible with democracy? Judicial review can be defined as the practice followed by our courts of passing on the constitutionality of laws and other governmental acts during the course of judicial proceedings.[1] In America, federal courts, and ultimately the Supreme Court, have the power to nullify state and federal laws as well as executive actions by declaring them contrary to the United States Constitution.

The central question of this chapter cannot be ignored by anyone who believes in democracy. Whatever else democracy means, it certainly means popular government. What kind of government is that which authorizes a nine-person Supreme Court, appointed for life, to nullify the will of the people's elected representatives?

It often seems that our attitude toward the practice of judicial review turns on the question of "whose ox is being gored." If *my* ox—a law favored by me—is the one struck down by the Supreme Court, am I not likely to denounce the rule of "nine old men"? But if the ox belongs to someone else, and it menaces *my* liberties, am I not likely to praise the activist Court as a "palladium of freedom"—or something like that? Judicial review, and the willingness of the Court to use it, has enjoyed a kind of seesaw celebration in American history. Business interests championed it during the early days of the Republic, and again during the first third of this century, as a safeguard against "radical" regulatory legislation. Civil libertarians became its defenders from the 1940s up to the present.

No matter what the year or era, someone can always be found to defend the Court or denounce it—depending on what the Court happens to be striking down. But the larger question remains: How can the Court presume to strike down *any* law, whether "good" or "bad," which has the support of a popular majority? This is not to suggest that democracy implies a subservient judiciary, like a khaki-clad "people's tribunal." In Great Britain the judges wear wigs, and maintain a tradition of independence that is at least the equal of their American counterparts. But no British court has the power to declare unconstitutional a statute passed by Parliament. British courts may interpret parliamentary statutes and (more commonly) administrative acts based upon these statutes, but the courts may never void such a statute. Parliament is supreme in Great Britain. In Walter Bagehot's words, "there is nothing the British Parliament cannot do except transform a man into a woman and a woman into a man."[2]

Legislative supremacy is not so difficult to reconcile with democratic theory, but what about judicial supremacy? What happens when the last word rests with five out of nine people, responsible to no one, and appointed years ago by Presidents we may now wish to forget? Is it not strange that we permit this five-person majority to reverse the decisions of a popular majority? Yet this is what happens every time the Supreme Court declares a law unconstitutional. Robert H. Jackson, a critic of judicial activism even after he was himself appointed to the Court, considered it "a doctrine wholly incompatible with faith in democracy."[3] Max Lerner put it more picturesquely: "Scratch a fervent believer in judicial supremacy, and like as not you will find someone with a bitterness about democracy. The two are as close as skin and skeleton."[4]

Is this bitterness necessarily in the bones of everyone who favors the active use of judicial review? We cannot X-ray or psychoanalyze them all, but we can at least take a closer look at the origins, the limitations, and the use of judicial review at various periods in our history. Then perhaps we can reach some conclusions about its compatibility with democracy.

ORIGINS OF JUDICIAL REVIEW

Although the Constitution does not explicitly provide for judicial review, the idea of courts overturning unconstitutional legislation seems to have been commonly accepted in eighteenth-century America; it was not considered controversial by the framers of the Constitution or by the conventions which ratified it.[5] The framers were worried about legislative, not judicial, tyranny. At the end of the Revolution the new state legislatures had passed a variety of measures—laws forgiving prerevolutionary debts, emitting paper money, taxing commerce which crossed their borders—which alarmed many of the participants in the Constitutional Convention. The judiciary, then, was to serve as a barrier against dangerous innovation, a protector of minorities, a guardian of the people's basic charter. In *Federalist 78,* Alexander Hamilton argued that judicial review was an essential means of enforcing the limitations on government prescribed in the Constitution.

> Limitations of this kind can be preserved in practice no other way than through the medium of courts of justice, whose duty it must be to declare all acts contrary to the manifest tenor of the Constitution void.[6]

This power to declare laws unconstitutional does not, Hamilton insisted, mean that the judicial branch is superior to the legislative branch. "It only supposes that the power of the people is superior to both. . . ."[7] The Constitution represents the settled and carefully considered will of the people. It is the basic charter under which the people have decided to govern themselves. The legislators are merely the agents of the people, acting with a temporary grant of power but acting *under* the Constitution. Legislators, as agents of the people, are bound to respect the people's charter, including the limitations on legislative power which are written into it. And if they refuse to? This is where the judiciary plays its vital role. By declaring unconstitutional acts to be null and void, the judiciary protects the people against their agents.

Hamilton anticipated two objections to this reasoning. First, what gives the judiciary such a special claim to protect the people against violations of the Constitution? His answer to this was that the "interpretation of the laws is the proper and peculiar province of the courts."[8] The Constitution must be regarded as a law. It follows, therefore, that the courts are the proper vehicles for interpreting both statutory and constitutional law. Judges are specially trained for this function, and life tenure lets them concentrate upon it without fear of political retribution.

The second objection anticipated by Hamilton turns upon the meaning of "the people." What if the people *themselves* authorize their agents to violate the Constitution? Hamilton's answer is to appeal from the people drunk to the people sober. James Russell Lowell once said that our written Constitution is an obstacle "to the whim, but not to the will of the people."[9] Hamilton's analysis proceeds along the same lines. Whatever "momentary inclination happens to lay hold of a majority" of the legislators' constituents, the courts have the duty to nullify laws if they violate the long-term will of the people as expressed in the Constitution.

> Until the people have, by some solemn and authoritative act, annulled or changed the established form, it is binding upon themselves collectively, as well as individually; and no presumption, or even knowledge, of their sentiments, can warrant their representatives in a departure from it, prior to such an act.[10]

In other words, if we want to change our basic charter, we must amend it. If our basic charter could be amended by any simple legislative act, it would no longer be basic: The people's long-term will would be sacrificed to transient passions and temporary majorities.

Marbury v. Madison

Chief Justice John Marshall used reasoning similar to Hamilton's in the landmark Supreme Court case *Marbury v. Madison* (1803),[11] which established judicial review as a precedent. The case arose out of the following circumstances. In the waning days of the Adams administration, the President, already defeated in the election by Jefferson, began appointing his fellow Federalists en masse to judicial posts before leaving office. "The Federalists," Jefferson complained, "have retired into the Judiciary as a stronghold . . . and from that battery all the works of republicanism are to be beaten down and erased."[12] In the last hours of the Adams administration the flood of appointments signed by the lame-duck President and sealed by his acting Secretary of State—who was none other than John Marshall—became so intense that Marshall mistakenly left some in his office before departing. The next day the new Secretary of State, James Madison, came upon them. One of the appointments, to the position of justice of the peace, belonged to one William Marbury, and this obscure individual began a legal action of profound significance, though it hardly seemed so at the time: He went directly to the Supreme Court and asked for a writ of mandamus, a court order commanding Madison to deliver the appointment to him. Acting Secretary of State John Marshall had now become Chief Justice John Marshall, and, unmindful of any possible conflict of interest, was now in the position of deciding on Marbury's application for the writ. Here, surely, was a perfect example of what Jefferson feared: a Federalist Chief Justice beating down and erasing the works of republicanism by deciding a case involving a fellow-Federalist.

Yet Marshall faced a dilemma. If he followed what would seem to be his political inclinations and granted Marbury his writ, there remained a distinct possibility that Jefferson would simply ignore it. Then what? Jefferson's administration had been carried into office by a large and triumphant majority. A similar majority now dominated Congress. Marshall's party was already in its dotage, while his Court was in its infancy. Both would be helpless against a defiant President, especially one as popular as Thomas Jefferson, and nothing could be more demoralizing for the Court than to issue an order and have it disobeyed with impunity. Yet the other horn of the dilemma was no more pleasant to contemplate. For if Marshall bowed to superior force and turned down Marbury's request for a writ, would this not be a concession of defeat?

Marshall sidestepped the dilemma by, in a sense, having it both ways. Much of the opinion in *Marbury v. Madison* was devoted to scolding Thomas Jefferson. Yes, Marbury had a right to the commission, which had been duly signed and sealed; Jefferson had no right to withhold it from him. Yes, since he has a right, and the right has been violated, the laws of this country should indeed afford him a remedy. But when it came to the question of the particular relief prayed for by Marbury—a writ of mandamus—Marshall concluded that the Court had no power to issue it. In denying himself this power, however, Marshall claimed for the Court a far greater power: the power to declare federal laws unconstitutional.

The Court's power to issue writs of mandamus "in cases warranted by the principles and usages of law" was granted in Section 13 of the Judiciary Act of 1789. Marshall found this section unconstitutional because it sought to add to the

Court's original jurisdiction. It is unnecessary for our purposes to examine Marshall's reasoning on this point. The enduring issue of the case is one which Marshall treated almost parenthetically: Where does the Court derive its authority to declare federal statutes unconstitutional? Let us see what sort of answers we can wring out of Marshall.

The question "whether an Act, repugnant to the Constitution, can become the law of the land," was, Marshall observed, "deeply interesting," but "happily, not of an intricacy proportioned to its interest." The answer was simple: If any ordinary statute could supersede the Constitution, there would be no point in having a written Constitution, since legislators would not be bound by it. The trouble with Marshall's argument, however, is that it avoided a direct confrontation with the *truly* "interesting" question of the case. It is not hard to find adherents to the position that the Constitution should be supreme over statutes; of course the Constitution should be supreme. But the real question is: Which branch of government has the sovereign power to *interpret* the often Delphic language of the Constitution? What does it mean by an "establishment of religion"? "Due process of law"? "Commerce among the several states"? The meaning of these and other key clauses in the Constitution is still being debated, and probably will as long as the Constitution endures. What gives the Court special insight into the meaning of this loose and elusive language? What entitles *it* to have the last word?

Marshall does not directly answer this question, for the simple reason that he does not raise it, but he does at least imply an answer. In doing so, he borrows heavily from Hamilton's argument in *Federalist 78:* the argument based upon expertise, or specialization. Hamilton had said that "interpretation of the laws is the peculiar province of the courts." Marshall said: "It is emphatically the province and duty of the judicial department to say what the law is." This was the major premise. The unspoken minor premise was that the Constitution is a law. Thus follows the conclusion that the courts have the peculiar duty, the sovereign authority, to interpret the Constitution.

The weakest link in the syllogism is its minor premise, that the Constitution is a "law." Marshall himself in a later case distinguished the Constitution from a "legal code." The distinguishing characteristic of a legal code, Marshall was to note in another landmark case, *McCulloch v. Maryland* (1819),[13] is "prolixity," i. e., its extensiveness, resulting from the need to spell out everything in detail. A Constitution, or at least our federal Constitution,* avoids this kind of precision. If it tried to spell out everything in the manner of a legal code, it could scarcely be embraced by the human mind and "would probably never be understood by the public." By its very nature a constitution "requires, that only its great outlines should be marked" and its important objects designated. In other words, Marshall was saying that the Constitution was a vernacular document (it should be "understood by the public"), and one which was made to be flexible if not delib-

---

* Some of our state constitutions *do* approach the "prolixity" of a legal code. (New York's is published as a paperback book.) For this reason they need frequent revisions. One of the reasons our federal Constitution remains relatively brief is that it remains vague enough to let the Court "interpret" it to suit the needs of the times.

erately vague. This raises the question whether the Constitution can be considered a "law," or at any rate a "law" of the kind which the judiciary has the peculiar "province and duty" to interpret. The legal training of judges may make them experts on prolix legal codes, but does it make them experts on a broadly worded document like the Constitution? Should not prudence and plain common sense play a great role in interpreting such a document? And do judges have a monopoly on prudence and common sense?

These questions, surprisingly enough, were not raised at the time by critics of *Marbury v. Madison*. Jefferson was furious at Marshall—not, however, for invalidating a section of the Judiciary Act or claiming the power of judicial review, but for presuming to lecture him in the opinion. Marshall had turned a dilemma into a victory. Nothing could be done to him, nor could he even be defied, since he had commanded no one to do anything. His opinion was, as Professor Robert G. McCloskey has written, "a masterwork of indirection, a brilliant example of Marshall's capacity to sidestep danger while seeming to court it, to advance in one direction while his opponents were looking in another." The Court was "in the delightful position . . . of rejecting and assuming power in a single breath."[14]

The real heart of *Marbury v. Madison*—its invalidation of a federal statute—thus lay unchallenged for half a century. Not until *Dred Scott v. Sanford* (1857)[15] did the Court do so again. *Dred Scott* is probably best remembered as the case in which the Court ruled that American Negroes were neither United States citizens nor even human beings (in the sense of the Declaration of Independence: "All men are created equal") but pieces of property to be bought and sold like cattle. But the decision's importance for our purposes here is that *Dred Scott* also marked the second time in our history that the Court invalidated a federal law. The Court held the Missouri Compromise of 1821 unconstitutional because it prohibited slavery in the territories and thus deprived slaveowners of their "property." This time the Court's assertion of judicial review could not be passed over: Chief Justice Taney's cataclysmic opinion upset a delicate accommodation between North and South, inflamed abolitionist sentiment, and helped precipitate the Civil War. Immediately following the decision, a newspaperman in Washington wrote: "If epithets and denunciation could sink a judicial body, the Supreme Court of the United States would never be heard of again."[16]

Dred Scott severely damaged the authority of the Court. It was endorsed wholeheartedly only by spokesmen for the slave-owning South, a minority of the nation which would soon go down to defeat in a bitter civil war. Even those Northerners who were generally sympathetic to the Southern cause, like Stephen A. Douglas of Illinois, were embarrassed by the decision. Douglas's position had been that the people of the territories may or may not prohibit slavery, as they chose, but *Dred Scott* made that position untenable: It had made it clear that neither Congress nor any other body could prohibit slavery in the territories without depriving the slaveowners of their lawful "property." Even as it made political compromise impossible, the opinion in *Dred Scott* shocked many Americans by its moral insensitivity. Here was the highest court in the land, supposedly the keeper of the nation's conscience, discussing slavery as if it were merely another commercial transaction, and talking about human beings as if they were cattle or bales of cotton. Putting together all these features of the decision—its political absolutism, its moral insensitivity, its reckless support of a slaveocracy which was to be crushed in the Civil War—*Dred Scott* could not but undermine the Court's claim to be the ultimate interpreter of the nation's highest law. Horace Greeley, writing in his *New York Tribune,* declared that the decision was "entitled to just so much moral weight as would be the judgment of a majority of those congregated in any Washington bar-room."[17] Not for another generation, when the passions of the Civil War began to cool, did the Court begin to recover its depleted authority.

And authority, after all, is the Court's only resource. The Court commands no armies, controls no purse strings. Authority is a peculiar element in political life; it occupies a very slender zone between persuasion and force.[18] Like a tough little school teacher, it neither pleads nor coerces: It gets its way because it commands respect. That respect is dissipated when the Court abuses its authority—when it uses it too much, or in the wrong areas, or without making clear why it is using it. A muddled court, a confused court, a court which collides head-on with the sentiments of the nation, cannot expect to have its decisions prevail for long. By one means or another the Court will be "put in its place," unless it finds some means of restraining itself.

This is perhaps the best place, then, to consider some of the checks on the Supreme Court. The Court may have the last legal word on the interpretation of the Constitution, but ultimate sovereignty resides outside of the Court, in the American political process, which checks judicial pretensions at least as effectively as it checks those of Presidents.

CHECKS ON THE COURT

1 Self-imposed Checks One category of checks can be classified as the self-imposed variety. It grows out of the Court's appreciation of its limited function (and perhaps its appreciation of its own inherent powerlessness). Even the most presumptuous judge will readily admit that judges are not legislators, that their duty is not to draft statutes. In theory, if not always in practice, the Supreme Court limits itself to deciding "cases and controversies" as provided in Article III of the Constitution. Courts are not supposed to issue advisory opinions, or stray from the issues of the immediate case. (Yet they depart from this rule often enough to make *obiter dictum*—Latin for "remark by the way"—an item in the lawyer's lexicon.) Parties to a suit must show that they have a substantial interest in the outcome of the case, that the whole controversy is not just a moot case in order to elicit the Court's opinion. Since 1849, in the case of *Luther v. Borden,* the Court has also refused to decide what it calls "political questions." In *Luther* the Court ruled that it had no authority to decide which of two governments struggling for supremacy in Rhode Island was the lawful one. Since then, the Court has invoked the doctrine of "political questions" in a number of cases. To cite one of the most prominent: Until 1962 the Court refused to decide on the constitutionality of legislative apportionment because "courts ought not to enter this political thicket."[19] But in *Baker v. Carr* (1962)[20] the Court in effect reversed itself by ruling that the constitutionality of Tennessee's apportionment was a "justiciable" issue, an issue which was proper for courts to resolve. In its opinion in *Baker* the Court tried to arrange into coherent categories the scattering of cases in which the Court had refused to rule on the grounds of "political" questions. The categories were boiled down to three: first, controversies which could better be resolved by a coequal branch of government (Congress or the President); second, controversies for which "judicially manageable" standards were lacking; third, controversies in which a judicial decision would risk embarrassment abroad or grave disturbance at home. In such cases as these, the Court was supposed to keep hands off, allowing the issues to be resolved by the political process.

Yet it was not long before the Court began whittling out exceptions. In 1969 the House of Representatives excluded Adam Clayton Powell, the flamboyant Harlem Congressman, from his seat in Congress. When Powell sued, the District Court ruled that the issue could not be decided by a court since it was "political." The District Court's dismissal was affirmed by the Court of Appeals on the grounds that a decision in Powell's favor would "bring about a direct confrontation with a coequal branch."[21] (The opinion was by Judge Warren Burger, who is now Chief Justice of the Supreme Court.) Yet the Supreme Court did exactly that—it reversed the lower courts and decided in favor of the Harlem Congressman.[22] "Political questions" thus remains an elusive doctrine in constitutional law. Evidently the Court still considers some issues as "political," though we are not exactly sure which issues. The question of a war's legality is still one in which the Court is unlikely to second-guess other branches of government.[23] On the other hand, a President's assertion of "executive privilege" does not prevent the Court from deciding on his claim to withhold information from a prosecutor.[24]

2 Legislation: Limiting the Court's Jurisdiction   Congress and/or the President have not always waited for the Court to restrain itself. The most direct and perhaps most regrettable act by Congress to clip the wings of the Court came during Reconstruction, when Congress passed a law removing a whole category of cases from the Court's appellate jurisdiction. Article III, Section 2, of the Constitution gives the Court appellate jurisdiction, both as to law and to fact, "with such exceptions and under such circumstances, as Congress shall make." On the face of it this "excepting clause" seems to give Congress the power to withdraw areas of law from the Court's jurisdiction.[25] In 1868, when the Court's reputation was at its nadir, Congress exercised this power by removing from the Court's jurisdiction a whole area of law involving habeas corpus. The following year, in *ex parte McCardle*[26]—which the Court obligingly held over for decision until Congress completed action—the Court meekly acquiesced: It refused to decide a case involving habeas corpus, citing the new law which removed it from the Court's jurisdiction. This was bitter medicine for the Court to swallow, and it has never had to do it again. Not until 1957 did either house of Congress come close to removing any area from the Court's jurisdiction. That was the year when Senator William E. Jenner of Indiana managed to get a jurisdiction-trimming bill reported out of the Senate Judiciary Committee. Complaining that recent decisions of the Court were "undermining the efforts of the people's representatives

... to meet and master the Communist plot," Senator Jenner proposed a long catalog of areas relating to "subversion" which would be outside the jurisdiction of federal courts.[27] The fact that the Senate did not pass the Jenner bill is less remarkable than the narrow margin by which it was rejected—forty-one to forty.

3 Impeachment Congress can impeach members of the Supreme Court. The method is the same as that for impeaching a President. The sun-bleached billboards in the South urging the impeachment of Earl Warren never did achieve their goal, but recent events make it clear that impeachment is more than a "rusted blunderbuss." Still, it seems unlikely that Congress today* would ever impeach a judge for no more than his or her opinions, so impeachment is probably not a very effective weapon against "judicial supremacy." The attempt to impeach Justice William O. Douglas in 1970 never went anywhere, even though the leader of the effort in the House, one Gerald R. Ford, assured his fellow members of Congress that they needed *no* grounds for impeaching a Supreme Court Justice—whim was sufficient. An "impeachable offense" Ford defined as "whatever the House of Representatives considers it to be at a given moment in history."[28] Some desultory charges concerning alleged conflicts of interest were made against Douglas, but, very clearly, it was the Justice's long record of liberal opinions on and off the bench which lay behind the impeachment effort—that, plus the Nixon team's desire to retaliate against liberals for leading the successful fight in the Senate to defeat two conservative Southerners nominated by Nixon to the Supreme Court.

4 Appointment The President, with Senate approval, can appoint new members to the Court. This does not assure that the President's appointees will be the President's puppets—far from it! This was made abundantly clear in the case of *United States v. Nixon*—the famous "Watergate tapes" case—when every one of Nixon's appointees who participated in the decision voted against the man who appointed them. But without being unduly loyal to his person, the President's appointees are likely to share his overall political views. Even this generalization must be regarded cautiously, because relatively conservative Presidents (like Eisenhower) have appointed justices who were liberals, or at least turned out to be liberals (like Earl Warren), and relatively liberal Presidents (like Kennedy) have appointed some rather conservative justices (like Byron White) to

---

* In times past, however, serious efforts have been made to remove federal judges because of their opinions. In the early 1800s, the anti-Republican opinions of certain Federalist judges provoked a Republican effort to remove them from the bench. Between 1803 and 1805 impeachment proceedings were instituted against John Pickering, a federal judge in New Hampshire, and against Supreme Court Justice Samuel Chase. Pickering was easily brought down, since he was not only an anti-Republican but an alcoholic and an incompetent. After being impeached by the House, he did not even show up for his trial in the Senate, and was removed from office after his counsel had pleaded his client's insanity. But Supreme Court Justice Samuel Chase—the Republicans' big game—got away. He had sorely vexed the Republicans by using his position on the bench to deliver lengthy harangues against the works of Republicanism in his opinions, and he had also played a prominent role in the sedition trials against Republican spokesmen. (See the account of the Alien and Sedition Acts in Chapter 1, above.) Chase was charged with a variety of offenses centering on trial misconduct, manifest partiality, and lack of respect for the dignity of his position. He was impeached by the House, but acquitted in the Senate.

the Court. Nevertheless, the generalization does hold up fairly well during crisis periods in the Court's history, when crusading Presidents show themselves ready to change the Court's direction by changing its personnel.

In this respect Nixon enjoyed a bonanza: four vacancies in three years. It usually takes many more years for so many justices to die or retire. Life tenure thus shields the Court from the political pressures of the moment. In *Federalist 78* Hamilton considered this to be the Court's special virtue, but seldom has a virtue been so frustrating. In the 1930s President Roosevelt watched with mounting anger as the "nine old men," as he called them, who were appointed by his predecessors, struck down a number of New Deal measures. After winning a landslide reelection in 1936, Roosevelt decided that he had a popular mandate to check the Court once and for all. He accordingly proposed legislation which would have had the effect of enlarging the Court from nine to fifteen members; Roosevelt would then be able to "pack" the Court with six new members of his own choosing. Somewhat disingenuously called a plan to "assist" the Court, it never got out of committee. Some of Roosevelt's warmest supporters were aghast, and one of his opponents in Congress read a letter from the Chief Justice declaring that the Court, thank you, needed no "assistance." As it turned out, the court-packing scheme proved unnecessary. While it was still being debated the Court's "swing" member, Justice Owen Roberts, who often voted with its conservative wing, voted to uphold a major New Deal measure, tipping the balance to the liberal side. (This was to be characterized derisively and probably unjustly as "the switch in time that saved nine.") Within a few years, moreover, some of the more rock-ribbed conservatives began to retire, permitting Roosevelt to change the Court's membership—and its opinions. Among the many lessons to be derived from the Court-packing attempt is a simple one in arithmetic: There is no constitutional reason why the Court's membership must be limited to nine. At various times in our history the Congress has enlarged or decreased the Court's membership; it could do so again, even though it declined the invitation in 1937.

5 Constitutional Amendment The most formal check on the Court's power, the legitimacy of which no one can question, is the amendment process. The method has been used in three instances: *Chisholm v. Georgia* in 1793 (which allowed a plaintiff living in one state to sue another state)[29] was nullified by the Eleventh Amendment five years later; *Dred Scott*, decided in 1857, was overturned by the Thirteenth and Fourteenth Amendments in 1865 and 1868; the *Income Tax Cases* in 1895 (which invalidated the tax)[30] were reversed by the Sixteenth Amendment in 1913. Among the more recent proposals for amendments to undo Court decisions have been ones which would allow prayers in public schools, modify the Court's decisions on apportionment, and permit states to forbid abortion. But checking the Court by means of amendment is an extremely cumbersome process. Amendments must be proposed by two-thirds of both houses of Congress or by a convention called by Congress upon the application of two-thirds of the state legislatures. The proposed amendment must then be ratified by three-quarters of the state legislatures, or by conventions in three-quarters of the states.

6 Inherent, or Structural, Checks Aside from the five specific checks listed above, other limitations on the Court's power grow out of the very nature of the judicial process, which is inherently *passive* and *negative*. It is *passive* in the sense that cases must come to it. Unlike a legislature, the Court may not reach out to pass a law or conduct an investigation. It must wait until a case reaches it through the process of litigation. Often, this simply does not happen. Ninety percent of lower court decisions are never appealed. Those cases which *are* appealed to the Court, about 2,000 to 3,000 per year, would represent an impossible demand on the justices' time, so the Court hears only about 7 percent of the cases it is asked to review. The Court's role is also inherently *negative*. In the words of Carl Brent Swisher, "Where government action is concerned, the options of the court are limited: it may merely refrain from interference with what the government wants to do, or it may hold such action unauthorized or forbidden by the Constitution. It cannot propose and initiate alternative programs."[31] It is true, of course, that in deciding cases which involve the implementation of previous decisions (such as school desegregation and apportionment) the Court has provided guidelines and hints about the kinds of plans it considers appropriate, but the decision itself can only approve or disapprove a particular plan.

DOES THE COURT "MAKE" LAWS?

In following the foregoing account of checks on the Court, the reader may have felt a growing sense of uneasiness. It appears that the Court's interpretation of the Constitution is subject to considerable discretion on the part of the justices. If the decisions of the Court can be affected by whoever sits on it, if its opinions on what constitutes a "political question" can vary over the years, if the Court seems at times to respond to outside political pressures, if the Court can reverse itself—if all of this is so, isn't the Court more like a legislature than a judicial institution? "The interpretation of the laws is the proper and peculiar province of the courts," said Hamilton in *Federalist 78*. But isn't the Court doing more than "interpreting" the laws? Isn't it *making* laws?

The question should trouble anyone who loves democracy. If the Court were merely interpreting our laws and our Constitution, and if it were using some neutral, value-free formula for doing so, then the people's representatives would remain the only real lawmakers. Judges, of course, could hold them within the bounds of the Constitution, but that would seem fair enough in a democracy which holds the Constitution to be the supreme law of the land. But if the Court is really *making* laws, if the Court is primarily a *legislative* forum, then what kind of democracy is it that permits five out of nine people, appointed for life, to make rules governing a nation of over two hundred million? "For myself," said the late Learned Hand, himself a Circuit Court judge,

> it would be most irksome to be ruled by a bevy of Platonic Guardians, even if I knew how to choose them, which I assuredly do not. If they were in charge, I should miss the stimulus of living in a society where I have, at least theoretically, some part in the direction of public affairs. Of course I know how illusory would be the belief that my vote determined anything; but nevertheless when I go to the polls I have a satisfac-

tion in the sense that we are all engaged in a common venture. If you retort that a sheep in the flock may feel something like it; I reply, following Saint Francis, "My brother, the Sheep."[32]

The problem suggested by Hand—who was one of our most distinguished jurists—is serious enough for anyone who does not share Plato's disdain for democracy: If judicial review really involves a degree of policymaking, are we not being ruled by a "bevy of Platonic Guardians"? Or, to put the problem less rhetorically, how do we reconcile judicial lawmaking and democratic government?

Reconciling Judicial Activism and Democracy: Three Approaches

1 The "Slot-Machine" Theory One answer to the problem is simply to deny that the Justices *do* make law. For years this was the approach of those who would defend the Court against its critics. "Judicial power is never exercised for the purpose of giving effect to the will of the judge," Chief Justice Marshall said in 1824, "always for the purpose of giving effect to the will of the legislature; or in other words to the will of the law."[33] A few years earlier another justice put it this way: "It is not for Judges to listen to the voice of persuasive eloquence or popular appeal. We have nothing to do but pronounce the law as we find it. . . ."[34] The most memorable elaboration of this view came many years later, when Justice Roberts said in *United States v. Butler* (1936):

> When an act of Congress is appropriately challenged in the Courts as not conforming to the constitutional mandate the judiciary branch of the government has only one duty—to lay the Article of the Constitution which is invoked beside the statute which is challenged and to decide whether the latter squares with the former. All that the Court does, or can do, is to announce its considered judgment upon the question. The only power it has, if such it may be called, is the power of judgment.[35]

This has been called the "matching colors" or "slot machine" theory of the Court's decision-making process, because it insists that its justices merely lay the statute and the Constitution side by side and, as it were, pull the lever in order to test a statute's constitutionality. If this theory were correct we could save taxpayers' money by firing all the justices except one. We might not even need one. We could fire them *all* and replace them with a computer, "which, having been fed all the pertinent data, would automatically render the one and only proper decision."[36] Of course the "slot machine" theory is nonsense; a judge's political philosophy is bound to color his or her interpretation of the Constitution. We have probably all heard this line: "By golly, we need judges who will interpret the Constitution 'strictly.'" It sounds pleasing to the ear, but what does it mean? That the Court must take a restrictive view of governmental power? But where does the Constitution say that? The answer is that the Constitution says it nowhere, so that the advocate of "strict" construction is reading a meaning into the Constitution that he thinks *should* be there. Actually, "strict interpretation" is so empty an expression that it now means exactly the opposite of what it used to mean. It used to stand for a restrictive view of governmental power and a correspondingly active use of judicial review to strike down "radical" laws, but in recent years it has come to mean an expansive view of governmental power, at least in the field of "law 'n' order," thus a reluctance to use judicial review against the actions of law enforcement officials. It is our political philosophy, then, which not only determines whether we interpret the Constitution "strictly" or "broadly," but actually fills in the meaning of these terms. Judges, then, simply cannot avoid using some sort of judicial philosophy as a guide to interpreting the Constitution.

2 Judicial Self-Restraint   But perhaps judges can keep their philosophies from getting out of hand. "The first requisite for one who sits in judgment on legislative acts is that he be a philosopher," Professor Paul Freund has written. The second, he added, "is that he be not too philosophical."[37] This suggests a second method of reconciling judicial review and democratic government, one which is far more candid than the futile attempt to deny that judges make law. This second method begins with a frank acknowledgment that a judge's political philosophy does play a role in constitutional interpretation. From this premise the argument goes on to conclude that the justices should therefore restrain themselves in the use of judicial review. The executive and Congress, Justice Stone said in 1936, are restrained by the ballot box, "but the only check upon our own exercise of power is our own self-restraint."[38] One advocate of judicial self-restraint, the late Professor Alexander Bickel, considered "judicial review a deviant institution in American democracy."[39] For the same reasons the late Justice Felix Frankfurter called the Supreme Court "the non-democratic organ of our government," adding that "the powers exercised by this Court are inherently oligarchic."[40] In this view, the worst mistake that the members of the Court could make is to strike down a law because they consider it unwise. The wisdom or unwisdom of a statute is a matter for legislators to decide; they are the ones elected by the people. Justice Frankfurter stated this view forcefully in a famous dissent:

> As a member of this Court I am not justified in writing my private notions of policy into the Constitution. . . . For the removal of unwise laws from the statute books lies not to the courts but to the Ballot and to the processes of democratic government. . . . In neither situation is our function comparable to that of a legislature or are we free to act as though we were a super-legislature . . . responsibility for legislation lies with the legislatures, answerable as they are directly to the people.[41]

Advocates of judicial self-restraint thus respond to the criticism that judicial review is undemocratic by admitting it. They do not, however, carry the logic of this admission to its conclusion by advocating the abolition of judicial review. They temper logic with realism—judicial review is here to stay, and, oligarchical or not, it needs to be used once in a while. They ask only that it be used sparingly, in extreme cases.

Philosophically, judicial self-restraint was an outgrowth of the movement toward "legal realism," a movement begun at the turn of the century, which found "the life of the law," as Oliver Wendell Holmes called it, not in logic but experience. The Constitution, therefore, should not be treated "as if it contained only the axioms and corollaries of a book of mathematics."[42] Politically, judicial self-restraint was a reaction to the various "nine old men" who sat on the Court during the first third of the twentieth century, the majority of whom did seem to regard the Constitution as a book of mathematics—or metaphysics—and thus managed to invalidate scores of important regulatory laws on the basis of subtle concepts and hairline distinctions. A state law regulating working hours was struck down because it violated "liberty of contract" (a phrase found nowhere in the Constitution);[43] a federal law prohibiting the interstate sale of products made by child labor was struck down because it interfered with state prerogatives.[44] Federal codes regulating prices and setting terms of fair competition were struck down for similar reasons.[45] For a time it seemed that the whole structure of the New Deal was about to be dismantled for offending the metaphysical canons of five Supreme Court justices. In this context judicial self-restraint appeared to many as the perfect antidote to what used to be called "judicial supremacy." The problem we have posed for ourselves in this chapter thus seems to admit of an easy solution. Judicial review can be reconciled with democracy—pragmatically, if not with iron logic—simply by not being used very often. "Put thy sword back into thy scabbard!" If the nine people on the Court will but heed this biblical injunction more often, they will get along tolerably well in a democracy. Judicial self-restraint is the ointment for healing the wounds inflicted by judicial supremacy.

But consider the fly in the ointment.

By the 1940s it had become obvious. World War II focused public attention on the need for "patriotism," and the public authorities reacted by fostering compulsory patriotism. The Pennsylvania legislature compelled all schoolchildren to salute the flag each morning. Saluting the flag violates the religious precepts of Jehovah's Witnesses (who consider the flag a "graven image" in terms of Exodus XX, 4), so one member of the sect brought a case to the Court under the First Amendment, which guarantees the "free exercise" of religion. Justice Frankfurter was perfectly consistent with his philosophy of self-restraint when he announced the Court's opinion upholding the compulsory flag salute:

> Perhaps it is best . . . to give to the least popular sect leave from conformities like those here in issue. But the courtroom is not the arena for debating issues of educational policy. . . . So to hold would in effect make us the school board for the country. That authority has not been given to this Court, nor should we assume it.[46]

The decision, though not important as a precedent—it was overturned two years later—points up a serious problem in the doctrine of judicial self-retraint: What about cases which involve civil liberties and the equal protection of the law? If the justices exercise self-restraint in those cases, don't they end up approving some pretty repressive laws? To arrange some of these draconic statutes or government procedures into approximate historical periods: In the forties the Court was called upon to consider compulsory flag salutes and the incarceration of Japanese-Americans in barbed-wire-enclosed detention camps; in the fifties Jim Crow laws and anticommunist statutes came under review; in the sixties the Court was preoccupied with legislative apportionment and criminal procedure. If the Court practiced "self-restraint" in all these cases, where would we be today? Would racial apartheid ever have been declared illegal in America? Would legislative malapportionment be corrected? Would the "red scare" or the "hippie scare," or whatever the latest "scare," be kept from generating legislative witch-hunts? Would free speech be protected? Would the evidence obtained from coerced confessions and illegal searches and seizures be kept out of the courtroom? Would Jehovah's Witnesses and other religious minorities be protected against those officials who like to fit everyone to their own model of "Americanism"? Not until the sixties did Congress enact meaningful civil rights legislation, and it is questionable whether Congress would have taken this step without the groundwork laid by the Court decisions of the fifties. As for the other areas mentioned above, if progress has been made in the direction of greater freedom, it has sometimes occurred despite, rather than because of, the elected branches of government.

3 "Preferred Position" During the forties and fifties a new breed of judicial activists appeared on the bench. Unlike the activists of the thirties, they were extremely reluctant to strike down economic legislation, or legislation regulating property rights; to such legislation they would grant the "presumption of constitutionality," and here they were in perfect agreement with the advocates of judicial self-restraint. But when it came to laws regulating speech, press, religion, or association, they believed that the Court must never presume constitutionality: A serious burden should then rest upon the government to show that such laws are constitutional. The new activists thus insisted that the Bill of Rights, and particularly the First Amendment, should occupy a "preferred position" in the hierarchy of liberties protected by the Constitution. Laws which touch upon "preferred liberties" must be given a much greater degree of judicial scrutiny than those which regulate other liberties. Property rights are one thing, but the right to speak is something far more precious.

But why? Why the double standard? Why should civil liberties be accorded a "preferred position"? For example, why should the right to say what I please be preferred over the right to pay what I please, charge what I please, and hire whom I please? What is so special about the freedoms spelled out in the Bill of Rights?

Why "Preferred"? (a) Justice Black's Answer One answer is that they *are* spelled out. The late Justice Hugo Black granted a preferred position to First Amendment freedoms because he believed that the language of the amendment left no room for interpretation. "Congress shall make no law [abridging freedom of speech] is composed of plain words easily understood."[47] Black's critics accused him of constitutional fundamentalism, and, while this criticism may be too harsh, it did seem at times as though Black read his Constitution much the same as William Jennings Bryan read his Bible: If the Bible says that Jonah was swallowed by a big fish, he was swallowed by a big fish. In an opinion on an obscenity case, Black said: "I read 'no law . . . abridging' to mean *no law abridging*"[48] (emphasis Black's). It is hard to quarrel with that, but the trouble comes when we try to go beyond it. The First Amendment also prohibits an "establishment of religion." What does that mean today? School prayers? Aid to parochial schools? The Constitution does not tell us. Even the guarantee of "freedom of speech" is more nebulous than it first appears. Does it protect false or harmful advertising? Should the Federal Trade Commission be prevented from regulating Madison Avenue hucksters? Or vicious, lying slander? The Constitution does not tell us. And what, after all, *is* speech? Does it include incitement—the right, for instance, to falsely shout "fire" in a crowded theater? Is there such a thing as "symbolic"speech, such as the burning of a flag or a draft card, which the First Amendment should protect? The Constitution does not tell us. The going gets even more slippery when we go beyond the First Amendment to the other amendments in the Bill of Rights. The Fourth Amendment, for example, guarantees our security against "unreasonable searches and seizures." What is "unreasonable"? And what is a "search" or a "seizure"? Tapping a phone? Bugging? No matter how many times we read over the Constitution, it refuses to answer these questions. If it did tell us, "in plain words, easily understood," how could the Justices disagree with each other—as they do so often? Justice Black's approach verges toward a liberal version of the "slot machine" theory, discussed earlier in this chapter in connection with the conservative Court of the thirties. In both the liberal and the conservative variants of the theory, a spurious objectivity is assigned to the language of the Constitution; in both variants the justice considers himself somewhat like an automaton, merely reading what is "there" in the document without any intrusion of the justice's own philosophy.

Why "Preferred"? (b) Justice Stone's Answer If the late Justice Black failed to provide a convincing argument for "preferred" liberties, is there any other defense for such a double standard? In a footnote to the Court's position in an otherwise obscure case, *United States v. Caroline Products* (1938), Justice Harlan Fiske Stone said:

> There may be narrower scope for operation of the presumption of constitutionality when legislation appears on its face to be within a specific prohibition of the Constitution, such as those of the first ten amendments, which are deemed equally specific when held to be embraced within the Fourteenth. . . .
>
> It is unnecessary to consider now whether legislation which restricts those *political processes which can ordinarily be expected to bring about repeal of undesirable legislation,* is to be subjected to more exacting judicial scrutiny under the general provisions of the Fourteenth Amendment than are most types of legislation. . . .
>
> Nor need we enquire whether similar considerations enter into review of statutes directed at particular religions, . . . or national, . . . or racial minorities, . . . whether prejudice against discrete and insular minorities may be a special condition, which tends seriously to *curtail the operation of those political processes* ordinarily to be relied upon to protect minorities and which may call for a correspondingly more searching judicial inquiry.[49]

Tentatively and parenthetically, Stone seemed to be moving toward grounding "preferred" freedom on something other than constitutional fundamentalism. What he seemed to be saying is that civil liberties are more precious than economic liberties because they are essential to the democratic process. If the state puts a crimp in people's profits, they still remain at liberty to seek legislative remedies: They can complain, petition, lobby, and support candidates pledged to repeal the offending statute. But if the state interferes with their civil rights and liberties—the right to speak, to vote, to get a decent education, to mingle with others on the basis of equality, to enjoy political and social rights—it has taken away the means of effective redress. Imagine Justice Frankfurter telling a Mississippi Negro in the 1950s that he should look "not to the courts but to the ballot and the processes of democratic government"! (To Frankfurter's credit he did not. He voted with the other members of the Warren Court in striking down Jim Crow laws. But it is hard to see how he reconciled his vote with his philosophy of self-restraint and his scorn for "preferred" liberties. In voting to compel the South to desegregate its schools, Frankfurter seemed to be disregarding his own earlier warning in the flag salute case—that the Court must not act as if it were a "school board for the country.")

Until the chief obstacles to democracy are removed, it is cruel and silly to expect people to find relief for injustice in the "processes of democratic government." Instead of merely accepting the fiction of democratic government, courts must inquire into the concrete facts. If robust speech is banned or discouraged, if would-be voters are terrorized, if legislative apportionment is wildly out of line, if police intimidation is a common occurrence (especially for the poor), if dissidents are forced into conformity, if racial minorities are treated unequally, then democracy is frustrated from the outset. In such situations it becomes necessary for the "oligarchy" on the Supreme Court to . . . to what? Not to rule others but to destroy the barriers to popular rule. In this role the Court is not a "bevy of Platonic Guardians" but a demolition team in the service of democracy.

THE WARREN COURT

It was characteristic of the late Chief Justice Warren that he considered his Court's most fundamental reform to be the decision in *Baker v. Carr* (1962),[50] the case which decided that courts could strike down the system of unequal voting resulting from malapportionment.

> If everyone in this country has an opportunity to participate in his government on equal terms with everyone else, and can share in electing representatives who will be truly representative of the entire community and not some special interest, then most of the problems that we are confronted with would be solved through the political process rather than through the courts.[51]

Warren believed that *Brown v. Board of Education,* perhaps the most memorable decision of his Court, might not have been necessary if the states had been apportioned properly in the first place. "If *Baker v. Carr* had been in existence 50 years ago, we would have saved ourself acute racial troubles. But as it was, the court just had to decide."[52]

"The court just had to decide." This sums up in capsule form the peculiar situation in which the Warren Court found itself. In 1953, when Earl Warren was appointed Chief Justice, Jim Crow was still a way of life in the South, and even in the North blacks were denied equal access to housing, schools, jobs, and public accommodations. The McCarthy period was at its zenith, and local authorities were enforcing "Americanism" with even greater zeal than their federal counterparts. Vaguely worded obscenity and slander laws chilled free speech a few more degrees. Rural-dominated state legislatures refused to reapportion themselves despite population shifts which were producing disparities of at least 2 to 1 between the least and most populated districts (in some states 223 and 242 to 1). The tactics of local law-enforcement authorities were often primitive and brutal. In some states a defendant in a criminal trial had to do without a lawyer if he or she had no money to afford one, and in many local areas defendants (usually the poor and uneducated) were convicted on the basis of coerced confessions and illegally seized evidence. Neither the President, nor Congress, nor the state and local authorities were doing anything to remove these obstacles to a working democracy. Vested interests, inertia, a failure of nerve, and a failure of imagination all conspired to produce what C. Wright Mills called "the conservative mood" which paralyzed the elected branches of government in the 1950s. In this context the Court's activism during this period was exactly the opposite of its activism during the thirties. In the latter case the Court was active in *preventing* change. The Court of the thirties was a dam holding back the flood of "socialistic" legislation enacted by the New Deal Congress.

But we must use an entirely different metaphor to describe the activist Court of the fifties: Far from being a dam, it was more like a dynamite charge for loosening a logjam. It opened up the possibility of basic reform of American institutions, and in some cases forced action out of the other branches, as when President Eisenhower had to send troops to Little Rock, Arkansas, to enforce school desegregation. (Eisenhower considered his appointment of Warren "the biggest damned-fool mistake I ever made.")[53] And while the Brown case was being argued before the Court, one of its justices remarked that "the reason this case is here was that action couldn't be obtained from Congress."[54] The Warren Court has been criticized for inconsistency and a failure to explain itself. Nevertheless,

> there was an underlying philosophy which bound much of the Warren Court's work: a philosophy which held that, when other branches of government are not capable of responding to the rightful demands and grievances of the people, it is the proper role of the Court to exercise leadership and initiate social change.[55]

The Warren Court had its weaknesses, which will be discussed shortly, but timidity was not one of them. Power, we have said repeatedly in this book, abhors a vacuum. The Warren Court stepped into the vacuum of power left by the President and Congress. It "seized the initiative in formulating solutions to pressing national problems which Congress and the White House had chosen largely to ignore."[56]

We have been considering solutions to the dilemma of judicial review *versus* democracy. One solution is to deny that the Court really makes law. The "slot machine" solution was rejected for the reasons given earlier in this chapter. The second solution admits that judicial review and popular government are irreconcilable, and therefore urges that judicial review be used sparingly in *all* cases, and that *all* statutes should enjoy the presumption of constitutionality. The third solution distinguishes between laws which regulate property as opposed to laws which interfere with foundations of effective participation: voting, petitioning, uninhibited discussion, education to the limit of our potential so that we can effectively participate in discussion, freedom from debilitating racial segregation, and security in our homes and private lives. Much of this can be placed under the heading of "minority rights," but here the minority is not an entrenched business minority, lording over the majority by its wealth and connections, but a beleaguered political minority seeking to be heard. One student of the Court's history put the question this way: "Can the Supreme Court block the will of the majority in the name of minorities and still remain a democratic institution?" His answer: It depends.

> When the minority rights protected are those of property, the answer is probably "no." Between 1890 and 1937, the Supreme Court actually retarded the growth of democracy. When, on the other hand, judicial review serves to give a minority, otherwise barred, access to the political process, it implements rather than limits free government. Majorities—and this is a key point of democratic theory—are in flux. Tomorrow's majority may have a different composition as well as different goals. Defense of the political rights of minorities thus becomes, not the antithesis of majority rule, but its very foundation. The majority must leave open the political process by which it can be replaced when no longer able to command majority support.[57]

Judicial review, then, need not be considered the enemy of democracy. Directed toward the proper ends it has proven to be an indispensable ally. In this respect the accomplishments of the Warren Court have been monumental. "There can be very few of us," Archibald Cox has observed, "who would wish to revive the caste system under the pretense of 'separate but equal'; to restore rural domination of state legislatures by systematic malapportionment; or to revive trial without the aid of counsel or through the psychological extortion of confessions."[58] The Warren Court, said another observer of it, "opened wide the judicial windows to allow the fresh, modern air of democracy to blow over and revitalize these blighted areas of state activities."[59]

Critics of the Warren Court

This does not mean that everyone who criticized the Warren Court wanted to close the window on democracy or turn back the clock on social progress. Many thoughtful and responsible critics—whose commitment to democratic values cannot be questioned—have pointed to the Warren Court's tendency to substitute rhetoric for careful reasoning, its inadequate legal craftsmanship, its excessive use of *per curiam* opinions (brief opinions which announce decisions without going into the reasons), its reliance upon preconceived ideas.[60] Professor Philip Kurland has pointed to the Court's tendency to strike out in new directions with scant regard for precedent.[61] Alexander Bickel noted the inconsistent and unpredictable course of its decisions, particularly those on obscenity.[62]

But carefully reasoned critiques of the Warren Court, such as those of Kurland and Bickel, are not the kind that play in Peoria. In the supercharged atmosphere of the 1960s, a highly emotional backlash was building against the Warren Court. It was to have a major effect upon the future of the Supreme Court.

By 1968 "law 'n' order" had become a staple of campaign rhetoric. The beauty of the expression was that, like "strict construction," it meant whatever the listener wanted it to mean. To some it meant "getting tough" or "cracking down" on muggers and rapists, to others it meant finally "cleaning out" organized crime, to others it meant jailing war resisters, or putting hippies to work or blacks "in their place." All these aspirations, and not all of them were ignoble, seemed to have been frustrated by the decisions of the Warren Court. Two decisions of the Warren Court's later years had become particularly controversial: the *Escobedo* and *Miranda* cases.

Danny Escobedo was arrested and interrogated about his brother-in-law's murder. Escobedo asked repeatedly to see his lawyer during the interrogation at the jailhouse, while his lawyer stood in the next room demanding to see his client. The requests were denied. He was then tricked into confessing complicity in the murder, and convicted on the basis of the confession. The Court in *Escobedo v. Illinois* (1964)[63] agreed with the petitioner that his Sixth Amendment right "to have the assistance of counsel for his defense" had been violated. But the Sixth Amendment is concerned with the right to fair *trials*. It says nothing about lawyers in the stationhouse. The court had extended the Sixth Amendment's right to counsel to cover any pretrial questioning which takes on an accusatory climate.

In *Miranda v. Arizona* (1966)[64] the Court spelled out the implications of *Escobedo* and other previous decisions. Any accused person must be given four specific warnings by the police:

1 He must be told that he has a right to remain silent.
2 He must be told that any statement he makes may be used against him.
3 He must be told that he has a right to have counsel present during the interrogation.
4 He must be told that if he cannot afford counsel, an attorney will be appointed for him.

The Court in *Miranda* went on to specify other safeguards for the protection of the accused. For example, when the suspect is alone with the police and in any way indicates that he does not wish to be interrogated, the police may not question him.

Even within the Court the *Escobedo* and *Miranda* decisions did not go down easily. Both were products of narrow 5-4 majorities, and the dissents were sometimes bitter. Dissenting in *Miranda,* Justice White declared that the Court's decision could very well "return a killer, a rapist or other criminal to the streets and to the environment which produced him, to repeat his crime whenever it pleases him."[65] Outside the Court, out on the political hustings, the decisions fueled many political campaigns, including the presidential campaign of Richard M. Nixon.

Nixon promised to get tough on lawbreakers by firing Ramsey Clark, President Johnsons's liberal Attorney General, and appointing a real "law 'n' order" man—John Mitchell. He promised an all-out war on crime by using wiretaps and electronic surveillance, which Clark had refused to use. And he promised to appoint to the Court "strict constructionists who saw their duty as interpreting and not making law."[66] We have already seen that these words have little meaning in themselves, but in the context of 1968 they were a signal that Nixon intended to appoint justices who would not be overly attached to "preferred freedoms."

THE BURGER COURT

Nixon's first opportunity to keep this promise came with the retirement of Chief Justice Earl Warren in June of 1969. In Warren's place Nixon appointed Circuit Judge Warren E. Burger, an outspoken critic of the Warren Court. Burger had caught Nixon's attention by a speech he made in 1968 which asserted that "a large measure of responsibility for much of the bitterness in American life today over the administration of criminal justice can fairly be laid to the Supreme Court. To put this in simple terms, the Supreme Court helped make the problems we now have."[67]

Warren's seat was not the only empty one on the bench during the first few months of the Nixon administration. A month before Warren's retirement, Associate Justice Abe Fortas, a Johnson appointee, resigned under a cloud of suspicion concerning payments he was receiving from a Wall Street financier while serving on the Court. To fill the vacancy Nixon first nominated Clement F. Haynsworth, a South Carolina Circuit judge. When Haynsworth's nomination was rejected by the Senate, he nominated G. Harrold Carswell, another Southerner, whose nomination was likewise rejected. (The Haynsworth-Carswell episode was recounted in the last chapter.) Nixon finally won Senate approval for his nomination of Circuit Judge Harry Blackmun, a lifelong friend of Chief Justice Burger. Then two more members of the Warren Court, Hugo Black and John Marshall Harlan, resigned while ill and died soon after, leaving two more vacancies. Nixon nominated Lewis Powell (a Southern conservative and a critic of the *Miranda* decision) and William H. Rehnquist (Nixon's assistant Attorney General, who often appeared before congressional committees to defend wiretapping, surveillance, and mass arrests of demonstrators). The Senate confirmed.

"The Nixon quads," as the four most recent appointees are sometimes called, have voted together in a number of key cases. With the additional weight of one or both of the Warren Court's "swing" members (Justices Stewart and White), they have been able to tilt the Court away from the direction it seemed to be headed in the sixties. Here are a few examples of Burger Court decisions:

Civil rights The Court ruled that the lower courts had no authority to order busing between city and suburb. The Nixon appointees voted together with Justice Stewart to form a 5-4 majority. In another case, involving racial discrimination at a Moose lodge which held a liquor license, the Court ruled that such discrimination was not "state action" within the reach of federal civil rights laws. In that case the Nixon appointees were joined by Stewart and White. In a case related to civil rights—the issue was not race but inequality of income—the Burger Court decided that school districts in a state could finance public schools unequally, with richer districts providing their children with better educational facilities than those which the poorer districts could afford for their children. This decision, which ratified existing practices throughout the nation, was made by the four Nixon justices plus Justice Stewart.

Civil liberties The Court refused to invalidate a state requirement that all state employees take an oath to oppose violent, illegal, or unconstitutional overthrow of the government. (The Nixon appointees plus White and Stewart prevailing.) In another case the Court denied the right to challenge military surveillance as unconstitutional. (The Nixon appointees plus White.) Then of course there was the *Caldwell* case, discussed in Chapter 1, in which the Court rejected the claim of a newspaper reporter that the First Amendment protected him against having to disclose his source of information, a source to whom he had promised anonymity. (The Nixon appointees plus White.)

Criminal procedures The Court allowed less-than-unanimous state juries to find defendants guilty in criminal cases. (The Nixon appointees plus White.) The Court narrowed the right to counsel by holding that it did not apply to preindictment proceedings such as lineups. (The Nixon appointees plus White.) The Court decided it was constitutional for grand juries to use illegally acquired evidence as a basis for questioning witnesses. (The Nixon appointees plus White and Stewart.)

The "Nixon quads" do not always agree, nor do they always favor the conservative side of civil-liberty cases. (A case in point: the "Keith" decision of 1972, denying the Attorney General the power to wiretap in domestic matters without a court warrant.)[68] But they have stuck together often enough, and tilted toward the right, to change the balance of power on the Court. They were the first admittedly ideological appointments, the first appointments made specifically for the purpose of changing the Court's direction, since Roosevelt's appointments began at the end of the thirties. But Roosevelt appointed men like Felix Frankfurter, Robert H. Jackson, and Hugo Black—men of enormous stature, honored even by those who sharply disagreed with their views. In contrast, what are we to make of Nixon's appointment of the genial William Rehnquist, "the President's lawyer's lawyer," as he was known in the Washington community? Readers of the White House tape transcripts may remember this exchange between *"P."* and John Ehrlichman:

> *P.* You remember the meeting we had when I told that group of clowns we had around there. Renchburg and that group.
> *E.* Renchquist.
> *P.* Yeah. Rehnquist.[69]

For Nixon, ideology seemed to be not only the prime consideration but the only one of any importance (except perhaps regional considerations, but these were related: Nixon wanted not Southerners, but conservative white Southerners, on the bench.) It almost seemed that the Court was being treated like a precinct caucus, to be stacked with people who would "vote right." For such purposes "clowns" are acceptable, provided that they are conservative clowns. Mediocrities may be all right too: Senator Roman Hruska, leader of the pro-Carswell forces in the Senate, said that even if Carswell were mediocre, "there are a lot of mediocre judges and people and lawyers. They are entitled to a little representation, aren't they?"[70] This is not to say that all four Nixon appointees have turned out to be mediocrities (Powell, for one, is regarded as a careful craftsman) but that for Nixon judicial stature seemed to be a purely accidental by-product of the selection process.

FUTURE OF THE COURT

It seems clear that the Court will pursue a more conservative course in the coming years than it did during the Warren period. By 1972 Professor Paul Bender had already detected a difference in overall philosophy:

> Underlying many of the Nixon Justices' opinions so far seems to be an attitude toward constitutional adjudication that is quite opposite to the philosophy that emerged during the Warren years. . . . Many of the Warren Court decisions . . . seemed grounded on a deep and growing skepticism about whether officials can really be expected, if left to their own devices, to be sensitive to individual constitutional rights in exercising their enormous powers over men's lives, liberty, and property. Because of this skepticism, the Warren Court often set up protective rules or presumptions, and authorized federal judicial scrutiny where none had existed before, to try to insure adherence to constitutional values. . . .
>
> The Nixon Justices, on the other hand, seem to assume that those in high places with power over their fellow men will almost inevitably act correctly and responsibly. This leads to the placing of enormous burdens on litigants and defendants to show that their rights have been violated, to the limitation of protective rules and presumptions, and to close restriction upon federal judicial inquiry into constitutional allegations. The new justices tend to see the Warren Court's safeguards as unwarranted intrusions into the activities of other branches of government.[71]

Perhaps it was inevitable that the Court should begin to retreat from the activism of the Warren years. American sentiment—from which courts are not forever isolated—travels in cycles, or, more precisely, pendulum swings, and the force which reverses a trend is the widespread feeling that "now they've gone too far." Back in 1966 Justice Harlan's dissent in *Miranda* struck a prophetic note: "This court is forever adding new stories to the temples of Constitutional law, and the temples have a way of collapsing when one story too many is added." Arguably, the retreat from the heyday of the Warren Court may even be considered prudent if, as some suspected, Warren's activism was on a collision course with public opinion. In the summer of 1974 Burger's court narrowly rejected city-suburban busing as a means of achieving racial balance. The decision probably would have gone the other way if the "Nixon quads" had not filled some vacancies formerly occupied by liberals. If the Court had approved this method of integrating schools, would the Court's authority have survived the inevitable uproar? Would we see revivals, this time successful revivals, of court-packing schemes, or new legislation to strip the Court of jurisdiction? Worse, would the decision simply be disobeyed by state and local authorities? Conceivably, the

1974 busing decision of the Burger Court was another historic "switch in time that saved nine." The Nixon appointees may have saved the Court from a fatal collision with public opinion.

But these are musings and speculations. What seems more certain is that the Warren Court left behind a rich legacy to democracy, a legacy which can be qualified but not erased. *Si monumentum requiris, circumspice,* reads the tomb of Sir Christopher Wren, the great British architect. "If you want to see his monument, look around." May not the same be said of the Warren Court? Men and women of all races and creeds are freer and more nearly equal because of the Court's decisions in the areas of civil liberties and civil rights. Our Congress and state legislatures are better linked to where the people are in modern America because of the Court's apportionment decisions. Indeed, unlike monuments of stone, the achievements of the Warren Court have acquired a life of their own. Even as the Burger Court falls back to a neo-Frankfurtian posture of "self-restraint," the possibility of legislative remedies is greater now than it was when Frankfurter expounded the doctrine; at least blacks can vote and all can expect to have their votes weighed equally. It also appears, when we compare the Watergate investigations with the investigations of alleged Communists of a generation past, that our elected branches have become more mature and responsible. Turning to the areas of civil rights and liberties, we see that blacks have found a new sense of pride which makes unthinkable any return to Jim Crow—whites, even Southern whites, now accept that fact—and today speech is freer and the rights of the accused more secure than at any period in our history.

Perhaps—and this must be considered with great caution—we have reached a point in the development of democracy where judicial review should be used sparingly. But if this is the case, it is partly because it was used so unsparingly, so boldly, during the years of legislative stagnation.

NOTES

1. Charles L. Black, Jr., *The People and the Court* (New York: The Macmillan Company, 1960), pp. 2–3. Some writers would restrict the meaning of judicial review only to those cases which involve coordinate branches (e.g., when a federal court declares the actions of the Congress or the President to be unconstitutional, not when it passes upon the constitutionality of state actions), but the broader definition seems more in keeping with general usage.
2. Quoted in Henry J. Abraham, *The Judicial Process* (New York: Oxford University Press, 1962), p. 260.
3. Robert H. Jackson, *The Supreme Court in the American System of Government* (Cambridge, Mass.: Harvard University Press, 1955), p. 58.
4. Max Lerner, *Ideas Are Weapons* (New York: The Viking Press, Inc., 1939), p. 474.
5. Raoul Berger, *Congress v. The Supreme Court* (Cambridge, Mass.: Harvard University Press, 1969), Chaps. 1–6, passim.
6. Alexander Hamilton, John Jay, James Madison, *The Federalist* (New York: The Modern Library, 1937), p. 505.
7. Ibid., p. 506.
8. Ibid.
9. Quoted in Charles Warren, *The Supreme Court in United States History* (Boston: Little, Brown and Company, 1926), II, p. 751.

10 Hamilton, op. cit., p. 509.
11 1 Cranch 137.
12 Warren, op. cit., I, p. 193
13 4 Wheat. 316.
14 Robert G. McCloskey, *The American Supreme Court* (Chicago: University of Chicago Press, 1960), pp. 40, 42, 43.
15 19 How. 393.
16 Quoted in Charles S. Hyneman, *The Supreme Court on Trial* (New York: Atherton Press, Inc., 1963), p. 31.
17 Quoted in Harry Carman and Harold Syrett, *A History of the American People* (New York: Alfred A. Knopf, Inc., 1957), II, p. 584.
18 Hannah Arendt, *Between Past and Future: Six Exercises in Political Thought* (New York: The Viking Press, Inc., 1961), p. 93.
19 *Colegrove v. Green,* 328 U. S. 549 (1946).
20 369 U. S. 186.
21 *Powell v. McCormack,* 395 F. 2nd, 577 (1968).
22 *Powell v. McCormack,* 395 U. S. 486 (1969).
23 See Chapter 9.
24 *United States v. Nixon* (1974).
25 But see Berger, op. cit., chap. 9. Berger concedes that "the inference is warranted if we look no further than the terms of the clause itself" (p. 285), but Berger's study of the historical background convinced him that the "exceptions" clause was intended to qualify the Court's appellate jurisdiction over matters of *fact* but not over matters of *law*
26 7 Wall. 506 91869).
27 *Limitation of Appellate Jurisdiction of the United States Supreme Court,* "Hearings before the Sub-Committee to Investigate the Administration of the Internal Security Act and Other Internal Security Laws of the Committee on the Judiciary," United States Senate, 85th Congress, 1st Sess., Part I, pp. 2–13.
28 *Congressional Record,* Apr. 15, 1970, pp. H3113–14.
29 2 Dall. 419 (1793).
30 *Pollock v. Farmer's Loan & Trust Co.,* 158 U. S. 601 (1895).
31 Carl Brent Swisher, *The Supreme Court in Modern Role* (New York: New York University Press, 1958), p. 64.
32 Learned Hand, *The Bill of Rights* (Cambridge, Mass.: Harvard University Press, 1958), n. 2 at pp. 73–74.
33 *Osborne v. Bank of United States,* 9 Wheat. 738 (1824).
34 Justice Story in *Dartmouth College v. Woodward,* 4 Wheat 518 (1819).
35 *United States v. Butler,* 297 U. S. 1 (1936).
36 Arthur A. North, S. J., *The Supreme Court: Judicial Process and Judicial Politics* (New York: Appleton-Century-Crofts, Inc., 1966), p. 7.
37 Paul A. Freund, *The Supreme Court of the United States* (Cleveland and New York: The World Publishing Company, 1961), p. 106.
38 *United States v. Butler,* 297 U. S. 1, 79.
39 Alexander M. Bickel, *The Least Dangerous Branch* (Indianapolis, Ind.: The Bobbs-Merrill Company, Inc., 1962), p. 18.
40 *American Federation of Labor v. American Sash and Door Co.,* 336 U. S. 538, 555 (1949).
41 *West Virginia State Board of Education v. Barnette,* 319 U. S. 624 (1943).
42 Oliver Wendell Holmes, Jr., *The Common Law* (Boston: Little, Brown and Company, 1881), p. 1.

43 *Lochner v. New York,* 198 U. S. 45 (1905).
44 *Hammer v. Dagenhart,* 247 U. S. 251 (1918).
45 *Carter v. Carter Coal Co.,* 298 U. S. 238 (1936); *Schechter Poultry Corp. v. United States,* 295 U. S. 495 (1935).
46 *Minersville School District v. Gobitis,* 310 U. S. 586 (1940).
47 Quoted in Bickel, op. cit., p. 88.
48 *Smith v. California,* 361 U. S. 147, 157 (1959).
49 *United States v. Caroline Products Co.,* 304 U. S. 144, 152–154 (1938).
50 369 U. S. 186.
51 Quoted in Warren's obituary, *New York Times.*
52 Ibid.
53 Ibid.
54 Leon Friedman, ed., *Argument: The Oral Argument before the Supreme Court in Brown v. Board of Education of Topeka,* 1952–1955 (New York: Chelsea House Publishers, 1969), pp. 243–244.
55 Louis M. Kohlmeier, Jr., *"God Save This Honorable Court!"* (New York: Charles Scribner's Sons, 1972), p. 44.
56 Ibid., p. 55.
57 Alpheus Thomas Mason, *The Supreme Court from Taft to Warren,* revised and enlarged edition (Baton Rouge: Louisiana State University Press, 1968), p. 201.
58 Archibald Cox, *The Warren Court: Constitutional Decision as an Instrument of Reform* (Cambridge, Mass.: Harvard University Press, 1968), p. 12.
59 North, op. cit., p. 180.
60 For a useful summary of these criticisms, see Clifford M. Lytle, *The Warren Court and Its Critics* (Tucson: University of Arizona Press, 1968), chap. 7, passim.
61 Philip B. Kurland, *Politics, the Constitution, and the Warren Court* (Chicago: The University of Chicago Press, 1970), p. 186.
62 Alexander M. Bickel, *The Supreme Court and the Idea of Progress* (New York: Harper & Row, Publishers, Incorporated, 1970), pp. 50 ff. and passim.
63 378 U. S. 478.
64 384 U. S. 436.
65 Ibid.
66 *Nixon on the Issues* (New York: Nixon-Agnew Campaign Committee, 1968), pp. 85–86.
67 Warren E. Burger, Address before the Ohio Judicial Conference, Columbus, Ohio, Sept. 4, 1968.
68 *United States v. United States District Court of Michigan, Southern Division,* 92 S. Ct. 2125 (1972).
69 Quoted in the *New York Times,* July 19, 1974, p. 14.
70 Quoted in Kohlmeier, op. cit., p. 154.
71 Paul Bender, "The Techniques of Subtle Erosion," *Harper's,* CCXLV (December 1972), pp. 25–26.

Conclusion: What Is America?

At a news conference on March 26, 1975, Secretary of State Henry Kissinger raised a basic and troubling question about the American people. In criticizing the reluctance of Congress to provide more military aid to the Thieu regime in South Vietnam, Kissinger said: "The problem we face in Indochina is an elementary problem of what kind of people we are. . . ." If we ever become known as a people who would "destroy our allies," he added, then we shall suffer "very serious consequences" in the world.[1] In the spring of 1975 Americans had reason to wonder whether any more donations—on top of the $150 billion and the 55,000 lives already donated—could possibly prop up South Vietnam, whose fleeing troops had just abandoned over $600 million in military equipment. Yet the Secretary's question, despite its rhetorical purposes, was still a very pertinent one: What kind of a people are we? What *is* America, and what are its true commitments?

We grope to find some sort of perspective for viewing ourselves today. One way to look at ourselves is to compare ourselves today with what we were in the not-so-distant past. If the Secretary's remarks were made at a news conference in 1960, they probably would have gotten a better reception from the press and public than they did in the spring of 1975. America was different at the beginning of the sixties, and it looked at itself very differently than it does today. To appreciate this difference, to get the feel of it, it might be useful to go back to a famous episode of 1960—and a famous contemporary account of that episode.

The Making of the President 1960 was the first of a series of books written by Theodore H. White on the quadrennial race for the American Presidency. It was a remarkable book, written with enormous gusto. It caught the flavor of one of the most exciting presidential campaigns in our history, a campaign which produced an unusually large voter turnout at election time, and which generated great hopes about America's future. White's book was on the best-seller list for more than forty weeks, and the critics were ecstatic. Yet in one sense the reviewer for the *New York Times* may actually have been understating matters when he said that "no book has caught the heartbeat of a campaign as strikingly. . . ." For White's book caught more than the heartbeat of a campaign. It seemed to expose the heart of the nation in the early sixties.

Eisenhower Doldrums

At the end of the fifties America was just emerging from eight years of the Eisenhower administration. Internationally these were years of almost constant tension—there was a cold war on—but domestically they were often called "the Eisenhower doldrums." The Democrats, after 1956, dominated Congress, and a Republican was in the White House. Not only was there little agreement between President and Congress in the area of domestic affairs, there was little definition of policy from either branch. The lack of clarity, the general fuzziness about domestic goals seemed to make many Americans uneasy and anxious. There was a sense of drift, of stagnation, even of decadence in that era of fishtail fenders and emerging suburbs. A Committee on National Goals was appointed by the President to come up with some answers, and *Life* magazine ran a whole series on "national purpose," but none of it seemed to help. Possibly the spirit of the times was personified in Bernard Mergendeiler, the anxious young man in Jules Feiffer's comic strips, who was constantly telling everybody of his self-doubts and his identity problems.

But the Communists seemed to have no Bernards in their midst. Steeled by the discipline of their ideology and their rulers, they were leaping forward confidently in armaments, space technology, and other critical areas of cold war competition.

It was not that America lacked the *potential* to win the cold war. There was plenty of raw energy among the young people in the land, but because of the lack of inspiring leadership this energy was being drained away into fraternity-boy hijinks, career-climbing, beatnik dissipations, or other forms of self-indulgence. There was also plenty of potential dedication in the land, but it was locked up. It needed to be tapped.

Enter Kennedy

A young and handsome war hero named John F. Kennedy was able to seize upon that combination of anxiety and restlessness which suffused the America of the early sixties, and he did it so well that he seemed to mesmerize his opponent, causing Richard Nixon to repeat the slogans and promises of Kennedy, lamely adding that he could perform them better. Kennedy's chief campaign theme was "we've got to get this country moving again." It was a sign of the times, and Kennedy's canny perception of those times, that nobody thought to ask: moving *where?*

Even if someone did ask, the question would have seemed irrelevant. The heart of the problem, Kennedy reminded his audiences in speech after speech, was the slow "spread of Communist influence" in the world. "Influence," as Kennedy used it, was broad enough to contain a variety of meanings: guerrilla insurgencies, weapons hegemony (a mythical "missile gap" was one of his campaign issues), and the fact that Russia was beating us to the moon. These Russian advances, Kennedy maintained, did not result from any inherent or insurmountable advantages on the Soviet side. They were achieved through default, they resulted from the erosion of America's influence and prestige. And what caused the erosion? Softness. After eight years of Eisenhower, America's muscles had grown slack. The solution, therefore, was obvious: Instead of sitting around worrying about our "national purpose," let us get up and find it—through action! "Let us begin," Kennedy later said in his inaugural address. Begin what? Begin moving. Moving where? But "where?" was not the right question. The question was "moving what?" and the answer was "moving our muscles." It is surely beside the point to ask the morning jogger where he is going. As Kennedy's administration was to emphasize the virtues of physical fitness, his campaign was structured around the need for political fitness, or "vigor"—especially vigor in the White House.

Need for "Crisis"

Only one obstacle stood in the way. In the past, great outbursts of presidential energy had been triggered by crisis. The drama of Roosevelt's first "hundred days," for example, had been in response to the nation's economic crisis. World War II and Korea had also elicited great acts from the White House. "But," said Theodore White, "John F. Kennedy was inaugurated in 1961, to preside over a nation to which no crisis was clear." True, the nation "sensed crisis," but it was a crisis "locked in the womb of time . . . whose countenance was still unclear."[2] Remote and unclear dangers do not make for good crises. So the difficulty remained: If Kennedy was to get America out of the slough of despondency he needed a crisis, but there wasn't any around.

We can only speculate about how Kennedy and his advisers tried to resolve this "crisis crisis." What is true beyond dispute is that, under Kennedy, the nation was suddenly confronted with a whole series of dramatic "crises" throughout the world. In his memoirs, Theodore Sorensen, Kennedy's special assistant, listed no less than fourteen of them during the first eight months of the Kennedy administration*—even before the most famous crisis of all, "the Cuban missile crisis," adrenalized the nation with images of nuclear apocalypse. Kennedy's "thousand days" were not very productive in the area of domestic legislation, but they were certainly rich in "crises."

Now let us turn to America today. If America seems to be suffering from anything in the late seventies, it is from a surfeit of political melodrama. After nearly twenty years of assassinations, riots, and wars, the nation has had quite

---

* Theodore C. Sorensen, *Kennedy* (New York: Harper & Row, Publishers, Incorporated, 1965), pp. 292–293. In retrospect, some of the "crises" on Sorensen's list, like the resignation of the President of Brazil, would seem to strain the term a bit, while others, like the Bay of Pigs disaster, were certainly crises—but crises of our own making.

enough of crisis—and of the crisis mentality that goes along with it. But what was it that charged up the atmosphere in the first place? What were the roots of the national nervousness that sometimes boiled over into frenzy? What was it that led to the urge always to "do something"—and fast—with little concern for *what* we were doing? No doubt the causes were many and varied. Only one possible source of the crisis mentality is suggested here: the problem of national identity and the false solution to the problem.

NATIONAL IDENTITY—A FALSE SOLUTION

The questions raised by Secretary of State Kissinger in 1975 were the same questions troubling America at the end of the fifties. What *is* America? What does it stand for? What role should it play in the world, and what are its responsibilities to its own people? At the end of the fifties, America, like Hamlet, seemed to be frozen into immobility by its failure to resolve these questions. To Kennedy and his New Frontiersmen the best tonic for a nation sicklied o'er with the pale cast of thought was red-blooded *action*. National identity? Whatever else America is, it is a nation of *doers*. Americans had performed many noble deeds in the world, and with a new infusion of vigor we would perform many more. *What,* exactly, those noble deeds were to be was less important than that they be noble, and deeds are noble when they are performed courageously, gracefully, neatly.[3] James Bond, one of Kennedy's favorite fictional heroes, did not worry his head about the morality or the ultimate purposes of his acts—he was in Her Majesty's Service, and that was enough. What he did was to carry out his missions with a maximum of coolness, style, and good cheer. For Kennedy, as for Bond, the ends themselves seemed to be subordinate to the daring process of securing them. Novelist Norman Mailer called him an "existential" President, and, while nobody, including Mailer, seemed to know exactly what that meant, it sounded like a good word to characterize the new activism which Kennedy brought to the Presidency: an idealization of sheer movement. It was as if the art of governing consisted only in "doing things," and never in wondering whether to do things, or in asking why some things had to be done. The spirit of Camelot was like a TV "action-drama," a tale with a very thin plot and hardly any dialogue—just terse, no-nonsense exchanges between the characters. And its spirit was contagious. With the help of the news media the public was soon caught up in the drama of hastily assembled meetings, around-the-clock vigils, men with briefcases and grave expressions entering, emerging, striding briskly from one crisis conference to another.

It was under Johnson and Nixon that the American people had to pay the bill for the unreflective activism which had become the hallmark of the American Presidency. Under Johnson they were dragged into the most tragically futile enterprise in the nation's history—a war which was conducted with an almost manic energy, but without any clear or consistent explanation as to *why* it had to be fought. (One day it was to protect American interests, the next day it might be to defend freedom, to honor treaty commitments, or simply to fight communism. The White House would select one or another of these excuses according to the occasion, without any apparent realization that each had different implications—in some cases conflicting implications.) Under Nixon the nation seemed to have no clearly defined policies at all[4] but not because of sloth in the White House. The President and his men worked day and night, but subordinated all goals to the highest one of keeping Richard Nixon in office. To attain that goal one member of the Nixon team, Charles Colson, said he would walk over his grandmother; the other members were probably not prepared to go that far, but they seemed to have no compunctions about trampling the Constitution and laws of the United States.

The mood of post-Watergate America is in some ways reminiscent of the fifties. Apathy, not hysteria, hangs over the land. Uncertainty, not precipitous action, is what Americans are witnessing in the highest councils of government. Government and people alike, after a twelve-year binge of activism, seem to be suffering a prolonged hangover. The old questions of the late fifties have come back to haunt us as well, the troubling questions about America's role and goals.

But this time around there is at least one important difference: The cold war is over. The world is as tense as ever, peace is just as fragile as it was in the fifties, and détente with the Soviet Union is shaky at best. But America is no longer the commander-in-chief of "the free world," nor does the world even seem to divide so neatly into hemispheres of good and evil as it once did. Americans, the public opinion polls show, would rather let the dominoes fall than to prop up any more corrupt "anticommunist" dictators.[5] The nation is thus brought face to face with the problem of its identity. Our leaders can no longer divert us from it by galloping us off into another round of global activism.

THE QUESTION AGAIN: WHAT ARE WE?

The argument running through the pages of this book is that America does not have to define itself as a "first-rate power" in the world; it is far more important for America to act decently and humanely toward its own people, for it to respect its Constitution and its traditions of self-government and civil liberties. The argument has not been for "neoisolationism" or unilateral disarmament. America must always protect its interests through diplomacy, and if necessary through force. But neither war nor the arming of others for war ought to be conducted in the name of "national honor." In 1811 Thomas Jefferson warned about the hazards of "honor":

> However . . . we may have been reproached for persuing our Quaker system, time will affix the stamp of wisdom on it and the happiness and prosperity of our citizens will attest its merit. And this, I believe, is the only legitimate object of government and the first duty of governors, and not the slaughter of men and devastation of the countries placed under their care in pursuit of a fantastic honor unallied to virtue or happiness. . . .[6]

After Vietnam and Cambodia Americans know all they need to about the slaughter of people and the devastation of countries in the name of "honor"; after Watergate Americans know the emptiness of "honor" when it is divorced from honesty and decency. This book, therefore, has supplied no startling new insights, but rather has tried to sum up some of the lessons so painfully learned about America's purposes and potentials. What is America? What does it stand for? What is it capable of? Henry Kissinger's question as to "what kind of people we are" can no longer be dodged. This book has suggested some answers, and by looking back over its chapters we can see how these answers contrast with the answers from the days of Camelot. America, we have tried to say, is—

1 A Multiethnic Society   It seems obvious today that America is a land of many peoples and cultures. This was not obvious to Theodore White in 1960. On the contrary:

> It was obvious that the nation could not any longer live as two communities bearing two separate cultures, white and Negro, in its bosom. It was obvious that only education could bring the two cultures together in common standards.[7]

The implicit, and sometimes explicit, arrogance in this approach to race relations was explored in Chapter 3. First of all, America is not just black and white, but also several shades of brown, yellow, red, beige, and pink, often corresponding to different cultures; second, America has, within limits, always been able to survive and even thrive with different cultures in its "bosom"; third, whenever it has attempted to assimilate everyone into "common standards" of culture, it has weakened the very fibers of the rich and variegated culture that is peculiarly America. The real task, it now appears, is not to melt everyone down into the same culture but to find a common *political* meeting ground between races and groups—convergence, not assimilation.

2 The Land of Opportunity   America is a country based upon a decent standard of living. Nothing in our tradition calls for an absolute equality of income, but America is certainly committed to equality of opportunity, to the idea that hard work will produce rewards—and that there will be jobs for those who want to work.

> The American is a new man, who acts upon new principles. . . . From involuntary idleness, servile dependency, penury, and useless labor, he has passed to toils of a very different nature rewarded by ample subsistence. This is an American.[8]

Yet in the cities and the rural hollows of America today one encounters all too much "involuntary idleness" and "servile dependence." It was there in 1960, too, yet neither in Kennedy's campaign nor in Theodore White's book about it was there any real understanding of what a scandal poverty is in this land, what an affront it is to the promise of America. White interviewed the President-elect shortly after his inauguration. He let Kennedy "relax in conversation," and the conversation soon drifted back to the themes of the campaign. Kennedy had made some desultory remarks during the campaign about the problem of poverty, and he now declared himself in favor of a housing program and an education bill pending in Congress. "But all of that . . . was not the real problem. The real problem was out there (with a wave of his hand) out there in Laos, in the Congo, in Africa."[9] Chapter 2 of this book focused on the problem *in here,* in the cities and the suburbs and the countryside of America, the unresolved problem of poverty in the land of affluence—a problem from which it is increasingly difficult for the President, "with a wave of his hand," to divert his fellow citizens.

3   Sweet Land of Liberty   "The right to speak my mind out, that's America to me."* The popular song of the forties honored an ideal that was placed under severe strain in the next three decades: in the fifties, when dissenters had to be careful lest they be labeled "Communists," in the sixties and seventies when dissenters were spied upon by the army, the FBI, and the CIA, when their names ended up in data banks and on "enemy lists," when official threats, denunciations, and even burglaries were used by the government against critics.

But the larger problem, which was explored in Chapter 1, concerns an aspect of liberty sometimes ignored by proponents of the need for diversity. "The right to speak my mind out" implies the right to be heard, the right to a forum for communication. Putting it another way, liberty of speech implies the right of the public to hear a variety of points of view. When the First Amendment was written this was not really a problem, since there was such a wide variety of newspapers in the land. But by 1960 the consolidation of newspapers and the growth of "natural monopolies" like television had created, not an arena for divergent communication, but a machine with enormous potential for manipulation. "The web of American communications, influence and politics is so sensitive that when touched in the right way by men who know how, it clangs with instant response."[10] White's observation was accurate, and still is today. The trouble was that White was not complaining, he was boasting. In their exuberance over the communications revolution, many Americans in the early sixties ignored the fact that the media were conditioning Americans toward accepting a superficial, one-dimensional picture of reality. We now recognize that monopoly control by elites—"the men who know"—is a major obstacle to the *effective* meaning of free speech.

4   Secular Government, Government of Laws   In the tradition of American thought, our Revolution has come to stand for more than merely the severance of our ties to the British Crown. It has come to mean the rejection of all mystical humbug once connected with monarchy: the sacredness of the royal person, the monarch as one who is above the law, the divine right of kings, and so on. Traditionally, Americans have treated this nonsense with the contempt it deserves. Men are not angels, James Madison observed, so let us be careful to check our governing officials—and encourage them to check one another.

But somewhere between Herbert Hoover and John Kennedy this healthy irreverence had given way to something close to awe. By 1960 White was writing effusively of "the immense and majestic forces and influence that belong to any President."[11] What should have been watched with a very jaundiced eye was now treated as a source of national grandeur: an unchecked power which could per-

---

* *The House I Live In.* Copyright © 1942 by Chappell & Co., Inc. Copyright renewed. All rights reserved. Used by permission of Chappell & Co., Inc.

mit the "great" President to live "beyond the law" and to act at once as "Chief Executive and High Priest of American life."[12] Chapters 7 through 10 of this book have been based upon the plain old American view of government as something less than holy, something profane in fact, which needs to be balanced off against itself and kept within the framework of law.

5 A Democracy Above all, America is a nation committed to self-government. This implies a good deal of faith in the wisdom of ordinary people. But by 1960 no one apparently thought to question the unabashed elitism which runs throughout White's book. Foreign policy was where the real action was in 1960, and foreign affairs were "too detailed, too complex, too sophisticated for the public at large to grasp." The people must follow the lead of their President. "Where he leads, his party, his instruments, *above all his reluctant people,* must be persuaded to follow."[13]

In discussing voting, campaigning, pressure groups, and political parties in Chapters 4 through 6 we have tried to look at things differently—in fact, from the opposite end. We have attempted to study political leadership not as something which percolates down from above but as a force which bubbles up from below. We have recognized, of course, that most people ordinarily are not active in politics, and we have called attention to the role played by "counterelites"—demonstrators, whistle-blowers, public interest lobbies—in getting the public at large involved in the political process. But citizen involvement does not have to mean involvement in organized groups like Common Cause or Ralph Nader's, nor does it have to become an obsession or a full-time avocation. Revolutions, as Lenin once noted, cannot be undertaken on a part-time basis, but citizen action can. At various places in this book—for instance, at the end of Chapters 4, 5, and 7—we have hinted at what citizens can do to lead their leaders. Let us now pause to elaborate.

CITIZEN LEADERSHIP: THE RANGE OF POSSIBILITIES

Not everyone writing in the early sixties was quite as ready as Theodore White to ignore the potential of grass-roots initiatives. In an essay published in 1962 the sociologists David Riesman and Michael Maccoby contrasted the "hypocrisy" of the modern era with that of the Victorian period:

> Whereas the hypocrisy of the Victorians consisted of concealing mean motives under noble rhetoric, our own hypocrisy often conceals a cankered decency beneath a cloak of *Realpolitik*.[14]

The authors' point, as it related to the possibility of citizen action, was that Americans had become so wary of lofty talk about "the people" that they had retreated behind a facade of pseudorealistic tough talk. Riesman and Maccoby described at length the cult of "toughness" in American policy making, the implications of which were spelled out in the introduction to this book. But what concerns us here is the optimistic side of their thesis. If Americans would just put aside their cynicism for a moment, the authors contended, they would discover that people—ordinary people—*can* influence their government.

The irony is that in an age when many feel so powerless a single irate letter can often have a totally unanticipated impact. The men in positions of power are often both divided and confused, and a "grass roots" complaint about a TV show or a congressional measure can, as often for the worse as for the better, show the fallacy of those who believe that there are no channels left for effective political action.[15]

Even the busiest of Americans, deeply immersed in studies or career, can manage to write a letter to an editor or a member of Congress. It takes only a slightly larger investment of time and/or courage to get on a local radio "hot line," or to speak out at a town or city council meeting. Picketing, lobbying, and organizing others to do so require greater investments, but the responses are likely to be greater, too. Back in 1965 a political scientist drew the chart, shown on this page, to illustrate the range of possibilities. Note that the chart lists voting among the "spectator activities," and puts it second from the bottom in terms of "involvement." To those who think they have performed the sum total of their "civic duty" by going to the polls, this may come as something of a shock. But consider: When we vote, the choices have already been laid in front of us; our contribution to the political process is the nearly passive one of flipping pointers and pulling a lever. Without disparaging the act of voting, we ought to keep in mind that the citizen can make more creative contributions to the political process by moving up the ladder of activism. Henry David Thoreau once urged us to "cast your whole vote, not a strip of paper merely, but your whole influence." [16] We need not follow Thoreau all the way—into civil disobedience and jail—in order to see his point. Citizenship in a democracy means more than just voting; it means getting *ourselves* involved in politics, and doing it *between* elections.

It is amazing what the spontaneous act of even one person can lead to. In 1955 one black woman, a forty-three-year-old seamstress named Rosa Parks, refused to move to the "colored" section at the back of a bus in Montgomery,

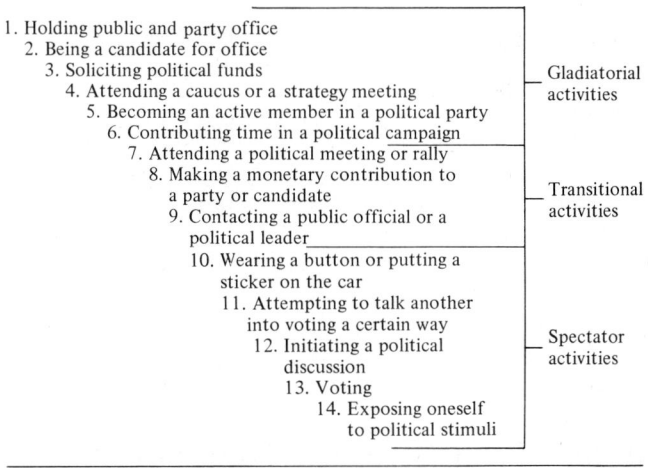

Hierarchy of political involvement. *(Source: Lester W. Milbrath,* Political Participation, *© 1965 by Rand McNally College Publishing Company, Chicago, Figure 3, p. 18)*

Alabama. She was arrested and fined, but her quiet refusal led to a boycott of the Montgomery bus lines by blacks. Within a year, the boycott led to a federal court injunction prohibiting segregation in the buses of Montgomery, and it set the pattern for future demonstrations all over the American South. In the introduction to this book we compared democracy to the widening rings in the water after a stone has been dropped. The solitary pebble dropped by Rosa Parks on the evening of December 1, 1955, was still making waves a decade later.

Not everyone can act as bravely as Rosa Parks, but the essential spirit of her act was not bravery per se; what her act really represented was the sudden awareness—not of the injustice of Jim Crow, for she must have known that for a long time—but of the *fact that she no longer had to tolerate it*. Every society, it seems, has its sages who patiently explain the facts of life to people who ask why we have to tolerate injustice and corruption. "Well, that's the way we do things here," says the sage. For generations of blacks in America, racial segregation—"knowing one's place"—was part of The Way We Do Things. But within fifteen years official apartheid had been swept away, and even George Wallace ("Segregation now, segregation tomorrow, segregation forever!") was talking as if it had never existed. But who had changed it? Certainly not those "moderate" clergymen who told Martin Luther King that his demonstrations were "unwise and untimely."[17] Certainly not our "centrist" politicians, who, fearful of losing Southern support, temporized and equivocated on civil rights.[18] Certainly not those social scientists who, with charts and statistical tables, were showing how beautifully the "normal system" works.[19] It was the dreamers who awakened America to the flaws in the "normal system." It was the idealists who changed the reality.

Yet the sages, the calm spirits who know everything and can imagine nothing, still take their motto from "the Frenchman who first said (in French, of course): 'The more things change, the more they stay the same.'"[20] They still sneer at the "wishful thinking" of reformers, still insist that it is not perverse people or institutions that stand in the way of any real improvement in society but changeless, ironclad "scientific laws."[21] Sages come in many varieties. Down at the bar, the neighborhood sage is holding forth:

> Who the hell cares about politics, anyway? I've got other things to do with my time.
>
> You can't beat the big-money boys. They've got everything fixed. Anyway, you can't do anything about the big corporations because your average American *likes* the system the way it is.
>
> People are dumb, right? They don't know what they're voting for. Just give 'em pabulum and they'll love you.

In a college classroom, the academic sage is preparing students for the "realistic" study of politics:

> It would clear the air of a good deal of cant if instead of assuming that politics is a normal and natural concern of human beings, one were to make the contrary assumption that whatever lip service citizens may pay to conventional attitudes, politics is a remote, alien, and unrewarding activity.[22]

> [M]ost Americans . . . display complacency about their economic institutions. Proposals for extensive reconstruction do not enjoy much support. The great corporations, it appears, have gained rather wide acceptance.[23]
>
> When the people at large get involved in politics, "emotion rises and reasoned discussion declines." The smart politician is one who has learned how to "finesse" tough issues, gloss over everything controversial, and stick with safe slogans like "law and order." The anti-Vietnam demonstrations were "walking political disasters."[24]

This book, on the contrary, has been based on the proposition that we do not have to accept The Way We Do Things. Such an acceptance would probably have doomed the American Revolution, stopped the abolitionists before they began, and chilled to death every reform movement over the past two centuries. Such an acceptance *did* help to keep the "white" and "colored" signs hanging in the South for a hundred years after the Civil War, and *did* silence many "centrist" Democrats who, it now appears, were secretly opposed to the Vietnam war during the critical years of its escalation.

The deepest roots in the American political tradition are opposed to fatalism and cynicism. America has been a land where people have dared to imagine that basic changes can be made in the human condition, and that they can be accomplished peacefully and deliberately—"from reflection and choice," as Hamilton said, not from "accident and force."[25] It has been a thesis of this book that each citizen can play a role in bringing about these changes. "I, myself, desegregated that lunch counter on Peachtree Street," the young man said to James Farmer one day, not so long ago, in the streets of Atlanta. "Nobody else. I did it by sitting in, walking the picket line, by marching. I didn't have to wait for any big shots to do it for me. I did it myself."[26]

WHAT IS AMERICA? SOME ANSWERS IN BRIEF

What, then, is America? Henry Kissinger's question invites a brief summary of what we have perhaps taken too long to say. America is a land of many peoples, who must learn to accept one another—as fellow citizens, if not as brothers and sisters. It is a land which has held out the hope of rising from poverty and servility; a land committed to free and robust discussion; a land where even the highest public officials are regarded as servants, not high priests. Most important, the Americans are a people who believe in democratic government and active citizenship.

Such answers, one suspects, would not have satisfied Secretary of State Kissinger in the spring of 1975. The real thrust of his question had to do with America's future as a world power. The imminent collapse of South Vietnam was obviously troubling the Secretary, as it was troubling so many other Americans. But Vietnam was the ultimate fruit of the cold war era, an era during which America seemed to forget about its own traditions in its effort to beat foreigners at foreign games. Now, perhaps more than ever, the question of what *we* are and what *we* want to be presses upon us. Archibald MacLeish, a poet who once served as Assistant Secretary of State in the Roosevelt administration, has asked:

Which are we—the old historic Republic conceived in the Declaration of Independence and dedicated to the belief in man, or the Great Power, conceived in the political intrigues of the Cold War, and dedicated to Security, meaning to still more power?

If America wants to be a superpower, then ideals are not really so important. Success is what counts. But if, MacLeish concluded,

> in spite of our childish power play in Southeast Asia, we are still the great Republic—great Republic first and power in the world afterward—then nothing matters as *much* as our passion for liberty, our belief in man, our love of humanity. For without them we will have no power. And will lose ourselves. [27]

NOTES

1. *New York Times,* Mar. 27, 1975, p. 1.
2. Theodore H. White, *The Making of the President 1960* (New York: Pocket Books, Inc., 1961), p. 452.
3. It was the moral indifference of the new, "tough-minded" liberals in the Kennedy administration, their constant readiness to subordinate principles to technique, which most troubled old-fashioned liberals like Chester Bowles. Bowles, a former Connecticut Congressman and Ambassador to India during the fifties, was a Presidential adviser at the time of the Bay of Pigs. When Bowles warned against the ill-fated venture he was derided as a "gutless wonder" by Robert Kennedy. Bowles and the other soft-liners were later eased out of the Kennedy administration, leaving the field open to cold warriors like Dean Rusk and Robert McNamara. What troubled Bowles about the Kennedy administration's fascination with gadgetry and hardware and James Bondian trickery was not only the silliness of it all but the fact that there seemed to be no guiding sense of morality in any of it. In his private diary he wrote: "The question which concerns me most about this new administration is whether it lacks a genuine sense of conviction about what is right and what is wrong." In fact, Bowles saw the two, the amorality and the silliness, as being linked together as cause and effect. "The Cuban fiasco demonstrates how far astray a man as brilliant and well intentioned as Kennedy can go who lacks a basic moral reference point." Quoted in David Halberstam, *The Best and the Brightest* (Greenwich, Conn.: Fawcett Publications, Inc., 1973), p. 88.
4. Nixon was not merely indifferent about goals, he seemed to be utterly contemptuous of anything resembling fixed principles. He had a peculiar way of making grandiose pronouncements and, a short time later, saying and doing the exact opposite. He was elected on the promise to "bring us together," but within a few months after his inauguration he sent Spiro Agnew out to practice and defend a policy of "positive polarization." In his inaugural speech he said that we should all "lower our voices," but he was soon doing everything he could to enflame public opinion against campus "bums." At Guam he declared that every nation must learn to defend itself, but made an open-ended commitment to defend the Thieu regime in South Vietnam (from the air if not from the ground), widened the war into Laos and Cambodia, and in the latter country committed America to the defense of the Lon Nol government. He emphasized the need for negotiation rather than confrontation, then threw down the gauntlet to the Russians by blockading North Vietnamese ports. He announced

that he was going to take special pains to choose a distinguished Cabinet in order to profit from its advice, then proceeded to wall himself off from any meaningful contact with his Cabinet officials, seeing hardly anyone outside a small circle of "special assistants." He spoke of returning government to the grass roots, yet went further than any of his predecessors in trying to centralize power in the White House. (He attempted to create a consolidated "super-Cabinet," to flush out every high-level bureaucrat not demonstrably loyal to Richard M. Nixon, to turn the Internal Revenue Service and other federal agencies into weapons for personal power, to supplement, if not supersede, the FBI and CIA with his own secret spy teams. He turned the Bureau of the Budget into a much more centralized Office of Management and Budget, and he impounded unprecedented sums of money appropriated by Congress—and intended for the very local communities he professed to champion!) He often said that social problems will not go away just because we throw money at them, yet he was the first President to propose a guaranteed annual income. For a far more thorough and systematic treatment of the substantive incoherence of the Nixon administration, see the six-part series by Jonathan Schell in the *New Yorker* (June 2 through July 7, 1975).

5   A Louis Harris poll taken in March of 1975 revealed the following:
By an overwhelming margin of 76 to 18 percent, those polled felt that "we should never again commit American soldiers to a war such as Vietnam."
A 74 to 17 percent majority opposed sending additional military aid to South Vietnam and a 68 to 21 percent majority opposed $220 million in emergency aid for Cambodia.
A 67 to 20 percent majority thought that "we should not commit American lives to the defense of corrupt governments abroad." *The Journal-News* (Rockland County, N. Y.), Mar. 21, 1975, p. 21A.

6   Edward Dumbauld, ed., *The Political Writings of Thomas Jefferson: Representative Selections* (Indianapolis, Ind.: The Bobbs-Merrill Company, Inc., 1955), p. 181.
7   White, op. cit., p. 455.
8   J. Hector St. John de Crevecoeur, *Letters from an American Farmer* (New York: E. P. Dutton & Co., Inc. 1957; originally published in 1782), p. 40.
9   White, op. cit., p. 450.
10 Ibid., pp. 31–32.
11 Ibid., p. 57.
12 Ibid., p. 441.
13 Ibid., p. 442. Emphasis added.
14 David Riesman and Michael Maccoby, "The American Crisis," in James Roosevelt, ed., *The Liberal Papers* (Garden City, N. Y.: Doubleday & Company, Inc., 1962), p. 32.
15 Ibid., p. 39.
16 Henry David Thoreau, "Civil Disobedience," in Robert A. Goldwin, ed., *On Civil Disobedience: Essays Old and New* (Chicago: Rand McNally & Company, 1968), p. 21.
17 "Letter to Martin Luther King," signed by eight Alabama clergymen, Apr. 12, 1963, in Hillman M. Bishop and Samuel Hendel, eds., *Basic Issues of American Democracy* (New York: Appleton-Century-Crofts, Inc., 1965), p. 287.
18 Theodore Sorensen, a friendly, not to say worshipful, observer-participant during the Kennedy years, revealed probably more than he realized about the way "centrism" works when he described how Kennedy reneged on his campaign promise to immediately, "with a stroke of the pen," ban discrimination in federally financed housing

just as soon as he entered the White House. Once in office, Sorensen wrote, Kennedy "moved cautiously":

> He waited until Congress acted on the nomination of Robert Weaver, who had previously spearheaded the drive for such an order, as head of the Housing and Home Finance Agency. Then he waited until Congress acted on his housing bill, of immense importance to Negro families in the low- and middle-income brackets. That bill, to be administered by Weaver, was dependent on Southern sponsorship and support in both the House and Senate. Then he waited for a full-scale report on housing from the Civil Rights Commission and for a more carefully drafted Executive Order to be prepared by the lawyers. Meanwhile he gave first priority to the Executive Order on employment and to administrative actions on voting, education and other areas.
> But now it was late November. The order had been largely drafted, its remaining issues refined if not resolved. Civil rights groups were clamoring for the promised stroke of the pen. A new dilemma, however, had arisen. . . .

There is much more of this, with Sorensen carefully accounting for each new "dilemma" and stumbling block. Not until the end of 1962 was the order finally issued, and then the announcement of it was made as quietly as possible. In a sentence which tells us much about the priorities of the Kennedy administration, Sorensen wrote: "The announcement was deliberately sandwiched in between a long, dramatic and widely hailed statement on Soviet bombers leaving Cuba and another major statement on the Indian border conflict with China." *Kennedy* (New York: Harper & Row, Publishers, Incorporated, 1965), pp. 480–481, 482.

19 "The full assimilation of Negroes into the normal system already has occurred in many northern states and now seems to be slowly taking place even in the South." Robert A. Dahl, *A Preface to Democratic Theory* (Chicago: The University of Chicago Press, 1956; Phoenix edition 1963), pp. 138–139.
20 Charles R. Adrian and Charles Press, *American Politics Reappraised: The Enchantment of Camelot Dispelled* (New York: McGraw-Hill Book Company, 1974), p. x.
21 Ibid., p. 260.
22 Robert A. Dahl, *Who Governs? Democracy and Power in an American City* (New Haven, Conn.: Yale University Press, 1961), p. 279.
23 Robert A. Dahl, *Pluralist Democracy in the United States: Conflict and Consensus* (Chicago: Rand McNally & Company, 1967), p. 331
24 The quoted section in the first sentence is taken from Dahl's *Who Governs?*, p. 322. The rest of the section summarizes one of the basic points made in Richard Scammon and Ben J. Wattenberg, *The Real Majority* (New York: Coward, McCann and Geoghegan, Inc., 1970), passim.
25 See *Federalist 1*.
26 James Farmer, *Freedom—When?* (New York: Random House, Inc., 1965), p. 81.
27 Archibald MacLeish, "A Great Power—Or a Great People?," *New York Times,* Nov. 19, 1972, sect. 4, p. 11.

Index

ABC, 46–47
Abzug, Bella, 9, 194
Activism:
   judicial, 296, 306–313, 317
   presidential, 322–325
Acton, Lord, 208–209
Adams, John, 29, 179, 181–182, 298
Adams, Sherman, 292n.
AFDC (see Aid to Families with Dependent Children)
AFL-CIO, 152
Agnew, Spiro, 16, 43, 52, 128, 190, 332n.
   attacks on the press, 39
   campaign against Senator Goodell, 148
   opposition to FAP, 77
Agriculture Department, 58, 60–61
Aid to the Blind (AB), 66
Aid to Families with Dependent Children (AFDC), 76, 79
   increased caseload during the sixties, 66–68
   weaknesses of, 68–69
Aid to the Permanently and Totally Disabled (APTD), 66
Aiken, George, 287n.
Alcohol, Tobacco and Firearms, Office of, 251n.
Alexander, Herbert E., 125, 133
Alien and Sedition Acts, 29
Allen, James B., 135
Allende, Salvatore, 154–157
Albert, Carl, 220, 231
Alsop, Joseph, 256
Amendments to the Constitution:
   amending process, 304
   Eleventh, 304
   Fifteenth, 98–99
   Fifth, 256, 273
   First, 25–26, 28, 30–31, 34, 37, 42, 50, 53, 136, 283, 308–310, 316, 327
   Fourteenth, 98, 304, 310
   Fourth, 237
   Sixteenth, 82, 304
   Sixth, 314
   Thirteenth, 29, 98, 34

American Federation of Labor-Congress of Industrial Organizations, 152
American Medical Association (AMA), 161
American Party (George Wallace's third party), 181, 195
   (See also Parties, political)
American Political Science Association (APSA), 175
Anderson, Jack, 128, 158
Anglo-Americans (see White Anglo-Saxon Protestants)
Anglo-French War, 248
Antilynching bill, 207
Antitrust laws, 250
Apathy, reasons for, 10
Apportionment, 301–302, 311, 318
Area Redevelopment Act (1961), 70
Arendt, Hannah, 263n.
Arthur, Chester A., 185
Articles of Confederation, 264
Ash, Roy L., 159–160

Baker v. Carr (1961), 301–302, 311
Baldwin, James, 90
Balkanization, 92
Barber, James David, 285–286
Barker, Ernest, 23
Barnburners, 179
Barth, Roger, 251n.
Bay of Pigs, 11, 238, 332n.
   invasion of, 284, 287
Beard, Dita, 128
Bender, Paul, 317
Benedict, Michael Les, 274
Bentley, Arthur F., 142
Bentsen, Lloyd, 289
Berger, Raoul, 292n., 319n.
Bernstein, Carl, 2, 18
Bickel, Alexander, 307, 313
Biden, Joseph R., Jr., 127
Bill of Rights, 277, 309–310
Bingham, Jonathan, 218
Black, Hugo, 309–310, 315–316

335

Black Americans, 97–107
 cultural oppression of, 104–107
 economic oppression of, 102–104
 legal oppression of, 97–102
 (*See also* Black Capitalism; Black Culture; Black
   Panthers; Black Power)
Black capitalism, 103
Black culture, 104
Black Panthers, 41, 100
Black power, 90, 92, 106, 111, 176
Blackmun, Harry, 34, 315
Blackstone, William, 274
Bolling, Richard, 223, 234, 235*n*.
Bolling proposals, 223
Bond, James, 6, 324
Boston Four, 32
Bowles, Chester, 332*n*.
Boxer Rebellion, 246*n*.
Bricker, John, 189
Brinegar, Claude, 159–160
Brinkley, David, 115
Britain, government of, 36–38, 43, 186, 211, 224, 287, 296
Broe, William, 155–157
Brown v. Board of Education of Topeka, Kansas (1954), 89, 99–100, 106, 311–312
Brown v. Board of Education of Topeka, Kansas (1955), 99
Buchanan, James, 230, 292*n*.
Buckley, James, 97, 136–137, 148, 218, 226
Budget and Accounting Act (1921), 221, 230
Bull-Moose Party, 181
 (*See also* Parties, political)
Burch, Dean, 273
Bureau of the Budget, 221, 280, 333*n*.
 [*See also* Office of Management and Budget (OMB)]
Bureaucracy, 221, 225
 as an amplifier of presidential power, 249
 as a check upon presidential power, 278–282
Burger, Warren, 34, 270, 302, 315
Burger Court, 128, 315–318
 and civil liberties, 316
 and civil rights, 315–316
 and criminal procedures, 316
Burke, Edmund, 224–225
Burns, James MacGregor, 172, 175, 177, 200*n*., 283
Burr, Aaron, 179
Busing, 105–106, 110, 317–318
Butterfield, Alexander B., 3, 268
Byrnes, Matthew, 36

Caldwell case, 41–42, 316
Calendar Wednesday, 212
Calhoun, John C., 142
Cambodia, 325, 332*n*.
 bombing of, 230, 244, 246, 267, 278, 283, 287
 invasion of, 247
Camelot, 240, 284, 324, 326
Campaign Act (1972), 133

Campaign contributions:
 devices for eliciting, 128–129
 laws regulating, 130–136
Campaign Finance Act (1972), 133
Campaigns, political, 121
 disclosure requirements, 132, 135
 large contributors, 130
 limits on contributions to, 130, 132–135
 1972 campaign, 117
 rising costs of, 130
 spending limits, 131–135
Carmichael, Stokeley, 111
Carswell, G. Harrold, 242, 267, 315, 317
Casework, 224, 226
Catholic(s), 107, 111, 189
 (*See also* White ethnics)
Catonsville Nine, 32
Caulfield, John, 2–3, 251*n*.
CBS, 39–40, 42*n.,* 47
Central Intelligence Agency (CIA), 2–3, 7, 18, 154–158, 160, 216, 279
 domestic spying, 40, 238, 327
 investigation of, 9
 lobbying for an "official secrets" act, 36
 misuse of, 237, 333*n*.
 overthrow of foreign governments, 246
 rationale for, 5
Centrism, 6, 122–123
Chase, Samuel, 292*n., *303*n*.
Chavez, Cesar, 90
Chicago Seven, 33
Chicago Tribune, 256
Chile, 154–157
Chiles, Lawton, 218
Chisolm v. Georgia (1793), 304
Christian Science Monitor, 46
Church, Frank, 156, 158, 161
CIA [*see* Central Intelligence Agency (CIA)]
Citizen involvement, 328
City University of New York (CUNY), faculty of, 108
Civil Aeronautics Board (CAB), 281
Civil liberties, 325
 and Burger Court, 316
 during cold war, 5, 8–9, 26, 281
 and judicial activism, 308–309
 as "preferred" freedoms, 309–311
 and Warren Court, 318
 (*See also* Free speech)
Civil rights, 98, 106, 207, 210, 309, 330
 and Burger Court, 315–316
 fate of bills for, 211
 and Senate filibuster, 215
 and Warren Court, 311–312
Civil Rights Commission, 101–102, 334
Civil rights legislation, 100
 Civil Rights Act (1875), 101
 Civil Rights Act (1957), 101
 Civil Rights Act (1960), 101
 Civil Rights Act (1964), 101–102

INDEX 337

Civil rights legislation:
  Civil Rights Bill (1968), 101
  Voting Rights Act (1965), 101
Civil Service, 185, 279, 281
Civil War, 12, 29, 97, 184, 218, 242–243, 253–254, 300–301, 331
Clark, Joseph, 215
Clark, Kenneth, 100
Clark, Ramsey, 314–315
Classification stamps (see Secrecy, government)
Clayton Antitrust Act (1914), 250
Cleveland, Grover, 253
Cloture, 214
Cohen, Benjamin V., 289
Cold war:
  effect on domestic politics, 4–6
  end of, 325
  habits of mind, 4–6, 322, 331–332
  and "politics as usual," 9–10
  and presidential aggrandizement, 7–8, 248–249
  and threats to civil liberties, 8–9, 31, 38
  and "toughness," 6–7, 12
Coleman Report, the, 104
Colson, Charles, 6, 39–40, 128, 325
Committee of the Whole, 213
Common Cause, 17–18, 78, 82, 132, 138, 164–165, 227–229, 232, 328
Communications, 327
Communications Act, "equal time" provisions, 124
Communism, 324
  and career of Richard Nixon, 38–39
  fear of, 154
  images of, in early sixties, 322
  imitation of its methods, 5–9
  influence of, 323
  prosecution of leaders, 30–31
  stigma of, 327
Community Action Agency (CAA), 72–73
Comprehensive Employment Program, 71
Conference Committee, 214
Congress:
  abdication of powers, 230–231
  casework, 224–227
  as check on president, 265–275
  committee system, 210–213
  Committee of the Whole House, 213
  Conference Committee, 214
  Congressional Budget and Impoundment Control Act (1974), 222–223
  contrasted with British Parliament, 211, 224
  Democratic caucus, 217–218
  folkways, 218–220
  fragmentation of authority, 220–224
  House Rules Committee, 212–213
  how a bill becomes law, 209–215
  impoundment controversy, 220–222
  investigatory power, 267–269
  negative checks, 215–216
  92d, 217
  93d, 231

Congress:
  94th, 217, 227, 231
  power of committee chairmen, 11
  power to impeach, 273–276
  public perceptions of, 205–206
  reforms, 229–231
  reorganization proposals, 223–224
  revenue bills, 210
  secrecy, 228–229
  Senate filibuster, 11, 105, 213–215
  seniority system, 11, 216–218, 227
  symptoms of decline, 207–208
Congress of Racial Equality (CORE), 106
Congressional Budget and Impoundments Act (1974), 222, 229
Congressional Quarterly, 148–149
Congressional Record, 211
Connally, John, 128, 152, 157
Conservative Party, 189
  (See also Parties, political)
Constitution, 110, 141–142, 210, 265, 267, 277, 296, 301–302, 305
  contrasted with ordinary law, 297, 299–300
  impeachable offenses, 272–275
  and judicial review, 296–297
    (See also Judicial review)
  "preferred liberties," 309
  presidential powers under, 239–243
  pro-slavery features of, 97
  "slot machine" interpretation, 306
  strict construction of, 306–307, 314–315
  vagueness of, 306–307, 310
Constitutional Convention, 247, 264
Conventions, 182–183, 186, 195
Corporation for Public Broadcasting (CPB), 50
Corrupt Practices Act (1925), 132–133, 138
Corwin, Edward S., 248–249, 277, 289, 290
Cox, Archibald, 15–16, 290, 291n., 313
"Crackpot realism," 7
Cronin, Thomas E., 258–259
Cronkite, Walter, 39, 46, 52, 187, 256, 285
Cuba:
  Bay of Pigs, 11, 238, 332n.
  invasion of, 231, 284, 287
  missile crisis, 7, 323
Curley, James M., 181

Daley, Richard J., 122, 193, 197
Dawes Act (1887), 94
Dean, John W., 3, 8, 39, 255–257, 267–268
Declaration of Independence, 12, 26, 252
Defense Department, 231
  spending, 81
DeFunis case, 108
Democracy, 328
  definitions, 24, 116
  prerequisites, 16, 24–27
  as a primitive football game, 16
  related to free speech, 26–27
  semantic roots, 25

Democracy:
  as the socialization of conflict, 13–16
Democratic Party, 175–176, 187, 195–196
  break-in of national headquarters, 1
  1968 Convention, 190
  1972 Convention, 190, 192–194
  origins of, 180
  reluctance to attack Nixon on Watergate, 282–283
  social welfare measures, 119–120
  (*See also* Parties, political)
Democratic Study Group, 223
Dennis v. United States (1951), 30, 32
Depression, 64, 154, 259
DeSapio, Carmine, 189*n*.
Détente, 6, 236
DeVries, Walter, 120
Discharge petition, 212
Disraeli, 173
Dominican Republic, 245–246
Donohue, Harold D., 228*n*.
Douglas, Stephen A., 300
Douglas, William O., 108, 293*n*., 303
Dred-Scott decision (1857), 97, 300, 304
DuBois, W. E., 102
Due process of law, 271

Eagleton, Thomas, 190, 266*n*.
Eastland, James O., 58
Economic Opportunity Act (1964), 70–71, 95, 145
Ehrlichman, John, 2–3, 34–35, 37, 39–40, 78, 128, 132, 208, 251*n*., 252, 254–255, 261*n*., 267, 316
Eisenhower, Dwight D., 38, 207, 231, 303, 312
  administration of, 322–323
  and executive privilege, 239, 269–270, 292*n*.
  and integration, 89
  and Little Rock, 99
  and Eugene McCarthy, 259
  as a "passive-negative" president, 286
  Republican Party programs, 144
  secrecy under, 36
  unilateral war-making, 246
  and Vietnam war, 245
  warning about military-industrial complex, 152, 160
"Elastic clause," of Constitution, 241
Elections Commission, 135
Electoral College, 184
Ellsberg, Daniel, 31, 34–39, 237, 254, 261*n*., 268
Emergency Price Control Act, 231
Environmental Defense Fund, 163
Environmental Protection Agency, 266
Equal Employment Opportunity Commission, 101–102
Ervin, Sam, 42, 268–269
Escobedo v. Illinois (1964), 314
Espionage and Sedition Acts, 29–30
Executive agreements, 248
Executive privilege, 302
  as an attempt to limit controversy, 15
  under Eisenhower, 269
  under Nixon, 270–271, 282, 290
  under Truman, 269

Fair Employment Practices Commission, 102
Family allowance, 74–75
Family Assistance Program (FAP), 68, 76–79, 82, 215
  advantages of, 76
  death of, 79
  Nixon's retreat from compromise version, 78
  possibility of revised FAP, 79–81, 84
  sliding scale of payments, 76
  support from mayors and governors, 76
FAP (*see* Family Assistance Program)
Farmer, James, 107, 331
FBI (*see* Federal Bureau of Investigation)
FCC (*see* Federal Communications Commission)
FDA (*see* Food and Drug Administration)
Federal Bureau of Investigation (FBI), 8, 36, 216, 225, 327, 333*n*.
  burglaries by, 238
  congressional probe of, 9
  effort by Nixon to thwart Watergate investigation, 256
  under L., Patrick Gray, 18, 267
  under J. Edgar Hoover, 280
  investigation of Watergate, 18, 272, 279
  Kennedy's use of, 250
  misuse of, 40, 275
Federal Communications Commission, 43, 48–49, 124–125, 160, 281
Federal Corrupt Practices Act (1925), 131
Federal Elections Campaign Act (1972), 131
Federal Housing Administration (FHA), 63, 225
Federal Power Commission (FPC), 281
Federalist, The, 142, 147, 162, 209, 241, 275, 288, 297, 299, 304–305
Federalist Party, 29, 179, 182
  (*See also* Parties, political)
Fein, Leonard J., 11
FHA (*see* Federal Housing Administration)
Filibuster, 11, 105, 213–215
Fitzgerald, A. Ernest, 160, 270
Flag, salute to, 308, 311
Food and Drug Administration (FDA), 164
Ford, Gerald, 303
  attempt to impeach William O. Douglas, 293*n*.
  brevity of presidential "honeymoon," 259–260
  comment on Boston busing violence, 106
  criticism of Congress, 206
  opinion poll ratings, 196
  opposition to amending Freedom of Information Act, 43
  pardon of Nixon, 242
  public expectations concerning, 62
Fortas, Abe, 315
Founding Fathers, 25, 141–142, 184
Fourteen Points, 246*n*.
FPC (*see* Federal Power Commission)
Frankel, Charles, 56, 92
Frankfurter, Felix, 171, 307–308, 311, 316, 318
Franklin, Benjamin, 93, 264, 291
Free-Soilers, 179
  (*See also* Parties, political)

INDEX 339

Free speech, 136, 327
  direct coercion as a threat to, 29–38
  as the dynamo of democracy, 26–27
  indirect coercion as a threat, 38–42
  monopoly as a threat to, 42–48
  (*See also* Civil liberties)
Freedom of Information Act (1966), 43
Friedman, Milton, 74, 76, 77
Friends of the Earth, 163, 165
Fulbright, William, 157–158, 231, 249

Gainesville Eight, 32
Galbraith, John Kenneth, 46, 197
Gandhi, Indira, 174
Gans, Herbert, 61
Gardner, John, 164–165
Garfield, James, 185
Geneen, Harold, 155, 157
Geneva Accords (1954), 245
Getty, J. Paul, 83
Goldwater, Barry, 101, 122–123, 176–177
  call for Nixon's resignation, 273, 283
  citations of undeclared wars, 246*n*.
  criticism of War Powers Act, 265
  promising "choice" between parties, 175
Goodell, Charles, 148
Gordon Rule, 160
Graham, Billy, 251
Grant, Ulysses S., 185, 230, 238
Gray, L. Patrick, 18, 267
Greeley, Andrew, 109, 301
Gross, Bertram, 60, 83–84
Gross, H. R., 222
Group theory:
  critics of, 144–147
  modern, 143–144
  origins of, 141–143
Guaranteed Annual Income, 74
Gulliver's Travels, 51, 147
Gun control legislation, 207

H. R. 1 (Social Security bill), 78
Habeus corpus, 253–254, 302
Haldeman, H. R., 2, 78, 132, 251, 272, 279
Hamilton, Alexander, 179, 241, 248, 258, 275, 288, 293*n*., 297, 299, 304–305, 331
Hamilton, Charles, 111
Hand, Learned, 305–306
Harding, Warren G., 230, 238
Harlan, John Marshall, 34, 98–99, 107, 315, 317
Harrington, Michael, 70–71
Harris, Fred, 82, 97, 164–165
Harris, Ladonna, 97
Harrisburg Seven, 32
Hart, Philip A., 128
Hauser, Rita E., 187
Hayden, Carl, 219
Hayes, Rutherford B., 253
Haynesworth, Clement F., 242, 267, 315
Health legislation, 207

Heart of Atlanta Motel v. U.S. (1966), 101
Hébert, F. Edward, 217–218
Helms, Richard, 155
Hersh, Seymour, 156
Hicks, Louise Day, 194
Highway Trust Fund, 159
Hill-Burton Construction, 81, 84
Hinkley, Barbara, 234*n*.
Hiss, Alger, 34, 36
Hitler, A., 286
Hoffa, James, 238
Hofstadter, Richard, 188, 191
Holmes, Oliver Wendell, Jr., 27, 29–30, 307
Holtzman, Elizabeth, 278
Homosexuals, 91
Hoover, J. Edgar, 175, 267, 286, 327
  rejection of "Huston Plan," 8, 280–281
House of Representatives (*see* Congress)
House Un-American Activities Committee, 269
Hruska, Roman, 317
Hughes, Emmet John, 205
Huitt, Ralph, 231, 232
Humphrey, Hubert, 122, 129, 194, 240
Humphrey's Executor v. United States, 281
Hunt, E. Howard, 2, 35, 39–40, 208, 267, 272
Huntington, Samuel P., 207, 259
"Huston Plan," 8, 40, 280–281

Impeachment, 230, 271–275, 282, 290, 292*n*.
  of Supreme Court members, 303
"Imperial Presidency," 230, 259
Impoundment, 231
"Income" strategy, 84
Income Tax Cases (1895), 304
Independent Regulatory Commissions, 281
Independent voters, 120
Indian Reorganization Act (1934), 94–95
Indians, American, 92–97
  communal approach to land, 93
  cultural differences from WASPS, 92–94
  cultural oppression of, 94–96
  effect of Termination Resolution, 95
  forceable removal from lands, 94
  oppression under Dawes Act, 94
  present condition of, 96
  and Reorganization Act, 94–95
Inherent power, 208, 252
Interest-Group Liberalism (*see* Group theory)
Interest groups (*see* Lobbies)
Intergroup coalition, 110
Internal Revenue Service (IRS), 60, 333*n*.
  misuse of, 39, 237–238, 250–252, 268, 275, 292*n*.
  resistance to misuse, 279, 281
International Telephone and Telegraph (ITT), 10
  activities in Allende's Chile, 154–158
  antitrust suit against, 249–250, 281
  collusion with CIA, 154–161
  IRS rulings in favor of, 251
  "noble commitment" of $400,000 to Republican National Convention in 1972, 128
  and "plumbers," 268

International Telephone and Telegraph (ITT):
    pressure to drop antitrust suit against, 128
Interstate Commerce Commission (ICC), 281
Irish, 105, 109, 111
IRS (*see* Internal Revenue Service)
Italians, 107–109

Jackson, Andrew, 12, 38, 184–185, 246*n*., 253
Jackson, Henry, 289
Jackson, Robert H., 255, 296, 316
Jacksonian Democrats, 182
    (*See also* Parties, political)
Jacksonian Revolution, 193
James, Dorothy, 87*n*.
James, Judson, 188, 198*n*.
Javits, Jacob, 175, 289
Jaworski, Leon, 272, 282, 290, 291*n*.
Jay, John, 275
Jay Treaty, 269
Jefferson, Thomas, 165, 178, 220, 246*n*., 276–277,
    288, 298, 300, 325
    ambivalent attitude toward majority rule, 25
    on the importance of newspapers, 44
Jeffersonians, 29
Jehovah's Witnesses, 308–309
Jenner, William E., 302–303
Jewish Defense League, 91
"Jim Crow" laws, 107, 308, 311, 318, 330
Job Corps, 71
John Birch Society, 129
Johnson, Andrew, 265, 273–274, 276
Johnson, Lyndon, 15, 26, 122, 128, 131, 177, 227, 286
    attitude toward Congress, 207–208
    avoidance of party identification, 176
    "can do" attitude of, 241
    and civil rights legislation, 101–102
    escalation of Vietnam war, 5, 245, 324
    Indian policy, 95
    invasion of Dominican Republic, 5, 245–246
    money in elections, 128
    "poverty," total war on, 62, 70–71, 84
    relationship with press, 284
    TV commercials for, in 1964, 122
    unreflective activism of, 324
Johnson, Nicholas, 43, 48, 159
Judicial review, 307, 313, 318
    attitudes toward, 295–296
    origins of, 296–301
    (*See also* Supreme Court)
Judicial self-restraint, 307–309, 318
    (*See also* Supreme Court)
Judiciary Act (1789), 298, 300
Justice Department, 128–129, 131, 133, 135, 158,
    237, 281, 289

Karp, Walter, 198*n*.
"Keith" ruling [*see U.S. v. U.S. District Court* (1972)]
Kemble, Penn, 190
Kennedy, Edward, 39, 135, 137, 196, 257

Kennedy, John F., 39, 63, 284, 303
    as an "active-positive" type, 286
    activism of, 322–323
    administration of, 332*n*., 334*n*.
    appeal to intellectuals, 239
    and Area Redevelopment Act (1961), 70
    as a "centrist" politician, 333, 334*n*.
    cold war thinking of, 4
    escalation of Vietnam war, 245
    Indian policy, 95
    invasion of Cuba, 231
    the "Irish Mafia," 149
    misuse of IRS, 252
    money in elections, 128
    and mystique of presidency, 257
    need for crises, 7, 323–324
    1960 campaign, 121
    promise of "vigor," 239
    seizing upon mood of early sixties, 322–323
    selective use of antitrust laws, 250
    TV debates, 124
Kennedy, Robert, 110, 332*n*.
Kent State University, 33, 41
Key, V. O., 17, 119, 126, 141, 177
Keyes v. School District No. 1, (1973), 104–105
King, Martin Luther, 90, 101, 238, 330
Kirkland, Lane, 193
Kissinger, Henry, 32, 244
    opposition to Allende regime in Chile, 154
    questioning America's identity, 321, 324, 326, 331
Kleindienst, Richard, 270, 293*n*.
Know-Nothing Party, 179, 181
    (*See also* Parties, political)
Koenig, Louis, 240
Korea, 246–247, 323
Korean War, 254, 277
Krough, Egil, 35, 37, 256
Ku Klux Klan, 98, 106
Kurland, Philip, 313
Kuttner, Robert, 251

Laissez faire, 63
Laos, 81, 244, 326, 332*n*.
Lasswell, Harold, 144
"Law 'n' order," 63, 314–315
League of Conservation Voters, 163
Lee, John Hancock, 180
Legislative Reorganization Act (1946), 210
Lenin, V. I., 328
Lerner, Max, 296
Library of Congress, 146
Liddy, G. Gordon, 35, 251*n*., 272
Lincoln, Abraham, 12, 185, 230, 242
    suspension of writ of habeus corpus, 253
    view of presidential warmaking while a congressman, 247
    and "war power," 246*n*., 253
Lindsay, John, 177
Link, Arthur S., 238
Litton Industries, 159

INDEX

Lobbies:
  citizens', 162–166
  impact on Congress, 151–154
  impact on Executive Branch, 154–161
  laws regulating, 150–151
  special-interest, 150–162
Locke, John, 252, 255
Lockheed Aircraft Corporation, 127, 151–153, 160
Long, Huey, 214, 258–259
Long, Russell, 66, 77, 79
Lowell, James Russell, 297
Lowi, Theodore J., 201n.
Lubell, Samuel, 107, 121, 195
Lurie, Leonard, 189
Luther v. Borden (1849), 301

McCardle, Ex Parte (1869), 302
McCarthy, Eugene, 5, 136, 189–190, 192, 197, 240
McCarthy, Joseph, 4, 11, 38, 40, 46, 258–259, 268–271, 312
Macchiarola, Frank, 54n.
McCloskey, Robert, 300
Maccoby, Michael, 328
McCone, James, 155, 157
McConnell, Grant, 250
McCord, James, 2–3
McCulloch v. Maryland (1819), 299
McGinnis, Joe, 117
McGovern, George, 123, 177, 189–190, 192–193, 240
  on the corruption of the Nixon administration, 128
  defeat in 1972, 5, 74, 78
  portrayed as radical by opponents, 122
McGovern Commission, 193
McKinley, William, 246n.
MacLaine, Shirley, 194
McLaurin v. Oklahoma (1950), 99
MacLeish, Archibald, 331
McNamara, Robert, 332n.
Madison, James, 142–143, 147, 151, 209, 239, 241, 247, 260, 275, 298, 327
Mailer, Norman, 324
Malcolm X, 90, 97, 102
Mansfield, Mike, 287n.
Marbury v. Madison, 298–300
  (*See also* Judicial review; Supreme Court)
"Mark up" session, 211, 228
Marshall, John, 276–278, 298–300, 307
Mason, George, 274
Mass media, 186
Meany, George, 152
Medicare, 223
Meiklejohn, Alexander, 26–27
Melman, Seymour, 81
Mercurio, 155
Mexican-Americans, 90
Mexican War, 246n., 247
Meyer v. U.S. (1926), 274
Miami Herald case, 52–53
Milbraith, Lester, 141, 150

Military-industrial complex, 152–153, 160
Military spending, 81
Milk deal, 128, 251n.
Mill, John Stuart, 126
Miller, Clem, 211n.
Milligan, Ex Parte, 254, 277
Mills, C. Wright, 7, 144, 312
Mills, Wilbur, 210, 217, 223, 235n.
Milton, John, 23
Milwaukee Fourteen, 32
Miranda v. Arizona (1966), 314, 317
Missouri Compromise (1821), 300
Missouri ex rel. Gaines v. Canada (1938), 99
Mitchell, John, 33–34, 39–40, 128, 132, 255, 268, 270, 272, 289, 292n., 314
Mondale, Walter, 136, 290
Money in politics (*see* Campaign contributions)
Monroe, James, 246n.
Morison, Samuel Eliot, 273
Morris, Jeffrey, 54n.
Moynihan, Daniel P., 66–68, 100
  family assistance program, 76
  proposal for family allowances, 74–75
Muravchik, Josh, 190

Nader, Ralph, 17, 163–165, 328
National Association for the Advancement of Colored People (NAACP):
  difference from Congress of Racial Equality (CORE) on busing issue, 106
  failure to pursue problem of economic oppression, 102
  series of lawsuits leading to school desegregation decision, 99
National identity, 324
National Welfare Rights Organization (NWRO), 67, 71, 77–79
NBC, 46
Neagle, In Re (1890), 254
Neal, Jack, 157
Negative checks, 215
Negative income tax, 74
Negroes (*see* Black Americans)
Neighborhood Youth Corps, 71
Nelson, Gaylord, 159, 289
Neustadt, Richard F., 9, 240, 246, 258
Neutrality Proclamation, 248
New Deal, 70, 109, 143, 145, 304, 308, 312
Newfield, Jack, 16
Newspapers, 44–45, 52–53
New York Times, The, 34–35, 41, 51–52, 239, 240, 244, 270, 284, 322
Nexon, David, 176
Niebuhr, Reinhold, 191, 193
Nieburg, H. L., 161
Nixon, Richard M., 215, 217, 230, 231, 303–304, 314–317
  an "active-negative" type, 286
  appointment of Claude Brinegar, 160
  appointments to Supreme Court, 315–317

Nixon, Richard M.:
  attempt to discredit Daniel Ellsberg, 34–36
  attempt to drop antitrust suit against ITT, 249
  attempt to politicize the IRS, 250–251
  attitude toward Congress, 208
  "black capitalism," 103
  bombing of Cambodia, 244, 278
  bombing escalation in Vietnam, 244
  book, *Six Crises*, 7, 34
  campaign against Senator Goodell, 148
  and campaign contributions, 151
  "can do" attitude of, 241
  and civil rights legislation, 100
  complaint about bureaucratic inertia, 280
  as congressman, 269
  demythifying of the presidency, 8, 258–260, 290
  discovery of his taping system, 3–4
  dismissal of Archibald Cox, 15, 290, 291
  events leading to *U.S. v. Nixon*, 291, 292*n*.
  and executive privilege, 270–272
  his administration as a culmination, 238–239, 252
  impeachment proceedings, 228*n*., 272–273, 283
  impoundments, 220–222
  Indian policy of, 96
  indifference about goals, 325, 352*n*.
  and inherent powers, 252–255
  invasion of Cambodia, 244
  invocation of "national security," 261, 262*n*.
  misdeeds of his administration, 237
  misunderstanding of appointment power, 242*n*.
  misuse of IRS, 279, 281
  1960 campaign, 121
  personality of, 237–238
  philosophy of Nixon White House, 237–238, 268
  proposal for six-year presidency, 287*n*.
  proposed Family Assistance Program (FAP), 68
  rating on opinion polls, 206
  red-baiting activities of, 38–39
  relationship with Congress, 266–267
  relationship with press, 283–285
  repeating Kennedy slogans in 1960 campaign, 322
  role in Watergate cover-up, 255–256
  Schlesinger's evaluation, 236
  and security stamps, 37
  strange case of, 236–237
  and "toughness," 6–7
  TV debates, 124
  "work ethic," 63
Norris, George, 186–187
Noto v. United States (1961), 31
Novak, Michael, 287–288
Nye, Gerald, 268

O'Brien, Lawrence, 251
Office of Economic Opportunity, 62, 68–69
  programs to help poor, 70, 129
Office of Management and Budget (OMB), 159, 221–222, 280, 333*n*.
Oil industry, 149
Old-Age Assistance (OAA), 66
Olney, Richard, 250

Omaha World-Herald, 256
OMB (*see* Office of Management and Budget)
Ombudsman, 225–226
Orlando v. Laird, (1970), 277
Orwell, George, 136

Parks, Rosa, 329–330
Parties, political:
  American parties contrasted with those of other countries, 174–175
  bosses, 180
  caucuses, 181–182
  check upon president, 282–283
  conventions, 182–183, 186, 195
  definition of, 173
  distinguished from pressure groups, movements, 173
  emergence of, 178–180
  functions of, 180–185
  officials of, 187
  patronage, 183
  primaries, 186
  "responsible" parties, 175–178
Party bosses, 180
Patman, Wright, 217, 218
Patronage, 185
Peace Corps, 70
Pechman, Joseph, 60
Pendleton Act (1883), 185, 191
Pentagon, 14, 15, 81, 151
Pentagon Papers, 15, 34–35, 41, 231, 246, 261*n*., 283
Percy, Charles, 175
Peretz, Martin, 171
Peterson, Henry, 18, 36
Philadelphia Plan, 102–103
Phillips, Kevin, 184, 196
Pickering, John, 274, 292*n*., 303*n*.
Plebiscitary presidency, 286
Plessy v. Ferguson (1896), 98–99, 107
Plural presidency, 287–288
Poage, W. R., 217, 218
Pocket veto, 214
Polish, 109
Political Broadcast Act (1970), 125
Polk, James K., 246*n*., 292*n*.
Pomper, Gerald, 119–120
Pope Pius XII, 276
Populism, 186
Poverty:
  difficulty in defining, 60–61
  gap between rich and poor, 59–61
  impediment to democracy, 62
  lack of progress in eliminating, 59, 61–62
  and laissez faire, 63
  and starvation, 57–59
Poverty programs, 71–72
Powell, Adam Clayton, 302
Powell, Lewis, 315
Powell v. McCormick (1969), 293*n*.
Preferred position, 309–311
  (*See also* Civil liberties; Supreme Court)

President:
    activism, 239–241, 324
    bureaucracy as check upon, 278–282
    checks on, 265–287
    as Chief Executive, 249–256
    as Chief Legislator, 207
    as Chief of State, 256–260
    as Commander-in-Chief, 244–249
    compared with British prime minister, 287–288
    Congress as a check upon, 265–275
    constitutional sources of power, 241–243
    contemporary roles, 243–260
    contrasted with executives in other countries, 256–257
    executive agreements, 248–249
    glorification of, 327–328
    impeachment of, 272–276
    imperial proportions, 7–8
    judicial checks upon, 276–278
    misdeeds during Nixon administration, 237
    plural presidency, 287–288
    pocket veto, 214
    political parties as a check upon, 282–283
    proposed checks upon, 287–290
    as Steward of the People, 253
    treaty-making power, 247–248
    veto power, 214
    voting as a check upon, 285–287
Pressure groups (*see* Lobbies)
Primaries, 186, 190
Prize cases, 254, 277
Progressivism, 186, 188–192
Project Headstart, 71, 72
Proxmire, William, 152–159
Public assistance, 65–66
Public Broadcasting Act (1967), 50
Public Broadcasting Service (PBS), 50
Public financing, 134
Public Health Service, 57
Puritan, 92, 93n., 97

Randolph, A. Philip, 102
Rayburn, Sam, 219, 227
Rebozo, Charles R., 251
Reconstruction, 97–98, 100, 101, 274, 302
Reedy, George, 257–258
Rees, Thomas M., 217
Rehnquist, William, 270, 315, 316
Repass, David, 119
Republican Party, 175, 176, 184, 187, 195
    members outnumbered by independents, 171
    1952 Convention, 189–190
    1964 Convention, 190
    origins of, 179
    pressure on Nixon during Watergate scandal, 282–283
    programs under Eisenhower, 144
    (*See also* Parties, political)
Republicans, Jeffersonian, 179
    (*See also* Parties, political)
Revenue Act (1971), 133

Revolution, American, 327, 331
Ribicoff, Abraham, 79, 80
Richardson, Elliot, 81, 290, 291n.
Riegle, Donald, 216n.
Riesman, David, 328
Roberts, Owen, 304, 306
Rodino, Peter, 228n.
Rogers, William, 269
Roosevelt, Eleanor, 188
Roosevelt, Franklin, 45, 64, 102, 230, 232, 304, 316
    an "active-positive" type, 286
    administration of, 154, 331
    anger at "nine old men," 304
    assertion of unilateral powers, 253–254
    attempt to sharpen party differences, 174–175
    "destroyer deal" executive agreement, 248
    FBI burglaries under, 238
    first "hundred days," 323
    "four freedoms," 23
    frustration with bureaucracy, 280
    and invocation of "national security," 261n.–262n.
    loyalty to his own interpretations of Constitution, 243
    and mystique of presidency, 259
    New Deal, 143
    relocation of Japanese, 277
    threatened unilateral repeal of statute, 230–231, 253–254
    view of president as moral leader, 257
Roosevelt, Theodore, 246n., 248, 257
    concept of "bully pulpit," 7
    "Stewardship" theory, 253
Rossiter, Clinton, 243, 257, 258, 266, 272, 288, 290
Rousseau, Jean-Jacques, 146, 232
Ruckelshaus, William, 291n.
Rusk, Dean, 332n.
Russo, Anthony, 35–36

Safe Streets Act (1968), 255
Sandburg, Carl, 136
Sandman, Charles, 272
Saxbe, William B., 40, 242
Scales v. United States (1961), 31
Scammon, Richard, 103, 196
Schattschneider, E. E., 144–145, 162
Schenck v. United States (1919), 29–30
Schlesinger, Arthur, 230, 236, 238–240, 248, 252, 254, 257, 261n., 271, 286
Secrecy, government, 35–37, 43
Securities and Exchange Commission (SEC), 281
Segregation, 98, 106, 330–331
    de facto, 100
    de jure, 100
Segretti, Donald, 40, 255
Self-restraint (*see* Judicial self-restraint)
Senate (*see* Congress)
Senate Select Committee on Nutrition and Human Needs, 59
Senate Select Committee on Presidential Campaign Activities (*see* Senate Watergate Committee)
Senate Watergate Committee, 231, 268

Seniority system, 11, 216–218, 227
Sherman Antitrust Act (1890), 250
Sherrill, Robert, 159
Shriver, R. Sargent, 70, 71
Sidey, Hugh, 285
Sierra Club, 163
Sirica, John J., 2–3, 290, 291*n*.
Slavery, 98
"Slot machine" theory, 306–307, 310, 312
  (*See also* Supreme Court)
Small Business Administration (SBA), 237
Smith, Al, 198*n*.
Smith, Howard, 212–213
Smith v. Allwright (1944), 99
Smith Act (1940), 30–31, 51
Social Security Act (1935), 64–66
Social Security Administration, 60, 64–65, 84
Sorenson, Theodore, 284, 289*n*., 323, 333*n*.
Southeast Asia Treaty Organization (SEATO), 245
Soviet Union, 4, 42, 323, 325
  détente with, 6, 236
Spanish-American War, 247
Speaker of the House, 210, 212–213, 224
Special Prosecutor, 282, 290, 291*n*.–292*n*.
Spock, Benjamin, 32, 33
Spot commercial, 125
Stalin, Joseph, 276
Stans, Maurice, 130, 132
Starvation, 57–59
Steinem, Gloria, 91, 94
Stennis, John, 291*n*.
Stern, Philip, 83
Stevenson, Adlai, 121, 188, 190, 195
Stewart, Potter, 315, 316
Stone, Harlan Fiske, 310
Stone, W. Clement, 130
Strict construction, 306–307, 314–315
  (*See also* Constitution; Supreme Court)
Supersonic Transport Plane (SST), 127, 167, 267
Supplementary Security Income Program (SSI), 65
Supreme Court:
  authority of, 276, 300–301, 317
  as a check on Presidential power, 276–278
  checks on, 301–305
  civil liberties, 309–311
  contrast with British judiciary, 296
  and democracy, 312–313
  judicial review, 295–301, 307, 313, 318
    (*See also* Judicial review; *Marbury v. Madison*)
  judicial self-restraint, 307–309, 318
  "making laws," 305–306
  political question, 301–302, 305
  preferred position, 309–311
  recent decisions of, 315–317
  reconciling judicial activism with democracy, 306–311
  "slot machine" theory, 306–307, 310, 312
  strict construction, 306–307, 314–315
Swann v. Charlotte-Mecklenburg Board of Education (1971), 104
Sweatt v. Painter (1950), 99

Swift, Jonathan, 147
Swisher, Carl Brent, 305

Taft, Robert, 175
Taft, William Howard, 257, 286
Taft-Hartley Act, 265
Talmadge, Herman, 252
Tammany, 189
Taney, Roger, 300
Tax Action, 164
Tax loopholes, 82–83
Tax shelters, 82
Taylor, Zachary, 266
Television, 45–51, 327
  cable, 48–49
  a "cool" medium, 46
  "equal time," 124–126
  FCC rulings, 124
  Kennedy-Nixon TV debates, 124
  oligopoly control, 46–48
  Political Broadcast Act (1970), 125
  political commercials, 117–118, 124–126
  spot commercials, 125
  Twentieth Century Fund's proposals, 125
Tenure of Office Act (1867), 274
Terrence, V. Lance, 120
Thieu, Nguyen Van, 244, 321, 332
Thoreau, Henry David, 16, 165, 329
Thurmond, Strom, 177
Tillman, Johnnie, 71–72
Tocqueville, Alexis de, 38, 275
Tonkin, Gulf of, 277–278
  resolution (1964), 245
"Toughness," pathology of, 6–7, 12
Treaties, 247
Truman, David, 143
Truman, Harry S, 7, 18, 161, 216, 265, 268
  an "active-positive" type, 286
  attitude toward Congress, 206
  and executive privilege, 269, 292*n*.
  frustration with bureaucracy, 280
  originated civilian secrecy system, 36
  tax scandals of his administration, 250
  unilateral war-making, 231
  Vietnam war, 245
  view of the presidency, 259
Tuchman, Barbara, 288
Tweed, William Marcy, 189

Ullman, Al, 210, 221–222, 231
Unemployment Compensation, 80
Unemployment Insurance, 65
Union Oil, 159
United Nations, 245
U.S. Bureau of Indian Affairs (BIA), 91, 96
United States Steel Corporation, 250
U.S. v. Caroline Products (1938), 310
U.S. v. Harriss (1954), 150
U.S. v. Nixon (1974), 270, 271, 292*n*., 303, 306
U.S. v. O'Brien (1968), 31
U.S. v. U.S. District Court (1972), 255

INDEX

Upward Bound, 71

Vietnam, North, 244, 245
Vietnam, South, 4, 321, 332*n*.
Vietnam war, 5–6, 39, 50, 81, 164, 207, 230, 246–247, 259
  belated criticism of, 331
  and Congressional abdication, 208
  cost of, 71
  escalation of, 238
  free speech during, 31–32
  Johnson's escalation of, 286
  Kennedy's escalation of, 284
  lies about, 238
  and "national honor," 325
  and Supreme Court, 277
Virginia Ratification Convention, 275
Volunteers in Service to America (VISTA), 70
Voters:
  decline of, 115
  rationality of, 117–121
Voting, as a check on the president, 285–287
Voting Rights Act (1964), 100–101
Voting Studies, discrepancy between. 121*n*.

Wallace, George, 105, 110, 125, 130, 181, 195, 330
War Powers Act (1973), 230, 231, 244, 247, 265–266
Warren, Earl, 99, 107, 126, 207, 303, 311, 315
Warren Court, 127, 317, 318
  civil rights, 311–312
  criminal procedures, 314–315
  critics of, 313–315
Washington, George, 257, 267, 269
  cabinet of, 179
  defense of bicameralism, 215
  farewell address, 178
  and treaty-making, 247–248
Washington Post, 1–2, 18, 39, 45, 51, 81, 151, 239, 270
Watergate, 206, 251, 259, 303, 318
  break-in, 1–2, 208
  burglars, 256
  and checks on the president, 290
  cover-up, 208, 255–256
  effect on bureaucracy, 280–281
  effect on Congress, 229–230
  effect on presidential power, 7–8, 229–230
  effect on public attitudes toward parties, 116
  end to an era, 4–6
  exposing the hazards of "politics as usual," 9–10
  investigation of, 3, 36, 132, 217, 231, 252, 255, 267–272, 279, 291*n*.–292*n*.
  lessons of, 6–10
  mood of post-Watergate America, 325

Watergate:
  as political issue, 196
  roots of, 230
  as socialization of conflict, 14–15
  as stimulus to reform, 6–11, 136–138
Watergate Committee (*see* Senate Watergate Committee)
Watkins v. U.S. (1957), 268–269
Wattenberg, Ben, 103, 196
Weaver, Robert, 334*n*.
Weber, Max, 279, 281
Weicker, Lowell, 9
Weinberger, Caspar, 221
Whips, majority and minority, 224
White, Byron, 34, 41, 303, 314–316
White, Theodore, 44, 284, 322, 323, 326–328
White Anglo-Saxon Protestants (WASPS), 92, 109, 111
White ethnics, 107–110
  definition of, 107*n*.
  media caricatures, 109–110
  myths about, 108–110
  under-representation at universities, 108
Whitman, Walt, 12
Whitten, Jamie, 58, 222
Wiggins, Charles, 283
Wiley, George, 66–68, 72, 74, 77–78
Wilkins, Roy, 106*n*.
Will, George, 272
Williams, John J., 78
Wills, Frank, 1
Wilson, James, 189, 195, 288
Wilson, Woodrow, 140, 210, 232, 268
  and political parties, 175
  shelving of Clayton Antitrust Act, 250
  unilateral war-making, 246*n*.
  views of the presidency, 239
Winter-Berger, Robert, 149–150
Wolff, Robert Paul, 144–145
Women's Liberation, 91
Woodward, Bob, 1–2, 18
Works Projects Administration (WPA), 80, 153
World War I, 29, 50, 246*n*., 250
World War II, 4, 30, 36, 45, 70, 82, 92, 95, 102, 141, 146, 154, 161, 215, 245, 247, 259, 261*n*., 277, 286, 308, 323
Wounded Knee, 97
Writ of mandamus, 298

Yates v. U.S. (1957), 31
Youngstown Sheet and Tube v. Sawyer (1952), 254

Ziegler, Ronald, 2, 18, 206, 273, 284